KV-645-171

# FIRMS, FARMS, AND THE STATE IN COLOMBIA

A Study of Rural, Urban, and Regional Dimensions of Change

*A.H.J. Helmsing*

BOSTON
ALLEN & UNWIN, INC.
London Sydney

Allen & Unwin, Inc.
8 Winchester Place, Winchester, MA 01890, USA

George Allen & Unwin (Publishers) Ltd
40 Museum Street, London WC1A 1LU, UK

George Allen & Unwin (Publishers) Ltd
Park Lane, Hemel Hempstead, Herts HP2 4TE, UK

George Allen & Unwin Australia Pty Ltd
8 Napier Street, North Sydney, NSW 2060, Australia

*First Published in 1986*

**Library of Congress Cataloging-in-Publication Data**

Helmsing, A. H. J., 1951–
Firms, farms, and the state in Colombia.

Bibliography: p.
Includes index.
1. Colombia—Economic conditions—Regional disparities. 2. Land use, Rural—Colombia. 3. Urbanization—Colombia. 4. Textile industry—Colombia—Location. 5. Rural development—Colombia. 6. Industry and state—Colombia. 7. Agricultural industries—Government policy—Colombia. I. Title.
HC197.H42 1986 338.9861 86–14098
ISBN 0–04–497003–X (alk. paper)



MANUFACTURED IN THE UNITED STATES OF AMERICA

*To Annèt*
*and my parents*

# CONTENTS



## PART ONE: INTRODUCTION



## PART TWO: ARGUMENTATION

# LIST OF TABLES

# ACKNOWLEDGMENTS

This book is a slightly revised version of the doctoral dissertation that I defended at Tilburg Catholic University in June 1985.

I wish in particular to acknowledge the stimulation provided by my promoters, Prof. J.G.M. Hilhorst and Prof. L.H. Janssen SJ, and by Prof. R.J. Apthorpe.

My colleagues at the Universidad de los Andes, Bogotá, particularly at the Centro Interdisciplinario de Estudios Regionales (CIDER), and at the Institute of Social Studies in The Hague have always given me support and encouragement, for which I am grateful.

Last but not least, I wish to thank Jean Sanders for her help in correcting this manuscript and reading the proofs, and Els Mulder and Peggy Haime, without whom I would not have been able to "deliver the goods" in the present format.

HARARE, ZIMBABWE
SEPTEMBER 1985

***A.H.J. Helmsing***

# LIST OF ABBREVIATIONS

| | |
|---|---|
| ACOPI | Asociación Colombiana de Pequeños Industriales (Colombian Association of Small Industrialists) |
| ANAPO | Alianza Nacional Popular (National Popular Alliance) |
| ANDI | Asociación Nacional de Industriales (National Association of Industrialists) |
| ANIF | Asociación Nacional de Instituciones Financieras (National Association of Financial Institutions) |
| ASCOFAME | Asociación Colombiana de Facultades de Medicina (Colombian Association of Faculties of Medicine) |
| ASOCANA | Asociación Nacional de Productores de Cana (National Association of Sugar Producers) |
| ASOCESAR | Asociación de Algodoneros del Cesar (Association of Cottongrowers of Cesar) |
| ASOBANCO | Asociación Bancaria de Colombia (Colombian Bankers Association) |
| CAJA | Caja Agraria (Agrarian Bank) |
| CAMACOL | Camara Colombiana de Construcción (Colombian Chambers of Construction) |
| CARBOCOL | Carbones de Colombia (Colombian Coal Company) |
| CEDE | Centro de Estudios sobre Desarrollo Económico (Center for the Study of Economic Development) |
| CEPAL | Comision Económica para America Latina (Economic Commission for Latin America) |
| CID | Centro de Investigaciones para el Desarrollo (Center for Development Research) |
| CIDER | Centro Interdisciplinario de Estudios Regionales (Interdisciplinary Center for Regional Studies) |
| COLCULTURA | Instituto Colombiana de Cultura (Colombian Institute of Culture) |
| COLPUERTOS | Empresa Puertos de Colombia (Colombian Port Enterprise) |
| CONALGO-DON | Confederación Colombiana de Algodon (Colombian Cotton Confederation) |
| CONFECA-MARAS | Confederación Colombiana de Camaras de Comercio (Colombian Confederation of Chambers of Commerce) |

| | |
|---|---|
| CONPES | Consejo Nacional de Politica Económico y Social (National Council for Economic and Social Policy) |
| CORAL | Corporación Algodonera del Litoral (Cotton Corporation of the Litoral) |
| CORELCA | Corporación Electrica de la Costa Atlantica (Electricity Corporation of the Costa Atlantica) |
| CSTC | Confederación Sindical de Trabajadores de Colombia (Confederation of Colombian Workers Unions) |
| CTC | Confederación de Trabajadores Colombianos (Confederation of Colombian Workers) |
| DANE | Departamento Administrativo Nacional de Estadística (National Department of Statistics) |
| DIAGONAL | Distribuidora Nacional de Algodon (National Cotton Distribution Company) |
| DIA | Departamento de Investigaciones Agricolas (Agricultural Research Department) |
| DNP | Departamento Nacional de Planeacion (National Planning Department) |
| ECOPETROL | Empresa Colombiana de Petróleos (Colombian Petroleum Company) |
| FASECOLDA | Union de Aseguradores Colombianos (Union of Colombian Insurance Companies) |
| FEDEALGO-DON | Federación Nacional de Algodoneros (National Federation of Cotton Growers) |
| FEDEARROZ | Federación Nacional de Arroceros (National Federation of Rice Growers) |
| FEDECAFE | Federación Nacional de Cafeteros de Colombia (National Federation of Coffee Growers) |
| FEDEGAN | Federación Nacional de Ganaderos (National Association of Livestock Farmers) |
| FEDEMETAL | Federación Colombiana de Industrias Metalúrgicas (Colombian Federation of Metallurgical Industries) |
| FENALCO | Federación Nacional de Comerciantes (National Federation of Merchants) |
| FESCOS | Friedrich Ebert Stiftung Colombia (Friedrich Ebert Foundation Colombia) |
| FONADE | Fondo Nacional de Proyectos de Desarrollo (National Fund for Development Projects) |
| FFA | Fondo Financiero Agropequario (Agriculture and Livestock Credit Fund) |
| FFCC | Ferrocariles Nacionales de Colombia (Colombian Railways) |
| HIMAT | Instituto Colombiano de Hidrología, Meteorología y Adecuación de Tierras (Colombian Institute of Hydrology, Meteorology and Land Improvement) |
| ICA | Instituto Colombiano de Agropequario (Colombian Agricultural Institute) |

| | |
|---|---|
| ICT | Instituto de Crédito Territorial (Urban Development and Credit Institute) |
| ICBF | Instituto Colombiano de Bienestar Familiar (Colombian Institute of Family Welfare) |
| ICEL | Instituto Colombiano de Energía Eléctrica (Colombian Institute of Electrial Energy) |
| ICSS | Instituto Colombiano de Seguro Social (Colombian Social Security Institute) |
| IDEMA | Instituto de Mercadeo Agropecuario (Agricultural Marketing Institute) |
| IFA | Instituto de Fomento Algodonero (Institute for Cotton Development) |
| IFI | Instituto de Fomento Industrial (Industrial Promotion Institute) |
| INA | Instituto Nacional de Abastecimiento Agricola (National Food Marketing Institute) |
| INCORA | Instituto Colombiano de Reforma Agraria (Colombian Agrarian Reform Agency) |
| INDERENA | Instituto de Desarrollo de Recursos Naturales Renovables y del Ambiente (Institute for the Development of Renewable Natural Resources and the Environment) |
| INGEOMINAS | Instituto Nacional de Investigaciones Geológico-Mineras (National Institute for Geological and Mining Research) |
| INRAVISION | Instituto Nacional de Radio y Television (National Institute of Radio and Television) |
| INSFOPAL | Instituto Nacional de Fomento Municipal (National Institute of Municipal Development) |
| INTRA | Instituto Nacional de Transporte y Tarifas (National Institute of Transport and Tariffs) |
| PREALC | Programa Regional de Empleo para America Latina y el Caribe (Regional Employment Program for Latin America and the Caribbean) |
| PROEXPO | Fondo de Promoción de Exportaciones (Export Promotion Fund) |
| SAC | Sociedad de Agricultores de Colombia (Colombian Agricultural Society) |
| SENA | Servicio Nacional de Aprendizaje (National Apprenticeship Service) |
| TELECOM | Empresa Nacional de Telecomunicaciones (National Telecommunications Company) |
| UNCTAD | United Nations Conference on Trade and Development |
| UNIANDES | Universidad de los Andes (University of the Andes) |
| UTC | Union de Trabajadores Colombianos (Union for Colombian Workers) |

# Map of Colombia



**Legend**

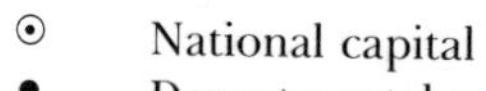

National capital
Departmental capital
International boundary
Departmental boundary

# PART ONE
# INTRODUCTION

# CHAPTER ONE
# REGIONAL STUDIES AND THE STUDY OF REGIONAL DEVELOPMENT

## Introduction

Recently, considerable effort has been made within the regional branch of development studies to reformulate the framework of regional development theory. During the 1960s, modernization–industrialization approaches established the interdisciplinary orientation of this field of studies, and the 1970s mainly were devoted to a critique of these approaches (for a discussion of Latin America see Helmsing and Uribe 1981). At present there are neither main currents nor countercurrents. However, there are over- and under-streams and they often create intellectual whirlpools that give rise to conceptual muddles. To escape these, normative approaches have lately become *en vogue,* such as the agropolitan approach (Friedmann and Douglass 1978), selective spatial closure (Stoehr and Toedtling 1976), and other often rural-oriented approaches. Although these have been and are being used to rationalize or guide regional planning practice, their contribution to theory and to the understanding of reality is limited.

This is not to say that real progress has not been made. On the contrary, new ways of thinking about regional development have been presented (see, for example, Smith 1976a, 1976b; Orlove 1977; Massey 1979; and Douglass 1984). In this research I hope to contribute to these efforts, and I shall attempt to set out some new lines along which further research may be directed. In this sense, this work is explorative and in need of further development.

Probably one of the most widely held suppositions in the social sciences is the presumed unilinearity of macrochange in past, present and, by inference, future. Changes over time are explained by what can be called *fixed continuous relationships* or a set of (mostly linear) functions. Any deviation from the defined pattern is explained by reference to exogenous factors. Broadly speaking, this applies to "development" as well as to "underdevelopment" theories of change.

This linearity is also widely accepted in regional studies, although some authors stress the conditional character of growth (e.g., Perloff and Wingo 1961; Hilhorst 1971; and Massey 1979). The discussion of regional disparities

is illustrative in this respect. Williamson's (1965) study points to the long-term reduction of regional income inequality while its ideological opponent—the concept of development of underdevelopment as formulated in the theory of internal colonialism—posits opposite conclusions. It could be argued that neither gives an adequate explanation. The critique of the former summarized by Gilbert and Goodman (1976), is too well known to be repeated here. With respect to the second, Crush (1980) has rightly criticized this theory for its failure to explain why conditions for accumulation in the periphery remain insufficient in comparison with those in the center. It is possible to go a step further and question the relevance of this approach. Here one may agree with Massey (1979) that regional inequalities have always existed. What matters most is not that they should be reduced *irrespective* of time and place, but that we should understand the role they play, if any, and their concrete form in the process of change.

The space dimension—an essential ingredient in the contribution of regional studies to the understanding of development—confronts us with a similar basic issue. Space is treated differently in the various contributions to regional development theory (Hinderink and Sterkenburg 1978). The basic distinction made in this context concerns the role of space as an explanatory variable in processes of regional development and the use of space in defining explicitly or implicitly an a priori framework of analysis. This gives rise to the problem of defining a *region*.

Different theories have been offered to explain the role of space variables. At one extreme is a so-called geographic determinism and at the other is economic determinism—representing spatial and aspatial theories of regional development, respectively. This controversy has been heavily debated in the recent past, although often indirectly. What is important to us is that both views hold an absolute notion of space (cf. Sack 1980). This is precisely what I question in this research. I propose instead a relative notion: The concept and the importance of space in (economic) behavior is not necessarily the same for all actors but may vary for each type of actor; the relation between economy and space is not homogeneous and uniform but heterogeneous and pluriform.

This reformulation of space has obvious consequences for the definition of region, the central element in frameworks of analysis. A remarkable ambiguity has always existed regarding the concept of region (cf. Hilhorst 1971). Regions have been recognized as *macro-socioeconomic entities* and defined by techniques that presume an absolute regional space. The problem in defining the relation between economy and space is expressed very clearly by the alleged vagueness of a region's boundaries, despite the high level of geographical precision obtainable with sophisticated delineation techniques.

Another way to approach this problem of a priori definition is to use sociospatial categories. For example, industrialization and urbanization are usually considered to go hand-in-hand, and by implication so do agricultural and rural development. Dichotomies such as "core–periphery," "rural–urban," and "town–countryside," in which macrosector and spatial categories coincide, are widespread. I contend that such conceptualizations unduly simplify the nature of (regional) development processes. Furthermore, they are becoming increasingly untenable in the face of the changes currently taking place in the organization of the economy.

At the same time, general development studies show growing appreciation of rural persistence and/or urban existence of multiple types of economic behavior that make broad-based sector generalizations increasingly difficult to sustain. A number of explanations have come to the fore, and are relevant to the regional social scientist particularly for their inclusion of a spatial dimension. Many of these continue to be based on sociospatial development dichotomies, however.

The aim of this research is to discuss these conceptualizations and to replace macro-sector spatial categorizations with a different perspective. This perspective has a dual foundation. First, economic behavior and space are integrated *at the micro-level*. Instead of disaggregating "from above," I try to build up "from below," from a microeconomic analysis. Second, the territorial organization of the state is integrated in the analysis of the role of the state in the economy. In the language of micro-economies, I consider both the internal and external organization of the "firm" and examine the interaction between the two.

In the next section of this chapter I summarize the main theoretical arguments presented in Chapters 2, 3, and 4 in order to support my basic contention and to develop the alternative perspective. The final section of the chapter presents case studies that will be discussed in Chapters 5, 6, and 7.

## Argumentation

I start with a discussion of theories of rural and urban change. Supposedly, both types of change are integrated parts of processes of regional development, but usually, not least due to wide recourse to an urban-rural dichotomy, they are treated independently. I do not devote separate analysis to theories of regional development; rather, specific aspects are treated where appropriate throughout the various chapters (for reviews of regional theories see, for example, Stoehr and Taylor 1981; Gore 1984; and for a discussion on Latin America, Boisier et al 1981).

With regard to rural change, I discuss some views on general and spatial conceptions of rural organization and development. A distinction is made between theories that consider rural people as agricultural producers and those that consider them as rural producers. In the first group, the agrarianists, I concentrate on the "organization-production" and "articulation" schools of thought, both of which recognize but do not incorporate regional diversity of rural change. I conclude that recent Latin Americanist contributions to the articulation debate, though disregarding independent peasant behavior, have made considerable progress in accepting that a variety of peasant situations may exist. When, however, the condition is dropped that capital has to control production, the key issues become to distinguish indirect or incomplete control (articulation) from none or little, and to determine how important the "squeeze" is for the accumulation of capital as well as for the survival of the peasantry. These issues remain unclear. The "independent peasant" economy view is still highly relevant as a general micro-economic framework of peasant economy. Independence in this context does not imply insensitivity to,or being unhampered by, capitalist enterprise, but refers to its decision-making framework, which has a logic and setting of its own.

The second group, that of the ruralists, generally departs from the wider framework and often discusses rural change in relation to "extrarural" processes that are either industrial (Kautsky 1970) or urban–industrial (Pearse 1968, Shanin 1972). A differentiation process is one of the results of incorporation, but differs in content from the "agrarian differentiation" discussed previously. Market incorporation exerts pressure on the peasants to reduce themselves to their role of agricultural producers only. In response, the peasants seek new economic activities or roles, rural and/or urban, in order to maintain a diversified pattern of activities that fully mobilize the resources of the household.

Lipton (1977), the last author discussed in this group, also recognizes the importance of industry for rural change, along Kautskian lines, but gives greater emphasis to the role of the state in causing "urban bias." Lipton is given individual treatment for his explicit and peculiar use of the urban–rural dichotomy.

I distinguish two levels of analysis in theories of rural spatial organization, namely, the micro-regional setting of (one) town and countryside and the macro-regional setting of central places. After a brief summary of main theoretical frameworks, I attempt to introduce into these frameworks some measure of socioeconomic differentiation.

The discussion of micro-regional spatial theories centers on Von Thuenen's (1966) theory. I attempt to carry this analytical framework beyond its original limits by replacing the economic homogeneity assumption, that is, by considering simultaneously big and small, landlord and peasant situations. I argue that opportunities for smallholders will vary in different locations.

While close-to-the-town smallholders may successfully transform into (partially) commercialized producers, in the outer periphery, smallholders' chances of survival as subsistence producers are greater, due to competition in the same crops by large-scale producers. In the middle area no clear position for smallholders can be established. By incorporating socioeconomic differentiation, the model loses locational precision. A second issue implicit in Von Thuenen's framework is the assumed complementarity of interest of farmers and town producers, a convergence that is locked into his framework. This becomes very clear in his analysis of (international) trade. When two "isolated states" are assumed, rather than one partitioned into two parts, a different conclusion can be drawn and a surprising parallel with Kautsky is found.

The discussion of macro-regional analysis centers on Smith (1976a, 1976b), who tries to link various situations of social differentiation with different types of central place systems. It is argued that these reformulations and elaborations are useful for indicating the regional diversity of processes of rural change. The static character of the analysis, however, limits the usefulness of these elaborations for improving our understanding of these processes.

I begin my review of theories of urban change, by reviewing general conceptions of urbanization that are inextricably linked with an explicit or implicit view on processes of rural change. Theories singling out urbanization as a prime variable in the development process generally depart from a rural-urban development dichotomy (industrialization equals urbanization equals development). I subscribe to Abrams's (1978) view that the social form of a town, which may concentrate essential elements of a larger process of change, should not be confused with that larger process. Urban change does not take place independently of rural processes of change but simultaneously, as evidenced by the urban expansion of (peasant) household or "traditional" production. In this context, informal sector-type explanations of this apparent anomaly are discussed. Finally, I review contributions by Santos (1977), Roberts (1978), Gilbert and Gugler (1982), who have in common their attempt to incorporate a greater diversity of urban situations and of rural-urban relationships. However, I question the "tight" domination–subordination or articulation framework that is put forward.

The notion of autonomous urban development is also at the core of various discussions on the role of towns, in which towns are also considered as a distinct sociospatial category. I briefly discuss propositions about the role of towns in agrarian societies, in the transition from feudalism to capitalism, and in colonial/postcolonial societies (with reference to Colombia). Towns are important to agriculture, even in agrarian societies, and town-based economic interests do not necessarily oppose rural/landed interests. In some instances, for example, in colonial situations, the unity of *some* urban and rural interests may be relevant. The absentee landlord personifies this particular rural–urban integration.

Continuing this line of reasoning, I discuss spatial conceptions of urbanization. These concentrate on the relationship between the evolution of the urban pattern (city size distribution) and the process of economic development. After a brief review, I criticize these theories for their implicit assumption of a single national urban system rather than various regional-localized and partially integrated systems. Moreover, the two "ideal type" city size distributions (rank size and primate city size distribution) are not mutually exclusive. Very little research has actually been devoted to the evolution of settlement patterns.

The conclusion I draw in Chapters 2 and 3 is that many urban and rural studies perhaps too easily take for granted a national framework for observation and analysis. These studies mostly disregard the dynamic effects of the integration of a great variety of local/regional economies. Furthermore, although in general development studies one tries to cope with regional variations in processes of social differentiation, in regional studies, dissatisfaction with existing explanations causes one to look for alternative answers by explicitly incorporating the spatial incidence of social differentiation. This might be considered a positive development leading to a convergence and eventually to synthesis. I argue, however, that conductors and mechanisms of rural and urban processes of change transcend both sectoral (agriculture–industry, formal–informal) and spatial divisions (urban–rural).

A new perspective is called for, and in Chapter 4 I present the first outlines of a possible alternative. Two central lines of argument are developed. One is based on the recognition that various forms of microeconomic organization are found in a particular regional economy, and that these differ among themselves as to their goals, internal organization, and spatial scales of operation. I propose a working typology of forms of microeconomic organization to capture (part of) this microeconomic pluriformity. Four forms are identified: household units, owner-operated firms, owner-managed enterprises, and manager-managed corporations. Each of these reacts differently to (spatial) changes in the distribution of demand, changes in conditions of production, and changes in coordination and exchange. Thus, if the microeconomic composition of an economy changes, say from household-type production to managerial corporations, then the mechanisms of rural, urban, and regional development processes will also change. The key to understanding this phenomenon is that new managerial microeconomic organizations have superseded town–country, urban–rural and even regional (core–periphery) divisions.

The second line of argument refers to the parallel process of the expansion of the role of the state. Although this issue has received considerable attention in the general literature (for example, O'Connor 1973), no explicit connection has been established between that expanding role and the simultaneous process of centralization within the government. Most economic activity is placebound and gives rise to positive and/or negative externalities; government action is then called for in order to settle conflicts regarding the distribution of social costs and benefits, to prevent negative externalities and to stimulate positive ones. Socioeconomic and physical infrastructures are provided for these ends. These provisions are also known as public goods. It should be recognized, however, that many externalities as well as public goods are impure, that is, they are not accessible to the entire public because of their localized character. As microeconomic organization and production become more complex and start operating on a larger spatial scale, not only are more infrastructures required to sustain it but these need to be made available on a larger spatial scale. The unification and/or compatibilization of socioeconomic and physical infrastructures, previously decided upon and provided locally, become necessary conditions for the unhampered development of microeconomic organizations. Thus, enlargement of the spatial scale at which activities are organized also influences the level at which government has to provide these infrastructures, from local to regional to (inter) national. In other words, there are implications not only for the size but also for the territorial organization of government. The forces that push for an expanding role of government also induce centralization within the government.

Having formulated this perspective, I seek to examine the implications for rural, urban, and regional development processes of the development of new forms of microeconomic organization and of changes in the role and organization of government. I single out and elaborate on three processes: the development of the agroindustrial complex and its implications for rural change; the consequences for urbanization of the development of a multilevel organization of government and enterprise; and, the effects on regionalism of verticalization of the regional economy.

The formation of the agroindustrial complex is the process that reshapes and restructures a rural economy, dominated by peasant household-type production, into an economy composed of owner-operated farms and managed forms of micro-organizations (agroenterprises). This process does not refer to "agrarian change" only but has multiple ramifications, industrial as well as spatial. In fact, the rural economy is reduced to agricultural activities which, in turn, become increasingly organized at national and international levels. Agricultural activities become sandwiched between two segments of industrial activities undertaken by specialized and (trans)nationally operating firms. "Upstream" firms engage in the production of capital and intermediate inputs, displacing household production. "Downstream" firms do the same with regard to conservation, transformation, and processing of agricultural output. The result is that agricultural activities are lifted out of their local and regional context and put into an (inter)national one.

Taking the existing rural structure into account, opportunities for microeconomic development are distributed unevenly. Transformation from hacienda to large-scale managerial production is favored. The transformation of diversified peasant household production to specialized owner-operated farms also comes to depend on the effective and unequal competition exercised by the larger managerial units. In this context, it should be recognized that, due to a number of factors, development of the agroindustrial complex does not occur in all products.

In various regional situations, the result of the general tendency toward incorporation into the agroindustrial complex and area specialization is the development of capitalist agricultural or managed enterprises and the survival of peasant households. Apart from an "industry-led incorporation" identified in the literature, there is an "agriculture-led" process that is of equal, if not greater, importance for the growth of intermediate and small towns in the region in question. It is argued that regional differentiation and diversity is an expected theoretical outcome.

Santos's (1977) work on the process of organization is singled out as an important attempt to integrate, within one framework, changes in the economic and spatial structure of a country. An asymmetry is advocated under which development of the "upper circuit" brings changes in the spatial organization, whereas "lower circuits," due to their localized character, can only react through migration. In this respect there is considerable convergence between the view held by Santos and the perspective elaborated in this research. However, I feel that the situation is more complex than the dual conception put forward by Santos. In addition, centralization of government is very much part of the same process. The state cannot be assumed as a given.

I put forward three propositions with regard to urbanization. I argue that the forces shaping the process of urban change in terms of pace and space are (1) the development of national and transnational oligopolistic corporations whose expansion is at the cost of smaller firms and households in both town and countryside; (2) the centralization-cum-concentration of decision-making powers vested in the central state and the restructuring of lower levels of government as extended rather than independent branches of government; and (3) the migrating responses of small firms and households to these two processes. Towns lose much of their relative socioeconomic autonomy as a result of centralization in both enterprises and government, and become mere nodes in multiple organizational networks. The development of large multiplant corporations has a two-pronged effect on urban and regional economies. Not only are locally operating firms displaced but, due to their selective use of local production requirements, intrafirm trade, and profit repatriation, a decline in local export-base multipliers also occurs. Less-localized activities can be sustained by the activities of the corporations. A verticalization takes place whereby the economy of a region is fragmented into parts that have little relation among themselves but, individually, have elaborate extraregional links. The process of concentration associated with centralization in government and enterprise stimulates the migration of households and small firms to the capital city to make use of numerous small opportunities. Economic and urban primacy go together. This does not mean that such processes are entirely unchallenged. First of all, we have seen that processes of "agriculture-led" incorporation and the related expansion of industrial, commercial, financial, and government services may stimulate the growth of (some) smaller and intermediate towns. Furthermore, local and regional groups may resist centralization processes. This leads us to a discussion of regionalism.

As stated earlier, I view regions as intermediate (supralocal) political–administrative territories of government that have evolved historicallly and at whose level the provision of public goods is organized. Processes of centralization of government cause regions to become less significant in this respect.

Regions, like towns, disappear as relatively independent entities. I view regionalism as a reaction against such a process. Local and regionally operating groups may resist the centralization tendency that reduces their access to government and weakens their capacity to withstand (by extra-economic means) competition from (inter)nationally operating corporations. However, regionalism does not occur in all or many regions simultaneously, nor is it necessarily supported from within. Expanding firms that have been successful, have gone (inter)national, and have outgrown their region of origin stand to gain from higher-level political–administrative integration. Because a large portion of their profits, wages, taxes and rents accrue to their particular region, these firms would have considerable local and regional political leverage. Regionalism may counterbalance some of these effects, but is unlikely to undo either verticalization of the economy or the tendency toward urban primacy.

## Case Studies

Three case studies are presented, all of which aim to illustrate, to verify where possible, and also to improve upon the theoretical propositions put forward in Chapter 4. The first attempts to examine, in an interpretive manner, the main interactions between economic and regional processes of change in Colombia over a period of 80 years (1900–1980). During this period, Colombia underwent several important economic and regional changes. Since the nineteenth century, when Colombia was an archipelago of relatively isolated and variously structured local regional economies, the Colombian economy and society have been reshaped by processes of economic, political, and physical integration that are still taking place. At different moments in history, these processes have been shaped by and have given direction to several factors and forces. In analyzing the expanding microeconomy and the increasingly centralized government in relation to these processes of integration, the intention is to learn more about the interaction between economic and regional change.

The second case study, which is more limited in scope, coverage, and time frame, but analyzes one particular case of economic and regional interaction in greater microcosmic detail, is a study of the development of the agroindustrial complex with respect to a single activity, the growing of cotton. In Chapter 4 it is argued that the development of the agroindustrial complex is a process of rural change having many ramifications—sectoral as well as regional, macro- as well as microeconomic. This is taken into account in the elaboration of this case study in Chapter 6. The process of rural change is multisectoral, in that it occurred among and was influenced by its interaction with industry, most notably the textile industries. The process is also multiregional, in that it involved considerable spatial reallocation of production. Macroeconomic conditions first restricted and later stimulated cotton-growing developments. Finally, the process involved important micro-level changes in the organization of production. The dynamics of the process are not only sectoral but also regional. In this case study I begin by analyzing sectoral interactions, which provides the setting for a comparative examination of some of the direct and indirect processes of the regional dynamics in the Costa Atlantica.

In the third case study I follow a somewhat different approach. It is confined to a single region, Antioquia, whose historical development provides the setting for an examination of intersectoral processes of change. Together with a few other cases elsewhere in Latin America, Antioquia is famous for its "autonomous industrialization" and "independent development"; as such, it continues to pose a challenge today, just as it formerly challenged many others. For these reasons, this case study is somewhat different from the other two in scope and purpose. Except for the primary data used in Chapter 5, this case study is largely based on a number of well-documented studies of the regional history of Antioquia. I also attempt to go one step further than most of the literature. Instead of concentrating on why Antioquia's development was exceptional, I focus on why it has ceased to be so. I argue that internal and external forces of integration and restructuring were involved and that the two questions are interrelated.

Before giving a preview of each case study, it is appropriate to stress some of their limitations with regard to my theoretical elaborations. Ideally, research is conducted in textbook-like fashion. A theoretical framework is constructed; hypotheses are formulated; data are gathered and interpreted; hypotheses are evaluated; and the (successful) proofs and disproofs are presented in a research publication. Such an ideal-type process seems overschematic; also in (my) experience, the course of events has turned out differently. In addition to the fact that this research has been carried out in a relatively disjointed (or, more euphemistically, dialectical) fashion of partial confrontations, revisions, and reformulations, we also have been constrained by a serious gap in development studies literature. Although much theoretical and empirical work has been done on macro-development patterns in countries as well as in particular regions, the field of micro-development studies is underresearched. Very little is known about development patterns of microeconomic organizations. The gap is even more serious because new forms of microeconomic organization have come to transcend conventional macro-sectoral and regional divisions. Not surprisingly, there is also a large gap in the empirical (firm- and farm-level) literature in this respect; the most important exceptions are studies on foreign (for example, transnational) enterprises and some on peasant households. Such a gap in the literature exists with regard to Colombia. As a result, one pillar of my reasoning cannot be sufficiently empirically anchored in my case studies. Finally, it is perhaps useful to state that although I have criticized sectoral and spatial approaches on theoretical grounds, I cannot ignore them, not least because much data and empirical analysis is expressed in these terms.

## Economic and Regional Change in Colombia: 1900–1980

This study begins by characterizing Colombia's initial situation as an archipelago of relatively isolated, rural regional economies within a federal state structure. Being "isolated" and "rural" does not mean that these regional economies were homogeneously poor and undeveloped. They showed considerable economic and political differentiation. Next, I turn to the conditions and processes that altered this situation and pushed for partial economic, physical, and political integration. The first thrust of these processes took place in the period before World War II, spurred by the development of coffee exports and early domestic industrialization. Neither of these developments was confined within sectoral limits, but had multiple ramifications.

Moreover, the two processes were partly interrelated and both took place in various regions.

The expansion of coffee production and exports created demand, and in some regions imports that were temporarily interrupted due to external factors, stimulated and partly financed a domestic-supply response in manufacturing and other activities. The infrastructure necessary for, and created in response to, the mobilization of coffee exports, unified and extended some regional product markets. In addition, these public works employed rural labor, which in turn stimulated migration and—together with other activities such as the processing of coffee, the import–export trade, finance, and support tasks—encouraged the growth of town populations. As a result, the demand for both manufactured and agricultural products increased. The demand for agricultural production primarily was met by peasant production drawn into market relationships. Consequently, a regional division of labor took place. Next, I turn to the new actors and groups that played a role in these processes: Nationally operating groups emerged as a result of concentration processess in industry, coffee growing, banking, and trade. I argue that these groups needed and pushed for consolidation and expansion of the central state and conclude with a brief characterization of the situations of the various regions.

The second thrust of the integration process took place after World War II. Two distinct subperiods can be identified: one in which the process occurred within a protected national market offering some import substitution, most notably in agricultural products; the other in which the national economy became more open via export orientation and some import liberalization, and foreign enterprise also came to play a leading role. Sectoral and regional patterns for both industry and agriculture are described. For industry, several techniques are applied to post-1945 census data. It is demonstrated that during the 1950s the pattern of regional change conformed to the core–periphery model, but that differentiation within core and periphery made this dichotomy less relevant during the 1960s and inapplicable during the 1970s, when internal differentiation had become too prominent. In the agricultural sphere we find that agroindustrial integration occurred for a number of crops, giving rise to a pattern of regional specialization and displacement. The internationalization of capitalist agriculture and the marginalization of peasant agriculture each reveals different regional patterns. In the former case, the process of specialization cum displacement continued; in the latter, no such process could be observed.

After discussing these broad patterns, I turn again to the actors in the processes: firms, farms, and state. Four processes are identified that have in common the characteristic of being conducive to what I call the *verticalization* of regional economies: (1) agroindustrial integration and farm-level specialization; (2) economic concentration and formation of national conglomerates; (3) the impact of foreign enterprises; and (4) centralization within the state.

Against the background of these organizing forces that reshaped regional economies, I look at the responses of small firms and households. I conclude the chapter with a characterization of the situation in the regions and the urban structure as each developed during the postwar period.

## Cotton and Textiles: A Case Study of Rural and Regional Change

Cotton is an example of import substitution in agriculture. In the early 1950s cotton production constituted only a small fraction of domestic demand, but by the late 1960s and early 1970s it had become one of Colombia's most important nontraditional export products.

Cotton production changed considerably during this period, both at the micro-level and in terms of the institutional environment in which it developed. Its regional division of labor also changed, which had considerable implications at the level of various regions. After an overview of the main trends, I first analyze the institutional environment, singling out three factors: the textile industry, which consolidated itself behind protective barriers; government, which provided key infrastructural provisions; and the cotton-grower associations, which, by organizing nationally, were able to counterbalance the monopsony of the textile companies.

Success in the rapid expansion of cotton production caused the development of cotton exports, which, in turn, led to a rearrangement of the institutional setting. Internationalization resulted, and was completed when the textile companies also became export oriented. The unified organization of cotton growers lost much of its significance and, partly because of other factors, a proliferation of growers resulted.

After elaborating on the institutional setting and the changes therein, I turn to shifts in the regional distribution of production toward the Costa Atlantica and to the changing composition of producers (marginalization of small producers). This analysis is followed by a discussion of some of the main impacts of cotton production within the Costa Atlantica (namely, in Cordoba and Cesar). I show that in Cesar cotton production triggered a number of developments including the creation of a new departmental government, commerce, personal services, and industry, and then compare these developments with those in Cordoba. Finally, I argue that these indirect effects, rather than the more regressively distributed direct effects, provide the key to understanding this case of regional change.

## Regional Development of Antioquia Reconsidered

Antioquia is famed for its regionalism, among other things. This reputed feature is what motivated me to examine Antioqueño development as a case study, to contrast it with common notions about regionalism and with factors that limit regionalism. I contend that, despite many exceptional circumstances, my propositions about the verticalization of regional economies, and in particular about the expanding microeconomic organizations and the role and organization of the state, also apply to Antioquia. These constitute factors that limit regionalism externally and internally.

A brief historical description begins with the colonial period, to which some of these exceptional circumstances can be traced (e.g., the weakness of colonial institutions, independent small gold mining, and the emergence of small traders). Independence enabled the small traders to obtain various privileges and powers and to consolidate and diversify their economic interests under the "protection" of the federal state structure. Land settlement was instrumental in these processes, and also in the creation of a large and independent peasant economy. It was possible for coffee production to expand rapidly in such a context.

If the Antioqueño traders had accumulated so many diverse interests, why did they move into industrial activities? This is the next issue that will be considered. It is not easy to answer this question because a number of factors prove to have played a role. Next, I discuss the process of national integration and the implications for the development of the region of the emerging of Antioqueño-led but nationally operating conglomerates. Together with the closure of the "small man's" frontier, these processes are singled out in the effort to explain the "normalization" of Antioqueño development.

Last, I review the literature that offers explanations of Antioquia's development, and identify three groups of theories: one centers the explanation around particular sociocultural values specific to the Antioqueños; the second group isolates a particular economic activity; the third group stresses the historical combination of events, without attempting to isolate any specific event but rather stressing their cumulative effects.

This study is intended as a contribution to the understanding of processes of rural, urban, and regional change, particularly those prevailing in Colombia. I try to pursue this goal, even though realizing that some simplifying notions are involved: although some may be more appropriate or more brilliant than others, they are merely intended to help in the understanding of reality, not to replace it.

# PART TWO
# ARGUMENTATION

# CHAPTER TWO
# FROM RURAL ECONOMY TO AGRICULTURAL DEVELOPMENT IN THE COUNTRYSIDE

## Introduction

Rural change is a complex process. This is evident not only in the generic sense of the term, but also in the way different disciplines and schools of thought within the social sciences define, dissect, describe, and try to explain it. Thus, it is fruitless to attempt to achieve some sort of general definition of *rural change*. At best, one can indicate differences of opinion in order to improve our understanding of the phenomenon and to realize its complexity from yet another angle. Although authors show such differences, basic commonalities can, of course, be found.

In the study of rural change, we refer to people who live in the countryside, whether in villages or dispersed, and who depend for their livelihood on a primary mode of production. This characterization is flexible enough to encompass a great variety of types and of organizational forms of production. The way in which rural production is organized in a particular area at a certain point in time is dependent on many factors, including the (historically evolved) general social structure and the specific geographical environment. This environment, in conjunction with general socioeconomic factors, explains part of the diverse range of rural situations. I emphasize the smallness of rural society in both the general and the spatial sense. There appears to be basic agreement that rural change is part of a larger process, but considerable differences exist among disciplines and schools of thought as to how this should be described.

In this chapter I discuss some general and spatial conceptions of rural organization and change. The first section deals with general conceptualizations, with a further subdivision based on whether rural people are seen as agricultural producers (sectoral view) or as rural producers (in which case a wider multisectoral view is taken). In the second section, spatial conceptualizations of rural change are discussed, and a distinction is made between concepts that focus on the classical (microregional) setting of a town and countryside and those that refer to larger countrywide settings.

This chapter sets the stage, as it were, for a differently structured analysis that is developed in Chapter 4—one that tries to come to grips with the major dimensions of change.

## Nature of Change in the Countryside

### Agrarian Change

In the opinion of many scholars, processes of agrarian change form the almost exclusive basis of rural transformation. The mass of rural people is thought to consist of peasants or petty commodity producers, and the central questions are what happens to them and how should the processes that affect their position be described? Proponents of this point of view identify different and competing processes with the common factor that change in the social organization of agricultural production is the fundamental dimension of agrarian development—as opposed to *other* aspects of agricultural production (e.g., environmental/ecological) and to nonagricultural production.

The Leninist view states that the process of differentiation of the peasantry ultimately leads to the proletarianization of poor and landless peasants and to further polarization, whereby rich peasants eventually may join the landlords to constitute the new dominant agrarian class (cf. Lenin 1964). The main cause of this differentiation is the inherent technological disadvantages of small-scale agricultural production. The necessary precondition for this process is differentiation in ownership relations. According to the Leninist view, the so-called middle peasants are caught in the middle and opt out (migrate). The factors in this process of agrarian change are essentially internal to the rural sector, that is, the initial distribution of property ownership and agricultural technology. Other factors outside the sector may either speed up the process (for example, create market demand for agricultural products through the process of proletarianization) or retard it (for example, expand the role of usury capital, which strengthens monopolies of local village shopkeepers and also traditional tenure).

The principal contesting view of agrarian change is the "independent peasant economy" or "organization-of-production" school of thought, for which Chayanov (1966) provides much of the analytical base. The basic points of departure are that peasant agriculture has a (noncapitalist) logic of its own which gives it its viability and ability for survival. Key to this independent logic of production in function of needs is the deployment of nonwage family labor. The degree to which such labor is put to work depends on the volume of consumption needs of the family. The fact that both vary over time as the family life cycle advances, is considered fundamental in explanations of differentiation among the peasantry (cyclical mobility).

This noncapitalist logic also explains the unique behavior of peasant agriculture in the context of the market. For instance, if the most basic consumption needs cannot be satisfied on a peasant's own holding, he will seek to acquire land in tenure and will be prepared to pay a higher price (rent or sharecropping arrangement) than one might expect from a capitalist farmer, or, for that matter, from a less-needy peasant. This preparedness to outbid and/or undersell capitalist farmers is the basis for the peasants' survival (cf. Shejtman 1975, 1980).[1]

Although the institutional framework of the peasant economy restricts differentiation, this does not mean that this school of thought views the peasant economy as homogeneous, either socially or geographically. Various members of the organization-of-production school recognize the enormous variety of agriculture across the Russian countryside. Regional analysis of agriculture has been an important component of their research (Solomon 1977). Chelintsev (1911), a major contributor to this research, concluded that these regional studies suggested an "evolution of Russian agriculture, with the various regions representing different stages of development" (quoted in Solomon 1977:67). Unlike Chayanov, he "did raise the possibility that the organization of peasant farms was influenced by certain factors external to it, namely the market and employment in crafts" (ibid.:63). However, as both conclusions threatened to undermine the very essence of the organization-of-production theory, both issues were downplayed and withdrawn from the entrenched debate with agrarian marxists in the Soviet Union during the 1920s.

Key factors governing the processes of change in the peasant economy were considered not only internal to the sector, but also internal to the individual family holding. Probably one could agree with Harriss (1982:212) that "the relative ease with which Chayanov's theory can be criticized has probably helped to create an impression that the 'differentiation thesis' is more or less correct." Yet, in contradiction to the latter thesis, peasant farming continues to exist, though not everywhere to the same extent. As a result, a number of intermediate positions have been elaborated; depending on which side of the debate they lean upon, these are either "theories of articulation" or "theories of incorporation."

Theories of incorporation emphasize nonagricultural factors and will be discussed in the next subsection; I limit myself here to a brief discussion of

1. In passing, it is perhaps relevant to add that this aspect of the behavior of peasants has nothing to do with their alleged efficiency in macroeconomic terms, as argued, for instance, in the CIDA studies on Latin American agriculture, nor with Schultz's (1964) 'efficient but poor' thesis.

theories of articulation. These recognize that capitalist and noncapitalist forms (modes) of production coexist, but this is an articulated coexistence. Noncapitalist production is dominated by, and restructured to, the interests and reproduction of capitalist development.

In the opinion of Goodman and Redclift, a capitalist agrarian transition does *not* require direct and supervisory control by capital and a consequent displacement (disappearance) of direct producers. In fact, this is not considered to be the dominant case: "rather the trend is to incorporate and maintain, not destroy rural petty commodity production and peasant family labour farms" (Goodman and Redclift 1981:71). In other words, the trend is to establish an articulated coexistence. The question now arises of how indirect control by capital is exercised, which brings several theoretical difficulties. Because generalized commodity production is no longer required as a precondition, in that some means of production are retained by the direct producers (the peasants), how much commodity production would be required to distinguish articulated from unarticulated and from precapitalist relations? Furthermore, if capital does not control production directly, how does surplus appropriation take place? Do peasants become "concealed wage workers" (Banaji 1976) or are they not-so-independent small producers suffering from a simple reproduction squeeze, through monetization of elements of the reproduction cycle and through actions of state and capital to regulate (rather than control) peasant commodity production and distribution? It is beyond my purpose to elaborate on all the alternative propositions that have been put forward on this issue of the position of the peasantry. For a detailed overview of this debate see Harriss (1981) and Goodman and Redclift (1981).

In my opinion, the problem is to distinguish indirect and incomplete control from none or little, and to determine how important the "squeeze" is for the accumulation of capital as well as for the survival of the peasantry. The articulation approach assumes that the indirect subordination of the peasant economy and the appropriation of its surplus is and *remains* vital for capital accumulation. The relative importance of this indirectly controlled sector in this respect and in comparison to the capitalist sector itself (developing in both agriculture and industry) is left unanswered.

The basic suppositions of the articulation approach are well summarized by Goodman and Redclift:

> Without entering the debate on the possibility of a "peasant mode of production", we would suggest that the general concept of peasantry and "peasant economy" cannot be sustained once the conditions of reproduction of household productive units are no longer independent of capital. The family-labour farm, admittedly with certain exceptions, is not the direct product of capital, nor does it depend for its reproduction on the realization of an average rate of

> profit. Nevertheless, once incorporated into commodity production, its conditions of existence are determined by the capitalist mode of production and the particular forms of capital to which it is subordinated . . . The dynamics of these household forms of production will be structured by the specific relations established with different capitals. The capitalist transformation of rural petty commodity production accordingly will be a diverse, differentiated process determined by the mix of capitals and their respective modes of expansion in agriculture. (Goodman and Redclift 1981:94)

Goodman and Redclift advance various concrete hypotheses to strengthen their claim of diversity. First, they postulate that "the introduction of wage labour marks a process of specialization, through which the 'polyvalency' or multiple role playing which characterizes the peasantry is replaced by fewer roles that are more clearly class-based" (ibid.:105). Their second hypothesis states "the penetration of capital leads to a convergence between the former estate and peasant smallholder systems of production" (ibid.:107), in the sense that the estate enterprise becomes more specialized and market oriented so that peasant and estate economy are forced apart, "making them more complementary but less dependent" (ibid.:107). The third hypothesis concerns the proliferation of *minifundia,* as a process of "agricultural involution" caused by the penetration of capitalism. The proliferation may result from the increased need to subdivide because of reduced possibilities of service tenure on the transforming estates and/or it may be made possible by the growing possibility of casual wage labor created by increasing specialization on the estates. Finally, a fourth hypothesis is put forward on the development of "peasant capitalism" in areas "where proximity to urban markets and freedom from the coercion of large landlords, has enabled families of middle peasants to accumulate capital" (ibid.:109). These small-scale enterprises, which are considered to be neither properly peasant nor properly capitalist, develop on the basis of family labor and regional networks of business contacts, and may become important within the context of the regional economy.

In addition to these empirically induced hypotheses, Goodman and Redclift indicate the importance of state-stimulated transition related to technological projects and land reform.

I have followed Goodman and Redclift rather extensively, not only because of their excellent review of the articulation literature, but also in order to point out that, curiously enough, the authors are caught between their own attempt to maintain articulation principles and their recognition of the varying experiences of diverse countries in Latin America, which are difficult to capture entirely under the single umbrella of articulation. The restatement of what articulation is, which we have quoted at length, does not fulfill two basic conditions: (1) that the articulation of the peasant economy is a profitable or necessary one for capital and (2) that articulation alters the behavior of the articulated in a fundamental way. Harrison (1982:248) rightly points out that Chayanov's theory of independent peasant economy operates *independently* of the presence or absence of generalized or partly commodity production. Also, although the limitation that only relations with capital (and state actions in the interests of capital) condition peasant existence is necessary to maintain articulation, it is perhaps too one-sided. Not only are peasants responsive to opportunities, as the "peasant capitalism" hypothesis seems to suggest, other factors and relations also play a role (see Chapter 2, pp. 30–38 and Chapter 4, pp 84–101).

Notwithstanding these criticisms—if we set aside the "articulation umbrella" for a moment—the empirically induced hypotheses of Goodman and Redclift represent an interesting and important attempt to cope with realities that reveal a clear heterogeneity of peasant situations. This heterogeneity arises not only from geographically varying distributions of landownership and combinations of agricultural enterprise and peasant production, but also from the fact that other activities outside the agrarian sector influence peasant behavior and position.

## Rural Transformation

The preceding theories are almost exclusively concerned with agricultural production, but others adopt a wider perspective on change. Peasant economy is not only agricultural economy; rural transformation entails nonagricultural dimensions as well. Moreover, the process of rural transformation may be shaped by factors from outside the agricultural sector.

In this general context, Kautsky occupies a special position, basically because he concludes that:

> *Industry* forms the motor force not only of its own development, but also of the development of agriculture. It was urban industry that smashed the unity of industry and agriculture in the countryside, that converted the peasant into a pure agriculturalist, a commodity producer tied to an unknown market, that established the possibility of his proletarianisation . . . [and] that produced the scientific and technical conditions of the new agriculture . . . and the dominance of large capitalist holdings over the small peasant exploitation. (Kautsky in Banaji 1976:45)

Kautsky's special position is also appreciated because of his attempt to integrate the urban–rural dimension into the analysis and explanation of the "agrarian question."

Capitalist industry and the growth of the communication system breaks the insularity of the countryside and eliminates peasant industry. Both peasants' and landlords' increased cash requirements alter tenancy contracts in the direction of payment of rent in money. The only way peasants can meet this demand is to expand their cash crops. Trade with the town brings along traders and users who exploit the now-important seasonality of peasant household production and cash income. The process continues by incorporating new regions, converting subsistence production into commodity production. Increasing improvements in transportation bring interregional specialization in agriculture, which further undermines the peasant household economy. "The growth of capitalism [in industry] in the towns is by itself sufficient to transform completely the peasantry's established way of life, even before capital has itself entered agricultural production and independently of the antagonism between big and small holdings" (ibid.:5). This antagonism is strengthened by the modernization of agriculture, which gives the large-scale holdings the advantage of being able to utilize large-scale technology. This does not lead to complete proletarianization, however, because the "resistance . . . the peasant farm puts up before the large holding is based not on its higher productivity but on its lesser needs" (ibid.:24).

Kautsky analyzes the development of capitalist agriculture and, on the basis of his analysis of 'ground rent' (absolute and differential), concludes that ground rent tends to grow at the expense of profits and wages. In effect, the terms of trade would turn to favor agriculture.

In Kautsky's view, however, other limits are placed on agricultural capitalism in general. First, continued centralization into larger holdings would meet physical barriers and diseconomies of scale. Second, there would be a continuous transfer of resources to the towns.

> As commodity production expands the demand for capital, an increasing mass of values flows to the towns by way of interest payments to the urban banks; with increasing urbanization and the growing attractions of the town, absenteeism expands and a larger portion of the rents generated in the countryside are consumed in the towns; the major share of the taxes which peasants pay becomes an expenditure on urban services such as the upkeep of the bureaucracy. (ibid.:39)

Kautsky also foresaw a progressive depopulation of the countryside following the extreme fragmentation of land held by the peasants, growing pressure on the land, and rising land prices, all of which militate against peasant reproduction and contribute to proletarianization. Ultimately, this would lead to a labor-shortage for capitalist agriculture. However, international trade would deal the deathblow to capitalist agriculture. On the one hand, rural markets would become less important for urban-based industry, which would then seek expansion overseas; on the other hand, competitive agricultural imports would turn terms of trade against domestic agriculture.

Although Kautsky's expectation of a shortage of labor may have been erroneous, the fact remains that peasant agriculture in general (i.e., middle peasants) is better able to withstand international competition than are large capitalist holdings (Djurfeldt 1982:143).

The three dimensions of the process of rural transformation (de-industrialization of the household economy, development of industrialized agriculture, and rural to urban transfer of capital) continue to be relevant, even though the results in Third World countries may not be the same, given the particular national and international conditions of those countries.

Shanin, a proponent of rural transformation, also starts from an independent peasant economy. He views family, farm, and village as the basic units of peasant economy and society (Shanin 1973/74). The family peasant farm forms a small production/consumption unit. Much in the tradition of the agrarian organization-of-production school, Shanin argues that the level of production is defined by family consumption needs and dues to the holders of political power. Unlike Chayanov, however, Shanin recognizes four basic patterns of mobility of peasant households: centrifugal, centripetal, multidirectional, and cyclical. Economic factors may encourage an accumulation of either negative or positive effects, resulting in a widening of the gap between households (centrifugal pattern), but other contributing factors have centripetal effects. Leveling factors arise largely from the internal dynamics of peasant holdings, such as the partitioning or merger of farms and families, extinction or migration, and land redistribution by the village. Thus, cyclical mobility can be seen as a combination of centrifugal and centripetal trends. Finally, and particularly if residual changes are included (e.g., natural calamity), the overall pattern may become multidirectional.

Although Chayanov's model explains these various factors of mobility through the family life cycle, it is important to appreciate the fundamental peculiarity of a smallholding economy: "The peasant household functions as a small production unit of extremely limited resources, greatly subject to the powerful forces of nature, the market and the state" (Shanin quoted by Harriss 1982:236).

The village plays an important role. First, it is a framework for traditional cooperation between peasants in production outside the farm; second, the redistribution of communal lands is decided at the village level, in order to reduce social polarization; and third, the village is a (periodic) marketplace.

It follows from Shanin's analysis that the study of rural transformation must consider not only the peasant farm, but also family households and the village, in relation to the three powerful forces just mentioned. In this context, Shanin emphasizes the impact on the peasant economy of processes of industrialization, commercialization, urbanization, and centralization, but does not elaborate very much on the nature of these processes. Although there may indeed be a trend toward the destruction of typically peasant social and economic structures, this has taken place much less rapidly than had been expected, and it has not occurred to exactly the same degree within individual Latin American countries.

Pearse (1968, 1975) focuses particularly on the Latin American peasantries. He begins with propositions that, in part, are very similar to Shanin's, but he is more elaborate and specific with respect to the forces and processes of change.

Pearse describes the peasant as an agricultural producer and cottage craftsman who produces for the provisioning of his own household and for market exchange, and who lives in land-groups (estate or *vereda*). The pursuit of livelihood, self-provisioning (subsistence) and the land-group are essential elements of peasant society and economy. Pearse adds to these the rural town *(municipio)*, through which peasant interaction with society at large is mediated, and Latin American–specific aspects of ethnicity and social ranking (*estamental* society).

Pearse emphasizes that market exchange as such is not the most fundamental aspect of rural transformation. Market incorporation is not new—it is a key feature of colonial and post colonial history. However, in the past, a rise in market integration was followed by decline related to (mis)fortunes in export crops, but at present one can speak about "a persistent process of penetration and incorporation of the rural areas in the system of market relations" (Pearse 1968:72). The main factors behind this process (and which together cause the alleged persistence) are the rapid growth of cities, rising populations, and growing internal markets which, enabled by expanding transport networks, introduce cheap manufactured consumer goods and agricultural inputs in exchange for increasing agricultural output needed to supply industry and the urban population.

One effect of this market incorporation is the elimination of local craft production, as cheap and often better-manufactured products replace locally made goods. This implies an increased demand for money, which can only be earned via an increase in market-oriented production on the peasant holding or via the sale of labor. The resulting reliance on market production exposes the peasant holding to the uncertainties of market prices and may cause a need for further market integration (e.g., if additional agricultural inputs must be purchased. The need generated in this way for consumption and production credit strengthens the foothold gained by market incorporation in the peasant economy. All this further undermines the subsistence system. The network of internal coordination and exchange of agricultural and craft products and of labor starts to crumble as each unit becomes increasingly market oriented. This expansion of the market economy, in which all goods and services have their price, leads to the progressive displacement of land-group institutions of exchange.

A process of institutional incorporation runs parallel to market incorporation. It brings

> a set of formally organized institutions (some part of the State apparatus and some not) which are characterized by national standardization, conformity to urban cultural norms and developmental aims, such as schooling, public health, agricultural development, provision of credit, education of adults, mobilization of peasants in community organization as voters or in political association, in football and sports clubs, as converts and as the recipients of charity. (Pearse 1975:75)

Institutional incorporation offers partial alternatives and palliatives to the dilemma of market incorporation. As national institutions advance, a further undermining of the land-group takes place. New distributive mechanisms begin to apply: "Under the new circumstances the primary asset is not the control of local resources but ability to manage the nexus with the town and the larger society, not only for obtaining credit and commercial advantage, but also for getting the benefits which the new agencies offer and the prestige which association with them confers locally" (ibid.:254–255).

The result of these incorportion processes is a tendency toward economic and social differentiation, but this process is different in content from the process discussed in the Russian agrarian debate. Market incorporation exerts pressure on the peasants to reduce themselves to their role of agricultural producers only. However, the increased pressure on the land caused by the incorporation process inhibits a change to agriculture as an *exclusive* occupation: in addition, this would not appear attractive in view of the higher risks involved. New economic roles are sought that will make it possible to *maintain a diversified pattern.* In part, these are made available by the institutional and market incorporation processes, which provide some self-employment and employment opportunities (e.g., local shops and commerce; occasional, part-time, and full-time jobs provided by public agencies and local government institutions, trade and services, etc.). But these new roles partly lie outside agriculture and the traditional realm and to some extent in the towns. Furthermore, "successful" or "progressive" smallholders need to establish and maintain contacts with the new institutions that are essential to their market operation.

> Social differentiation follows the economic, and the cut between social strata no longer divides land-group from town, but passes through the land group and

> lines up the "progressive" smallholders with the townfolk stratum. Increasingly they adopt elements of urban culture and their town acquaintances provide an alternative reference group for their conduct. (Ibid.:255)

Those that are unable to (let themselves be) incorporate(d) are forced to rely on old and new social groups or to opt out altogether and migrate to the large city. Consequently, although the process of differentiation brings in elements of country-wide social class differentiation, it does not necessarily create conditions for class-based conflicts.

An altogether different view of rural differentiation is put forward by Lipton. He formulates a hypothesis of urban bias based on experience in Africa and Asia (Lipton 1977). In his view, the main conflict in most Third World countries—and particularly in the recently decolonized ones—is not based on classical class divisions but on rural–urban opposition. Because small interlocking urban elites have developed a strong capacity to organize, centralize, and control the economy and to appropriate surplus far in excess of their own economic contribution, Lipton argues, in the name of efficiency and equity, that more resources should be distributed to the rural areas where the great mass of poor people live. However, urban bias and power prevent this. Instead, there is a drain of rural savings and skills, and additional price twists are imposed that have a similar effect.

The urban bias is also responsible for growing rural differentiation (cf. Lipton 1982). The commercial farmers receive preferential treatment and are heavily subsidized, in the effort to ensure cheap food for the cities. In contrast to Lenin's dictum—a poor peasant consumes less but buys more—urban-biased agricultural policy realizes that if more resources were distributed to the poor peasants they would end up "consuming more and selling less." This would endanger the very basis on which urban bias rests.

Lipton has attracted much criticism (cf. Moore 1984),not so much for calling attention to the urban–rural contrasts and gaps as a major development issue, but for proposing an urban–rural dichotomy as the core of the explanation of underdevelopment and for rejecting any alternative dichotomy, such as labor versus capital; rich versus poor; core versus periphery; or domestic versus foreign (cf. Lipton 1984). In my opinion, a major problem in Lipton's hypothesis is his formulation of this dichotomy. Although at first sight, it seems that a geographical dimension is converted into a class division, this is not the case at all. Lipton states: "'Rural–urban' is not a categorization of space alone. . . . The overlap 'rural, agricultural, labour using, dispersed' vis-à-vis the overlap 'urban, non-farm, capital using, concentrated', while imperfect (and complex in operation) does define a central class conflict" (Lipton 1984:155). As the rural elite adopts capital-using farm technologies and becomes an "urbanizing class," the dichotomy between urban and rural ceases to be valid and becomes instead an obstacle to the analysis of rural–urban interrelationships.

Lipton does acknowledge the importance of industry for rural change, particularly along Kautskian lines, but he gives relatively more weight to the state as a driving force for rural differentiation (cf. Corbridge 1982). In this respect his analysis is quite distinct from that of Pearse, who attributes a greater role to industry and, not taking a sectoral approach, comes to opposite conclusions regarding the rural social structure. Pearse concludes that instead of a continued rural–urban bias, there is growing social polarization in the countryside and a movement away from the 'structural peninsularity' of rural land-groups toward a national class society.

## Relations between Town and Countryside

### Micro-Regional Relations between Town and Countryside

Exchange relationships are the central element around which relations between town and countryside develop. One may agree with Smith:

> Market exchange occurs sporadically in all kinds of societies, with a distinct class of non-food producers who are situated in urban or at least nucleated centers. The centers and the elite class may arise as a result of endogenous or exogenous forces that transform the local social order, but in any event the internal market system is instituted by an elite class that requires regular and efficient food provisioning. Smith 1976a:51)

Such a provisioning may develop or be arranged in different ways. One way is to rely entirely on commercial farming. Another is to arrange adequate provisioning through extra-economic means, for example, the feudalistic solar system.

> Imagine a very large town, at the centre of a fertile plain which is crossed by no navigable river or canal . . . There are no other towns on the plain. The central town must therefore supply the rural areas with all manufactured products, and in return it will obtain all its provisions from the surrounding countryside. (Von Thuenen 1966:7)

This hypothetical isolated local state underlies Von Thuenen's analysis. The farmer's income or rent for each crop or agricultural product varies with distance from the market center, depending on costs. For each crop, a net income per ton per hectare curve can be identified. These curves vary from each other due to different prices per ton per hectare for each crop, different ton/ha production costs, and different gradients due to differences in transport rates, resulting in intersections of the curves. Assuming rational economic behavior, that is, behavior directed at maximizing net income, a specific pattern of land use emerges. Those products with high net income per hectare will be produced near the market center, whereas products with lower net income per hectare will be found in the outer rings.

In addition to this crop theory, Von Thuenen also elaborates an "intensity" theory. Given the availability of alternative farm technologies of varying intensities, which is the most rational under a given set of conditions? At the time of Von Thuenen's study, three alternative technologies were available: The three-field system, the improved system, and the crop alternation system, distinguished from one another by the amount of nonfarm material inputs that would need to be purchased (in the town) per hectare. The effect of rising prices or, for that matter, of moving closer to town, is that "the soil becomes too valuable and productive to permit any portion of it to lie idle. With the consequent break-up of the fallow, the improved system changes into the system of crop alternation which at this stage will yield a larger land rent than the former system" (ibid.:227). The famous presentation of the rings of land use results from the application of both theories.

Von Thuenen's model is quite abstract and its setting is distinctly European. Many of the assumptions underlying the model do not apply to the present-day reality of Third World countries where uniform farm sizes, uniformity of soil and other farming conditions, and so forth, are not present.[2]

If we want to consider the interdependence among factors that affect the social organization of physical space, our picture necessarily is less precise in locational terms than in the case of abstraction from these kinds of factors. Before doing so, it is important to consider the three principal limitations to Von Thuenen's model. First, there seems to be no quantitative or institutional restriction to access to land. At the fringe, land is free and abundant. Rent arising from ownership is not considered. Second, the assumption is made that a micro-regional setting is isolated from the rest of the world. In particular, Von Thuenen is led to questionable conclusions when he addresses broader issues such as international trade and the natural wage.

2. Von Thuenen apparently was aware of these limitations and attempted to cope with some of them, but without leaving his method of analysis: "Without abstracting from reality, we can attain no scientific knowledge" (Von Thuenen 1966:229). At the same time he admitted that "This process presents a twofold danger: (1) that mentally we separate what in reality is interdependent; and (2) that we base our findings on assumptions which, not being fully conscious of them, we fail to make explicit; and that we then regard as generally valid, what is valid only under these assumptions" (ibid.: 229).

Finally, there is the assumed ultimate rationality of economic behavior. A fully commercialized system is taken for granted, rather than partially commercialized or subsistence peasant production. The notion of a specialist farmer may be less relevant to peasant economies, however.

Despite these criticisms, we need not abandon the useful insights of Von Thuenen's model. One could argue, for instance, that unequal competition between small peasants and large-scale capitalist farmers causes the former to content themselves with crop production generating lower net incomes per hectare than they potentially might achieve given their distance from the main market, that is, if no agrarian differentiation had occurred. For small peasants in the periphery of the "isolated state," however, there are even fewer feasible options—crops yielding positive net incomes—than for those in the center, resulting in greater competition in the *same* crops from large-scale holdings in the *same* area. In other words, commercial small-scale farming is less feasible in the periphery.

Apart from Von Thuenen's crops theory, one may also argue on the basis of his "intensity theory." Differing technologies may be available that give varying intensities of production. These differences in land productivity are a consequence of differences in the amount of "town-based material inputs"; that is, differences in productivity are related to the amount of capital employed per hectare. Because peasants would have less access to capital (or access at higher costs), they would also have less access to the higher-intensity technologies. Only peasants who enjoy locational rents near the urban centers would have the opportunity to switch to such higher-intensity technologies. The argument can also be reversed: traditional peasant technologies consist of a diversified farming system and have lower land intensities and aim at minimizing risks, even if this implies lower monetary income per hectare (Lipton 1968). In this case, peasants are also better able to withstand local market contractions arising from declining demand or from competing trade. They can survive where large-scale capitalist farms would probably perish, and consequently would not compete for the land.

As a general conclusion, it seems that smallholders would be better able to survive, at the two extremes, but in a *different* role at each end of the spectrum. Smallholders near the urban market may be able to survive despite relatively high land prices, as small commercial producers adopting high-intensity technologies, whereas those at the other extreme, the periphery, may (continue to) subsist using their traditional survival technology. The absence of opportunities for large-scale capitalist production in the periphery causes land prices to remain low—in the intermediate area, however, it will be more difficult to determine opportunities and chances of survival because several factors work in opposite directions. In this way we have been able to deal to some extent with the third limitation of Von Thuenen's theory.

As regards the quantity or institutional restriction to access to land, and in relation to absolute land rents in particular, it could be argued that, to the farmer, land rental constitutes a cost whose level is determined by the general political and economic conditions. The workings of the model may then help to explain local *variations* in levels of land rentals (and land prices for that matter). These variations can be seen as attempts on the part of the landowner to appropriate fully or partially the differential land rent. In other words, if the differential land rent increases because of such factors as the adoption of higher-intensity technology, or decreases in transport rates or marketing costs, the landlords will attempt to capture part of this increased differential rent by raising the land rental, such that in the next round it would be necessary to include a higher land rental as higher cost. Consequently, a lower land rent or net income will result. The greater the monopoly power of the landlords, the smaller the net income of the tenant farmers and the variations in net income among them.

Von Thuenen stays very close to the localized setting of his analysis. This is clearly illustrated when he deals with external trade and particularly with the effects of (artificial) barriers to free trade. For the purpose of his analysis, he divides the local state into two sectors: one encompasses a fraction of the hinterland and the other takes in the town and the remainder of the hinterland (a poor and entirely rural sector). The imposition of a barrier to trade between the two would harm both states, in the sense that farmers in the poorer (entirely rural) state would be left without an income and would "have to choose between emigration or starvation" (Von Thuenen 1966:193), whereas the artisans, factory workers, and miners of the town (the other state), who previously supplied the farmers with urban-made goods, would lose their livelihood. Consequently, both would lose.

What would happen, one might ask, if the area available for potential cultivation was not curtailed as a result of cutting one isolated state into two, but if more imports from another isolated state become available which are produced at lower cost? To answer this question it is necessary first to realize the consequences of a "closing frontier." If no more land is available in an isolated state, a *generalized* increase will occur in the prices of agricultural products (for the sake of simplicity I do not consider here the normal tendency of rising urban prices due to higher average transport costs, which in any case may be counteracted by improvements in transport). The shortage of land will reveal itself first in the outer ring in terms of higher prices, and its effects will translate into the inner rings until a new and stable situation is obtained. The farmers and particularly the landlords would benefit from such a situation, but it would be disadvantageous to the town population: the latter's real income would decline. Now if the town should succeed in importing from another isolated state and at competitive prices one *single* agricultural product (that hitherto yielded high land rent)—that is, if the product concerned is produced at lower absolute cost because of superior agronomic or inferior social conditions—this would cause locally a *generalized* decrease in urban prices of agricultural commodities, and, of course, a *contraction* of the cultivated area. Those who will then be most seriously affected are the farmers (or their landowners instead) who enjoy the highest land rent(al). As mentioned earlier, these are the high-intensity capitalist farmers rather than the (partially commercialized) peasants, who are less affected. This is clearly a different conclusion than Von Thuenen's own conclusion regarding international trade—that international trade, or interregional trade for that matter, is beneficial to the town population and detrimental to the surrounding agriculture, rather than having the same negative effect on both.

This last conclusion may also be what Kautsky had in mind when he stated:

> The expansion of the railways and reduction of transport cost achieved in the latter part of the nineteenth century expanded the urban market and accelerated the growth of the industrial population which thus called for a larger volume of imports into Europe from the overseas territories. The threat to European agriculture came not from the volume of agricultural imports so much as the conditions under which they had been produced. *As they appeared on the market, they made it progressively less possible for European agriculture to shift the burden of its own charges* (a rising absolute rent, etc.) *back on to consumers by way of price increases.* (Kautsky in Banaji 1976:42; italics added)

One conclusion that may be drawn from the preceding analysis is that town-based economic elites rather than landed elites are interested in trade integration with other isolated states, and in the emergence of specialized production in the countryside.

## Macro-Regional Relations between Town and Countryside

Trade and exchange in general between town and countryside tend to expand beyond an isolated micro-regional framework. This brings us automatically to the question of the sociospatial evolution of trade systems. Before dealing with this complex issue, however, it is useful to examine some of the known central-place models of spatial organization.

Formally, the central-place models of Christaller (1966) and Loesch (1954) employ two key concepts: (1) minimum economic size of activity (threshold of supply) and (2) maximum range of a good in terms of demand, that is, the maximum distance consumers would be prepared to travel for it. The underlying operational assumption is that the minimum supply surface is always smaller than or equal to the surface of the circle delimiting the maximum range. In the reverse case, only mobile traders would survive. Furthermore, goods and services can be grouped in varying orders of threshold and range. Under the assumptions of an isotropic plane nested hierarchies of central places emerge, central places being the centers where suppliers concentrate.

The principal difference between the Christaller and the Loesch models is the way in which the system is built up. Whereas Christaller works downward from highest-order facility, Loesch works upward, and because he considers thresholds in more variable orders, the result is a less rigid system of central places. Christaller developed three types of hierarchies, each of which differs in spatial arrangement: the landscape based on the marketing principle ($K = 3$); the landscape based on the transport principle ($K = 4$); and the administrative landscape ($K = 7$). The variable $K$ refers to the number of hexagons that can be included within a hexagon of next higher order. For a graphical presentation of marketing systems based on these principles see Figure 2.1.

The question which of these types would apply under what general conditions is answered somewhat superficially. On the basis of empirical findings, Christaller considers the marketing principle to be the "primary and chief law of distribution of central places" (1966:192). The principles underlying the other two types are considered secondary laws causing deviations that apply only under certain incidental noneconomic or natural conditions.

The models discussed here, like Von Theuenen's model, are subject to restrictive assumptions that do not apply easily to the historical, economic, and geographical features of most Third World countries. We shall not further elaborate on these, but refer the reader to the literature (cf. Chisholm 1962; or Berry 1967).

As in the preceding discussion of Von Thuenen, I turn now to consideration of some of the social implications of the way in which trade is spatially organized. Let us compare, for instance, the topological structure of the three systems (Smith 1976a). Apart from the obvious difference that the $K = 3$ system lies in a more dispersed rural population than do the other two, the rural producers in this system are better placed vis-à-vis urban traders (see Figure 2.1). In the $K = 3$ system a rural producer has equal access to three towns of the same order, whereas in the $K = 7$ system he has close association with only one town. In the latter there is no interlocking competition, whereas the former encourages such competition, which is clearly to the advantage of rural producers. The $K = 4$ system takes an intermediate position regarding interlocking competition, because lower-order centers are located along transport links originating from higher-order centers, and this

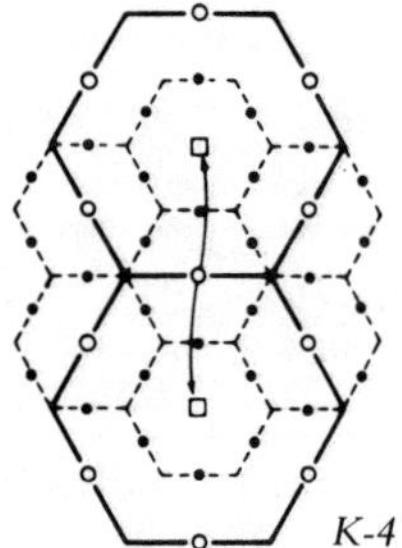


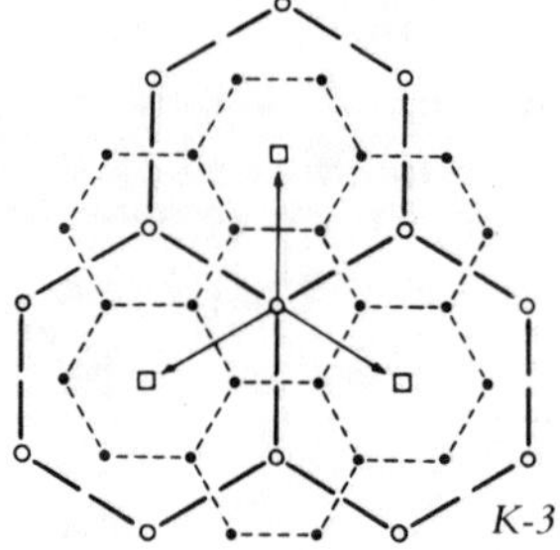


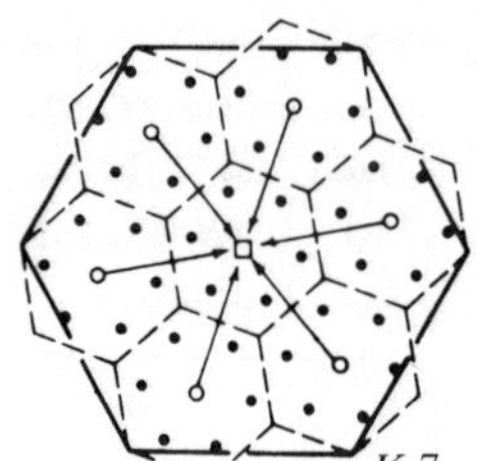


*Christaller Center Place Systems*

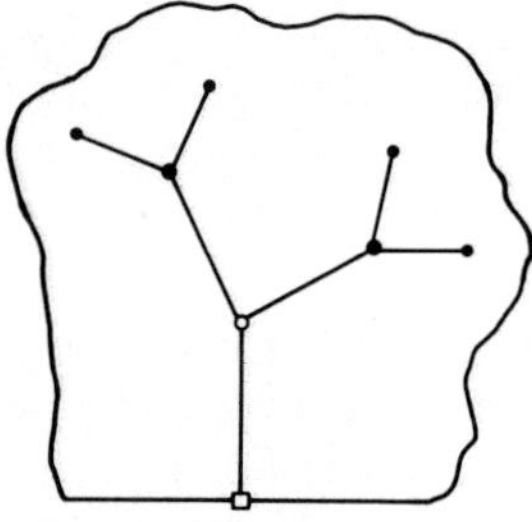

*Dendritic System*

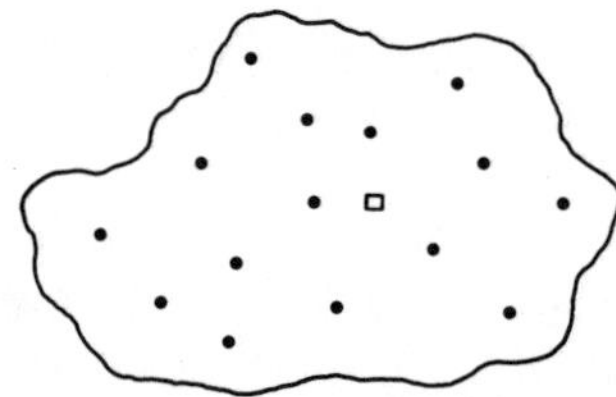

*Solar System*

□ *First-order center*

○ *Second-order center*

● *Third-order center*

FIGURE 2.1. Central place systems.

system appears to be efficient for the distribution of urban goods. In the $K = 7$ system, trade areas are administered—that is, completely divided up into discrete areas without overlap—a phenomenon that is familiar as a monopolistic practice. Thus, one may conclude:

> The marketing pattern is most efficient for rural consumers and for the distribution of rurally produced goods. The transport pattern is most efficient for urban distributors and for the distribution of urban goods . . . And the administrative pattern is most efficient for urban-based bureaucrats or monopolists, who are attempting to control a region. It is not well suited, from the point of view of the consumer, for the distribution of rural commodities. (Smith 1976a:20)

Furthermore, there is no reason to assume that at the level of a country as a whole, only one single system—of what ever *K* order—would apply. On the contrary, there is every reason to assume that there will be significant (historical) differences depending on the role that various micro-regions play in the process of national integration and the historically evolved socioeconomic structure in each region.

To complete this brief socioeconomic appraisal of spatial structures, it is important to deal briefly with a fourth type of central-place system: the dendritic market structure (Johnson 1970).

As a topological structure, this system has the following characteristics: First, lower-order centers are associated with only one single higher-order center, and second, there is an absence of a nested pattern. Most of the small centers are found in a few areas at a great distance from the largest urban center. The latter, according to Johnson, is usually a port or the national capital. The system is efficient in channelling rural goods up the hierarchy and for export, and similarly in distributing imported goods downward. The system would clearly be inefficient for the distribution of rural goods domestically and among the various regions.

One problem of these central-place models is that, given their static and descriptive nature, they are of little use for analyzing the evolution of market systems. Attempts to dynamize such models by introducing stages of filling in an iostropic plane, so as to generate a trajectory, remain unsatisfactory (cf. Abler, Adams, and Gould 1971).

The development of market systems cannot be seen separately from the development of market exchange itself and the particular conditions under which this takes place. Market systems do not appear instantly, and whether they are externally imposed or endogenously brought about is likely to produce different results. Equally, new market-system developments are shaped by the previous market structure (inertia of spatial–physical structure).

In his study of marketing in rural China, Skinner (1964, 1965) attempts to describe the development of an interlocking central place system on the basis of periodic markets. He considers population growth to be the stimulus to commercialization of the peasant economy, and argues that the market system that evolves is entirely functional to the peasant economy. Urban centers develop only as a result of rural market intensification. Therefore, because the system's emphasis is on the rural redistribution of rural goods, peasants can specialize their production, increase their productivity, and so forth.

Periodic market systems do not necessarily evolve in this way. Instead of integrating both horizontally and vertically, vertical integration alone may take place, such that the system develops toward a dentritic system that permits urban–rural exchange but at the same time isolates local (rural) markets. The importance of external forces in separating rural–urban from rural–rural exchange contrasts with the process as described by Skinner.

Similarly, solar systems may either be molded into a dendritic structure of external linkage or be integrated into an administrative central-place system (Smith 1976b). The former case, being selective in terms of the area where the export product is grown or mined, presents a process of simultaneous international integration and national disintegration (Slater 1975). The process of creation of the national state usually involves the centralization of political and administrative control, which effectively implies a loss of power—including that of raising taxes—by local and regional authorities in favor of the central government. Finally, one can conclude from the preceding discussion that a national spatial structure may best be viewed historically as a composite structure of partially separated and separately organized systems rather than as an instant and unified one. It is only under new development processes that powerful forces emerge that seek to integrate the entire country and beyond. For an analysis of this phenomenon, however, the framework of market and marketplace becomes inadequate, because towns then have become part of the urban economy.

## Regional Diversity of Rural Change

The most important aspect of the rural transformation is that the rural society and economy are reduced to agriculture in the countryside. In this chapter I have explored various theories, concepts, and insights that are necessary and useful for an elaboration of my general thesis. I have briefly reviewed and discussed some general theories of agrarian and rural change as well as some theories of rural spatial organization.

It is already possible to draw one preliminary conclusion: general theories of agrarian and rural change give relatively little attention to the territorial dimensions of rural transformation, although ruralists clearly have been more sensitive to this than the agrarianists.

As regards the agrarianists, we have concentrated on the organization-of-production and the articulation schools of thought. Recent Latin Americanist contributions to the articulation debate, though disregarding independent peasant behavior, have made considerable progress in accepting that a variety of peasant situations may exist. When the condition is dropped that capital has to control production, however, the key issues are to distinguish indirect or incomplete control from none or little, and to determine how important the squeeze is for the accumulation of capital as well as for the survival of the peasantry. These distinctions remain unclear. The independent peasant economy view remains highly relevant as a general microeconomic framework of peasant economy. Independence in this context does not imply that the independent peasant economy is insensitive to, or unhampered by, capitalist enterprise, but applies to its decision-making framework, which has a logic and setting of its own.

The ruralists generally depart from a wider framework and often discuss rural change in relation to extrarural processes that are either industrial (Kautsky) or urban–industrial (Pearse, Shanin). A differentiation process is one of the results of incorporation, but differs in content from the agrarian differentiation discussed earlier. Market incorporation exerts pressure on the peasants to reduce themselves to the role of agricultural producer only. In response, peasants seek new economic roles, rural and/or urban, in order to maintain a diversified pattern of activities that fully mobilize the resources of the household.

In this context one cannot escape an often-overlooked truism, namely, that rural and urban processes of change occur simultaneously and in interaction with each other. "Peasant capitalism" cannot be explained without invoking the "urban connection," one should not speculate about "agricultural involution" without considering "urban involution," and so forth.

It can be concluded that the principal difficulty with spatial organization theories is that they isolate spatial factors underlying regional diversity, and give too little attention to the social organization of rural activities and their effect in encouraging or inhibiting the spatial/regional specialization of economic activities. Attempts have been made to analyze the interaction between the two kinds of factors by exploring the economic and social implications of spatial-organization theories. In the case of Von Thuenen's land-use theory, in particular, some advances have been made; in the case of central-place models, I have discussed contributions by others, notably Smith. Yet notwithstanding important advances that have been made, much of the understanding and explanation of processes of rural change lies beyond these theories. It should be recognized, of course, that the original aims of these theories were also more restricted; basically, the theories were meant to explain how spatial concentration/differentiation could result from a socially homogeneous setting. If one now wants to analyze from a socially differentiated setting, these postulated outcomes do not emerge. Moreover, the key variables considered in the spatial theories become less important.

The regional diversity of rural transformation is thus seen as a complex interplay between social–economic factors and the geographical environment. Rural transformation has a social-economic component insofar as regional differences exist in the historically evolved social organization of rural activities. Moreover, forces of change also have a spatial dimension, such that they act differentially upon these various regions, notwithstanding the fact that some forces of change reveal strong homogenizing tendencies. This dual interaction will be further elaborated upon in Chapter 4, after I have discussed the main approaches to processes of urban change.

# CHAPTER THREE
# FROM TOWN TO URBAN ECONOMY

## Introduction

Having discussed some of the most important processes of rural change, I turn now to the processes of urban change. In reviewing some of the views offered in the literature, one is struck by the varying importance attributed to urbanization. For some, urbanization is a demographic phenomenon, whereas others consider political and/or economic and/or social aspects as the overriding feature(s) of urban change.

Urbanization is associated with the rise of capitalism in general and the industrial revolution in particular. More recently, under-urbanization is seen to have important implications for transitions to socialism in Eastern Europe as well as in the Third World. Finally, in an all-comprehensive way, urbanization has been equated with modernization/development. At the risk of being polemical, one could say, paraphrasing Wildavsky (1973): "if urbanization is everything, maybe it is nothing." General conceptions of urbanization are linked inextricably to an implicit or explicit view of processes of rural change. In fact, if urbanization is singled out as a prime variable, a rural–urban dichotomy is often found at the base.

Taking these observations into account, I have organized this chapter as follows: First, I discuss general theories of urban change, followed by spatial theories of urbanization. In the next section I examine urban change in relation to the process of rural change, analyzing the relationship between town and countryside from an urban point of view. In the last section I draw some preliminary conclusions.

## General Conceptions of Urbanization

It is not surprising that, in the study of urbanization, the demographic dimension has received considerable attention (Davies 1969, 1972). Migration and the so-called demographic transition fuel the process of urban growth. Whereas in the past towns had low and even negative rates of natural increase and migration was needed in order to maintain town populations, urbanization denotes a change whereby urban life expectancy and natural growth exceed those in the rural areas and are further amplified by rural-to-urban migration.

In the conceptualization of urbanization as a process of intersectoral change, urbanization is equated with industrial or rather nonagricultural growth. The basis for the intersectoral shift is the classical precondition that agricultural production needs to rise above subsistence levels before specialization and urbanization can take place. Specialization and productivity, augmenting (nonagricultural) activities, set in motion an upward process that enables and stimulates the expansion of nonagricultural activities in cities. High income elasticities of demand further support this process. Because towns offer more advantageous locations for manufacturing and trade than does a dispersed distribution, the urbanization process becomes a corollary of industrial change (Currie 1976). A somewhat different interpretation holds that industrialization (and also commercial agriculture) has a high labor productivity and can draw upon a supply of labor that in principle is unlimited, and which originates largely from the countryside. The intersectoral shift from subsistence agriculture to industrial economy implies the creation of an urban unlimited supply of wage labor.

The concept of urbanization as a process of social and political change is firmly embedded in modernization studies (cf. Friedmann and Wulff 1976). Urbanization becomes a causal rather than derived factor of political and social change (Friedmann 1968). It signifies the breaking up of traditional values and forms of exchange and the creation of new ones. Fast processes of urbanization may even cause crises of inclusion when the political system is unable to accommodate the new demands that are put on it. This view of urbanization relies very heavily on cultural ecology ("urban way of life") and on cities as a locus of innovation (Germani 1973). With particular reference to Latin America, and on the basis of his vast knowledge of its settlement history, Richard Morse was one of the first to reject this particular conception of urbanization, although he prefers to call his critique a "lens correction" (Morse 1971:189). His main contention is that

> Friedmann's vision of the innovative potential of the metropolitan center and his generous appraisal of possibilities for the spatial organization of communities must be deepened—though not necessarily effaced—by the image of the large Latin American city as a basis of privilege and conservatism whose wealth and opportunities are denied to increasing numbers of its poor. (Ibid.: 198)

Setting aside for the moment the Latin American historical evidence, the key issues are really that physical factors such as size are seen as the universal conductors for social change and innovation. However, formulated very succinctly by Abrams (1978:10), the "trouble, perhaps, is that the town is a social form in which the essential properties of larger systems of social relations are grossly concentrated and intensified to a point where residential size, density and heterogeneity, the formal characteristics of the town, appear to be themselves constitutional properties of a distinct social order."

Somewhat earlier, and from a different and more empirical angle, some of the weaknesses of the preceding concept were laid bare in a discussion on "over-urbanization." This proposition was intended to convey the idea that Third World countries were experiencing very high rates of urban population growth, whereas statistical analyses of population data from developed countries revealed that the level of urbanization was already much higher in the developing countries than was to be expected in view of their levels of economic development. Sovani (1964) demonstrates the empirical inconsistencies in the analysis of over-urbanization (the correlation between urbanization and occupational structure or industrialization is not stable over time), and argues that the concept does not fit Third World realities very well.

This inconclusive situation may well have had the effect that, almost by default, alternative and new approaches obtained credibility. Two powerful and apparently attractive explanations came to the fore, namely, the dependency and the informal-sector concepts of urbanization. Both address the same questions, which over-urbanization protagonists had unsuccessfully attempted to answer.

Although there are many dependency views and versions, the dependent-urbanization concept can be considered neo-Marxist because it departs from a basic feature of the Marxist point of view, namely, that urbanization is a mode of economic integration of capitalist development. In capitalist societies, as distinct from that in precapitalist societies, the city not only appropriates surplus product but also, because it has become a locus for production, extracts surplus value through production and exchange (Harvey 1973:232). Urbanization in the Third World then connotes the specific pattern of capitalist development whereby this transfer of surplus takes place in international center–periphery structures (Frank 1969). Urbanization also takes on a different physical shape—that of "metropolitanization" (or urban primacy).

Further neo-Marxist interpretations focus on the distortions brought about by dependent capitalist industry and capitalist agriculture, which cause the elimination of artisan crafts and peasant agriculture. At the same time, industry is unable to absorb the growing mass of urban labor which, as a consequence, becomes increasingly marginalized. Because of the international center–periphery structures, urbanization assumes a specific social form, that is, dependent urbanization, where locally disintegrating social formations are subordinated to foreign-dominated capitalist sectors (Castells 1973).

This dependency view has rightly been criticized by Singer (1973) for its almost exclusive emphasis on external factors and its failure to examine internal factors. With regard to the significance of dependency for Latin American historical developments, Singer stresses, "Although it is possible to line up dependency as *one* of the factors in a series of events, the size, the strength and interests of the different classes and regional groups within each country and between the collating countries were certainly decisive in many other instances" (Singer 1973:96). Similarly, it would be an unwarranted simplification to argue that foreign capital prevented an urbanization process which, until then, was said to have been unbalanced. Singer adopts a contrasting position and argues that there has been *too little* migration. The problem is the continued existence in urban *and* rural areas of low-productive precapitalist sectors, *in spite of* modern capitalist developments. Singer does not elaborate on the nature of urbanization, other than saying that it correlates with the (mal-)development of productive forces. The particular characteristics of the urban structure (primacy and disarticulation) are attributed to the same general cause, complemented with considerations from industrial and central-place location theories.

The recognition that urbanization is neither a homogeneous nor a universal process brought new insights to the fore. McGee (1971), an early author who contributed to this view, argues that neither (early) dependency nor modernizationist urbanization theories are adequate to explain the Third World urbanization process. Both are considered "city dominant" theories. McGee proposes a theory of urban involution whereby the economic structure of the Third World city is examined in light of its relationships with its hinterland and with international capitalism. He draws on Geertz's (1963) description of the bazaar economy. Relationships with the city hinterland are established by the transactions that take place between the peasant and bazaar economy (or nonagricultural and food products, respectively). Both are based on the same principles of survival. Thus, agricultural involution and urban involution are, apparently, two sides of the same process of change. This connection, however, is not drawn explicitly by McGee, who concentrates exclusively on the city. In any case, it is the involution of the bazaar economy (including the sharing of poverty) that sustains the urbanization process, rather than the development of the "firm sector." In the long run, the penetration by the firm sector of the interlinked bazaar and peasant economies would undermine the involuted system. For example, elimination of the peasant economy would reduce the supply of products and inputs for the urban bazaar economy. "At the same time landless peasants pour into the city looking for work, which neither the capitalist nor weakened bazaar sector can provide in sufficient quantity, [causing] . . . a gradual transformation of the indigenous economy from traditional to capitalist modes of production" (McGee 1971:

86). Therefore, it is basically through actions of the firm sector that the system breaks down and acquires "revolutionary potential."

A number of dualistic informal-sector formulations can be identified for Latin America, which are different from those perceived by McGee's "geographer's eye." They are more employment oriented and can be considered to have terminated the inconclusive debate on open and disguised under- and unemployment. These unwieldy categories were initially defined as the informal sector, a "waiting room" for employment in the formal sector. A collection of articles published in the 1970s and republished by PREALC (1978) gives a good impression of how the concept has changed over time. Together with Todaro's (1969) migration model, the informal sector apparently became a rational explanation of an anomaly to established convention. The informal sector "emerges as a new traditional sector—which it is in terms of income and productivity—and constitutes a way in which migrants subsist who do not find employment in the organized part of the labour market" (PREALC 1978; translation by the author).

Very quickly, however, the informal-sector discussion became rather confusing in that the same concept was used for dualist *and* nondualist conceptions (cf Moser 1978); in the latter case, relations with other sectors vary from complementary (Webb 1975), exploitative (Bienefeld 1975), and marginal subordination (Quijano 1974) to heterogenous dependency (Tokman and Souza 1976). What initially was considered a fairly straightforward conceptual solution became progressively unwieldy. Sinclair (1978) summarizes the general criticisms under three points: (a) as a prior generalization this conceptualization is too aggregate to capture the complexity and internal variety; (b) as a dichotomy it emphasizes differences of separated wholes rather than recognizing the urban economy as an "ensemble of production"; and (c) as a static conception it is difficult to use in dealing with what, in reality, is a dynamic situation. Furthermore, Sinclair wonders correctly whether the urban-rural dichotomy that implicitly precedes and overlaps with that of the informal sector is an appropriate one. With these critiques the discussion has gradually turned away from urbanization and has focused more and more on the organization of the urban labor market per se and on the structure of urban poverty.

In the context of the informal-sector discussion in Latin America, special mention should be made of Milton Santos, who presents a particular view of his own and attempts to integrate—following the thinking of McGee—the general economic and spatial dimensions of the process of urban change. The pattern of "distorted" development of countries of the Third World entails that the city "[can] no longer be studied as a single homogeneous entity, but should be thought of as two subsystems, namely the 'upper' or 'modern' circuit and the 'lower circuit' " (Santos 1977:8). The international demonstration effect coupled with the post–World War II technological modernization created an upper circuit alongside the existing lower circuit. The upper circuit evolved with import-substituting industrialization, the expansion of banking and commerce, the increasing involvement of the state, and the dependency on multinational corporations. Technological factors cause market conditions to become predominantly monopolistic or oligopolistic, and this has a profound impact on entry to and behavior in the upper circuit as distinct from the lower circuit. Although Santos is careful to avoid the term *dualism* and prefers to speak of *bi-polarity,* a number of dichotomic variables are listed to describe each circuit: "The two circuits thus represent opposite forms of division of labour. In the upper circuit, it is imposed by the necessity of capital accumulation; in the lower circuit, by the need for the survival of a numerous labour force" (ibid.:91). The relations between the two circuits can be both complementary and competitive, but in all cases in a domination–subordination framework: "As the economy becomes more modern, and as different intermediate and final consumer goods are demanded, the lower circuit must increasingly turn to inputs from the upper circuit. Equally, upper circuit demand for lower circuit outputs decreases as the economy becomes more complex" (ibid.:140). Polarization between the two circuits would increase.

Santos's contribution differs significantly from other theories using an informal-sector conceptualization, in the sense that he looks at the organization of the urban economy not only in terms of production but also in terms of market and credit institutions and the state. However, basic problems inherent in this conceptualiztion remain, such as the level of aggregation, linkage, and dynamisms (see Chapter 4, pp. 92-98).

More recently, students of urbanization have taken a new look at the processes involved, and also have turned to other important aspects of the urban economy, including issues such as the political economy of the city and of urban planning (Castells 1978; Harloe 1977), and the analysis of urban forms of casual work (Bromley 1979; Bromley and Gerry 1979), etc. With regard to the processes of urban change, it is important to refer to Roberts (1975, 1978, 1982) and to Gilbert and Gugler (1982), whose analyses of urbanization share in common that they are not burdened by an a priori hypothesis of an urban–rural division, whether as a dualism or a continuum.

A more open and eclectic approach to urban and rural relations is taken by Gugler, who argues that rural–urban migrants are often well-informed, by kin or local migrants who return (temporarily), about opportunities available in the city. Only those without sufficient connections may have to content themselves with less-attractive opportunities and these individuals become part of what Quijano (1974) calls the "marginalized labour force." Kinship and other local-level closely knit networks play an important role in migrant adaptation to the urban economy. These close ties do not necessarily break down in the city. On the contrary, for the urban poor who cannot secure a stable livelihood, they constitute an important basis for distributive exchange:

> What distinguishes the city from rural areas are the options it provides. There is not one urban lifestyle distinct from a rural way of life but a variety of lifestyles unknown in the village community. Some urbanites lead encapsulated lives, nearly as if they were in a village community, but others strike out, associate with like-minded persons, separate when they no longer agree, become individualists. The bigger the city, the better the chance for even the most unusual mind to find others so inclined . . . Cities are centres of innovation because it is in cities that innovators can constitute a critical mass. (Gugler 1982:124)

Gugler reiterates Friedmann's views which, in their most complete version, were expressed in 1972 in his *General Theory of Polarized Development.* A similar reorientation is found in Butterworth and Chance 1981:90–94).

Roberts (1975, 1978) relies and elaborates on the approach taken by Paul Singer (1974), and also underlines the historical fact that dependency in Latin America had taken a variety of forms. Furthermore, he draws attention to the importance of (urban) primacy resulting from industrial concentration, adding that the

> period of capital-intensive industrialization has, however, changed the nature of the articulation between the capital city and other large cities and provincial places. Rapid urbanization and the development of capitalist production in agriculture have increased the importance of the internal market for both agricultural and industrial production. Improvements in communications and the penetration of government, commerce and the mass media to even the remotest areas of a country are other factors increasing economic and political integration. (Roberts 1978:82)

Consequently, "internal colonialism is an inadequate concept to explain contemporary provincial underdevelopment" (ibid.:82).

Roberts also supports Singer's position, that the central issue of Latin American urbanization is why the process has *not* led to the modernization of agriculture. The question is not why so many leave the land but why more have not done so. According to Roberts, this is because peasants have become more diversified in their off-farm nonagricultural activities. In view of the increasing population pressure on the land, such diversification is also a necessity. Migration to urban areas, even if temporary, is part of such a diversification strategy. Migration, then, is not necessarily a signal of local stagnation but of local enterprise. Robert's basic arguments may be summarized as follows:

> In Latin America, the counterpart to the concentration of economic activities in urban–industrial centres is an increasing diversification of the agrarian structure. The transformation of that structure by the infusion of capitalism remains a partial one, which is likely to be felt most sharply in the rural areas close to the most dynamic cities. Elsewhere, various forms of agricultural production coexist and complement each other: peasant farming expands as a means of colonizing new regions or of exploiting crops which are not commercially viable under other forms of production. The improvement of communications and the generalization of money wages have commercialized the village-level economy, but without transforming it completely into capitalist production. Seasonal labour, often provided by peasant farmers or at times by agricultural workers residing in towns, powers plantations and commercial farms. The result is a situation in which the rural areas retain part of the natural increase in their population and their characteristic economic activities become those of petty trading, petty commodity production and labour intensive farming. The household remains a significant unit in the local economy, but the migration of family members and the fragmentation of economic enterprise undermines its basis as a unit of production. (ibid.:107)

Furthermore, these enterprises may span urban *and* rural locations.

Roberts defines these enterprises primarily as being small in scale, although he follows very closely the Geertz–McGee dualistic model of the urban economy. He puts more emphasis on the linkage between them, in the sense that in terms of either inputs (including credit) or outputs or both, the small-scale sector is dependent on large enterprises: "The basic reason for survival of the small-scale sector of the urban economy is that it is a convenient complement to the large-scale sector" (Roberts 1978:117). As a consequence, this "articulated coexistence" becomes a characteristic feature of the firm sector, where it reduces the need for rationalization and further technological improvement.

I have quoted from Roberts's contribution at some length, not only because of its importance, but also to be able to make some observations. First, it is somewhat surprising that he puts so much emphasis on the links between urbanization, industrialization, and agriculture, whereby the latter two are understood as aggregate sectors. The historical facts—that in England an agricultural revolution preceded the industrial and urban one, and that in the United States urbanization stimulated both the industrial and agricultural sectors—are perhaps not particularly relevant, because neither holds true for Latin America (as Roberts also argues). The fundamental reason for this is that at the microeconomic level, both large and small enterprises *simultaneously* operate agricultural and nonagricultural activities. As Roberts (1978) himself points out, the fact that peasant households (rural or not) hold onto their land is because they are *diversified* enterprises.

Second, in Latin America, not only the urban–rural distinction but also the intersectoral one is less marked. This brings us to another point, which is directly concerned with this diversification of activities. In Chapter 2 I review some pertinent theories on rural change, showing that the "ruralists" in particular—in contrast with the "agrarianists"—emphasize this diversity as an essential (and existing) feature of the peasant household. Therefore, the issue is not so much that peasant households now increasingly must rely on nonagricultural activities, *but that these nonagricultural activities and opportunities became increasingly urban based.*

Third, the articulation view held by Roberts stands somewhat in contrast to his careful and critical approach to dualistic conceptions. To label these urban-based activities entirely as an articulated sector seems to deny the active and entrepreneurial dynamism of this social group. How important are the purchase/sale of inputs/outputs for these households, or for the large firms, for that matter? How vital to the continued existence and growth of each of the two sectors is subordination? Dynamism in the small-scale sector is demonstrated by the fact that unequal market conditions and the resulting low incomes and high uncertainty are counteracted by the household, by means of diversification into other activities, either formal or informal, agricultural or nonagricultural. Notwithstanding these unanswered questions, Roberts's contribution is highly relevant and stands out for its supradisciplinary grasp of the varied and complex realities of Latin America.

## Spatial Conceptions of Urbanization

The early spatial conceptions of urbanization were concerned with city size distribution. They sought to relate these to aggregate dimensions of the development process, particularly to what are considered two opposite types of city size distribution, namely, the rank size and its corresponding lognormal distribution of cities by city size, and the primate city size distribution. The rank size can be stated as follows:

$$P_r^q = P_1/r \ ,$$

Where $P_1$ is the population of the largest or first-ranking city under the strict formulation and a general constant under the general formulation of the rule; $P_r$ is the population of a city with rank $r$; and $q$ is an exponential constant, or:

$$\log r = \log P_1 - q \log P_r \ .$$

The rank size rule posits a stable relation between the size of a city and its importance in the urban (size) hierarchy (Abler, Adams, and Gould 1971). The primate city size distribution refers to those distributions where a considerable gap exists between the population size of the largest city in the country and that of the second, third, etc., largest city. Primacy is usually expressed as a ratio of the largest town divided by the next largest town ($P_1/P_n$), or by the sum of $n$ next larger towns $(P_1/^nP_n)$.

Research has concentrated on establishing the causes of the existence of either city size distribution *at the national level* and on relations with the level of development. Berry (1961), in his influential article, "City size distribution and economic development," rejects on empirical grounds the earlier view that primacy is associated with underdevelopment, and rank size rule with economic maturity. He formulates a general descriptive model, characteristic of his time, according to which a country with a primate city size distribution passes through various and alternative intermediate distributions (stages). He argues that "fewer forces will affect the urban structure of a country [conducing to primacy], (a) the smaller is that country; (b) the shorter is the history of urbanization in the country; and (c) the simpler is the economic and political life of the country and the lower its degree of economic development" (Berry 1961:149). This model was criticized at the theoretical (starting from primacy) and the empirical levels, such that the author revised his view and maintained that an urban system develops from "a low-level equilibrium distribution" (many small-sized places) via urban primacy to the "high-level equilibrium" of a lognormal distribution (Berry 1971).

This revised model has several characteristics in common with El-Shakhs's (1972) proposition: using an average primacy ratio, he found an association between primacy distribution and the economic development pattern, namely, a "peak of primacy at the height of socioeconomic transition". Initially, nonagricultural activities and population will concentrate in a few cities surrounded by dispersed and isolated settlements. Primacy reaches a peak as economic development advances, but "eventually, with the increasing influence and importance of the periphery and structural changes in the pattern of authority (as a result of conflict resolution in favor of the periphery), deviation-counteracting processes induce a decentralization and spread effect in the development process" and "the degree of primacy begins to decline" (1972:31). Once this process is set in motion, further transport and communication improvements will stimulate further decentralization and urban diseconomies of scale will push for a steady increase in primacy. Although El-Shakhs recognized that his propositions closely resemble the pattern of regional income inequality postulated by Williamson (1965), he relies more on a presumed positive outcome of Friedmann's (1972) theory of polarized development. The latter stresses the importance of the spatial organization of power and government for the development of the urban system, which he hypothesized in the same year.

> The spatial distribution of governmental power influences the location decisions of entrepreneurs during the early phases of industrialization and . . . the

> growing interpenetration of governmental and private economic institutions channels the subsequent location decisions of individuals and households to locations of central power in excess of objective opportunities for productive employment. The resulting polarized pattern of urbanization tends to be self-perpetuating, whereas the eventual decentralization of productive activities into the passive periphery of major core regions tends to leave essential relations of power virtually unchanged. (Friedmann 1972–73:16)

Consequently, the principal way in which this pattern can be changed is when the organization of power is challenged, both socially and spatially, by counter-innovative elites. The possibilities for the emergence of such elites, outside the existing social and spatial core, depend very much on the processes of diffusion and adoption of (entrepreneurial) innovations, which in turn are themselves heavily influenced by the (existing) urban system.

Although the authors mentioned so far focus almost exclusively on the relationships between city size distribution and processes of internal or national development and integration, Vapñarski (1969 attempts to incorporate the international dimension. He argues that city size distributions are affected by two key variables: the degree of closure of the system (the dependence of the national economy on international trade) and the degree of interdependence, which refers to the interregional linkages within the national economy (a highly or lowly structured system). He argues on the basis of general ecology principles that primacy is (inversely) associated with the degree of closure of the system, and that rank size is associated with the degree of internal interdependence. Postulating various combinations of closure and interdependence, he arrives at changes in the urban structure running from a primate distribution, through a rank size distribution of all centers below the primate center, to a final position of a complete rank size distribution.

The earlier view of primacy as a factor related to underdevelopment gained renewed credibility, but was now expressed in a dependency perspective. Further research was done on international dependency. For instance, McGreevey (1971) argues this on the basis of an association that he established for Latin America between the level of per capita exports and the degree of primacy in the urban system.

Johnston argues that Berry's rejection of the relation between underdevelopment and primacy had to do with the fact that "the countries whose urban size distribution are currently analyzed frequently are not spatially coincident with the original colonies within which urban patterns developed" (Johnston 1977:5). According to Johnston, the role of the town in colonialism has a gateway function; it is "an organizing nexus, a concentration of merchants and associated non-productive workers such as those involved in transport and others administering the colony for the 'homeland elite' " (ibid.:4). Primacy emerges by virtue of the lack of development of other towns: "Most colonization was at low rural densities and demanded few settlements of any size inland of the gateway, except in a few cases where very large-scale mining developments encouraged large city growth" (ibid.:5). Thus, he concludes that primacy is normal rather than lognormal. Although one could improve on Johnston's analysis, which is somewhat limited due to his exclusive reference to United Kingdom settler colonies, the basic criticism of Berry seems justified.

Three criticisms can be raised against these spatial concepts of urbanization. First, the question arises, What is it that is being observed: a nation-state or a colony, where the former may consist of several colonies or a part of an earlier colony? In any analysis of a national city size distribution, due attention should be given to the fact that physical structures, products of urbanization, normally are highly inert and are subject only to long-term processes of change.

A second criticism parallel to that just raised is the implicit assumption of Berry and almost all others that there is one *single* and *national* urban *system,* rather than various regionally localized and partially integrated *systems.* Although the city was the point of departure for Spanish colonial settlement in Latin America, it did not produce an urban system. On the contrary, "the urban network was weakly developed. The lack of commercial reciprocity among the cities, which was accentuated by Iberian mercantilist policies, insulated them and tied them individually to Lisbon and Seville" (Morse 1962:363). Cities remained the bureaucratic, commercial, and cultural outposts of Europe.

Independence in the nineteenth century did not alter the basic economic structures. Increasing but unstable dependence on a few, now-agricultural export staples militated against the creation and development of a stable network of towns and villages. This was in particularly true when one staple followed the other, creating short-lived processes of growth and expansion in various successive regions, as was the case in Colombia. Thus, the appearance of lognormality in that country is due not so much to the existence of a complex or structured system but rather to the historical (mis)fortunes of international linkages of regional economies that were only weakly organized and structured at the national level.

Although this would be an inadequate account of the Colombian urbanization and industrialization pattern (see Chapter 5), it serves to illustrate the argument that it would be historically incorrect to speak of a process of national urbanization and of a national city size distribution as meaningful analytical categories.

Third, the view predominates that there is a loose continuum from primacy to rank size distribution. In fact, as Vapñarsky (1969) hints and Carroll demonstrates, the two distributions are *not* mutually exclusive. "City size distributions which conform to the general rank size rule, can generate widely varying primacy ratios" (Carroll 1982:3). A somewhat similar point is independently raised by Ettlinger (1981), who argues that such a continuum, if it exists, is not necessarily unidirectional.

The present state of empirical findings on national city size distribution is neatly summarized by Carroll as follows: "(1) the lack of association between primacy and economic development and urbanization; (2) the high level of association between primacy and small area and population size; and (3) the association of primacy with economic export orientation" (1982:20).

These criticisms of the analysis of city size distribution should not be taken to mean tacit agreement with the "dependent urbanization" view, which considers metropolitanization (growing primacy) to be explained by layers of (sub)national center–periphery structures, dominated and imposed by international relations of dependency. Dependent urbanization has already been criticized in the previous section, and it is unnecessary to repeat the arguments here.

Perhaps one of the surprising gaps in the development literature is the lack of either theoretical or empirical studies of the historical evolution of urban or settlement patterns. Major review articles such as that by Harvey (1967) indicate that apart from a number of stochastic models and the familiar deterministic central place models, there are virtually no general propositions concerning the evolution of settlement patterns. Although a few isolated exceptions exist (e.g., Meyer 1980), this is still true today. At the empirical level, the situation is little different. For instance, one widely distributed standard introductory text on the geography of Latin American development does not mention a single study (Gilbert 1974).

Of course, the tremendous difficulties involved in such research constitute an enormous barrier, but however difficult such an analysis would be, it would undoubtedly yield important new insights. In the case of Colombia, for example, it has been established that prior to independence only some 56% of the *cabeceras municipales* (municipal towns) were in existence. The remaining 44% were founded in land colonization processes in various parts of the country at different periods of time (Hemsing 1984). Although it is fair to say that colonial (under)development had a major impact, this is also a general truism that must be complemented with a detailed analysis of internal processes in order to reach a meaningful understanding of urbanization: "the unobjectionable idea of urbanization under peripheral capitalism should convey a great deal more than domination from afar. The emergent city of the Third World shows us a complex mixture of distant and local influences that defy additive or linear interpretations" (Walton 1982:133). The same applies by implication to the urbanization process as a whole.

## Towns and the Relations between Town and Countryside

There is little disagreement in the literature that towns have played a central role in important historical processes of development and change in Europe and that they continue to play such a role in Third World development. There is a great deal of disagreement, however, as to what actually comprises that role. Towns have distinct spatial as well as social characteristics, and the disagreement arises from the difficulties in relating spatial and social characteristics at the aggregate level.

One position, that considers the town as a distinct sociospatial category, is remarkably persistent and widely accepted, not only with regard to the economic history of Europe and the transition from feudalism to capitalism, but also with regard to development in the Third World. Before discussing these issues, I will briefly review some general notions about towns and development.

### General Propositions about Towns and Development

The fact that towns were and are found in diverse social and economic settings has induced many social scientists to attempt to uncover common features of the town and its origins.

On the one hand, we find broad-based generalizations, and on the other, general and cross-sectional typologies of towns. To the former belong a number of broad statements, such as Harvey's (1973) statement that the town is associated with social differentiation and the social division of labor between producers and nonproducers, between food and nonfood producers.

Others emphasize demand factors, that is, the higher income elasticities for nonagricultural (urban-produced) goods and services. Such a generalization can be traced back to Adam Smith, who, in this context, stresses the role of the market and of town-based improvements in agricultural productivity (1970: 352–375). This view, with a different emphasis, is held by Johnston and Kilby who argue, with respect to agriculture: "Although a substantial part of the diminution in the importance of agriculture can be attributed to the relatively greater demand for non-agricultural goods with rising incomes, the more fundamental cause is the transfer of functions from generalist producers in the countryside to specialist firms in the towns" (1975: 34–35).

Broad generalizations are indeed no more than that. However, Johnston and Kilby implicitly shift from a spatial and all-encompassing definition of agriculture (everything that is located in rural areas) to a sectoral definition (see also Johnston 1970).

It may be incorrect to link towns exclusively with a market-based social division of labor, in the sense that towns emerge in other non-market-based social divisions of labor. This, however, is a moot point. The question is to determine the role that is played by the towns and the answer does not always involve a town–country opposition or dichotomy.

Hoselitz (1954), in his well-known distinction between parasitic and generative cities, recognizes the difficulty of generalizing the role of towns and seeks to circumvent this problem by means of a typology of towns. Generative cities were those that stimulated economic growth in their surrounding hinterland or region, whereas parasitic cities constitute the opposite, that is, they form an obstacle, draining resources from the countryside rather than stimulating innovation and change.

A somewhat different typology is elaborated by Sjoberg (1965), who distinguishes three "constructed types" of cities: the preindustrial, the industrializing, and the industrial city. Unlike Hoselitz, Sjoberg considers these types of cities to be "subsystems of a larger social order" namely, the feudal, the modernizing, and the industrial society. According to Sjoberg, technology in its widest sense is the key variable, and has a fundamental impact on the urban social structure. The preindustrial city functions primarily as a governmental and religious center, and its commercial role is of secondary importance. Although a high socioeconomic differentiation exists in preindustrial cities with an upper class that is almost exclusively urban, division of labor involves little specialization: standardization is virtually lacking and technology is in the hands of the lower class, by whom it is developed. The upper class is very little involved in economic activities and maintains its position through political control. The industrial city is part of the industrial order and, as such, is very much the opposite of the preindustrial city. In the industrializing city, which constitutes an intermediary, transitional link between the preindustrial and the industrial city, technology is the principal element: "Traditional arrangements most closely associated with the economic technological order seem to buckle under the impact of industrial urbanization" (Sjoberg 1965:224). In this way, a type of three-stage model results which, like many other cross-sectional models, constitutes a concept of development that is too rigid.

The city—as towns are usually called by modernizationists—is the center of social change, and city people set out to transform the traditional countryside. Friedmann's (1972) model is widely known in this context. He distinguishes three kinds of actors: the entrepreneur, the administrator, and the "disaffected intellectual." Each acts on traditional society in his own action space. A progressive integration in both the socioeconomic and the spatial sense, via heightened interaction channelled through the matrix of urban centers, makes society move toward a modern *urban* society. In subsequent articles Friedmann elaborates and refines his analysis, which in its most complete form is known as the "general theory of polarized develoment." In this version, the original town–country framework disappears, and is replaced by a core–periphery framework (Friedmann 1973). However, he retains his general conclusions that the city is devoid of traditional elements and that the direction of change is "city outward" and "country inward."

These generalizations and typologies seem to suggest that towns in predominantly agricultural societies had little economic or developmental significance, were largely parasitic, and consumers of rural surplus—a picture that seems somewhat oversimplified. As discussed in Chapter 2, the countryside in such economies was not only agricultural; rather, industrial activities were agriculturally based, that is, dependent on organic materials as material inputs and as source of energy. This is one reason why many, though not all, industrial activities formerly were carried out in the countryside. As Wrigley (1978) rightly points out, the contribution of towns to preindustrial growth was crucial. Towns facilitated specialization of the countryside in the economy; through market integration towns enabled a certain degree of specialization in agricultural *and* industrial products in the countryside, on the basis of local availability of raw materials and/or water power, and so forth. The increased exchange of goods and services was organized through trade or administered by the state, mostly at a short distance from the town but also from further away. In this respect, the role of towns was greatly strengthened by transport improvements. The key point, and the major difference between preindustrial and industrial economies, is that in the rural society all major industries depended on the land for most of their major material inputs (textiles, leather, wood for construction) and also on wood as source of energy; thus, anything that raised the productive capacity of the land improved prospects for industrialization (cf. Wrigley 1978:300 ff). Consequently, land was the major source of wealth and accumulation, and circumscribed the secondary but nonetheless crucial role of the towns.

It seems reasonable to conclude, therefore, that the development of agrarian societies would be difficult *without* the development of town-based activities.

## Towns and Transition

The progressive role of the towns, coupled with a dualistic view of town–country relations, is an issue in the Marxist debate on transition. Sweezy attributes an autonomous role to the towns, which came about through long-distance trade: the external pull of urban markets based on long-distance trade acts as the motor and dissolvant of the feudal mode (cf. Sweezy et al.

1978:41ff). Dobb (1978) challenges this position, arguing that towns have feudal origins. In his view, the transition was the outcome of the rural class struggle between feudal lords and serfs. Nevertheless, he recognizes, but as an internal contradiction, the role played by towns and trade in fostering the decline of the feudal economy through the socioeconomic differentiation that accompanied this decline in both town and country.

If one rejects dualism by arguing that towns (and merchant capital) already existed in the feudal economy, what the "are the determinants of the 'urban revolution' in Western Europe which allowed the dissolution of this mode to lead to the ulterior conquest of the countryside by the city?" (Merrington 1978). As regards the relation between towns and feudalism, Merrington went on to argue, "Far from being immobile, let alone exclusively 'rural,' feudalism was the first mode of production in history to allow, by its very absence of sovereignty, an autonomous structural place to urban production and merchant capital" (ibid.:178)—this in contrast to other cities that did not have some form of autonomy. "This position of the town as a 'collective seigneur' was—and remained backed by the absolutist state—that of a corporate economic and social unit just when and because certain places were set apart and defended by laws and privileges making them market or production centers and denying some or all such rights to the countryside around" (ibid.:180).

One might ask why Western European feudalism had such a remarkable property. Abrams (1978) argues "It was not really the towns that caused the West to advance, but the peculiar inability of western feudalism to prevent these people [merchant entrepreneurs] from maximizing their advantage which they did typically within the institutional form of a closed town" (1978:25). The move from open to closed corporate towns was their attempt to consolidate their power vis-à-vis feudal and landed authority as well as against artisans and laborers in the towns.

Thus, during the decline of western feudalism there was a changing relationship between the landed authorities and the town merchants. In addition, the transformation of feudal rent from labor services to rent in kind to money rent stimulated independent commodity production and commercial exchange which, apart from causing differentiation among the peasantry, strengthened the role and the position of the town merchants. Urban–rural as well as rural–rural but urban-mediated exchange became more important. This geographical extension of the market enabled the merchants to move *beyond* guilds and local exclusivism, that is, to production of high-quality goods for a small urban market, through the growth of manufactures first by rural industries (proto-industrialization) and then by machine production. The latter, together with capitalist agriculture, enabled the development of factories, which in turn enabled capitalist cities to overcome the limits of corporate urban development. According to Merrington, these two factors (extension of the market and elimination of the barriers imposed by a guild-based urban economy) constitute two major discontinuities that cannot be accounted for by either unilinear concepts of urbanization or dualist views of town–country relations.

Holton (1984) voices a similar critique of the autonomous role of under-urbanization and the implied rural–urban dichotomy in relation to the transition to socialism, as postulated by Szelenyi (1981) and Szelenyi and Pearse (1983).

## Towns in Colonial/Postcolonial Societies

One could argue that such town–countryside dualism is no longer applicable to Western Europe, but what about those Third World countries that underwent colonialism? For instance, and with respect to Latin America, it is generally argued that colonial society was a town society (Morse 1962) and that towns were a key instrument of colonial occupation: "The town was point of departure for the exploitation of mineral and land resources" (Houston 1968:352). These towns were bureaucratic, commercial, and cultural outposts of Europe. This implied dualistic conception is aptly formulated by Gilbert in his statement, "European cities prospered throughout the Third World" (Gilbert in Gilbert and Gugler 1982:15). This may be correct in terms of physical appearance, particularly for the administrative centers of the *Audiencias,* but is much less correct in a socioeconomic sense. Most industry was forbidden by Spanish colonial policy, which reduced the craft guilds to minor significance, and the merchants explicitly were forbidden to sit on the town council. Thus, the towns were in the hands of the landed oligarchy (the *latifundistas-encomenderos*) and the Church (Houston 1968). We should not lose sight of the fact, of course, that in colonial Latin America the landed elite also had important trade interests, but this only further strengthens my point. Furthermore, the *indigenas* constituted a large proportion of the town populations. Due to the *mita urbana* (forced labor conscription) to which these people were subjected, they can hardly be seen as European town citizens. Finally, the stagnation of the town population was due not so much to guild exclusivism as to the decimation (in the towns as well as in the countryside) of indigenous peoples who were not resistant to European diseases, and the like.

It is clear that the town–country configuration of colonial Latin America was quite different from that in Europe. In Latin America, town and countryside relations were defined by a *unity of purpose,* namely, the colonial extraction and exploitation of (nonurban) primary resources, for example, sugar.

The opposition created by Singer is equally artificial. He argues that the division between town and country in Latin America during the colonial period was caused by the absence of agriculture in the town: "The town practically always depends for its subsistence on the countryside, whereas the countryside only starts to depend on the town as from a certain degree of specialization of town-based activities" (Singer 1974:10). For this reason, the town had to dominate the countryside.

Another phenomenon that played a role, at least in Colombia, in the colonial period, particularly in the second half of the eighteenth century and with even more vigor in the nineteenth century, was the foundation and development of towns based on expansion of the peasant economy. In contrast to the *latifundista* or former colonial towns these towns developed out of land-settlement efforts by the *mestizo* and by poor white immigrants. The expansion of the land frontier was an important factor in the emergence and growth of independent peasant production. Domestic trade increased as a result, strengthening the commercial function of such towns and the position of the small traders.

If one wishes to maintain a dualistic view, then, a cross-town-countryside conceptualization would probably be more appropriate, certainly for Colombia, whereby some areas (town *and* countryside) would orbit more firmly in the colonial economy than would others (e.g., the mining areas, the colonial administrative centers).

The independence of Colombia in the early nineteenth century altered the colonial configuration insofar as merchants became politically and economically much more important. Town–country relations were affected by liberal trade policies that encouraged the creation of an agrarian export economy. Artisan industry in both town and countryside were affected by competing English imports. Notable in this respect was the strong opposition of the artisan guilds in Bogotá, and the depopulation between 1800–1810 and 1850–1870 of important former colonial centers such as Popayan, Cartagena, and Bogotá (although in the interim years Bogotá grew because it was made the national capital) and of towns in Santander where the peasant economy had reached a certain degree of specialization in hat making for export but which, as consequence of liberalizing trade, entered into a deep crisis and collapsed (Villegas 1978).

Because the development of export staples in the nineteenth century was erratic, short-lived, and took place in different regions, town–countryside relations continued to be consolidated at the intermediate level, producing temporarily strong regional elites who contested each other for control of the central government (Palacios 1981). The change to a federal political structure in 1851 may be considered a clear sign of this domestic nonintegration. Regional elites dominated town and country. It was only as coffee developed into a fast-growing export crop at the end of the century that this situation changed (see Chapter 5).

I have briefly dwelt on aspects of Colombian economic history to indicate that colonial dualism did not necessarily produce a town–country dualism or reflect an opposition of urban and rural interests.

## Some Conclusions on Socioeconomic and Spatial Change

In this chapter, I have reviewed some major concepts of urbanization from a general and from a specific spatial point of view, and have discussed various points of view about the role of towns in relation to changes in the countryside. Although general theories of urbanization were abandoned fairly soon after their inception and the role of urbanization subsequently was somewhat scaled down, town–country dichotomies persisted. Sectoral points of view on urban and rural change became more dominant. Urbanization was associated with industrialization, with or without the informal sector, and rural change was reduced to agrarian change.

In the latter part of the 1970s and in the early 1980s the urban–rural dichotomy began to lose credibility in the face of the persistence of traditional, peasant, precapitalist, petty forms of life in the countryside and of its growing equivalent—the informal sector—in the towns. This point is illustrated by the fact that, in addition to "agricultural involution," "urban involution" was put forward and "articulation" was seen as the key to understanding the anomaly of the rural persistence and urban expansion of the small–scale, traditional, precapitalist or petty sector.

In this and the preceding chapter, I try to show that alternative propositions are being put forward that supersede the urban–rural division. In discussions of theories of rural change, there also has emerged a reappreciation of the importance of nonagricultural dimensions, a growing recognition of the regional diversity of rural change and social differentiation in particular, and recognition of the interrelation between rural and urban processes of change.

In the analysis of urbanization, not only is the importance of towns in preindustrial or predominantly agrarian societies realized, but there is also increasing acceptance that urbanization is only one dimension of development and should not be equated with it. Towns cannot be seen as a distinct sociospatial category.

Finally, from the urban perspective also, it is increasingly recognized that urban and rural changes occur simultaneously. In this respect there is a surprising coincidence between the urban studies of Roberts (1978) and

Gilbert and Gugler (1982) on the one hand, and the rural studies of Goodman and Redclift (1981) on the other.

New contributions to the spatial conceptions of urban and rural change call for greater attention to the role of social differentiation in the understanding of spatial variations in urban and rural processes of change, and a more integrated analysis is called for from this side.

Many urban and rural studies have taken for granted, perhaps too easily, a *national framework* for analysis and observation, although international effects are increasingly incorporated. Most of these studies, however, have disregarded the effects of the development, disruption, integration, or other changes in what is sometimes a great variety of local regional economies.

Therefore, after surveying both approaches, I come to the conclusion that the general study of social differentiation tries to cope with regional variation, but regional studies, dissatisfied with existing explanations, seek alternative answers by explicitly incorporating the spatial incidence of social differentiation. At first, this apears to be a favorable development, in the sense that different disciplines of development studies approach each other. However,it becomes increasingly apparent that neither the sectoral (agriculture, industry, formal, informal) nor the spatial (urban–rural) divisions are useful analytical classifications, as development phenomena increasingly cut across and transcend types of division.

The realization of this problem has induced many authors to take an "open," "realistic," or "balanced" approach to rural and urban issues. For example, Gilbert and Gugler (1982), Johnston and Clark (1982), and Chambers (1984). In this context, eclecticism is an oft-heard criticism; in view of the obsoleteness of key concepts, perhaps this is not a vice but a virtue. In any case, it seems that a need exists for new perspectives with which to analyze both urban and rural change.

# CHAPTER FOUR
# MICRO ORGANIZATION AND MACRO CHANGE: A PERSPECTIVE

## Introduction

In the previous chapters I discuss and argue that neither a sectoral nor a spatial approach, nor a complementation of one by the other, can offer any considerable improvement to current understanding of (regional) development and change. I argue that conductors and mechanisms of change have come to transcend sectoral, spatial, and spatio-sectoral divisions and dichotomies and that, therefore, a different perspective is needed.

This chapter offers some basic elements for the design of a new perspective. Instead of seeking to integrate spatial and sectoral approaches at the aggregate or macro level, my analysis concentrates on the micro level. Nowadays, various forms of microeconomic organization can be identified, varying not only in their behavior but also in the spatial scale at which they operate. Although some forms are local, others operate regionally, nationally or transnationally. Space and economy are integrated within the micro level. Sectors and regions have ceased to be homogeneous with regard to the microeconomic actors, whose supposed homogeneous or at least similar behavior is at the basis of these macro concepts. The implied problem of aggregation has worsened: not only have new forms of microeconomic production developed, but the relative economic weight has shifted over time from one type of micro unit to another. This calls for more attention to the microeconomic dimension of the development. To come to grips with this problem, I propose a working typology in the following section.

The second basic element that I elaborate upon in this chapter concerns the institutional environment in which the microeconomy functions. This environment is not static, but is the subject of and active in the process of change. Here I refer in particular to the growing importance of the state in the economy. I argue in the third section of this chapter that as the economy becomes more complex, in terms of both microeconomic organization and the technology of production, the state not only must provide more public goods (infrastructure), but the level at which these must be provided changes from local to regional to (supra)national. The state is neither a holistic nor a given entity but is composed of various layers or levels. The creation of a multilevel system of government is very much part of the same process that causes the economic role of the state to expand.

Thus, at the micro level, I seek to examine the relation between space and economy; emphasis on the territorial organization of the state will allow a more thorough discussion of the interaction between state and private economy. In the fourth section of this chapter, I elaborate on three partly overlapping issues; that is, the impact of the agroindustrial complex on the rural economy; the impact of multilevel organization on the urbanization process; and the effects of verticalization of the regional economy on regionalism.

With regard to the first of these issues, I postulate the formation of the agroindustrial complex as the development of a new set of macro and micro relationships. In the process, the rural economy is reduced to agricultural activities that become increasingly organized at (inter)national levels. The resulting general tendencies of micro and regional specialization result in varius regional situations where development of capitalist agricultural enterprises occurs simultaneously with the survival of peasant households.

With respect to urbanization, I argue that the multilevel organization of enterprises and the centralization of government are conducive to the insertion of towns as nodes in multiple organizational and spatial networks. As a result, towns cease to be relatively autonomous sociopolitical entities.

Last, I examine some economic and political effects of the verticalization of regional economies resulting from changes in the organization of government and enterprise. I argue that both enterprises and government are prime causes of uneven regional development. I conclude with a discussion of regionalism. Although the importance of this phenomenon in counterbalancing some effects of the preceding processes is recognized, I argue that those same processes impose limitations that severely reduce the effectiveness of regionalism.

## Expanding Microeconomy

The basic point of departure in the analysis that follows is that in most mixed or market economies in the Third World, several forms of microeconomic organization can be distinguished. By this I mean the institutions in which people use their labor and other resources to produce goods and services for the achievement of a particular goal. I postulate that microeconomic forms of organizations distinguish themselves in several respects, namely, their goals and internal organization, and the spatial scale at which they operate.

The explicit recognition of space in microeconomic behavior—the firm—is not entirely new. In the 1950s the link between microeconomic organization, its growth, and the spatial scale at which it operates was recognized in regional studies related to the evolution of the geography of the enterprise (McNee 1958, cited by Hayter and Watts 1983). Important advances were made in studies on locational hierarchies, locational adjustment of firms, and models of the spatial evolution of firms, but the principal concern was with spatial aspects.

In another context, namely, the theory of oligopolistic competition, there is a similar link between economic organization and spatial scale. Sylos-Labine (1969) for instance, considers the reduction of transport costs of critical importance:

> Production units which enjoyed certain monopoly powers in limited areas gradually lost the natural protection of high transport costs: new firms were able to start up and the strongest among the existing firms were able to expand and so invade the markets hitherto closed to them . . . However, the very same process which destroyed local monopolies, created . . . more enduring monopolistic and oligopolistic positions embracing whole countries. (1969:3)

Thus, imperfect competition at one scale is carried over to a higher spatial scale. Apart from this explicit recognition, little has been done to clarify the role of this link in the dynamics of oligopolistic competition, nor have the implications for uneven development systematically been made clear.

The link has also been recognized in business administration studies on the growth of the firm. Chandler (1977), in comparing the traditional American owner-operated firm with the modern enterprise, states:

> This type of firm handled only a *single economic function,* dealt in a *single production line* in *one geographic area.* Before the rise of the modern firm, the activities of these small, personally owned and managed enterprises were coordinated and monitored by market and price mechanisms. Modern enterprise, by bringing many units under its control, began to operate in *different locations,* often carrying on *different types of economic activities* and handling *different lines of goods and services.* (1977:3; italics added)

The activities of each type of enterprise and the transactions between them thus became internalized. They became organized by managers rather than market mechanisms. Market-displacing administrative coordination entails imperfect competition in the areas in which the firm remains operative. It should be stressed that the large, modern enteprise is not merely bigger than a small firm but also is a qualitatively different unit.

A central and methodological problem in the study of Third World mixed or market economies is that production organization does not move gradually or homogenously from one single form of micro-organization to another. In addition to production organized on a household basis, there is transnationally organized production with other forms inbetween. An additional complication is that the microeconomic branch of development studies is rather undeveloped itself. Little is known, for instance, about the evolution of microeconomic organizations in the Third World.

Although I have signalled this gap in the literature, it would be beyond the scope of this research to try to fill it here. Instead, I formulate a working typology of microeconomic organizations that will constitute a building block for my theoretical perspective.

## Microeconomic Organizations and Space

In most Third World mixed economies nowadays, at least four kinds of microeconomic organization exist.

First, there are the so-called household units, which can be seen as a noncapitalist form of organization and decision making. These operate in both rural and urban contexts, and basically consist of microeconomic units in which production and consumption decisions are taken within a single framework. All household resources—mainly labor—are deployed in rural and/or urban activities. The fact that survival is often emphasized as the main objective should be interpreted with care. There is no reason why a household should not seek prosperity, but poverty of resources and opportunities and the general precariousness of the situation make survival the most immediate aim. Survival is a prerequisite to prosperity. The microeconomic behavior posited in Chayanov's theory of peasant economy (see Chapter 2) is of particular relevance here in that it attempts to deal with houehold behavior under varying conditions. Household production units tend to be small in size and essentially have a local scale of operation. Thus, local conditions provide the basic frame of reference for their day-to-day decision making (cf. Ortiz 1973).

The second type of microeconomic organization is the owner-operated micro-organization. An important difference between household units and owner-operated micro-organizations is that, in the latter, craft or technical sophistication causes family labor to recede into the background, whereas more extrafamily (semi-skilled) labor is engaged in different ways. Another difference is that the direct link of production-in-kind to satisfy own consumption needs no longer constitutes a principal component of total household income. Owner-operated microeconomic organizations, however, continue to be owned by the household or family. In this sense, their objectives are similar. When extrafamily labor is employed, profit seeking becomes the means by which this is partly achieved. Profits, just as much as household or family considerations, influence decision making. This mixture of "pure economic calculus" and family ties keeps the unit in business. Owner-operated units also tend to remain relatively small and to operate at local and regional scales. The vast majority of agricultural (farms) and industrial (crafts and workshops) activities and shopkeepers and holders of other service establishments are organized in this form of enterprise. The greater majority of such owner-operators accumulate not for growth but for "decent survival."

Owner-managed firms constitute the third form of microeconomic organization. In contrast to owner-operated units, the household or family has only supervisory or managerial control over the unit's activities. Household or family labor has largely disappeared from the shop floor, if indeed it was ever there, and remains in management. The consequent separation of the household from the production unit causes profit making to become the declared objective of the enterprise. This does not mean that this type represents the idealized nuclear family-based economic man managing his firm in holistic fashion. Two distinct subgroups may be identified: the 'older aged' firms that have been developed by enterprising landed or otherwise established elites who have created a regional empire of diversified activities in their respective areas, and the middle-class professional, skill or technology-based enterprise in agriculture, industry, personal services, or trade.

The first of these subgroups has been described by Leff (1979) as the so-called economic group in which capital is mobilized from families and others with close ties. By putting their kin and near kin in key managerial positions in each operation, the group owners operate as an interrelated unit (cf. Tangri 1982). An economic group is "a multicompany firm" that invests and produces in several product lines involving vertical integration or other economic and technological complementarities (Leff 1979b:722). These units tend to operate mainly on a regional or a national scale.

The fourth type of microeconomic organization is the manager-managed corporation, a complex organization that can no longer be run by a small group of owners. The growing role of salaried managers, first in middle management and later also in top managerial functions, alters the behavior and the decision-making process of such units in a bureaucratic direction. Motives for corporate growth now include the pecuniary and personal interests of executives, the reduction of uncertainty and risk, and also the existence of unused or underutilized resources (Hakanson 1979). Managers, rather than being profit maximizers per se, tend to opt for the long-term market position and growth of the firm in accordance with their own career perspectives and forms of remuneration (Chandler and Daems 1980). The multinational corporations constitute a distinct subgroup here (Hymer 1971), but may also be found at the national scale.

The micro units I have enumerated are summarized briefly in Table 4.1.

The main point is not to establish the number of admissible combinations, or to argue that the preceding classification is the only one possible. More sophisticated and refined general typologies may be and have been devised (e.g. Taylor and Thrift 1983). The principal message to be conveyed is that *a relationship exists between the form of microeconomic organization and the spatial scale at which it is organized.* Transnational corporations, a type of manager-managed company by definition, cannot be local, nor will any peasant household unit operate transnationally. This has important implications for processes of competition and for the analysis of the process of geographically uneven development, which I will further elaborate in the following section.

First, however, it is perhaps useful to note some differences between my typology and other spatio-economic typologies. My typology should not be confused with the product-market classification devised by Mennes, Tinbergen, and Waardenburg (1969) on the basis of the spatial extent to which products are traded or tradeable. Peasant agricultural produce, which in my microeconomic unit classification can be considered as localized household production insofar as all relevant conditions for production are locally given to that household, may become a regional or national product through regionally or nationally operating intermediaries. Even further, the peasant produce becomes an international product in the Tinbergen classification if it is bought up by internationally operating foreign trading houses, or sold by internationally operating home agencies. Similarly, in a given Third World country, a transnational corporation may establish a production facility intended only for that country's internal market. In the Tinbergen classification, the product may then be considered a national one, but this situation differs from one in which the product is supplied by firms that operate exclusively on the national level (owner-managed and national corporations).

TABLE 4.1
Microeconomic Organization and Space: A Working Typology

| | *Scale of operation* | | | |
|---|---|---|---|---|
| *Microeconomic organization* | *Local* | *Regional* | *National* | *International* |
| Household unit | X | | | |
| Owner-operated firm | X | X | | |
| Owner-managed enterprise | | X | X | |
| Manager-managed corporation | | | X | X |

For instance, in the latter case the government has more effective means of economic control than in the former.

With respect to theories of spatial organization, particularly that of Loesch (1956), it is important to emphasize that the spatial scale at which a firm operates, as defined in my typology, is not the market area of a spatial monopolist. The spatial scale does not refer to the geographical contact area of the firm: it is an action space, *without* assuming the firm to be necessarily a monopolist in that same area. For example, the contact area may be within the local political/administrative unit or it may extend regionally. Within the latter, other firms having different spatial scales, smaller *and* larger, may be operating. It is precisely this phenomenon that complicates any analysis of interrelationships between these units. It also follows that (geographical) barriers of transport cost are not the only ones that count. Rather, transport-cost barriers—which are applicable to all firms in an area—are replaced by other barriers to entry and competition that are beneficial to some firms but not to others. In spatial-price theory, on which the analysis of market areas is based, only the former are taken into account (cf. Richardson 1969).

In examining the interrelationships among the various microeconomic units, it is useful to distinguish two types of competitive processes: horizontal and vertical. By *horizontal competition* I mean struggles between firms with similar (microeconomic) organization operating at a similar level. Each firm will then face more or less the same conditions. Although some firms may be better able to respond to these conditions (e.g., due to individual or localized locational advantages), all firms basically face the same *set* of conditions.

By *vertical competition* I mean the competition between units of differing organization and level, for example, between a regional and a national firm, or a regional and a transnational one. The very fact that the transnational corporation not only produces the particular product on a technically large scale, but also internalizes part of the technological and/or trade linkages, means the factors that condition competitive struggle are likely to be (in part) different from those facing regional firms. Because the international firm operates in more markets, both geographically *and* product-wise, it has superior market information and market power (in each component market). The advantages of superior organization give such firms dominance over their smaller competitors. The concept of domination used here is similar to that introduced by Perroux in the 1950s in the analysis of firm behavior (cf. Perroux 1964).

Vertical competition is always unequal, oligopolistic competition; its key aspect is that it entails a nonhomogeneous set of microeconomic units. The higher-level unit has a partly different and a greater number of activities in comparison with a lower-level unit. Vertical competition assumes an unequal relation, whereby inequality in market power arises not from a superior characteristic of the product concerned but foremost from superior organization.

Similarly, differences in microeconomic behavior affect competitive struggles. A case in point is the differences in behavior of a managed enterprise, a household, and an own-account producer in a competitive struggle in a homogeneous product market. In a situation in which basic consumption needs have not yet been satisfied, the household may be prepared and (structurally) able to undersell its own product. The own-account producer and the enterprise will be able to do so only in the short run, but in the long run they will not be able to sustain this activitiy and will be forced out of this particular business.

To appreciate the implications of these various competitive situations, it is perhaps useful to recall some aspects of the theory of oligopolistic competition. Technical discontinuities imply a limited number of technical alternatives (and possibilities of substitution). This has several implications: all production factors are not always fully utilized (indivisibilities) and give rise to a fixed cost, irrespective of the actual volume of operation; the technology and organization of large-scale production tends to create more indivisibilities and, as a result, the proportion of fixed costs increases. At the same time and as a corollary of this, the full realization of large-scale production capacity enables economies of scale that are reflected in lower unit costs. Large-scale firms are thus more sensitive to relative variations in sales volume than are small firms, which can more easily compensate lower sales with lower costs due to their lower overheads. Seen from this point of view, managers of large-scale firms are more intent on controlling the market than are owner-operators. Moreover, they are better able to do so because of their technical concentration and potential economies of scale.

The core of the theory of oligopolistic competition is analysis of the market structure in terms of a pre-existing distribution of market shares over variously sized firms, with a given set of demand conditions (absorption capacity and extension of market).

Following earlier theorists, Sylos-Labini (1969) emphasizes the importance of market entry by new firms. (In this context, the role of new entrants need not necessarily refer to entirely new producers; existing experienced producers may enter a new national, regional, or local market area.) By introducing minimum, exclusion, and elimination prices that vary according to the size of the firm, the structure of the market can be analyzed. An important theoretical conclusion is that a stable "live and let live" market situation may be reached, in which the oligopolistic leader firm *cannot* improve its own rate of profit by expanding its market share at the cost of small firms. When put in the real context of location and market areas, such a conclusion seems plausible. Communication and transport costs and difficulties would further narrow the margin in which any improvement in the market share could be realized.

In a restricted case of an undifferentiated oligopoly in a closed economy, it has been argued that the introduction of spatial monopolies, given unequally developed regions in combination with a process of "rich to poor" national integration, leads to the formation of national oligopolies, and that firms located in the central region are in the best position to assume the leader role in such national oligopolistic market structures (Helmsing 1978).

When considering differentiated oligopolistic structures, non-price strategies, and transnational firms, it is less easy to draw such conclusions. Differentiated products and non-price barriers to entry and to exclusion and elimination seemingly reinforce the argument that market areas are discrete. The situation in which one firm has a dominant share in a particular area (whether local, regional, or national) appears to be the most usual one (Watts 1975; Dorward 1979). In the literature and in my Colombian case study (see Part III) support can be found for such suppositions. Studies of acquisitions and mergers stress the importance of a strong home-based market position and also tend to support the regional sequence in the process (Scherer et al. 1975).

If we consider new products and multinational corporations, the process of formation of national oligopolistic structures may be very short indeed. Such firms operate in the entire national market area, and local or regional demand differentiation plays almost no role. Nonspatial barriers to competition are important in this context, and derive not only from superior technology but also from superior size and organization. In his Brazilian study, Newfarmer concludes:

> TNCs exhibit strong propensities towards organizing and preserving various forms of market power in host economies. These tactics are often based on the advantages of global financial strength [such as in the case of cross-subsidization or acquisition] or perceived international and local dependence [such as interlocking directorates, mutual forbearance or collusion] . . . Clearly, barriers to entry which protect the monopolistic advantage of TNCs are solely based on superior technology, but include specific corporate practices designed to deter new entry. (Newfarmer 1979:135)

Finally, there is a whole range of non-price barriers to competition that are or may be established by government action. These refer to favorable or unfavorable conditions of production and exchange. Thus, access to government, and the ability to influence it to erect such barriers, whether locally, regionally, or nationally, is an imperative (see pp. 78–84).

## Processes of Micro and Spatial Change

Analysis of the evolution or transformation of microeconomic organization might be expected to constitute the centerpiece of development theory, but this expectation seems unfounded in reality. In comparison to macroeconomic organization, the field has so far received only scant attention.

In general, three sets of factors are often mentioned in relation to the development of the enterprise: first, sociopsychological factors underlying entrepreneurship, capitalist spirit, and so forth; second, technological–economic factors such as mass production, mass distribution techniques, and organization; and third, spatial factors of communication and transport technology and infrastructure.

My concern here is not to elaborate on such factors or to fill the signalled gap in microeconomic development theory, but simply to establish the fact that links between micro-organization and regional development are twofold. I emphasize here the role of (historical) factors and processes of regional, urban, and rural change in the development of microeconomic organizations; later, I explore the consequences of changes in microeconomic organizations for opportunities for development in the regions (see pp. 84–101).

In this section I identify three broad areas in which factors of urban, rural, and regional change may influence the development of microeconomic organizations: (1) the distribution of demand; (2) the distribution of conditions for *profitable* production; and (3) the distribution of conditions for exchange and coordination. These factors, and their effects on the various forms of microeconomic organization, are discussed in the following section.

### DISTRIBUTION OF DEMAND

Two distinct sources of change in the geographical distribution of demand can be identified: changes in the income distribution among social classes, and the transfer of demand arising from the migration of those who exercise it.

The significance of this second factor is recognized by Gunnar Myrdal (1957) as an important source of cumulative imbalance. On the basis of my typology of microeconomic organization, I am able to give transfer of demand a further characterization—for instance, by considering the two major migration processes, that is, migration from the rural area to the towns and from the smaller towns to the larger metropolitan cities. This distinction is a relevant one in view of the accumulating evidence that migration is stepwise and often is structured in this manner (cf. Connel et al. 1976 for a recent review). What are the implications of these migratory processes for the development opportunities of the different microeconomic organizations? I consider the smaller organizations first.

Migration from rural areas to the towns is usually of intra-regional scope, and implies a transfer of demand that favors town-based owner-operated small firms. For the same reason, rural artisans and households see their external sales dwindle in accordance with the pace of rural depopulation. The diversified base of rural household production is thus undermined. This, together with the increased competition from larger town-based production, forces rural households to specialize in agricultural production, which they must commercialize in increasing proportion in order to cover basic needs. Those households that have (access to) some land will cling to it more than before (Figueroa 1984). The alternative, to relocate the entire household in a vain attempt to follow demand, is not attractive in view of the considerable uncertainties this entails. It may be more feasible to diversify into other opportunities, particularly those offered in town (cf. Morrison 1980). Rural households may thus adjust by extending into the towns. Household members will be sent to town temporarily, to start urban business activities, to find wage-labor employment, and the like. This was found by Roberts (1975) and by Long and Roberts (1978), for example, in Peru.

Town-based owner-operated firms are without doubt in a favorable position to respond to the transferred demand. Their long presence in town often gives them local political, economic, and locational advantages over new entrants in the town markets, whether household or owner-operated.

Some owner-operated firms may be stimulated to transform themselves into larger owner-managed firms, but this is not necessarily the case. Family considerations, such as having a successor, may play an important role, together with economic barriers (capital requirements, managerial and technological know-how, etc.). Moreover, because migration tends to be stepwise, people also leave the towns, and as a result urban demand as a whole may not grow very much.

The extent to which town-based small firms benefit also depends largely on the presence-cum-penetration of larger firms operating on a regional and national scale. Rural–urban migration does not strategically alter their overall market position, although they will derive certain advantages, such as rationalization of distribution and sales networks, as demand becomes concentrated in fewer market areas of higher density.

Interregional migration clearly has a differential effect on owner-managed and larger manager-managed firms. The latter are able to absorb interregional changes in the demand surface via a corresponding interregional reassignment of product flows and a complementary market network strategy. Insofar as regionally operating firms are concerned, it is important to distinguish between the regions that lose and those that receive the migratory flows. Firms in the losing regions will see their market volume decline, in relative if not in absolute terms, making it difficult for them to adjust via an expansion of their spatial scale of operation—unless opportunely anticipated—enabling them to become nationally operating firms. It is very unlikely that the banks would be prepared to finance such operations. Relocation is equally or even more difficult, because of the risks it involves.

Instead, when confronted with a threat or offer of take-over by a rival firm, such firms eventually may be willing to accept the offer, particularly if family considerations favor selling out. As is often pointed out in the literature, the buying firm is intent on expanding or consolidating its *overall* market network and market position and usually is less interested in the production facilities than in the market share and distribution network of the acquired firm (Scherer et al. 1975).

Owner-managed firms based in the demand-receiving region will see their market opportunities improve. Depending on their competitive struggles with rival nationally operating firms in the same region, they may be able to capitalize on their increased market share. In a comparative sense, their enlarged home base might then enable them to transform themselves into managed corporations with an extended spatial scale of operations.

The preliminary conclusion may be drawn that the *concentration of demand* following migration into towns, into large cities in metropolitan regions *ceteris paribus* tends to contribute to decentralization of production from small household and owner-operated into large owner-managed and manager-managed firms.

So far I have addressed final product markets only, but it is also necessary to consider the effects in intermediate product markets. In this respect it is useful to keep in mind that an important characteristic of household production is its integrated and diversified character. Material intermediate inputs and capital goods are mostly self-made. Contact with intermediate markets, though normally not totally absent, often is minimal. As we have seen, competition from outside undermines the degree of integration and diversification at the household production unit level.

At the other extreme, however, the success of the large corporation is based on the integration and internal coordination of numerous activities in many places. The integration of firms with intermediate production of goods and services, via the internalization of backward and forward linkages, constitutes vertical integration. The drive to maintain or to strengthen an oligopolistic position in a particular output market often induces these firms to move forward or backward in attempts to ensure demand for their output or to control the supply of inputs. A strong position in one product market will certainly pay off in terms of a high rate of accumulation. The profitable investment of resources will enable the firm to seek other investment opportunities, particularly when demand in the original market area threatens to become saturated. Penetration of the market in other places is one alternative;

depending on the barriers encountered, including the cost of entry, the firm may instead opt to diversify into other products. Particularly if the firm has elaborate political links with local authorities, it may prefer local diversification over continued specialization in a larger area, perhaps obtaining more favorable conditions of production thanks to preferential treatment by the local government.

Although it would be difficult to provide concrete evidence, it might be argued that a manager-managed firm would seek the latter policy, which would be consistent with the career aspirations of the managers. The owner-managed firm with local family and political ties may prefer local diversification, even if in quite unrelated fields (in agricultural, industrial, or service-type activities). Vertical integration and diversification tend to strengthen the position of the firm in intermediate markets, making it more immune to rival actions.

The most important indirect effect will be the increased frequency of oligopolistic/oligopsonistic market forms, that is, many small buyers/sellers and a few large sellers/buyers. The second indirect effect is the classic case of backwardly linked satellite firms that supply oligopsonistic firms. Recently, it has been shown that such satellite firms tend to follow the relocation and locational adjustment strategies of the oligopsonistic leader firm (Suzman & Schultz 1983). Modern forms of "putting out systems," whereby large firms subcontract assembly-type parts of production processes to owner-operated firms and own-account workers, represent another way in which managerial firms use their organizational efficiency. Relations of dependence, or even dominance, can be enforced in numerous ways, ranging from price fixing to more subtle quality and other control schemes.

## DISTRIBUTION OF CONDITIONS FOR PRODUCTION

It would be a simplification to maintain that demand conditions are the sole factors that alter the structure of microeconomic organization. Equally if not more important are the conditions for profitable production. The analysis of geographical conditions for production traditionally has been the domain of location theory, and location theory contributions have undergone considerable changes over the last 20 years or so (cf. Storper 1981; Hayter and Watts 1983). First, they moved away from the traditional framework of isolated locational decision making toward theories of growth of the firm and growth of production; in such theories, location and relocation of plants or functions are part of growth or survival strategies. A second important change is that the focus moved away from the small-scale, holistic, entrepreneurial, single-plant firm to the corporate multiplant and multinational firm.

Nowadays it is also recognized that requirements for profitable production have changed over time, to some degree because of changes in the microeconomic organization of production. For example, for a household-operated unit, *all* requirements for profitable production have to be met within the area in which it operates—not only availability of material and other inputs but also local demand. Local availability of (external) labor is less important. A nationally operating multiplant firm, on the other hand, does *not* need all requirements to be met in a single area, but can exploit one production requirement in one region (e.g., a cheap and reliable labor force), and another in a different region (e.g., market availability). By virtue of its managed organization, it can relocate high-skill functions to high-amenity areas, etc. In other words, the larger, multiregional, managed firm can respond more *selectively* to the particular conditions of production existing in each region. By decentralizing production plants to the low-labor-cost periphery and by concentrating management and higher-order functions in core regional centers of decision making, these firms have made use of the advantages of both. On the other hand, locally operating firms must accept the production condition of a region, lock, stock, and barrel. Only through trade can they compensate for some unfavorable conditions, such as insufficent demand or inadequate supply of material inputs. As Norcliffe correctly argues, transport costs are becoming less important due to technical progress. More efficient use of higher-grade raw materials, improved transport technology (containerization), and more ubiquitous energy inputs are the principal factors involved (Norcliffe 1975).

Technical change in production must also be taken into consideration. Machine-intensive production and further automation of production alter its occupational structure: de-skilling takes place on the shop floor. At the same time, highly skilled white-collar employment increases more than proportionally in managerial and higher-order technical and engineering functions. It is in these latter functions that needs for horizontal communication rapidly increase, and for which access to specialized services becomes more and more important (cf. Jansen 1974; Norcliffe 1975).

Currently, regions offering only a limited range of favorable production conditions can less easily capitalize on them and compensate for less-favorable factors. For example, a large firm may be induced, perhaps with the aid of central government incentives, to set up a branch plant operation in a certain region of high unemployment. The firm will benefit from a relatively low-wage advantage in the area by setting up a low-skill production operation; little demand will be generated for highly skilled labor. Furthermore, most material and sevice inputs will be obtained elsewhere from existing suppliers or through intrafirm trade. Thus, few dynamic impulses will be given to the area, and highly skilled labor and small (would-be) entrepreneurs will contine to migrate, whereas the large microeconomic corporations are able to exploit the particular advantage offered. Spillover effects and agglomeration economies do not materialize, however, and no new advantages are created to compensate for the disadvantages. Existing regional resource endowments will become less significant in changing the economic structure of the region, as a consequence of the increasingly selective use made of them.

Finally, it is important in this context to refer to state-determined conditions of production. It is argued that centralization of government reduces the discretion of local and regional governments to alter conditions of production. This applies not only to the main types of company taxation, but also to current and capital expenditures, including special incentives, which, increasingly, have become the domain of central government. For several reasons, central government bureaucracies, however large, cannot easily respond to the particular needs of a multitude of small firms. Instead, fewer and large corporations tend to become the main beneficiaries of state intervention. This is also true of regional policy (Stoehr and Toedtling 1976). Moreover, as central government starts to regulate more and more, issuing titles, deeds, certificates, licences and so on, locational access to central government offices becomes an essential precondition for production.

## CONDITIONS FOR COORDINATION AND EXCHANGE

Economic activity requires coordination among actors and acting organizations: markets usually are considered the principal mechanism of coordination among producers and consumers. It should be added, however, that the role and importance of markets varies greatly in different types of microeconomic organization.

For the houehold units, markets are of less importance. The household internally coordinates production and production-consumption decisions, often on the basis of long-established cultural traditions of division of labor. The impact of economic change, however, undermines the capacity for internal coordination. Production inputs and consumption needs are externally provided and more output is sold through market exchange, a process that makes the household units more dependent on other coordinating agents, mainly traders and government.

Owner-operated establishments differ in this respect: they are more dependent on coordinating actors and agencies and have less opportunity to withdraw into internal subsistence activities. To specialize as a small producer, a corresponding specialization in the environment is needed. As long as this specialization remains localized, traders perform the key function of coordination among producers in different places, and may make use of their position to impose terms of trade that are beneficial to themselves. The specialization of trade into wholesale and retail organization is a development associated with owner-operated organization of production.

The development of large-scale managerial organizations breaks this wholesale–retail organization, because such firms often undertake their own direct marketing and distribution. Large-scale managed organizations have a double advantage: technologically based economies of scale and coordination, and information economies arising from their larger spatial scale. (The latter previously were obtained by traders and trade organizations.) The larger managed organization is able to strike a better deal not only because it is a "bigger customer" and the market structure becomes monopolistic, but also because it is a "better informed customer."

A second, often overlooked, aspect of coordination and exchange is the unification of norms and standards of goods and services. At the early phase of the product cycle, market segmentation by the deliberate adoption of a different standard often forms part of the marketing strategy. At the later stage of mass production (and mass distribution), standardization becomes more profitable. The unification of standards allows for more efficient handling, processing, repair, and so forth, and its advantages are generally recognized. The key issue in competition is that of whose standards are to prevail. The company that developed the standards has a competitive (time and cost) advantage, because others must realize additional investments to retool their products and production processes in accordance with the changed specifications. The greater the spatial scale and size of the market, the more important this becomes. Although in many instances firms may agree among themselves, the territorial authority of government is important for the enactment and, if necessary, the enforcement of standards within that particular territory.

## Development of the Territorial System of Government

The political integration of a territory into a single system of government and the increasing role of the state in economic development are often singled out as dominant features of development processes. By *political integration* I mean the process by which smaller local and regional communities are consolidated into a territorially larger and multilevel system of government. Local and regional political institutions and loyalties are altered and become secondary to national ones. There are many interpretations of how "early states" were formed and which factors have influenced the integration process (cf. Johnston 1982). What is important here is to stress that rarely were these states well integrated.

> Organization of the territories was not usually strong, however, especially in the larger states, because of the difficulties of maintaining contact and control. Each state tended to have a single major core, which was the focus of state power and the home of the sovereign. Beyond the core, the territory was organized in a series of substates who owed fealty and tribute to the sovereign, but were in certain respects, independent. (Johnston 1981:41)

Certain state functions were centralized at the national level (e.g., the army), whereas others were left entirely to the substates. There was a hierarchy but no coordinated multilevel system of government. The latter developed with the expanding role of the state in development processes.

## State and Economy

There are many different approaches to the economic role of the state (cf. Jansen 1982). Most theories concentrate on the functional aspect, and little is said about the important territorial changes that have taken place. In regional studies this second dimension is given more attention. One approach has been to relate to urbanization the enlargement of the action space of private activities and the concomitant spatial concentration of public decision making (cf. Hilhorst and Lambooy 1974). The general, functional interplay between public and private sector has received less attention.

The literature also leaves largely unanswered the question of why, in many mixed economies, the public sector has the tendency to increase in importance. A clear exception in this respect is O'Connor (1973), who has attempted to establish a new framework. He argues that the state essentially has two functions: to maintain or create conditions in which private capital accumulation can profitably take place, and to maintain or create conditions for social harmony. He also distinguishes two private sectors: a competitive sector (with low productivity, low capital intensity, low barriers to entry, small industries and businesses that operate primarily in local and regional markets), and a capital-intensive and large-scale sector (with high barriers to entry and operating primarily in national and international markets). Due to the increasingly complex technology and division of labor, the growth of this monopoly sector requires increasing amounts of social investment in physical infrastructure and related social expenditures in proportion to its own investment. O'Connor found the monopoly sector to receive a lower than proportional share of total domestic demand, because competitive-sector productivities (especially in services and trade) and in the state sector increase relatively slowly, and thus the costs of production rise more rapidly. Competitive and state sectors absorb an ever-larger share of total demand, thus depriving the monopoly sector of markets (ibid.:25). Furthermore, the monoply sector tends to generate surplus production capacity and surplus population (technological unemployment). Markets need to be expanded, either domestically via social expenditures of the "welfare" state, or abroad requiring "warfare" state expenditures (including aid).

Because the monopoly sector and its trade unions resist the appropriation of surplus to finance social expenditures, a structural gap and fiscal crisis is caused. An additional crisis results from the "private appropriation of state power for particularistic ends" (O'Connor 1973:9).

The centralization of government is duly noted by O'Connor:

> Because of growing regional and national economic intergration, the development of regional economic units with distinct social and economic problems, and increasing economic concentration and centralization, monopoly capital requires more top down administration and budgetary planning, especially around regional needs. But because of the persistence of small business control of state and local governments, the proliferation of special districts and authorities, and the general fragmentation of local political and budgetary power. . . . the struggle for centralized political administration and fiscal planning has been a protracted one. (ibid.:89)

This conflict over the influence on government at various levels inevitably leads to centralization, as "monopoly capitalist groups and the federal executive have been working together to increase federal power in local affairs and, step by step, to dismantle local government" (ibid.:90).

O'Connor's important contribution has subsequently stimulated considerable urban research (Schwartz 1983). What does not seem entirely plausible, however, is the relation of his model to the two private sectors. Why should the monopoly sector lose demand to the competitive sector when, historically, it grew out of this sector in the first place? One may agree that in the long run the monopoly sector creates technological unemployment that requires social (harmony) expenditures. But O'Connor's assumption that this sector loses demand to the competitive sector and that therefore it must rely on expanded state-sector demand to prevent productive capacity becoming idle, seems doubtful. In many activities the monopoly-sector products and services actually displace the competitive sector. In others there is no longer any competitive-sector equivalent. This, of course, does not conflict with his central contention: the growing need for social investment in economic and physical infrastructure is due to the increasing technological and organizational complexities of the monopoly sector.

O'Connor sees fiscal crisis and the centralization of government as part of the same problem, namely, the relation between the monopoly and the state sector, but he does not integrate these two tendencies. In the next section, I argue first that centralization of government is necessary for the development of large-scale managed firms and, second, that the fiscal crisis itself contributes to the furtherance of this process.

## Externalities and Impure Public Goods

Most activities are carried out in a more or less permanent way in a certain place, and cause positive and negative externalities for other activities carried out in other (nearby) places. As I will show, the existence of these externalities normally promotes or restricts activities in the same area. Many examples can be given of externalities, including also the familiar economies of agglomeration. Pollution and congestion are typical examples of negative externalities. Labor-market advantages and other relatively place-bound localization economies are examples of positive externalities.

Externalities must be dealt with through political decision making, and the increasing role of the state will be analyzed from this perspective. The case for government intervention is made by and pushed for different groups in society, to stimulate positive or to prevent negative externalities. The government invests and regulates or otherwise addresses conflicts that arise from these externalities, providing socioeconomic and physical infrastructures to improve the situation.

These provisions are also known as public goods, but most of the latter are *impure*; that is to say, they are not accessible to the entire public due to their localized character.

Two further considerations must be taken into account with regard to the growing importance of the state sector. The first is the fact that the density and (Von Thuenen-like) intensity of activities in an area increases over time. Consequently, externalities become more important and also the need for government intervention to address them.

A second and related aspect concerns scale enlargement. When firms develop more specialized production and operate on a larger spatial scale, they tend to require not only more public goods but, in addition, these are made available at the higher spatial scale. In other words, an essential prerequisite for economic integration at a given level is the unification or compatibility of socioeconomic and physical infrastructures in the areas involved in the integration process. This applies to day-to-day conventions such as weights and measures, to legal systems concerning property and trade, to transport and communication systems, education and health, and other social and economic institutions. Thus, the enlargement of the spatial scale at which activities are organized also influences the level at which government has to provide these infrastructures. In other words, it has implications not only for the size but also for the territorial organization of government.

## Centralization of Government and the Provision of Public Goods

It would be self-defeating to try to draw up general propositions regarding the organization of government and the provision of public goods. Many internal and external factors, such as war, conquest, colonization, liberation, decolonization, and even historical accidents shape the boundaries of states and their basic internal organization (cf. Short 1982). However, some general observations may be offered on long-term processes that exert pressure to alter internal government structures.

In economies where most activity is local and where there is little exchange, the provision of public goods is extremely limited, and mostly provided by local (self-)government. With market exchange and private property, externalities and therefore public goods become part and parcel of economic and political life. The role of local governments begins to increase and they become more firmly institutionalized throughout the country. The entire territory of the country gradually will be divided up administratively into areas of local government, exact boundaries forming the spatial limits of their legitimacy, that is, the right to provide physical and social infrastructure and to levy taxes. The public nature of such provisions entails that political administrative areas will be contiguous, in other words, that there is no "free rider" no-man's land. Eventually, the territory will become entirely covered by a "layer" of (local) government.

Local political pressures will determine what infrastructures are to be provided and where. With regard to impure public goods, in particular, these tend to influence the value of the land as a location and also the uses that can be made of it. Therefore, the distribution of the financial burdens and also of the benefits become stakes in local political power struggles.

Local political power structures, institutions, and processes become established, and vested interests are generated with which to maintain them.

As the microeconomy expands and firms organize their activities at a higher spatial scale, pressures will be exerted for infrastructures to be unified.

> The specialist [firms] in the center whose activity spaces include the non-central villages have a series of common interests, even if they are in direct competition. They will therefore tend to cooperate with or at least support any effort to establish law and order in the plain—at least insofar as these efforts cover their activity spaces. (Hilhorst and Lambooy 1974:153)

What applies to law and order also applies to other public goods, such as transport, communication, physical infrastructure, trade institutions, and the like. In the first instance, coordination by and among local "states" may be all that is needed (federative structures). As more economic activities are carried on at this larger spatial scale, however, further integration will become necessary.

The process of political integration is of singular importance in this respect: as it evolves, it will have decisive influence on the processes of competition that will develop between firms originating in the various participating territories. Whose cultural, economic, and technological norms, standards, social institutions, and so forth will (be made to) apply to the others? Such struggles for dominance are likely to be less far reaching when they concern integration at local levels, for example, from city "states" to small regional "states." The economy is largely organized at the household and owner-operated levels where economic (inter)dependence among micro units is relatively limited. As activities become more and more specialized and organized by larger managerial organizations, however, and relatively more and new infrastructures are needed at higher spatial scales, the potential impacts become greater and the stakes higher.

Only the larger managed firms will push for and need this organization for production and for markets at the next higher spatial scale, and the traditional smaller firms and businesses may therefore resist, particularly if they stand to lose due to processes of uneven development in space (see pp. 72–78).

The majority of the activities will remain localized and organized by locally operating microeconomic organizations, and the infrastructures catering for these therefore will also remain organized at this level, that is, the local-government level. The next level of government caters, coordinates, and controls the new infrastructural provisions needed for the expanding microeconomy.

As more and more activities become organized at the regional level, the weights and balance of power between the two levels of government will shift in favor of the higher level. Local infrastructures will be brought in line with higher-level needs. Advances in technology and in the management and organization of production require and supply a vast impulse to extension of the spatial scale at which economic activities are organized. For agricultural activities,in the past, the spatial change may have been more from local to regional; for industrial activities, the change was rather from regional to national to international. However, the impact was no less dramatic. The national level of government becomes more important and is entrusted with many of the infrastructural exigencies of industrialization, both physical and, above all, socioeconomic. Unification and integration at this third level produces a new balance of power in its favor, at the cost of the local and intermediate levels. The degree to which the balance shifts will depend largely on the existing level of development and its geographic unevenness.

At this stage, three levels of government provide public goods, partly in the same field or complementary to each other. The multiplication, duplication, and maladjustment of government functions performed at the various levels is therefore an *expected* historical outcome. Rationalization of the state sector—administrative reform—with the purpose of eliminating such "inefficiencies" during periods of severe fiscal crisis becomes necessary, and will inevitably favor further centralization of government. In this respect, it should be taken into account that certain public goods can be provided more efficiently if their production is organized on a larger scale. Even localized public goods can be catered for more efficiently by higher levels of government. Local governments then become "branch plant and field offices" of the centrally organized production of impure public goods, such as health care, education, law and order. Not only do regional and local groups and polities resist these multiple breaks in their autonomy for the reasons discussed above, but regional and local bureaucracies may also resist, though less openly, such reductions in their powers of decision making. Some degree of decentralization, particularly of the implementation of newly created infrastructures, may be offered as a palliative and/or partial compensation for the relative but often absolute loss in public decision-making power.

## Organizing Forces and Rural, Urban, and Regional Change

In previous sections of this chapter, I have attempted to uncover two important and related processes of change. The first concerns the microeconomic basis of the economy. Various forms of micro organization are of relevance to us insofar as they also concern differences in the spatial scale, that is, the activity space, at which they are organized. The industrial and, later, the managerial revolution made it possible to enlarge the activity space and to create new forms of microeconomic organization.

Compared to household and owner-operated forms of economic organization, managerial organizations have transcended town, countryside, and even regional divisions. National boundaries may be formidable to peasant households, obstacles to be passed (illegally) as *contrabandista,* migrant, or refugee. The managed corporations, however, have many ways by which to cross frontiers; some of them consider the world to be their domain.

In any given territory various kinds of micro organizations operate at different levels. The development or entry of large micro units in a territory induces a verticalization of relations among them. The managed corporation dominates over smaller micro units, not only because of its size but also because of its superior organization in space. The managerial corporation is increasingly becoming a force that shapes the structure of the regional economy. Because the area involved is only a small part of its total activity space, the corporation can make partial or selective use of it via branch plants and offices. The corporation's presence and behavior in the area, however, influences the conditions of production and exchange of smaller units operating in its neighborhood. The significance of the managerial corporation as an organizing force is dependent on many factors. Some of these relate to its own size and development as well as to that of other smaller units, whether these are very small and operate exclusively in that area, or are larger and have the capacity to counteract the larger corporation elsewhere or in other products or markets. Perhaps the general point to be made on this issue is that functional and spatial processes of change are linked to each other in a dynamic interaction.

The second process of change concerns the role and organization of government. In general, the case for state intervention is related to the distribution of costs and benefits of externalities arising from private activities. The increasing role of the state largely relates to the provision of infrastructure that is functional to the unification and integration of economies and markets. This is required and it sustains the development of (new) micro organization at a larger spatial scale. We have seen that the centralization of government at higher levels, at the cost of local and regional levels, is part and parcel of that same process. The roles of local and regional governments increasingly are being narrowed down and regulated, causing them to become "branch plants" and "field offices" in the centrally organized production and provision of public goods.

Although the two processes discussed here could each be said to be moving in the same direction and linked to one another, *they do not necessarily depart from the same level.*

The preceding analysis presumes an uninterrupted and gradual process. Indeed, such a process perhaps may have taken place in some "first world" countries. Many countries in the Third World, however, show considerable disjunctures in the process of government formation, largely as a result of their colonial past. In particular, those peoples who have only recently liberated themselves tend to adopt a highly centralized government structure. Thus, centralization often has a purely political imperative, namely, to maintain or create national unity. At the same time, much of the private sector may consist of households and owner-managed businesses operating on a local and/or regional level, possibly with some transnational corporations in key sectors. This lack of correspondence between the two processes and the tensions that arise from it constitute a key issue of development.

In our context, the specific question could be asked: What are the socioeconomic consequences for local/regional (urban and rural) opportunities of development? Not least because of the dynamics involved, it is extremely difficult to give a general answer to this question. Historical factors such as the preexisting territorial formation must be taken into account. What would apply to Colombia would not apply in the same way to another country. Moreover, the framework is still too crude to generate very detailed propositions: it serves as a perspective only.

In the remainder of this section, and with particular reference to Colombia, I shall elaborate my framework on three partially overlapping issues: the formation of the agroindustrial complex and the process of rural change; the process of urbanization as shaped by the development of multilevel organizations; and the process of verticalization of the regional economy and its implications for regionalism.

## Formation of the Agroindustrial Complex and Rural Change

The basic starting point of the analysis that follows is that in the past, and in predominantly agrarian societies, activities usually have been organized, under traditional tenure, at the houehold level by independent peasants and on self-provisioning estates. The rural economy is composed of both agricultural and nonagricultural activities. The peasant household is simultaneously a unit of consumption and a unit of production, and nonagricultural activities generate an intrinsic part of its income. Artisan household production may include consumer, capital, and intermediate goods.

Any analysis of the process of rural change should therefore consider all these dimensions. In this respect, we may remember the controversies discussed in Chapter 2: the supposed ability of the peasant to outbid/undersell capitalist farmers, the diversity of agricultural and nonagricultural activities that is the key to rural livelihood, and which is undermined by industrialization. In this context, industrialization is understood as a process by which material production is developed with mass-production techniques and managerial forms of microeconomic organization.

The effect of industrialization on rural-household consumption is that mass-produced consumer goods will compete with and effectively displace local artisan and household-made goods, with the immediate effect of eliminating an important source of rural income. In addition, new consumer wants are usually created and new manufactured products enter into the rural-household consumption basket.

This impact of industry cannot be realized without a change in the organization and structure of trade and services. Mass production calls for mass distribution (Chandler 1977). That is to say, new products bring new trade structures. Fairs and periodic markets of local origin and scale are partly replaced by permanent multilevel trade systems (wholesale, retail, and market chains), usually brought in, controlled, and operated from outside. The peasant household is pushed from self-provisioning toward the market development of its agricultural activities, to enable it to acquire these manufactured goods; alternatively, it has to find off-farm wage employment.

The dynamics of the process of rural change consists, on the one hand, of the push for restricted market incorporation, and, on the other hand, of growing opportunities for agricultural activities derived from the growing demand by town-based industries and populations for food and agricultural raw materials.

The impact of industrialization, however, is not limited to the rural consumption side. The push to reduce subsistence production is accompanied by a push to reduce the household production of capital and intermediate inputs. Furthermore, it will cause a change in crop composition and displacement, which will result in a tendency toward specialization.

At the macro level, this process is accompanied by the development of relations between agriculture and manufacturing industry.[1] Agriculture becomes sandwiched between two segments of industrial activities, the entire sandwich being the agroindustrial complex of highly interrelated and organized activities (Bye 1975). The upper or upstream segment is composed of firms that produce capital and intermediate inputs for agriculture and also provide other specialized service inputs. The lower or downstream segment consists of firms that process and transform agricultural produce and of others that provide specialized transport, storage, finance, and other specialized services.

The preindustrialization rural economy is characterized by a high degree of household production, not only of consumer goods but also of intermediate and capital inputs, such as seeds, tools, and implements; organic fertilizer; animal traction. A similar situation holds with respect to the processing and transformation of agricultural output, for example, the milling of grains, the processing of milk and milk derivates, the processing of hides in leather and leather products, vegetable oils, textiles, and so forth. Increasingly, however, these products are made by manufacturing firms located upstream and

1. For the concept of agroindustrial complex and the general analysis of intersectoral relations, I have drawn from Pascal Bye (1975).

downstream. When metal making, machinery, and chemical industries displace the original rurally produced, lower-productivity equivalents, not only is the composition of rural activity affected but the generation of agricultural innovation is externalized. In seeking their own expansion, such industries become a propulsive force in agricultural development.

This macro process has two important microeconomic consequences: first, agricultural activities increasingly become capital-using; second, non-agricultural activities previously undertaken by the rural unit in periods of low-intensity work on the land, are replaced by industrially produced inputs that must be purchased. Both consequences imply an increase of capital intensity.

Development of the lower or downstream segment of the agroindustrial complex is related to the proportion of food products that is processed and transformed by industry. This proportion increases as the level of income rises, new tastes often being introduced from abroad. Urbanization creates a further stimulus. The growing gap between concentrated urban demand and dispersed agriculture increases the complexity of organizing (continuous) supply, making it necessary to reduce the perishability of agricultural production through more advanced methods of storage, conservation, processing, and packing, which require standardization and quality control on the production side. Finally, efficient distribution and transport systems become necessary.

Considering these processes from another angle, it could be argued that the greater proportion of agricultural produce passes first through this lower or downstream segment before it reaches the final (urban) consumer. A general conclusion can be drawn that activities are eliminated that previously were locally organized at the level of the rural economy. The industrial development of these activities is similar to that in other fields. That is to say, large multiplant and national operating corporations emerge as leading firms in oligopolistic market structures. As I have shown, this process takes place through the integration of markets at higher levels, moving from local and regional to national levels (and beyond).

The dynamics of oligopolistic competition lead generally to diversification and/or vertical integration. The latter implies that downstream firms have the tendency to move closer to the source of supply so as to ensure or control it and to establish quality standards. As a consequence, there is a stimulus for industry to establish direct contact with agricultural producers through contract schemes, technical assistance, seed supply and credit schemes. Trade becomes internalized and directly managed by these firms without the interference from commercial intermediaries. In some cases, the firms may even assume direct agricultural production (plantations). This tendency has an important implication: namely, that in order to keep down the costs of such operations, industry will prefer to mobilize a limited number of large agricultural producers rather than a large number of small and dispersed producers. In other words, the formation of the agroindustrial complex may generate a bias toward large-scale specialized agricultural production.

A proportion of agricultural production will remain unprocessed, making it necessary to consider distribution activities as well. Suffice it to say here that as more agricultural surplus is needed to meet rising urban demand, the organization of the marketing/distribution becomes more complex. The chains of intermediation become longer and the margin of commercialization tends to increase, leading to greater differences between urban consumer and farmgate price. Intermediation also becomes organized at a higher spatial scale, that is, from locally to regionally and from regionally to nationally operating firms.

The growing complexity of distribution has two effects on the rural economy. First, it can be concluded that *due to the changes in market organization, the prices of agricultural products are no longer determined by local conditions but increasingly by those on the national level.* Second, the growing differences between farmgate and urban prices caused by the growing complexity of small-scale organization of distribution may stimulate the emergence of mass-distribution firms that will increase the size of individual transactions so as to reduce costs. In effect, some intermediary links are then bypassed by means of direct farm-to-wholesale or market-chain contractual deliveries. Again, a greater proportion of agricultural output becomes administered trade. The effect of increasing the size of individual transactions is a scale bias.

The impact of industrialization on the rural economy can be summarized as follows. The incorporation of rural markets by manufacturing firms results in the elimination of nonagricultural activities that had formed an integral part of rural livelihood. In addition, it induces further commercialization of agricultural production. The industrialization of agriculture itself is based on the development of the agroindustrial complex generating further specialization in agricultural activities. The development of upstream industries has a labor-saving effect in that it absorbs activities that previously were integrated in rural-household production, and has a capital-using effect through the delivery/sale of manufactured inputs to the farms. The development of downstream industries that process, transform, and distribute agricultural produce causes agricultural activities to be lifted out of their local and regional context and put into a national one.

In terms of the organization of agricultural activities and the preexisting rural structure (*hacienda* 'peasant household'), it may be concluded that formation of the agroindustrial complex generates an uneven distribution of opportunities. Transformation of the *hacienda* toward large-scale managerial production is favored. From another angle, the transformtion of diversified peasant households into specialized owner-operated farms depends on the effective (and unequal) competition exercised by the larger managerial units.

Although opportunities are unevenly distributed, this does not necessarily imply the elimination of peasant-household economies. It could be argued, for instance, that the ability of the peasant to outbid or undersell his competitors would ensure his survival. However, in the process previously described, the terms of competition are changing. By undermining the diversity of household production, the possibilities for cross-subsidization among the various activities and for pooling resources are also reduced, although this naturally varies from crop to crop. Moreover, there may be extra-household opportunities for diversification, particularly in off-farm wage employment and in the vicinity of the larger cities. Furthermore, formation of an agroindustrial complex does not occur in all products, neither upstream (because of absence of new varieties and methods), nor downstream agriculture (because of absence of processing and transformation caused by the structure of demand related to income distribution). In such cases, it is likely that there will be little competition, if any, between large-scale managerial and peasant farming, though the unequal competition for land and capital will remain. For those products around which an agroindusrial complex is developed, peasant farming will essentially play a secondary role, largely dependent on what happens on the transformed estates.

Formation of the agroindustrial complex would imply that farms become boxed in, squeezed, suffering the effects of vertical competition in their relations with (inter)nationally operating upstream and downstream industries. Although, in this context, there is a clear difference between the small owner-operated farm and the large managed-farm enterprise, the (national) organization of farmers can be seen as an attempt to counterbalance the market power of the enterprises, either directly or through influence on government policy. The more centralized the industries, the greater this need.

One of the conclusions drawn earlier is that development of the agro-industrial complex lifts agriculture out of its local context into an interregional or even international context of specialized production. To put this in different and contrasting terms, in the traditional rural economy the crop pattern is determined by local needs, and is relatively diversified. All products that can be locally produced will be produced in that region, sometimes irrespective of their yield or "profitability." At the other extreme, in a completely industrialized agricultural setting, only those products are produced in the region which in the (inter)national context are the most profitable, given differences in costs, soil suitability, and so forth. All other products will be supplied through interregional or international trade.

When considering the regional implications of this process, the following general tendencies may be observed. First, the development of manufacturing industry tends to be restricted primarily to the most developed region(s). Its expansion there will in part be based on the penetration of markets in other rural regions where it reduces nonagricultural activities. Also, commercialization of agriculture initially will be limited to the core region where it induces transformation of the estates. Peasants will be evicted and/or turned into wage labor, either on the capitalist farms or in the cities where they become absorbed into the urban economy in one way or another. As productivity increases due to this process, land prices in the area will tend to rise, in turn putting a brake on expansion possibilities of the peasant economy. Rural–urban migration extends the labor market for industry. The development of the agroindustrial complex leads to a process whereby the more-profitable crops displace the less-profitable ones in that area—the core region. The less-profitable crops will be the basis upon which transformation of the estates in other regions will take place. In this way, industrialized agriculture extends itself in successive waves toward various regions, within each of which it tends to produce a homogenization of conditions for agricultural production for each type of farm unit. Depending on the preexisting agrarian structure, further social polarization may result.

Two processes occur simultaneously. First, more land is incorporated into capitalist or managerial forms of agriculture, and the *haciendas* disappear. Second, within that expanding group, the crop pattern in each region is continually adjusted because of the changing interregional circumstances. In other words, a certain sequence in the process of regional specialization is likely. The share of a region in national production will increase and, in complementary fashion, the level of agricultural diversification in each of the "incorporated" regions will decline as the process advances.

Essential to the process of interregional displacement cum advancement is the "opening-up" of the regions—that is to say, creation of the necessary physical infrastructure and the building up of the institutional and organizational support that will enable the effective incorporation into the agro-industrial complex. The largely urban-based institutions and organizations stimulate nonagricultural employment and the growth of towns in these areas, without which the process of rural change would not be possible, a fact that underlines the role of towns in rural development.

Taking the analysis of "industry-led incorporation" into account, as Pearse (1968) calls it, we can now identify an "agriculture-led incorporation" process. Whereas the former is guided by the market and by profit considerations of consumer-goods industries, the latter is guided by agronomic and profit considerations underlying the agroindustrial complex. The two incorporation processes do not necessarily go together, nor do they occur in a spatially continuous fashion. Each is selective according to its own guiding principles.

Various kinds of regional situations may exist at a given point in time. In the core region, the *rural* nonagricultural (self)employment opportunities of rural households are reduced. The industry-led market incorporation forces them to sell more of their food products on the growing urban food market. Peasants are likely to become cornered in a situation in which their existing economic organization is undermined, while their poverty of resources does not permit transformation into an owner-operated organization of their agricultural production. There is little scope for expansion of their holdings (because of rising prices of land and land rentals); in fact, the fragmentation of their holdings under the impact of demographic pressure may further reduce their income basis. Only by a timely adjustment to exploit *urban* employment and income opportunities will some households be in a position to offset, wholly or partially, the loss of rural nonagricultural activities and to continue their mode of life, albeit in adjusted form. In other regions to which industrial agriculture is extended (agriculture-led incorporation) the process just outlined is repeated but, depending on the growth of urban food demand in the core region, the impact on the peasant economy will range from partial or complete. Finally, in the most peripheral regions, the peasant economy may be preserved for the time being and/or decay under general population pressure.

The principal conclusion that must be emphasized in this context of interregional changes is that regional differentiation is an *expected* theoretical outcome. Regional diversity is the *rule* rather than an accidental or empirically observed exception.

In this section I have tried to highlight how the rural economy is subject to change. It becomes increasingly agricultural, lifted out of its local regional setting and surrounded by nationally or internationally operating firms and organizations. In much the same manner and largely as a function of it, national government presence becomes increasingly felt on the local level. The insularity of the countryside breaks down, and people find themselves increasingly involved in complex webs of organizations whose decision making is not located nor exclusively attuned to that area or region. Depending on the specific regional situation, some people may adjust successfully, others will see their livelihood undermined, and yet others will migrate to the towns.

## Urbanization and the Development of Multilevel Organizations

Some years ago, Milton Santos made an important contribution to integrating the analysis of the economic structure with that of the spatial organization.

He argues that "new economic demands are superimposed over existing 'traditional' ones. The economic system is thus forced to accommodate both new and inherited social realities, and faces the need for dynamic modernization. . . . Two economic circuits are created, responsible not only for the economic process, but also the process of spatial organization" (Santos 1979:8).

From this perspective, neither the economy nor the city can be seen as single homogeneous entities; rather, each should be thought of as two subsystems, namely, the upper (or modern) circuit and the lower circuit. Monopolies are seen as the representative elements of the upper circuit, operating largely beyond the city and its surrounding area, in a national and international framework. The lower circuit, on the other hand, consists of small-scale localized activities entrenched in the city.

According to Santos, the "two circuits . . . represent opposite forms of division of labour. In the upper circuit, it is imposed by the necessity of capital accumulation; in the lower circuit, by the need for the survival of a numerous labour force" (ibid.:91). He emphasizes that relations between the two circuits crystallize at the local level, because the lower circuit operates only at this level. These relations may vary from complementarity to competition but always occur in a domination–subordination framework. Moreover, as "an economy becomes more modern, and as different intermediate and final consumer goods are demanded, the lower circuit must increasingly turn to inputs from the upper circuit. Equally, upper circuit demand for lower circuit outputs decreases as the economy becomes more complex" (ibid.:140). Santos does not spell out the final implications of these trends.

Thus, the economy of a Third World country is characterized by a bipolar structure. So also is the spatial organization. Because the lower circuit functions only locally, the spatial organization of a country is orchestrated by the upper circuit. This circuit, as it develops on imported technology, is largely concentrated in the metropolis, from where it extends, in "internal colonialist" manner, into the regions, intensifying regional inequalities. The position of the capital city is further strengthened because of the role played by the (central) state in this process, directly through state enterprises and indirectly through the creation and organization of infrastructure. Asymmetry typifies the evolving spatial organization: "The large city is the starting point for *downward* and *outward* migrations of agents of the State and important economic interests, and the focus for *upward* migrations from rural areas and smaller cities. Downward migrations are in harmony with modernization and economic progress. . . . [However,] . . . upward migrations merely represent a response to extremes of rural poverty" (ibid.:167). Urbanization becomes a "macrocephalous" process.

With the development of the upper circuit, the relation between town and countryside also alters. Asymmetry develops: although lower-circuit rural activities continue to have limited but necessary relations with similar activities in towns, this "cannot be said for modern rural activities whose ancillary services are normally only carried out by enterprises in the national metropolis' (ibid.:180). Smaller towns are thus completely bypassed.

This explanation of spatial discontinuity is one of the most important, but little emphasized, features of Santos's analysis. Upper and lower circuits may share the same place or area, yet they may be(come) entirely separate. Upper-circuit activities in the area may have intense linkages with activities that are located elsewhere and may therefore develop without specific regard for local conditions and opportunities. This is in contrast to lower-circuit activities that are and can only be locally integrated and hence depend on the supply and demand fortunes of the area. In this regard, there is considerable convergence between Santos's analysis and that elaborated in previous sections. In my view, however, the situation is more complex than the dual structure put forward by Santos. First, the definition of the two circuits as macro sectors suffers from the same deficiencies as other dichotomies (see pp. 41–49).

A second problem, in my view, is that Santos's analysis does not include the organization of the state as an integrative element of both circuits: the development of the state sector is largely taken for granted.

A third problem is that Santos adopts largely a top-down analysis that assumes the a priori existence of an excessively centralized state, of national monopolies of either national or transnational origin, and of a primate urban structure which, in the process of "internal colonialism," only becomes a more perverse structure. Such an analysis does not explain why such structures come about in the first place, but only why a process continues in one way and not another.

In stating my perspective on urban change, it is perhaps useful to begin by formulating the principal propositions. I contend that the development of an urban system is the result of the creation and outgrowth of multilevel economic and political–administrative organizations of state and enterprise, and of the displacement and relocation of small local firms and households. The forces that shape the process of urban change in pace and space include the development of national and transnational oligopolistic firms whose expansion is at the cost of small firms and households in both town and countryside; the centralization cum concentration of decision-making powers vested in the central state and the restructuring of lower levels of government as extended rather than independent branches of government; and the migratory responses of small firms and households to these processes.

Stuart Holland (1976) is one of the first to recognize the importance of multinational corporations that, as (micro)economic organizations, transcend conventional analytical divisions. Holland tries to capture the phenomenon by creating an additional category, the mesoeconomic sector, composed of "big league" or oligopolistic leader firms. Because these firms organize themselves and operate multinationally, conventional instruments of regional policy are no longer able to work. The alternative to locating a plant in a domestic peripheral region is to expand operations abroad.

Being used to a *national* framework of analysis, the transnational corporations were of course the first to attract attention in this respect. My contention is that this phenomenon is widespread and is part of a general process of development of the microeconomy from household and owner-operated to owner-managed to manager-managed forms of microeconomic organization. The industrial revolution led to specialization of production embedded in wholesale and retail structures of market-based distribution. The managerial revolution enabled the internalization at company level of large-scale mass distribution and handling, along with mass production.

In this context, it is useful to recall the four strategies of corporate growth identified by Hakanson (1979): (1) market penetration, as when a firm seeks to increase sales volume or market share in its present products and (market) area; (2) product development when firms seek to increase their market share in the area by means of improved versions of the present products; (3) market development whereby the firms take their present products into new market areas; and (4) diversification by adding new products and/or markets that differ from existing product and market combinations. The same strategies can be said to apply to owner-managed firms, with the important difference that this happens at a much smaller (regional or national) scale. As discussed earlier (see pp. 64–78), these firms probably will be deterred from expanding beyond existing markets and product lines in the face of competition from the large corporations that occupy oligopolistic leadership positions (cf. Holland 1976).

When examining the regional dimension, it should be recalled that the more-developed regions offer the best conditions for domestic oligopolistic leader firms to emerge due to their relatively larger and better integrated labor, product, and input markets, their superior infrastructure, and their access to the various levels of government. Insofar as foreign "big league" firms are concerned, they will also quite naturally prefer central regional locations, from the point of view of both the domestic market and global cost strategies. Also, face-to-face access to the government bureaucracy is a relevant factor for such firms.

Earlier in this chapter I discussed competition between various kinds of firms. I drew several conclusions that are important in the present context. First, small-household and family-owned firms may *not necessarily* be in direct competition with large corporations, because they operate in smaller isolated, marginal, or otherwise well-protected local and regional markets. Instead of attempting to break into larger national markets, these smaller firms may prefer to capitalize on their local control and, in accordance with their typical characteristics, to diversify their activities in the area. A second conclusion is that "big league" firms make selective use of production conditions prevailing in a region, whereas smaller firms must take the production environment largely as given. With this strategic advantage, the large firms can assume market leadership and impose a vertical structure of competition. Some time ago, Westaway (1972) pointed to the lopsided labor market and social effects of such verticalization. The urban labor market in the central locations becomes more polarized in high- and low-wage occupations, whereas the urban labor market in the peripheral regions becomes biased toward blue-collar occupations.

The process of development of multilevel managerial organizations that centralize and concentrate production cannot be separated from the process of centralization in government. Friedmann & Weaver (1979) and Holland (1976) not only view transnational corporations as the organizations primarily responsible for uneven development, but consider government exempt from the underlying process of change. Hilhorst rightly criticizes this view and agues that government as producer of goods and services undergoes the same process. Consequently, government is part of the problem. I extend this line of argument. Earlier, I discussed the role of the state in relation to the growing need for the provision of public goods (see pp. 78–84), arguing that this is not merely a question of more of the same, but that a growing proportion of economic, social, and economic infrastructural provisions and services must be made available and be organized at a higher spatial scale. The centralization of government is part and parcel of the same process that demands greater government involvement.

In terms of urban change, two important consequences can be seen. First and rather obviously, the outgrowth of the public sector stimulates urbanization, directly and indirectly, as part of the *urban* economic base. Second, the centralization will cause increased geographical concentration. The balance of power in decision making on public goods shifts from many dispersed municipalities to fewer but concentrated provincial units to a single level of central government.

The indirect effects of this centralization process can be summarized under three points. First, as already noted, managerial firms will expand their operations, preferably in the metropolitan center, to facilitate direct access to the increasingly important central government bureaucracy. Second, current government expenditures will be heavily biased toward a few places, most notably the metropolis. Public-sector employment will be similarly biased. Government thus contributes to the (rural–urban, urban–urban) metropolitan brain drain. Third, the process (further) undermines essential features underlying the notion of a town, namely, the local political autonomy of self-government, even if these communities show strong social divisions internally. Many towns disappear, as it were, to become nodes in multiple organizational and spatial networks. It seems justified to conclude that government is a major force integrating individual towns into one urban system and shaping that system toward primacy.[2]

The degree to which the balance of power shifts between levels of government will depend on specific historical developments and geographical differences. Moreover, the centralization process may be resisted by certain regional groups and polities that wish to maintain a certain level of relative autonomy in order to protect their respective economic and political spheres of influence. In particular, one can think here of situations where, for historical reasons, enterprises have centralized in a region or regions other than the seat of central government.

The third proposition concerning urban change refers to the responses of households and small firms to these processes. How will rural households react to penetration of the countryside by industry? What will be the effects of the formation of the agroindustrial complex? Similarly, what will be the reactions of small producing households and families in the towns?

The picture is endemically complex: much depends on historically specific, timed and spaced conditions. A general answer to these questions is thus apparently ruled out. Yet, on the basis of my analysis, two opposing factors may be identified: the lure of the metropolis provides a powerful and attractive force, but regional cultural factors may successfully prevent or counteract such a force. The expansion of government employment and of multilevel organizations in industry and services in metropolitan centers will cause the economic base of these cities to grow and will allow for a greater expansion of small localized activities. Migration to the center is partly self-propelling, in the sense that migrant households that come to make use of this *large* number of individually *small* opportunities will create additioinal opportunities.

We should not lose sight of the fact, however, that in Latin America, most migration is basically a rural exodus caused by unequal access to land, by economic and demographic pressure on the land (Shaw 1976), and by the impact on the rural economy of the agroindustrial complex. In other words, location of industry in the city is *not* the prime cause—something that would be difficult, in any case, given the relatively small size of industry (Gilbert 1970:387)—but a rurally pushed flow. The centralization of government and enterprises is a powerful force to (re)direct this flow into the big cities.

2. Hilhorst (1971) was one of the first to postulate a relationship, albeit a static one, between the shape of the urban system (primate or rank-size) and the organization of government (centralized or decentralized).

The penetration of multilevel enterprises in regional markets, their selective use of local production requirements, and their profit repatriation, cause *local* export-base multipliers to decline. In other words, less localized urban activity can be sustained and this will reduce the absorption capacity of intermediate cities.

The overall result is not influenced by industry and government alone. It is important here to stress the urban effects of the formation of the agroindustrial complex, which may in part compensate the tendency of declining absorption capacity with regard to (some) smaller towns. In absolute terms, the expansion of government services and industrial, commercial, and financial activities may be sufficiently substantial to sustain the growth of urban centers in the regions, but this does not alter the verticalization of the regional economic structure.

## Verticalization of the Regional Economy and Regionalism

In the literature, *regions* are defined either as social or as economic spaces that rarely coincide with political administrative boundaries. This is somewhat peculiar, in view of the fact that political administrative units are often used as a basis for analysis. I contend that regions are intermediate (supralocal) political administrative territories of government that have evolved historically and at which level the provision of public goods is organized. As more and more economic activities and social institutions become organized on larger spatial scales, many regions tend to disappear as important levels of both public and private decision making, just as many municipalities have already largely lost such significance (except where multilevel organizations are located).

Although this is the predominant trend, under the impact of the development of the agroindustrial complex, new intermediate and local territories of government may be created in land settlement and other hitherto "unincorporated" areas. As argued previously, the agroindustrial complex may produce situations where crops will be displaced and new areas will be entered into, requiring that government should provide and/or improve infrastructural facilities. Local/regional groups, emerging from the same process of economic expansion, may push for the creation of separate local/regional government entities in order to consolidate their own political power base.

At the other end and in other regions, local and regional government may be reorganized into a single lower level of government that is charged with maintenance of centrally provided infrastructures. The extent to which this may materialize will depend on many factors, including the resistance of local/regional power groups. This brings us to the issue of regionalism, which in recent years has received much (renewed) attention (for a review see Abalos 1982; Stein, Rokkan, and Urwin 1982). In the present context, it is particularly relevant to ask whether regionalism—which can be defined as a group or class alliance based on territorial social identity—would be able to counteract economic and urban centralization processes.

Before treating this question, it is useful to refer to Gourevitch's analysis of the conditions under which "peripheral nationalism" would emerge in particular regions. Gourevitch focuses on the relationship between ethnic potential (regionally distinct cultural features) and the geographical (in)congruence between two functions of the modern state, namely, the provision of national political leadership (strong central institutions), and the stimulation of economic development for the country as a whole. He argues, for example, that if the political leadership is concentrated in one region and economic development is centered in another, and one of the two has ethnic potential, then politically relevant "peripheral nationalism" may emerge. This may happen "if the original economic or political core falters; that is, if it stops promoting economic growth or providing political leadership for the whole country" (Gourevitch 1979:306). Based on a review of cases of regionalism in a number of western countries, some further conditions are specified:

> First, the more severe the core's weakness, the stronger is the peripheral nationalism. . . . Second, the more valuable the economic trumps available to the peripheral region the stronger is the nationalism there. . . . Third . . . the stronger the ethnic potential or the sense of ethnic grievance, the weaker the economic tension between core and periphery needs to be to produce nationalism. (ibid.:319–320)

Gourevitch also argues that the more open the economy of a country, the less effective will be the state in performing its functions, and the more peripheral nationalism will be encouraged. Finally, the significance of the attitude of the peripheral region's elite is stressed. Does it prefer the national or the local/regional political option?

Although Gourevitch may be correct in stressing the differences between core and periphery, he underestimates the importance of integrating elements. Just as the international mobility of labor and capital undermines the effectiveness of national government policies, so the regional integration and interregional mobility of labor, capital, and firms undermine the viability of regionalism. Moreover, the state is made up of more than the national government alone; to what extent are regionalist movements born by the economic success of groups in the periphery or a response to the failure to withstand extraregional penetration? Finally, if "peripheral nationalism" (re)emerges in a region, what will be the outcome?

In dealing with these issues it is important to recall the role played by access to and influence in the provision and maintenance of economic and physical infrastructures in processes of oligopolistic competition. Local, regional, and national oligopolies may be created on the basis of technological advantages, but in large measure they will be maintained and consolidated by the exploitation of infrastructural advantages. The directing, spacing, and sequencing of infrastructural provisions in the various regions creates these advantages: market and managerial integration cannot take place without them.

One implication of this is that local/regional firms having technological disadvantages with respect to (inter)nationally operating firms can resist or alter the terms of their integration through their influence on local/regional governments. To what extent this will be successful will depend partly on the relative position of these governments vis-à-vis central government, and the degree to which the process of centralization referred to earlier has advanced. Both types of firms will make use of their direct and indirect links with government, with the difference that the larger (inter)national firms have access to *more* and *higher* levels of government.

Regionalism can be seen as an attempt to resist the loss of (local/regional) control over local/regional government. The existence of historically developed, regionally specific cultural values may thus be of strategic importance in forging a political basis of multigroup or class alliances, but they do not constitute a sufficient condition. The key issue will be the existence of a broad front of regionally operating microeconomic units. Historically, many of these have been commercial and industrial; nowadays, many industrial and commercial firms operate nationally or internationally. The development of the agroindustrial complex in a particular region may thus stimulate new firms and groups to operate on the regional level.

The political processes related to regionalism are not merely struggles among *levels* of a territorial–political hierarchy. Firms that are expanding and in the process of achieving control over the national market stand to gain from higher-level integration. These firms, like the transnational corporations, have outgrown the region in which they are located, but because a large portion of their profits, wages, taxes, and rents accrues to that region, they have the leverage with which to influence their regional government to cooperate. The basis for a regional alliance in such regions will be smaller and weaker. Thus, although regionalism may occur in some regions, it is unlikely to occur simultaneously in all.

Regionalism often results in the creation of new political administrative units or in their separation. The expansion of the public sector in the new regional capital city will have a lasting effect on the urban structure.

It seems reasonable to conclude that regionalism can be a powerful force against primacy, but at the same time its limitations must be stressed. Given the factors and processes that shape primacy, regionalism is limited in scope and frequency.

## By Way of Preliminary Conclusion

The growing appreciation of historical and new developments in the micro-organization of production has brought the recognition that the basis for economic analysis is more heterogeneous than most theories can handle. At the lower levels of analysis, in particular, it becomes difficult to sustain conventional homogeneous behavior of functional sectors (agriculture, industry) or spatial–social segments (rural, urban). Town–country divisions "evaporate" when supralocal managerial enterprises take predominance over household and owner-operated firms operating almost exclusively at a small but above all localized scale. Similarly, regional divisions are altered fundamentally by the development of multilevel, multiplant managerial corporations that operate either nationally or internationally. A verticalization of regional economic structures results. The increasing sophistication and complexity of microeconomic organization and production demands greater government intervention, but at higher levels of spatial organization. Centralization and concentration of the public sector is the outcome of the process.

In previous sections, I examined the consequences of these tendencies in terms of processes of rural, urban, and regional change. I analyzed the implications of the development of the agroindustrial complex, and tried to show that the rural economy is reduced to agricultural activities that, in turn, become increasingly organized at national and international levels. The general tendency toward regional specialization and incorporation in the agroindustrial complex results in varying regional situations of the development of capitalist agricultural enterprises and the survival of peasant households. Apart from an "industry-led" incorporation process, there is an "agriculture-led" one, which is of equal if not greater importance for the growth of intermediate and small towns in the regions.

In considering the urbanization process, the most revealing factor is the disappearance of towns as independent social and political entities. The development of multilevel microeconomic organizations and the centralization of government lead to the insertion of urban centers as nodes in multiple organizational and spatial networks. In this respect, I agree with Castells's statement that "the development of industrial capitalism, contrary to an all too widespread view, did not bring a strengthening of the city, but its virtual disappearance as an institutional and relatively autonomous social system, organized around specific objectives" (Castells 1977:14).

The verticalization of regional economic structures differentiates the ability to internalize economic growth. Multilevel managerial firms make selective use of conditions for production prevailing in the various regions. The consequence is that *local* economic-base multipliers decline, and fewer localized activities can be sustained. This reduces the growth capacity of intermediate urban centers.

The centralization of government and enterprises foments the tendency for the national metropolitan center to grow relatively faster than the other urban centers. Centralization in government also has the important direct effect that a greater proportion of government expenditure and employment will be effectuated in this center.

Rural–urban migration is largely a response to the direct and indirect effects of the process of development of the agroindustrial complex and the penetration of "big league" industrial and trade firms into local and regional markets. Many people will migrate to the metropolis, where the greatest concentration of small opportunities and perhaps a few major chances are found. Migration in this context is self-propelling, not only because in the process new small opportunities are created, but also because of the rural–urban continuity in social networks and the household deployment of resources.

Finally not only towns but also regions are disappearing, a conclusion that should be seen in light of the emergence of regionalism as a reaction *against* their disappearance. Local and regionally operating groups resist the centralization tendency because it reduces their access to government and weakens their capacity to resist (by extra-economic means) competition by (inter)nationally operating corporations. Regionalism may be able to counteract some of the centralization effects, but it is unlikely that it will redress the verticalization of the economy or urban primacy.

# PART THREE

# CASE STUDIES

# CHAPTER FIVE
# ECONOMIC AND REGIONAL CHANGE IN COLOMBIA: 1900–1980

## Introduction

In this part of the study I describe the changes that have taken place in the economic and regional structure of Colombia. The central aim of this chapter is to analyze the interrelations between expansion of the microeconomy and the process of (re)centralization at the national level of government institutions and the implications for regional development.

Change is a dynamic process. New actors, factors, and forces emerge and alter the roles and behavior of those that already exist. Some preexisting actors disappear, others adjust and restructure to fit the new circumstances. My aim is to examine some of these actors, factors, and forces in an attempt to understand the dynamics of regional, rural, and urban change in Colombia.

I concentrate on twentieth-century Colombia, but where appropriate will refer to earlier periods of the country's history. I do not pretend to "regionalize" the entire modern history of the country; rather, the analysis should be seen as an interpretive essay intended to enable a better understanding of some of the major processes of regional economic change.

To highlight these major changes, I begin this chapter with a description of the general economic and regional situation as it existed at the end of the nineteenth century. This initial situation is characterized as an economic archipelago of relatively isolated rural regional economies within a federal state structure. This archipelago was by no means honogeneously (un)developed; on the contrary, there were considerable economic and political differences. This initial situation was drastically altered by several factors and processes that pushed for national economic, physical, and political integration. The first thrust of these processes took place in the pre–World War II period, which will be examined in the third section of the chapter.

The expansion of coffee production and exports at the end of the nineteenth century created demand and, in various regions, the temporary interruption of imports due to external factors that stimulated a domestic supply response in manufacturing activities financed by capital accumulated in the coffee trade. Some regional product markets were unified and extended by the infrastructure made possible by and necessary for the mobilization of coffee exports. Public works, employing rural labor, also stimulated migration to the towns and the emergence of urban labor markets, and as a result demand for manufacturing and agricultural products increased. Agricultural demand was met mostly by peasant production drawn into market relationships. A regional division of labor began to emerge.

All these changes had profound political implications. To understand these, I turn in the fourth section of this chapter to new actors, namely, nationally operating groups that emerged as a result of concentration processes in industry, banking, coffee, and trade. These groups needed and pushed for the consolidation and expansion of central state institutions. I illustrate this development by describing the process of (re)centralization and internal restructuring of the Colombian state. I conclude my analysis of this period in the fifth section with a brief characterization of the regional situation.

My analysis of economic and regional change in the post–World War II period (1945–1980) is broken down into two time periods covering the change in economic policy from import substitution (1945–1967) to export promotion (1967–1980).

In the sixth section, we shall see that in the first period protection played a more important role for industry than did actual import substitution. Behind protective walls, the process of national market integration could be completed without external interruption by the end of the 1950s. In the 1960s, foreign enterprise came to play a more significant role through the expansion of intermediate production. The regional pattern of industrialization is described through the shift-and-share technique and a variant of export-base analysis. I show that the pattern of change during the 1950s conformed to the core–periphery model, but that differentiation within the core and the periphery made this dichotomy less relevant in the following decade.

It will be argued that, in contrast to industry, import substitution played an important role in (tropical) agriculture. The main features of agricultural development in the period are summarized and its regional pattern described by means of an analysis of land-use specialization and concentration. For a number of crops, a process of agroindustrial integration is found to have given rise to a pattern of regional specialization-cum-displacement of other land uses.

In the seventh section, the period of export orientation (1967–1980) is analyzed, showing that although exports become a significant source of growth, domestic demand remained the most important source. Import liberalization cancelled out the export growth effect and, as a result, the economy became more international—a change in which foreign enterprise played a significant role.

Using the same techniques, I describe the regional patterns. It is found that the core–periphery pattern no longer holds for industry, differentiation within core and periphery having become prominent. In agriculture, the internationalization of capitalist agriculture and the marginalization of peasant production each reveal different regional patterns. In the former, the process of specialization and displacement is continued; in the latter, such changes are not observed.

In the eighth section, I consider the patterns of regional differentiation. Four processes are identified, all having the common element that they lead toward fragmentation of regional economies into parts that have little interrelation among themselves, but which individually have elaborate extra-regional links. These are (1) agricultural specialization and agroindustrial integration; (2) economic concentration and development of multilevel managerial organizations; (3) the extension of foreign enterprise into the country; and (4) (re)centralization within the state sector. Together, these processes cause the verticalization of the regional economy. A fifth process concerns local/regional (small firm and household) responses to the verticalization processes.

This chapter concludes with a brief review of the urban and regional situation as it has evolved during the postwar period.

## Nineteenth-Century Colombian Economic Archipelago

In many respects, nineteenth-century Colombia can hardly be described as a single national society. When the Republic of Gran Colombia—comprising present-day Colombia, Ecuador, Venezuela, and later also Panama—was proclaimed after the victorious but not very bloody battle of independence, the unity forged under the leadership of Bolivar in 1819 quickly started to break down. Soon after liberation, Ecuador and Venezuela separated from Gran Colombia. The political cohesion within the remaining territory of the newly proclaimed Nueva Granada (1831) was not very strong, however. A series of constitutional changes followed, leading in 1863 to the adoption of a federal structure—the Estados Unidos de Colombia—composed of the states of Bolivar, Antioquia, Cundinamarca, Santander, and Cauca.

The lack of a dynamic export base can be related to the absence of any nationally dominant elite after independence and helps to explain the inability to create a strong central state. The country lacked the resources with which to build and maintain such a state. A number of short-lived attempts were made to replace gold production, which had started to decline even before independence, but none of these (tobacco, quina, and some textile products) were successful. The pre-independence landed regional oligarchies were able to recoup political power, and the adoption of a federal structure minimized any conflict among them (Tirado Mejia 1978).

Nieto Arteta (1975a) aptly describes the nineteenth-century economic structure of Colombia as an "economic archipelago," composed of a number of isolated regions with little economic interaction among themselves. The geography of the country contributed to this situation. The country is carved up by three north–south spurs of the Andes mountains. There are a number of large and natural regions, namely the Western Andes region formed by the Cauca river basin, the Eastern Andes region formed by the Magdalena river basin, the Atlantic Coast, the Pacific Coast including Panama, and the Orinoco and Amazon river basins east of the Andes. At the end of the nineteenth century, a number of local regional formations occurred within these major natural regions. In the eastern highlands, which are the most populated part of the country, two regional formations roughly tallied with the present departments of Cundinamarca/Boyaca and Santander/Norte de Santander. In the western Andes, the Antioquian regional economy was considerably enlarged in the second half of the century by new land-settlement processes, particularly in a southward direction. The second important regional formation in the western part was the Valle del Cauca, of which Popayan was the traditional political center. Between the eastern and western regions is the interior local formation, situated around the valleys of the upper Magdalena (Tolima/Huila). In the north, the Andes give way to the Atlantic Coast region, some parts of which, due to their location along the Magdalena river transport system, have a long development history. Finally, the remaining vast natural regions are sparsely settled, mostly by indigenous peoples.

These geographical features constitute formidable barriers to communication and movement. At the end of the nineteenth century, for instance, it was cheaper to transport a commodity from Liverpool to Medellin than from Medellin to Bogotá (Ospina Vazquez 1974; McGreevey 1975). There was relatively little to unite the various regional economies, but this does not mean they were "homogeneously small." In fact, they showed considerable (historical) differences (cf. Kalmanovitz 1978b; Nieto Arteta 1975a; Escorcia 1978). First of all, some regions were characterized by traditional *haciendas* that had developed from the colonial *encomiendas* and through which the local indigenous and mestizo peoples were subjected via traditional forms of land tenure. I refer in particular to the high plains of Cundinamarca/Boyaca, the southwestern region of Valle del Cauca/Narino and, since the end of the eighteenth century, the interior region (Tolima/Huila). Population growth and the dissolution of the *Resguardos* caused *minifundio* to develop alongside these haciendas and on the marginal lands and mountain slopes.[1] In the colonial period, gold was mined in Choco and in the Valle del Cauca with the aid of slave labor, and led to the formation of slave plantations. In Antioquia, however, the low population density caused gold mining to be organized on a small scale; for the same reason, there was little development of haciendas. This also applied to Santander, where peasant settlement of the land by poor inmigrants and mestizos from the early eighteenth century onward, had created a more independent peasantry, which achieved a considerable level of artisan development in the following century. A similar process of land settlement, but at a quicker pace and on a greater scale, took place in Antioquia in the nineteenth century (Parsons 1950). Finally, the Costa Atlantica and the Llanos, to the extent that they were populated, were characterized by extensive livestock estates.

For most of the five decades after independence, the political scene was dominated by the landed oligarchies of the states of Cundinamarca and Cauca, the two most populous regions, which also provided most of the federal presidents in this era (McGreevey 1975). According to Martinez (1979), there were fundamental differences in political structure, in particular between Cundinamarca and Cauca, on the one hand, and Antioquia and Santander, on the other. In the former, the hacienda system created and maintained an adscriptive loyalty of the subjected population, the origin of which goes back to the colonial *encomendero* system of labor obligation. The political power of the *hacendados* was based on their capacity to be "generals." Civil conflict and violence were means with which to enforce both political power and the loyalty of the *peones*: by calling on their respective (private) armies of *peones,* these *hacendados-generals* could confront any major political difference of opinion. From the list of eight major civil wars and many more localized conflicts, it seems that political differences were quite common (Tirado Mejia 1978). In contrast, in those regions where the *encomendero–hacienda* did not develop historically and where land settlement occurred in later periods, that is, Santander and Antioquia, political power was less authoritarian and was based on negotiated political pacts *(Pacto Libre).*

On the whole, towns developed very little in the nineteenth century. With the exception of Bogotá, Medellin, Cali, and Bucaramanga, not much about the towns was "urban" (Melo 1979:143): they were mostly places of residence for the various landed elites and seats of government. The economic base of the towns consisted mostly of the conspicuous consumption of the landed rich, which generated some additional (self-)employment opportuni-

1. *Resguardos* (indigenous reserves) date back to the colonial era. In these areas, land is held communally and customary law and institutions apply.

ties for the poor and mestizo population. Only the larger towns had sizable artisan populations, but the import of manufactures eroded much of their growth potential. Urban population growth throughout the century was very limited indeed, except towns that were developing in relation to land-settlement processes, such as Medellin, Manizales, Pasto, and Cucuta. Only in the last quarter of the century did towns grow mainly in relation to the increasing internal and external trade generated by the coffee expansion.

The economic and regional structures of the nineteenth century were affected by two processes, namely, the import of (European) manufactures and the expansion of coffee production and exports. The import of European manufactures, largely controlled by *hacendado*/traders in Antioquia and Cundinamarca, undermined artisan production in Santander in the second half of the century and, together with civil wars, stimulated migration toward Antioquia. The ascendance of the latter region is thus connected, though not exclusively, with the decline of Santander and Boyaca. Two additional factors favoured the rise of the Antioqueño elite relative to the established centers of power: gold mining and coffee (see Chapter 7). The first gave Antioqueño traders a certain predominance in interregional trade because they possessed the scarce means of circulation. The development of coffee production started to be significant from 1870 onward, and although initially most production was concentrated in Santander (88% in 1874), its greatest expansion was in Antioquia/Caldas, which moved from 2% in that year to 35% in 1913.

The development of coffee as the major export product generated new forces that called for a unitary system of government. In this context, an important factor is that coffee was grown on a considerable though changing scale in three of the major regions (states) of the country—Santander/Norte Santander, Antioquia/Caldas, and Cundinamarca/Boyaca. In other words, many but not all regional landed groups and newly emerging traders supported such a government. The Regeneration movement led by Nuñez achieved a constitutional reform in 1886, although considerable powers were still vested in the new departments, which were patterned closely on the previous federal states (Ruiz 1982). The departments continued to have a large resource base and controlled such key functions as police, education, immigration, land settlement, roads, and railways (Tirado Mejia 1981). Moreover, Nuñez's attempts to establish a central bank that would have a monopoly over the emission of banknotes were resisted. A national army was established, and the growing strength of the export sector directly and indirectly gave further support to the development of central state power and institutions. It became urgently necessary to develop infrastructure on a large and interregional or national scale (railways, roads, harbors, monetary system, and so forth); this called for greater powers for central government at the cost of the departments, although without any considerable expansion of the role of the state as a whole. The War of a Thousand Days (1899–1902) brought the defeat of traditional regional power. Although Nuñez and the radical liberals were defeated, and the conservative General Rafael Reyes came to power, in effect the development of central state institutions was enhanced at the cost of the departments. Five new departments were created after the war: Narino, Caldas, Atlantico, Huila, and Norte Santander. The department of Boyaca, earlier separated from Cundinamarca, underwent considerable internal restructuring during Reyes's dictatorial administration. With this fundamental internal political restructuring, the country entered the twentieth century.

## Coffee and Early Industrialization (1900–1950)

The country needed some time to recover from the ravages of the War of a Thousand Days. The eastern departments in particular were severely affected by the disruption and destruction that had been caused. Recuperation was aided by favorable developments in coffee prices and exports. In the first decade of the twentieth century, coffee came to constitute around one-third of total exports. Partly due to the changing world market of coffee in favor of the fast-growing post–World War I economy of the United States, the share of coffee in total Colombian exports rose rapidly during the 1920s to around 70%. This share dropped during the Great Depression, recovered again after World War II, and rose to more than 75% in the 1950s.

The expansion of coffee production is a key factor in the emerging regional divison of labor in this period. Historically, coffee was first introduced in the state of Santander, where the initial wave of expansion took place (1840–1900). A second expansionary movement occurred in Cundinamarca and Tolima and also in Antioquia in the last quarter of the nineteenth century. The third wave of expansion took place in the first decades of the present century, during which coffee cultivation pushed the land settlement frontier of Antioquia further south toward Tolima (Palacios 1979).

Although, in general, coffee cultivation did not displace agricultural activities—at best it displaced some extensive livestock rearing—and aided in the settlement of new land and/or the incorporation of hitherto idle land, the way in which the expansion occurred differed markedly between western and eastern regions. In the latter, large coffee haciendas coexisted with independent and tenant-peasant production. It will be recalled that population densities were relatively high in the east. Furthermore, the crisis in tobacco growing and in rural-household textile manufacture created a large rural labor surplus that could be employed on the coffee haciendas (particularly in Santander). In the western regions, peasant land colonization had created a large medium-sized and independent peasantry. Coffee cultivation had no particular scale advantages and its direct and indirect labor requirements enabled the full utilization of family labor. In this sense it was preeminently a peasant crop. According to Palacios (1979), this was also the reason why, in the 1930s, the coffee haciendas in Cundinamarca lost out and moved into the commercialization of coffee, trade, and industry, leaving production to tenured and *minifundio* peasants.

Table 5.1 shows that the center of coffee production moved from Santander and Cundinamarca in the east to Antioquia/Caldas, Tolima, and Valle. The differences in agrarian structure were made very clear in the first Coffee Census in 1932. In Santander, 48% of the coffee production came from holdings of over 35 ha, constituting only 3.2% of all coffee holdings. A similar concentration of very large holdings is found in Cundinamarca, where this group controlled 55% of production but constituted only 5% of the total number. In Tolima, the figures were somewhat smaller: the large holdings represented almost 3% of all coffee holdings and provided 38% of annual output. In Antioquia, by contrast, large holdings constituted only 1.1% and controlled 20%. The share of the larger holdings in Valle and Caldas was even less (0.6–11.0% and 0.3–7.0% respectively) (Machado 1977:131, Table 13).

The introduction and expansion of coffee production meant not only agricultural and rural growth and development; it also required a basic physical and economic infrastructure, which was lacking in most areas, that is roads and railways, import and export trade establishments, banking and transport, and facilities for processing coffee. In other words, coffee required and brought about a considerable local regional economic transformation (cf.

TABLE 5.1
Coffee Production by Region, Colombia, 1874–1943 (thousands of 60-kg bags)

| | *1874* | | *1913* | | *1932* | | *1943* | |
|---|---|---|---|---|---|---|---|---|
| Magdalena | 0.2 | ( 0.2) | 25 | ( 2.4) | 21 | ( 0.6) | 25 | ( 0.5) |
| Antioquia/Caldas | 2.5 | ( 2.2) | 384 | (35.4) | 1,621 | (46.9) | 2,532 | (48.9) |
| Cauca/Nar/Valle | 1.9 | ( 1.7) | 85 | ( 7.8) | 430 | (12.4) | 865 | (16.7) |
| Tolima/Huila | 1.0 | ( 0.9) | 60 | ( 5.5) | 499 | (14.4) | 800 | (15.5) |
| Cund'ca/Boyaca | 8.6 | ( 7.5) | 203 | (18.7) | 428 | (12.4) | 495 | ( 9.6) |
| Santder/NorSan | 100.0 | (87.6) | 328 | (30.2) | 420 | (12.2) | 460 | ( 8.9) |
| Others | — | — | — | — | 36 | ( 1.0) | — | — |
| Total | 114.2 | (100.0) | 1,085 | (100.0) | 3,455 | (100.0) | 5,177 | (100.0) |

*Source:* Urrutia and Arrubla (1970:210)

Garcia 1937 on Caldas). This also explains why considerable capital investments were necessary; in part these were taken care of by the state but the remainder came from the private sector. Thus, even if coffee production was democratic, as it was characterized to be in Antioquia/Caldas, local elites made large investments in the reorganization of the local regional economy, both in the east and west, and were well rewarded economically and politically (Palacios 1979).

## Industrialization

The development of the coffee export sector in no way implied that Colombia was moving toward becoming a classic mono-agricultural export-producing country. On the contrary, the strong development of coffee production and exports enabled diversification toward industrial activities and stimulated it in various ways (Urrutia 1979). First, the structure of coffee production was less concentrated than that of any other export crop, generating a more favorable distribution of (monetary) income, thus constituting an important source of demand for manufactured products. Second, increasing coffee exports contributed the foreign exchange necessary to finance the imports of industrial machinery and raw materials. To this a third point may be added, namely, that the mobilization of coffee exports needed and stimulated the creation of the transport infrastructure, which naturally also enabled the physical entry and movement of industrial equipment and commodities. During the first three decades of the twentieth century, great advances were made in the expansion of the various railway sytems (McGreevey 1975). Finally, the emergence of the industrial bourgeoisie is related, though not exclusively, with coffee production and trade (Brew 1977). The accumulation of coffee capital partly financed other industrial enterprises, while the industrial processing of coffee beans stimulated industrial relations and entrepreneurial experience (Arango 1977).

In addition to coffee, a number of other factors contributed to the establishment and later consolidation (after 1930) of industrial enterprises. For example, the temporary interruption of competitive imports created a similar effect during the first and second world wars and during the Depression, when protective measures were needed because of the reduced capacity to import. Furthermore, and not without importance, the development of a viable export sector directly and indirectly strengthened the state. Customs duties came to constitute the major source of government revenue, displacing the traditional state monopolies (Melo 1979). Foreign loans had an indirect effect. Together with the indemnification paid by the United States for the independence of Panama (agreed to in 1923), they enabled the government to finance major public works programs which, among other things, helped to expand domestic consumer demand.

The regional significance of the public works programs was considerable. They not only boosted (market-based) consumer demand, but also helped to reduce transport costs, thus extending the local regional input and output markets of town-based industrial and trade activities. The expansion of the railways has been fairly well documented (McGreevey 1975). As shown in Table 5.2, the total railway length increased almost sixfold in a period of 30 years. Much less systematic information is available with regard to roads. The data presented in Table 5.3 give some approximation, showing that Cundinamarca, Antioquia/Caldas, and Valle at that stage became the best internally integrated and externally connected regions, (the first two via the Magdalena river, the third via the Pacific), not only by rail but also by road [see Figure 5.3, p. 162].

Because, on the whole, specialized artisan manufacturing was relatively small and limited to a few towns, and because much specialized rural-household manufacturing had already been eliminated many years earlier (e.g., the Santander textile manufactures) as a result of free trade policies and the ravages of civil war, industrial growth between the two world wars was largely at the expense of the expansion of foreign imports. Industrialization thus internalized the growth effects of coffee and increased the dynamic effects on the economy as a whole.

Although the second half of the 1920s and the entire 1930s clearly were periods of the greatest growth of industrial activities, a number of industrial establishments had been founded earlier in the century (cf. Ospina Vasquez 1974). Apparently, it took some time before full use could be made of the generally favorable economic climate, which is understandable when one takes into account that industry had to be built up from scratch and without

TABLE 5.2
Railway Length, by Main Region, Colombia, 1885–1945 (in kilometers)

| | *1885* | *1904* | *1909* | *1914* | *1922* | *1934* | *1949* |
|---|---|---|---|---|---|---|---|
| Costa Atlantica | 27 | 199 | 238 | 261 | 313 | 486 | 201 |
| Antioquia/Caldas | 37 | 66 | 102 | 205 | 281 | 556 | 449 |
| Pacifico/Valle | 37 | 43 | 94 | 234 | 341 | 678 | 824 |
| Tolima | 15 | 50 | 144 | 141 | 205 | 310 | 347 |
| Cundinamarca | 31 | 136 | 234 | 234 | 249 | 626 | 556 |
| Santander | 54 | 77 | 89 | 91 | 92 | 192 | 177 |
| Total: | 201 | 571 | 901 | 1,166 | 1,481 | 2,848 | 2,554 |

*Source:* McGreevey (1975:262).

TABLE 5.3
Road Length, by Department, Colombia, 1922–1936 (in kilometers)

| | *All types of roads* | *National and departmental roads only* | |
|---|---|---|---|
| | *1922*[a] | *1930*[b] | *1936*[c] |
| Antioquia | 234 | 667 | 981 |
| Atlantico | — | 165 | 148 |
| Bolivar | 30 | 152 | 64 |
| Boyaca | 367 | 621 | 847 |
| Caldas | — | 430 | 587 |
| Cauca | 120 | 311 | 436 |
| Cundinamarca | 1683 | 920 | 1628 |
| Huila | 30 | 373 | 332 |
| Magdalena | 4 | 234 | 240 |
| Narino | 240 | 436 | 699 |
| Norte Santander | 302 | 307 | 943 |
| Tolima | 49 | 428 | 390 |
| Valle | 298 | 394 | 1235 |
| Other | — | — | 147 |
| | 3,357 | 5,438 | 8,677 |

*Sources:* [a]Pardo Pardo (1972:414).
[b]Pardo Pardo (1972:415).
[c]Medina (1936:512).

any significant direct foreign participation. Industrial activity developed in most basic consumer goods, for example, food products, soft drinks and beer, tobacco, textiles and clothing, furniture, leather and shoe manufacture, ceramics and earthenware, matches, soaps and detergents, some metal products, and the like. In addition and not surprisingly, the building materials industry, particularly cement and brick making, developed rapidly. In most branches only a few firms developed at a time; most were relatively small, in terms of both capital investment and employment, catering to no more than small and localized, mostly urban markets. In those days, capitalist industrial organization was most advanced in the textile, tobacco, and beer and soft drinks industries, where individual enterprises became fairly large, employing more than 250 workers each (cf. Montenegro 1982:132; Brew 1977:392–403; Ricaurte Montoya 1936:156–160). These firms mainly were found in the largest towns such as Medellin, Barranquilla, and Bogotá. The increased industrial activity in the second half of the 1920s was in all probability due not only to the growth of coffee and coffee-related activities of trade and transport, but also to the large volume of public works.

The immediate effect of the Great Depression was not only a temporary decline in prices and stagnation in the volume of exports, but also a virtual cessation of central government public works programs. Industry soon recuperated, however, and experienced a very high rate of growth, estimated for the period 1932–1939 at as high as 10.6% per annum. The strongly reduced presence of competitive foreign imports proved a greater stimulus to expansion than was the scarcity of foreign exchange for the import of capital goods and raw materials, which was a barrier to growth (Montenegro 1982: 149). The strongest firms were able to ensure their access to the necessary foreign exchange. In this context it is revealing that the textile industry grew at an impressive 20% per year in the same period. By 1939 the share of industrial activity in GDP was already almost 15%. Although industrial expansion was constrained during the World War II period due to the relative scarcity of foreign exchange, the protected market must have favored capital accumulation: an impressive investment boom took place immediately after the war and annual growth rates in the order of 11% were achieved (Poveda Ramos 1967).

In 1945 the industrial structure was dominated by textiles, food, beverages, and nonmetallic minerals (building materials), industries which together accounted for 58% of factory value added and 57% of factory employment (Table 5.4).

The growth of coffee-related activities of processing, transport, and trade, as well as the expansion of infrastructural works and growing industrial employment, all stimulated the growth of towns. The rate of urban population growth (Table 5.5) in the period 1905–1918 was still lower than that of rural population (1.3% versus 3%); in the next intercensal period (1918–1938), however, urban population increased at an average of 5.9% per annum, whereas rural growth dropped to a low of 0.4%.[2] Finally, in the period 1938–1951 urban population growth continued at a relatively high rate while rural growth stayed fairly low (1.0%). Industry, trade, and state needed and fomented the growth of towns. The share of urban population rose from 21% in 1918 to 29% in 1938 and 39% in 1951. If we look at the proportion of the four largest towns (Bogotá, Medellin, Barranquilla, Cali) in the total urban population, we find that their share increased continually, rising from 24% in 1918 to 30% in 1938 to 37% in 1951 (DANE Census of Population 1976:125, DNP 1977:27). Throughout the period these towns grew more than twice as rapidly as the average town (see Table 5.6). Those four largest towns also accounted for 70% of the factory labor force.

2. It is generally agreed that since 1938 the population censuses are fairly reliable and consistent in their definitions. Caution is needed when drawing comparisons based on earlier census information.

TABLE 5.4
Census of Manufacturing Industry, by Sector and by Region, Colombia 1945

| | *Establishments* | *Employment* | *Value added (Thousands of Columbian $)* |
|---|---|---|---|
| **A. By Sector of Activity** | | | |
| Oils and Fats | 2 | 11 | 9.4 |
| Food | 2,020 | 27,493 | 24,869.3 |
| Paper & products | 38 | 594 | 594.6 |
| Printing & Publ. | 295 | 5,189 | 7,828.5 |
| Rubber & related | 42 | 978 | 1,673.1 |
| Beverages | 422 | 9,389 | 18,026.8 |
| Leather | 919 | 8,919 | 7,988.7 |
| Oil derivatives | 2 | 1,140 | 2,393.8 |
| Precision instruments | 162 | 1,385 | 1,923.2 |
| Wood & products | 821 | 8,323 | 7,393.8 |
| Metallurgical & mach. | 546 | 8,481 | 9,973.5 |
| Nonmetallic minerals | 556 | 11,204 | 13,221.7 |
| Chemicals & pharm's | 381 | 5,443 | 6,553.3 |
| Tobacco | 293 | 7,643 | 5,264.9 |
| Textiles | 337 | 28,726 | 29,003.7 |
| Clothing | 963 | 9,648 | 7,479.8 |
| Other | 54 | 834 | 605.3 |
| Total | 7,853 | 135,400 | 144,803.6 |
| **B. By Region** | | | |
| Antioquia | 1,288 | 34,648 | 36,473.6 |
| Atlantico | 595 | 14,405 | 18,881.1 |
| Bolivar | 346 | 5,649 | 4,760.3 |
| Boyaca | 663 | 4,657 | 3,172.6 |
| Caldas | 620 | 8,660 | 8,694.2 |
| Cauca | 158 | 1,761 | 1,563.6 |
| Cundinamarca | 1,569 | 27,694 | 36,602.3 |
| Huila | 81 | 787 | 506.5 |
| Magdalena | 133 | 1,237 | 1,326.5 |
| Narino | 175 | 1,811 | 971.5 |
| Norte Santander | 251 | 2,200 | 1,623.4 |
| Santander | 796 | 9,989 | 7,664.2 |
| Tolima | 320 | 3,575 | 3,914.6 |
| Valle | 800 | 17,979 | 18,241.9 |
| Other | 58 | 345 | 407.8 |
| Total | 7,853 | 135,400 | 144,803.6 |

*Source:* Ospina Vasquez (1974:547–548).

TABLE 5.5
Population Growth, Total, Rural, Urban Municipal, and of Bogotá, Colombia, 1905–1983 (in thousands)

| Year | Total pop. | Annual growth % | Urban pop. | Annual growth % | Rural pop. | Annual growth % | Urban share % | Share mpls. % | Pop. Bogotá | Share Bogotá % |
|---|---|---|---|---|---|---|---|---|---|---|
| 1905 | 4,135 | | | | | | | 10.5 | 100 | 2.3 |
| 1912 | 5,073 | 2.9 | — | — | — | — | — | 10.5 | 121 | 2.4 |
| 1918 | 5,855 | 2.2 | — | — | — | — | — | 11.6 | 144 | 2.5 |
| 1938 | 8,702 | 2.0 | 2,534 | — | 6,168 | — | 29 | 16.6 | 330 | 3.8 |
| 1951 | 11,548 | 2.2 | 4,469 | 4.5 | 7,080 | 1.1 | 39 | 23.1 | 648 | 5.6 |
| 1964 | 17,485 | 3.1 | 9,093 | 5.4 | 8,391 | 1.3 | 52 | 37.5 | 1,697 | 9.7 |
| 1973 | 22,487 | 2.8 | 13,719 | 4.3 | 8,781 | 1.0 | 59 | 37.5 | 2,811 | 12.5 |
| 1983[a] | 27,503 | 1.9 | 18,207 | 3.0 | 9,296 | 0.1 | 66 | — | 4,163[b] | 15.4 |

[a]Estimates
[b]Figure 1980
*Sources:* McGreevey (1971:110); DANE (Census of Population 1977:29); Florez & Gonzalez (1983:52).

## Agriculture

With regard to agriculture, it is important to recall some fundamental historical aspects (cf. Kalmanovitz 1978a; Palacios 1979). In the most populated Andean regions the agrarian structure is dominated by the *latifundium–minifundium* complex (Pearse 1975). In general, large haciendas are found in the fertile valleys, the high plains, and the lowlands, with peasant holdings situated alongside them on less fertile land and on the mountain slopes (Fals Borda 1957). Relatively speaking, agricultural activities were most developed in the more temporate Andean regions, though the degree of commercialization of produce of both hacienda and *minifundio* was very low.

As we have seen, some subtropical regions have only recently been colonized (e.g., Antioquia). However, except for some commercialization of cattle, pig raising, and coffee, most agricultural production has been of a household subsistence nature.

Early in the twentieth century, tropical agriculture was virtually undeveloped. If it existed at all, extensive livestock production prevailed in regions such as the Costa Atlantica and the Llanos Orientales. On the whole, however, the productive development of the land was relatively low. Moreover, large parts of the country were hardly populated: at the turn of the century, for instance, only 7% of the land was used for crops and livestock, 40% was owned but unused, and another 34% was not even effectively settled (Bejarano 1979:142). The expansion of coffee production had no major impact on agricultural production. As we have seen, coffee production could

TABLE 5.6
Population of Main Urban Centers and Their Intercensal Annual Growth Rates, Colombia, 1918–1973

| | *1918* | *1938* | *1951* | *1964* | *1973* | *1918–38* | *1938–51* | *1951–64* | *1964–73* |
|---|---|---|---|---|---|---|---|---|---|
| Bogotá | 143,994 | 330,312 | 664,506 | 1,673,370 | 2,885,576 | 4.2 | 5.5 | 7.4 | 6.2 |
| Medellin | 79,146 | 168,266 | 397,738 | 948,025 | 1,473,572 | 3.8 | 12.6 | 6.9 | 5.0 |
| Cali | 45,525 | 101,883 | 245,568 | 663,485 | 998,011 | 4.1 | 7.0 | 7.9 | 4.6 |
| B'quilla | 64,543 | 152,348 | 269,537 | 530,651 | 755,935 | 4.4 | 4.5 | 5.3 | 4.0 |
| B'manga | 24,919 | 51,283 | 107,517 | 224,676 | 366,888 | 3.7 | 5.7 | 5.8 | 5.6 |
| Cartagena | 51,382 | 84,937 | 111,291 | 217,910 | 309,422 | 2.5 | 2.1 | 5.3 | 3.9 |
| Pereira | na | na | 89,275 | 179,133 | 259,031 | na | na | 5.5 | 4.1 |
| Cucuta | 29,490 | 57,248 | 70,375 | 147,176 | 223,833 | 3.3 | 1.6 | 5.8 | 4.8 |
| Manizales | 43,203 | 86,027 | 92,030 | 195,542 | 213,185 | 3.5 | 0.5 | 5.9 | 0.9 |
| Ibague | 30,255 | 61,447 | 54,347 | 125,233 | 193,879 | 3.6 | 5.6 | 6.6 | 4.9 |
| Armenia | na | na | 72,805 | 155,364 | 177,105 | na | na | 6.0 | 1.5 |
| Pasto | 29,035 | 49,644 | 48,853 | 82,546 | 128,285 | 2.6 | −0.1 | 4.1 | 5.0 |
| Neiva | 25,185 | 34,294 | 33,040 | 75,886 | 112,479 | 1.5 | −0.2 | 6.6 | 4.5 |
| Sta Marta | 18,040 | 33,245 | 37,005 | 89,161 | 108,007 | 3.1 | 0.1 | 7.0 | 2.1 |
| Popayan | 20,235 | 30,038 | 31,866 | 58,500 | 79,490 | 1.9 | 0.4 | 4.8 | 3.4 |
| Total | 604,952 | 1,240,972 | 2,325,753 | 5,211,294 | 8,284,698 | | | | |
| Urban (in thousands) | na | 2,534 | 4,469 | 9,093 | 13,719 | na | | 5.4 | 4.3 |
| Share main towns in total urban population | | 49% | 52% | 57% | 60% | | | | |

*Sources:* McGreevey (1975:113); DNP (1979).

easily be incorporated into peasant-household production. Furthermore, and particularly at this stage, the increase in land needed for coffee trees was met by an extension of the land-settlement frontier. Only when production gradually became more intensified toward the end of the 1900–1950 period could an effect be expected in terms of increased demand for food and labor. In this context, it is interesting to observe that the literature makes no mention of any severe shortages of labor during coffee harvests, although in the eastern region there were greater problems of labor recruitment. The direct effect of the expanding coffee production on other rural activities was limited.

In the 1920s and 1930s, the main effects on rural production came from public works and industrialization. On the one hand, there was a strong demand for rural labor to work on infrastructural projects and in the factories, transport, and trade. This demand had the immediate consequence of uprooting traditional forms of tenure that for many years had tied rural labor to the haciendas. On the other hand, there was a local–regional impact in terms of growth of demand for food and agricultural raw materials. The importance of the demand for labor is indicated by the scarce data on wages. Wages started to increase rapidly in the 1920s, but because considerable increases in food prices occurred simultaneously, real wages began to increase somewhat only in the second part of the decade. Not only did food prices increase but also the imports of food (Rodriguez 1981:43-45). In other words, early industrialization had little impact on agriculture. The *hacendados* resisted the disruption of traditional tenure and blamed the growing food shortages on the public works that had drained away rural labor with higher wages (Bejarano 1979; Diot 1976).

Although many new opportunities were created on the demand side, relatively little had changed on the production side, in the sense that traditional technologies remained unaltered and favored peasant production. For the peasantry, however, much had changed. Several new opportunities, varied for the different regions, came within reach. One was coffee production, which could yield a considerable monetary income. The second was related to the commercialization of subsistence crops for the growing and favorable town markets. The rapid extension of the rail-and-road networks, particularly in Cundinamarca and Valle, made this a viable option. Finally, there was the possibility of employment in public works, trade and transport, and industry.

Prior to World War II, the government had minimal policy on agricultural production. If we disregard emergency measures, such as the elimination of duties on food imports in the 1920s, there remains only the attempt to stimulate agricultural production via the private settlement of public land. During the period 1910–1937, more than one million hectares of public land were converted into private property, mostly in very large tracts of land: only 9% of the land thus acquired was in lots of less than 20 has (Bejarano 1979:159). Moreover, no conditions were attached regarding its productive use.

In the 1930s, liberal governments changed their attitude somewhat in reaction to the growing rural conflict, especially in Cundinamarca, and to the changing overall political situation (cf. Urrutia 1969). Rural conflicts mainly were due to the fact that the deflation of food and coffee prices immediately following the Great Crash of 1929 made it very difficult for many food and coffee-producing tenants to pay their rents (Palacios 1979). Many laborers were laid off in both public works and industry and landlords were temporarily able to recoup part of their rural power by replacing emancipated tenants by other peasants. When landlords threatened to evict tenants who were unable to pay their rents, peasant leagues were organized with the help of the socialist and communist parties (Gaitan 1976). In an attempt to neutralize the socialist party and to reduce rural conflict, government then proposed some measures of land reform, including the buying out of some large coffee estates in Cundinamarca and the selling of small holdings through the newly created Agricultural Mortgage Bank. In 1932 the government responded to the peasant credit problem by creating the Agrarian Bank.

If land use within agriculture is analyzed on the basis of available but fragmentary statistics, it appears that in 1915, 66% of total crop land was devoted to food crops for direct consumption, some 25% to crops requiring some form of processing before use (particularly sugar),and 9% to export crops (mainly coffee). By 1938 the distribution had changed in favor of export crops, whose share increased to 26% Bejarano 1979, quoting Kathryn 1952). Not only most food crops but also the industrial crops seem to have remained within the realm of small-scale peasant production, often on a sharecropping basis. The most notable exception concerns the production of sugar. The present-day sugar cartel—dominated by only four families—developed on the basis of integrated sugar plantations that were established in the first three decades of the twentieth century. Finally, many coffee haciendas encountered difficulties as the Great Depression began and many *hacendados* withdrew from coffee production to concentrate on processing and trade. The share of small and medium-sized peasant holdings in total production consequently increased considerably (Machado 1977; Palacios 1979).

The regional distribution of agricultural land use shows that most agricultural developments took place in the regions of the interior, most notably Cundinamarca, with the United Fruit export enclave and some cotton in the Costa Atlantica as the main exceptions. In 1925, Cundinamarca was among the 3 largest producers of 7 of the 12 crops surveyed. By 1937, consistent with the pattern of industrialization and the shift in coffee cultivation toward the western regions, these regions (notably Antioquia) also had become more important in the production of marketable surplus in other agricultural crops. The geogaphical base of agricultural market production was extended. Even taking regional differences in climate into account, a definite process of regional specialization is not observable—with the clear exception of coffee. The data on agricultural land use in 1925 and 1937 (see Table 5.7) show that the share of the three largest production areas declined, though in varying degrees for most crops, namely 8 of the 12.

I mentioned earlier that food imports reached considerable levels, and the situation was only somewhat better with regard to livestock production. Cattle were imported mostly from Venezuela. Therefore, in this respect also, rural production could not keep pace with the growing demand from the towns. Table 5.8 summarizes the main data available. In a period of nine years, total stock expanded at a rate of 3.4% per annum.

With regard to the regional distibution, we find that livestock production extended into more departments. An interesting finding is that in the eastern coffee departments of Cundinamarca, Tolima, and Santander, cattle stock

TABLE 5.7
Agricultural Land Use, Colombia, 1925 and 1937. Area Cultivated in Main Crops in Three Largest Producing Departments

| *Crop* | *1925* | | | *1937* | | |
|---|---|---|---|---|---|---|
| Banana | Magdelana | 20,408 | ha | Magdalena | 60,705 | ha |
| | Valle | 1,200 | | | | |
| | Narino | 924 | | | | |
| | Total | 23,594 | 95%[a] | Total | 60,705 | 100% |
| Cacao | Valle | 7,537 | | Huila | 9,900 | |
| | Cauca | 5,342 | | Valle | 7,988 | |
| | Huila | 1,966 | | Cauca | 6,819 | |
| | Total | 16,432 | 90% | Total | 32,821 | 75% |
| Coffee | Cund'ca | 28,571 | | Caldas | 86,283 | |
| | Nor. San. | 21,106 | | Antioq. | 70,157 | |
| | Caldas | 15,381 | | Tolima | 65,795 | |
| | Total | 105,325 | 62% | Total | 391,881 | 57% |
| Cotton | Atlant. | 9,050 | | Atlant. | 22,486 | |
| | Magdal. | 4,325 | | Magdal. | 9,236 | |
| | Cauca | 2,655 | | Bolivar | 4,059 | |
| | Total | 17,892 | 89% | Total | 43,281 | 83% |

TABLE 5.7 *(Continued)*

| *Crop* | *1925* | | | *1937* | | |
|---|---|---|---|---|---|---|
| Sisal | Nor. San. | 3,360 | | Santander | 8,715 | |
| | Cauca | 1,435 | | Antioq. | 2,586 | |
| | Boyaca | 1,270 | | Boyaca | 2,293 | |
| | Total | 7,781 | 78% | Total | 18,459 | 74% |
| Maize | Cund'ca | 60,000 | | Antioq. | 97,493 | |
| | Antioq. | 29,639 | | Cund'ca | 91,792 | |
| | Caldas | 16,103 | | Bolivar | 80,602 | |
| | Total | 161,609 | 65% | Total | 551,075 | 49% |
| Peas & beans | Cund'ca | 42,700 | | Antioq. | 28,498 | |
| | Antioq. | 4,962 | | Caldas | 11,378 | |
| | Boyaca | 3,522 | | Valle | 5,673 | |
| | Total | 58,894 | 87% | Total | 72,060 | 63% |
| Potato | Cund'ca | 90,000 | | Narino | 25,252 | |
| | Boyaca | 11,632 | | Cund'ca | 14,401 | |
| | Narino | 5,000 | | Boyaca | 11,721 | |
| | Total | 116,390 | 92% | Total | 67,446 | 76% |
| Rice | Valle | 9,506 | | Bolivar | 28,582 | |
| | Cund'ca | 2,500 | | Valle | 9,530 | |
| | Boyaca | 1,902 | | Santander | 4,266 | |
| | Total | 20,613 | 67% | Total | 61,306 | 69% |
| Sugar (refined & brown sugar) (*panela*) | Cund'ca | 35,000 | | Cund'ca | 70,869 | |
| | Valle | 30,979 | | Huila | 33,747 | |
| | Boyaca | 14,963 | | Santander | 31,016 | |
| | Total | 125,767 | 64% | Total | 302,359 | 45% |
| Tobacco | Antioq. | 2,308 | | Santander | 6,218 | |
| | Valle | 1,733 | | Bolivar | 3,656 | |
| | Nor. San. | 500 | | Antioq. | 1,458 | |
| | Total | 4,561 | 99% | Total | 14,899 | 76% |
| Wheat | Cund'ca | 27,500 | | Boyaca | 88,866 | |
| | Boyaca | 9,525 | | Cund'ca | 73,902 | |
| | Narino | 6,514 | | Narino | 16,893 | |
| | Total | 48,289 | 90% | Total | 199,640 | 90% |

[a]Percentage share of the three largest producing regions in total national cultivated area. It should be noted that "total" is national cultivated area and not a sum total. For example: 20,408 + 1,200 + 924 = 22,532. (22,532/23,594) × 100 = 95%.

*Note*: Data on Bolivar and Santander are not available for 1925

*Sources:* Bejarano 1979, Tables A-7 and A-15. Diot, 1976, Table 11.2, p. 134.

TABLE 5.8
Regional Distribution of Livestock, Colombia, 1925 and 1934

| | *1925* | | *1934* | |
|---|---|---|---|---|
| | *No.* | *(%)* | *No.* | *(%)* |
| Bolivar | 1,789,000 | 29 | 1,768,961 | 20 |
| Antioquia | 575,000 | 9 | 822,126 | 9 |
| Boyaca | 320,000 | 5 | 767,000 | 9 |
| Magdalena | 186,000 | 3 | 757,150 | 9 |
| Tolima | 734,000 | 12 | 652,690 | 7 |
| Valle | 500,000 | 8 | 560,037 | 6 |
| Cundinamarca | 560,000 | 9 | 547,817 | 6 |
| Caldas | 336,000 | 5 | 467,203 | 5 |
| Cauca | 361,000 | 6 | 339,288 | 4 |
| Huila | 147,000 | 2 | 263,716 | 3 |
| Narino | 215,000 | 3 | 237,769 | 3 |
| Santander | 241,000 | 4 | 224,071 | 2 |
| Norte San. | 61,000 | 1 | 180,009 | 2 |
| Atlantico | 150,000 | 2 | 164,179 | 2 |
| Terr. Nac. | — | — | 338,916 | 4 |
| Total | 6,176,000 | 100 | 8,090,932 | 100 |

*Sources:* 1925 from Sanchez Santamaria (1925); 1934 from Morillo (1942:301–302).

went down in absolute terms. This may indicate a de facto displacement of livestock by agricultural activities and hence the beginning of specialization.

With regard to the regional distribution of the country's international exports (see pp. 180–184), it is not surprising that by 1950 Caldas and Antioquia were the major contributors, 37% and 21%, respectively, of total Colombian exports. The third coffee region, Cundinamarca, ranked third, with 12%. Other regions contributed with secondary exports, for example, Magdalena bananas), Santander (tobacco).

Consistent with the overall pattern of development, the four departments of Cundinamarca, Antioquia, Atlantico, and Valle absorbed 83% of international imports, but they show a manifest differentiation in that Cundinamarca alone accounted for almost one-third (31%) of total imports. In all probability, the relatively prominent role played by ports and port-related towns such as Barranquilla and Cali is due to the fact that more specialized import trade firms were located in those towns.

The net interregional flow of foreign exchange that now can be calculated shows that Caldas contributed 64% and the two Santanderes another 22%. The largest net user is Cundinamarca (38%), followed immediately by Atlantico and, at a lower level, by Valle (19%). In this context, it is interesting to observe that Antioquia, in line with its independent reputation, generated within its own department the foreign exchange it required to finance its international imports (see Table 5.13, p. 142).

Finally, a number of departments had little if any direct international trade participation. This refers not only to distant frontier regions such as Choco and Meta, but also to long-established but still predominantly subsistence regions such as Narino, Huila, Boyaca, and Cauca.

This brief account shows that the first half of the twentieth century was a very dynamic period during which various processes of change reinforced one another. The production and export of coffee created demand, and the reduction of competitive imports resulting from external factors stimulated a domestic supply response in manufacturing. Furthermore, coffee production or rather its trade enabled an accumulation of capital which, under prevailing circumstances, could best be profitably invested in domestic industry. Some regional markets for industrial products were unified and extended by the infrastructure made possible by and necessary for the mobilization of coffee exports. Infrastructural works employed rural labor, stimulated migration to the towns, and contributed to the formation of urban labor markets. Migration fueled the growth of towns which, in turn, amplified the demand not only for industrial products but also for agriculture. Given the technological conditions of agriculture in the first half of the twentieth century, these new opportunities could best be met through increasing local regional peasant production. Development as an agricultural mono-exporting and industrializing economy also meant the emergence of a new regional division of labor and had profound effects on the country's internal political structure, which hitherto had been dominated by regional power groups.

## Central State, Oligopolies, and Regions

It took more than 20 years, a traumatic civil war, and the virtual dictatorial administration of Nuñez and General Reyes, for Colombia to come to terms with the unitary system of government that was established in 1886. Central government institutions initially were extremely weak, and it was several decades before the central state became consolidated vis-à-vis the regions. In the following section, I explain how the economic changes discussed previously stimulated the strengthening of central state institutions and how the central state, backed in this way, gradually took over functions from the departmental and local levels of government. The simultaneous processes of concentration in industry, banking, trade, and transport resulted in the emergence of nationally operating firms. As government centralized, central government institutions expanded at the cost of local and regional governments and in response to the needs of nationally operating groups and firms. The result was a growing tension, as local/regional scope for maneuver narrowed. To some extent, the *Violencia* was related to the collapse of government in several regions.

It is extremely difficult to analyze this process in purely political terms. For one thing, the most important political parties in Colombia, the conservatives and liberals, are not formal organizations with a regular western democratic-type party machinery, nor did program politics play much of a role. Both parties had become "polyclass," and it is difficult to find a single decisive criterion as to their origin (Safford 1977a:153–201). Some go so far as to state that these parties are no more or less than the means by which various dominant groups seek to control the resources of the state (Martinez 1979). More often than not, conflicts between party factions predominate, such that the least divided party or coalitions between factions of the two parties come to power (Leal 1973; Kline 1983). Finally, it is often claimed that the liberal governments of the 1930s were the propagators of industrialization, but the most prominent and outstanding industrialists who led the transformation were active members of the Conservative party, which is usually associated with the vanishing traditional order (Montenegro 1982:137–138). Similarly, it will be recalled that coffee had become a profitable business for many, conservatives and liberals alike, during the first three decades of this century (Palacios 1979). Party divisions are extremely hazy, and if any rule applies, it is that party affiliation is inherited. The lack of ideological and social distinction does not mean that intense conflict does not occur. Particularly at the end of a period of hegemony of one party, interparty rivalries generate massive popular mobilization and civil conflict, apparently reinforcing hereditary affiliations.

## Central State

As coffee production and trade and industry developed, new economically powerful groups came to the fore, seeking to improve the conditions of accumulation. The fact that these developments took place in several regions gave them a new political dimension. Although theoretically the two groups may not have had identical interests (for example, on issues such as protectionism), in practice they agreed on the need for the physical and economic integration of the country and for the strengthening of the central state.

The expansion of coffee trade and exports generated a large increase in central government revenues and made the country increasingly eligible for foreign loans. On the other hand, the demands on the central state also increased. In addition to infrastructural works, which also were carried out by the departmental governments, there was a great need to rationalize the banking system. The Kemmerer Mission advised not only on the banking system but also on the administrative and financial organization of central government—for example, the reorganization of the ministries on sectoral lines, the centralization in the Ministry of Finance of all national taxes, the introduction of a comprehensive national budget and the establishment of an audit department to control its execution (Ruiz 1982:86–87). The Banco de la Republica—the central bank—was created in 1922. The process of administrative centralization increased departmental and municipal government responsibilities (in the fields of education, health, services such as water and sewage systems, etc.) without allowing them to extend or raise taxes, so that they became more dependent on central government allocations (Ruiz 1982: 88–90). For these purposes, special central state institutions were created: Fondo de Fomento Municipal (1940), Caja Nacional de Prevision (1945), Instituto Colombiano de los Seguros Sociales (1946). Financial responsibility for education and electricity supply was shared between central and departmental government (decrees of 1913, 1918, 1936, and 1938).

Similarly, central state institutions moved out to establish field offices and branches in various departments and towns. The Caja Agraria and the Banco Agricola Hipotecario, as well as the Banco de la Republica, established nationwide networks (cf. Medina 1936; Garcia 1937).

Finally, the tax reform of 1935 established new (national) taxes on internal activities: this helped to stabilize national tax revenues, because these now depended less on customs duties (Bejarano 1980:59).

Table 5.9 shows that local and regional government received more income and spent more on investment and consumption in the 1930s than did central government. A decade later this situation had drastically changed. Central government received 56% of all government revenues (compared with 42% in 1930–1932), and took care of 58% of total government expenditures (compared with 42%). The centralization was particularly strong in investment activities, where central government's share increased from 44% to 71%.

The centralization in government did not stand on its own. The 1930s also showed the beginning of a process of economic concentration in the various sectors of activity. Unfortunately, very limited information is available, so we are only able to construct a fragmented and partial picture. Nevertheless, the message is loud and clear: unmistakable tendencies of concentration in banking, industry, trade, and transport. The main evidence is summarized in the following sections.

TABLE 5.9
Distribution of Income and Expenditures by Government Level, Colombia, Selected Years, 1930–1952, percentages

| | *1930–32* | *1940–42* | *1950–52* |
|---|---|---|---|
| | | **A. Income** | |
| National | 42 | 56 | 62 |
| Dec. Ag's | — | — | — |
| subtotal | 42 | 56 | 62 |
| Departmental | 30 | 27 | 22 |
| Municipal | 28 | 17 | 16 |
| | | **B. Total Expenditure** | |
| National | 42 | 58 | 61 |
| Dec. Ag's | — | — | — |
| subtotal | 42 | 58 | 61 |
| Departmental | 34 | 26 | 21 |
| Municipal | 24 | 16 | 18 |
| | | **C. Current Expenditure** | |
| National | 44 | 47 | 57 |
| Dec. Ag's | — | — | — |
| subtotal | 44 | 47 | 57 |
| Departmental | 33 | 34 | 24 |
| Municipal | 23 | 19 | 19 |
| | | **D. Investment Expenditure** | |
| National | 44 | 71 | 74 |
| Dec. Ag's | — | — | — |
| subtotal | 44 | 71 | 74 |
| Departmental | 31 | 16 | 10 |
| Municipal | 25 | 10 | 15 |

*Sources:* 1930–1932 to 1950–1952 calculated from CEPAL/ONU estimates published in 1955 and reprinted in DANE (1970:152–182).

## Concentration in Banking

The nineteenth-century history of banking in Colombia is characterized by as many foundations as failures. The lack of any regulation, the coin shortage and speculation, and civil conflict and wars that interrupted the conduct of banking affairs, were the main causes of failure (Child and Arango 1984). After the expansion of coffee trade in the 1870s and the increase in prosperity, a new series of banks was started. In 1870 the Banco de Bogotá opened to soon become the government cashier, in the absence of a central bank. With some interruptions, such as during the Regeneration, this bank remained the central government's cashier and principal creditor until 1923. In the short span of 15 years, some 12 banks were created: 5 in Bogotá, 3 in Medellin, 2 in Bucaramanga (Santander), and 1 each in Popayan and Cartagena. Just before and during the first two decades of the present century, an additional 10 banks were created, 2 of which were in Caldas, 2 in Medellin, and the remainder in Bogotá, Barranquilla, Tunja, Honda, Ibague, and Cucuta. Although some banks disappeared rather quickly, there were one or more banks in most centers of trade of the era. Almost all of them were founded by local people. The banks that developed beyond this level were those engaged in the coffee trade and with government. The Banco the Bogotá began to expand its geographical area of operation during the 1920s. In 1922 it opened branches in Girardot (from where Cundinamarca coffee was shipped) and Neiva, and in 1926 it took over the Banco Social del Tolima in Ibague, which placed it at the center of the Tolima coffee area. In 1928 the Banco de Bogotá went national. In exchange for shares, it took over local regional banks in Honda, Bucaramanga, Cucuta, Medellin, and Pereira, which all became branch offices. The bank completed its national network by absorbing a bank in Tunja and by creating branches in Cali and Barranquilla (Banco de Bogotá 1960). Although we do not have similar information for any other bank, sources indicate that others were expanding into new regions (cf. Garcia 1937: 463–467). In Tolima, for instance, branches were established in the same period by the Banco Aleman Antioqueño of Medellin and by the Banco Dugand of Barranquilla. Similarly, the Banco Comercial Antioqueño, the Banco Aleman-Antioqueño from Medellin, and the Banco de Bogotá and Banco de Colombia, both from Bogotá, established branches in Santander (Galan Gomez 1947:537–538). These two banks and the Comercial Antioqueño also established themselves in the Costa Atlantica (Morillo 1942). It seems reasonable to conclude that, in the 1920s, regional banks were being absorbed into nationally operating banks originating in the main economic centers of the country.

During the Depression, the banks were unable to expand their networks to any great degree. The major banks again increased their branches in the 1940s and 1950s. In this context it is interesting that the expansion of the network of the Banco de Bogotá very closely followed the regional development of agriculture (Figure 5.4, p. 163).

## Concentration in Coffee Trade and Transport

Processes of concentration in trade and transport were intimately linked with coffee. Colombian traders had moved into coffee production by establishing haciendas when the coffee trade first started to expand, and they relied largely on North American trading houses and banks for the commercialization and export of their product. After the first coffee crisis of declining prices following World War I, a number withdrew from production and concentrated on processing and trade. Four major coffee trading houses emerged. By 1923—just before it suffered financial difficulties due to the failure of its bank—one of these, the Casa Comercial Lopez, was able to control 70% of coffee exports. Lopez had a network of storage facilities, drying and threshing installations, and also owned the shipping company Naviera Colombiana (Bejarano 1980). The concentration in coffee trade became permanently established when the Federacion Nacional de Cafeteros de Colombia was created in 1927 and became consolidated by 1937 (Palacios 1979). During the 1930s, a national commercialization, storage, and threshing network was established by this rather peculiar privately constituted and managed organization with state-recognized public functions of trade negotiation, price stabilization, and coffee product and area development. Coffee marketing became rationalized, that is, internal regional price differentials were eliminated (Palacios 1979:325). The federation finances its operations via the Fondo Nacional del Cafe, a tax on coffee that it manages.

River transport, which in the early twentieth century was the principal way of moving import and export trade (mainly the Magdalena river), showed some signs of a concentration process. In 1915, 11 companies were registered; one of these owned 13 of the 39 steamships with almost half of the total tonnage. In the 1920s, just before the Great Depression, transport expanded considerably: 37 companies owned 133 steamships with a total tonnage of slightly over 25,000 tons. The largest two companies controlled 25% of the total. Trade volume declined considerably during the recession and a process of restructuring must have taken place, because in 1935 only 20 companies existed, the largest two of which controlled 29 of the remaining 71 steamships and 48% of total tonnage (Ricaurte Montoya 1936: 185–190). During the 1940s and 1950s, the rail–river transport system increasingly was displaced by road transport, but the preceding serves as an indication that concentration processes were taking place in other than the financial and industrial sectors.

Soon after the inception of industrialization, a process of economic concentration also occurred in this sector, as a result of several factors, including technological (scale of production) and market reasons. Market reasons constitute a particularly powerful incentive for concentration, even if there are no specific technological advantages. The principal advantages seem to have been access to foreign exchange and raw materials in times of shortage. These become even more important when the domestic market becomes very favorable because of external reasons.

## Concentration in Industry

As economic and physical integration took place within regions and gradually also between economic centers of the most developed regions, this reduced the effective (transport cost) protection of regional markets. The development of transport technology was another powerful force in this process. For example, the cost of transporting one 125-kilo bag of coffee on a particular route in Antioquia dropped from seven pesos in 1927 (by donkey) to slightly over one peso in 1933–1935 (when transport by truck was introduced). To meet the growing competition from this new medium, rail tariffs for cargo were reduced by 40% in the same period (Garcia 1937: 396–397). The potential market for an individual firm thus increased considerably; competition might be strong during a short interregnum, leading ultimately to an oligopolistic market structure.

In Chapter 7, I examine the process of concentration in the textile industry in more detail. Suffice it to say here that the process of concentration by means of merger and takeover of firms is of early origin. In the 1920s and even earlier, this process was taking place first at a regional scale (in Antioquia) and later nationwide.

The Great Depression, as well as the period of relative protection of domestic markets, were powerful stimulants to economic concentration. This is clearly shown in the beverages sector. The Bavaria Company, founded in 1889, merged in 1930 with Cerveceria Continental of Barranquilla, which was in financial difficulties. Cerveceria also had breweries in Bogotá, Medellin, and Pereira. In 1931 a number of local breweries were taken over by the new consortium in Manizales, Honda, and Santa Marta, and two in Cali. After consolidating as a nationally operating firm, Bavaria S.A. established new factories in Barranquilla (1934), Cucuta (1935), and Duitama (1940). By the end of the 1940s the company entered a new round of expansion, establishing factories in 10 other towns. In the process, a number of local breweries had to close down, until only one major competitor existed in the Costa Atlantica (Bavaria 1966; Ogliastri 1976).

A similar process can be traced in other industrial activities. For example, Colcurtidos, at present a conglomerate based on the leather industry, had achieved a dominant market position by the end of the 1930s, and in 1944 took over a rival firm located in Medellin. In 1941, the Cia Nacional de Chocolates, a conglomerate based on cacao and coffee products and located in Medellin, established factories in Bogotá and Manizales. In other cases industry remained largely organized around regional markets, but even for typically regional products concentration processes can be found, though on a more limited scale. An interesting example in the building material industry is Cemetos Argos, manufacturer of cement and later bricks and prefabricated concrete structures. This company, established in Medellin in 1933, established cement factories in Barranquilla (1934 and 1944) and in Montebello (1939). Similarly, a cement company in Bogotá established a subsidiary factory in Santander. The dispersed pattern of location of this industry due to high transport costs did not prevent oligopolization of the market. Finally, it is of interest that, of the 24 industrial conglomerates that now exist, 10 of the parent companies were founded *before* 1930 (see also pp. 161–166).

## Political Implications

The development of the coffee export complex and the process of early industrialization had significant political implications. The regional landed oligarchies that traditionally had dominated the political order were now joined by two new nationally powerful groups which, although they partly arose from the former, set out to displace them. The coffee complex was organized and represented by the Coffee Growers Federation, while the industrialists organized themselves as a lobby in 1944 (National Association of Industrialists–ANDI). These 3 groups largely cut across the two main political parties. One can argue that for this reason a relatively smooth political transformation should have occurred, but this was far from the case. Two reasons were of importance here: one concerns the political entry of new groups; the other refers to the political transformations at the regional level.

The development of a town-based or urban proletariat in industry, trade, and transport, and a peasantry partly organized by the socialist party constituted a serious political problem for the dominant groups. According to Urrutia, a key role was played by the Liberal Party: "It appears that the Liberal Party, in order to ensure for itself the vote of the growing mass of industrial workers, adopted the reformist ideals of the Colombian Socialist Party. Thus, the historic function of the Socialist Party was to make the Liberals abandon their individualistic free enterprise and free trade ideology" (Urrutia 1969:75). After a series of conservative governments during the 1920s and growing divisions among conservative factions, the Liberal party managed to come to power and Lopez Pumarejo began to support the labor movement, to achieve reform as well as to strengthen his own political position, also neutralizing the newly arrived political parties.

Given the fact that industry already was achieving considerable degrees of monopoly, unions were organized at enterprise rather than nationwide level and by occupation. In no small degree this resulted from the labor legislation that was introduced and which protected enterprise unions (ibid.). The reform-mindedness of the elite was limited, however, and when the labor movement threatened to escape elite control in the 1940s with the emergence of the populist Gaitan, much of the protection that labor unions had enjoyed disappeared together with much of the organized labor movement.

We already have seen that the organization of the peasantry into peasant leagues was particularly effective in areas where coffee-producing tenants sought better terms of tenure. Although the reform laws of the 1930s brought some improvements, the main response of the Liberal government was the parcellation of large coffee estates in Cundinamarca, where the original owners offered no strong opposition. The large coffee estates became less profitable and increasingly difficult to manage.

Perhaps the most salient aspect of the Liberal Revolution on the March was that central government intervened actively in problems that were in part regional issues (the Cundinamarca coffee estates) or occurred in only a few regions (industrial labor disputes). In other words, it does not seem that the limited reform objectives were shared at all levels.

This bring us to a key issue of the period. Although the economic development processes stimulated central institutions at the top, very little restructuring and reform took place at the regional level. The political system still depended on regional bosses *(gamonales)* and on local political chiefs to deliver the votes in national elections (cf. Ruiz 1982). To function, this system depended on local and regional room for maneuver (departmental administration). The expansion of central state functions, the growing dependence of regional administration on central state institutions, and the national organization of enterprise that bypassed the regional level, all undermined the political system at that level.

The collapse of the government in some regions has been seen by some as the principal cause of the *Violencia,* which started in 1949 (Oquist 1978). This period of vicious violence continued through most of the 1950s and resulted in more than 200,000 deaths and the desertion of 400,000 rural holdings (Guzman et al. 1977). Ultimately, it caused the migration of two million people (Oquist 1978). The *Violencia* had many dimensions: land, religious, political, and others. At the regional level, the government system collapsed, whereas part of the severe division at the national level, which prevented any containment and resolution of the conflict, was that the Liberal hegemony viz. the central state showed that "the stakes had increased so much" (Kline 1983:51). The fight for control of the (central) state became too fierce for any accommodation or compromise.

## Regions and the Emerging Division of Labor

The economic development of the country was thus in a state of considerable imbalance. On the one hand, coffee and industry enabled a massive accumulation of capital and prosperity, which was shared by some sections of the peasantry and urban worker, to some extent at least. On the other hand, the masses of the (rural) population continued to be illiterate and to suffer from malnutrition and disease. Agricultural development lagged considerably. The basic imbalance that characterized the country in economic and political terms also had a clearly regional dimension. So far, I have alluded to this where appropriate, but we have not recapitulated the processes of change in regional terms.

Throughout the period up to World War II, three major development regions emerged, each with a relatively well-developed transport system, and began to evolve links among themselves. At a second level was the Caldas coffee region and, on the Atlantic Coast, Barranquilla, the country's principal port, which was able to become a center of accumulation and growth. By 1938 these regions contained 46% of the total population. Within their boundaries were the largest and fastest growing towns with the best infrastructural facilities. Illiteracy was lowest in these regions— in 1938 it was less than 25% in all except one of these regions. (Urrutia 1979:147). At the other extreme, regions in the north, northeast, south, and eastern lowlands (Llanos and Amazonas) and the Pacific Coast had hardly entered the twentieth century. The Gran Cauca, the last bastion of traditional landed power, was divided under Reyes's "new nationalism" into four parts, and took little part in the new developments. The relatively dense rural and *minifundio* population of Narino extended the rural frontier via settlements of new lands in the direction of Putumayo and the Pacific. Illiteracy was fairly high, particularly in Cauca. On the basis of estimates made by Urrutia, it seems that there was considerable artisan development in the region (Urrutia 1979: 220–250).

In other more densely populated regions such as Boyaca the situation was broadly similar, perhaps with the relative difference that the settlement pattern was more dense due to historical reasons (Medina 1936). The main changes were agricultural. The great economic expansion in the neighboring region of Cundinamarca brought growing opportunities for the commercialization of agricultural produce, particularly because the regions were connected by rail and by a growing road network. The principal cash crops were part of the basic food staple, namely, wheat, maize, beans, and potatoes. Finally, sisal production prospered, making bags for coffee. Illiteracy was almost as high as in Bolivar. The lack of industrial development and the consequent need to import the major part of manufactured products from other regions or from abroad had already been noted in 1936 (Medina 1936:464). On the other hand, the region had very considerable household and craft industries in basic consumer items, such as ceramic products, clothing including hats and *ruanas*, candles, tobacco, baskets, and so forth (ibid.:469). A somewhat similar situation was found in Norte Santander, although thanks to the earlier colonization and trade related to the development of coffee, a somewhat better overall situation had been created.

The department of Bolivar, which included what were later to become the departments of Cordoba and Sucre, had experienced some mainly foreign-controlled agro-enclave type developments (Fals Borda 1976). Domestically, these were limited to declining port services (Nichols 1973), and extensive livestock production. The department had one of the highest illiteracy rates (more than 55%). The old landed oligarchy of Cartagena, though anxious about the rise of rival groups in Barranquilla, seems to have played no role of importance. The situation was very similar in Magdalena, with perhaps the sole difference that there was only one foreign enclave, that of United Fruit. This enclave dominated departmental affairs and, in 1922, was the site of one of the first major organized strikes in which central government and the army intervened (Botero and Guzman 1977).

This sketch of the various regions is too restricted to allow any firm conclusion to be drawn. It does indicate, however, that regional situations were heterogeneous and that this increased throughout the period under study. The central regions in which most coffee and industrial developments took place came to spearhead the emergent capitalist regional division of labor (cf. Davila 1976). Migration processes in the 1938–1951 intercensal period provide a first glimpse of the cumulative effects that were to develop in the following period. The *Violencia* greatly affected migrational processes, however. In any case, all major central regions, with the clear exception of Antioquia, are large net receivers of migrants (Berry 1965; Gilbert 1970). Another net receiver was Caqueta, which became a focus for land settlement as a result of the *Violencia* (cf. Helmsing 1984).

## Import Substitution in Agriculture and Industry

The change from one period to the next was marked by two main events: (1) a spectacular investment boom in the immediate post–World War II period (1945–1950), during which annual growth rates were achieved in the order of 11% (Poveda Ramos 1967, 1970), and (2) the early years of rural conflict, the *Violencia*.

During the period considered in this section (1950–1968), the nature of the industrialization process underwent various and fundamental changes. At first sight the pattern seems to have followed very closely the import substitution model. Periods of boom and recession followed each other in accordance with changes in the earning capacity of exports (coffee). Government responded to balance-of-payments problems with new protectionist measures, which in turn stimulated the emergence of new activities. The recurrent and in some respects systematic government intervention marks an important difference with the preceding period, although this policy was more concerned with the balance of payments than guided by conscious and deliberate goals of industrial development (Montes and Candelo 1981).

For the period as a whole (1950–1968), manufacturing industry grew at an average annual rate of 8.1%. The greatest contribution to growth came from the intermediate products, namely 3.7%, whereas consumer goods contributed 2.7% and capital goods only 1.7% (ibid.). Given the level of industrial development that had already been achieved in the country, import substitution, though important, was not the main source of growth. This is clearly seen if a sector's changes in domestic production are broken down into changes in components of demand of that sector.[3] The results of such calculations for the subperiod 1950–1958 are summarized in Table 5.10.

3. The analysis is based on the following methodology (cf. Montes & Candelo 1981:96–97): total supply ($Z$) can be divided into domestic supply ($X$) and imports ($M$); total demand ($Q$) also have several components, namely, final demand by government and private sector ($D$), intermediate demand ($W$), and exports ($E$). Assuming $Z$ and $Q$ to be an identity, $X$ can be expressed as follows:

$$X = D + W + E - M$$

The change over a period can be expressed as follows:

$$dX = dD + dW + dE - dM$$

As domestic supply is only a proportion of total supply ($u = X/Z$), only a certain proportion of the change in these demand components can be attributed to it.

$$\text{Let } u_O = X_O/Z_O \text{, then } dX_d = u_O\, dD \qquad dX_w = u_O\, dW \qquad dX_e = u_O\, dE$$

Import substitution can be seen as the change in the proportion of domestic in total supply: $(u_t - u_O)\, Z_t$.

The changes in domestic supply can be formulated as follows:

$$dX = u_O dD + u_O dW + u_O dE + (u_t - u_O)\, Z_t$$

or,

$$dX = dX_d + dX_w + dX_e + dX_m\ .$$

TABLE 5.10
Decomposition of Growth in Manufacturing Industry by Main Economic Use, Colombia, 1950–1968 (percentages)

| | *Change in domestic demand* | *Change in exports* | *Import substitution* |
|---|---|---|---|
| Consumer goods | 93.5 | 3.6 | 3.1 |
| Intermediate goods | 71.8 | −0.5 | 28.7 |
| Capital goods | 53.3 | 0.6 | 46.1 |
| Total manufacturing | 84.2 | 1.1 | 14.7 |

*Source:* Montes and Candelo (1981: Table 6, p. 100).

Although the pattern conforms sector-wise to the import substitution model, changes in domestic demand (final and intermediate) on the whole are far more important than the external sector on the side of both imports and exports. In fact, the increase of protection on consumer goods produced very little growth effect, and consequently should be seen in the context of domestic price rises and, in all likelihood, increases in profitability. The growing protection of the domestic market facilitated the process of oligopoly formation that had already started but which now became related more to technological advantages of large-scale production in a market that was generally restricted due to a skewed income distribution (Misas 1975a; Bejarano 1978b).

With the exception of petroleum, early industrialization had been largely undertaken and controlled by Colombian groups, but from 1950 to 1968, foreign investment and multinational firms became more important, particularly in the intermediate and consumer-durable branches (Arango 1976). However, foreign firms also penetrated into activities that were traditionally Colombian owned, such as textiles, clothing (see Chapter 6), and food (Ayala et al. 1978).

By the end of the 1960s, the limitations of the domestic market became more and more evident. The unequal distribution of income in favor of high and middle incomes altered the orientation of industry, because of different

---

By using first–last year averages, the problems related with the choice of period may be reduced. Finally, we obtain:

$$dX = u^{\star}dD + u^{\star}dW + u^{\star}dE + (u_t - u_O)\, Z^{\star}$$

where

$$u^{\star} = (u_t + u_O) / 2 \qquad Z^{\star} = (Z_t + Z_O) / 2$$

demand schedules, away from mass production for low-income demand to small production runs for high-income demand. This was not only the case in consumer durables but also in "early" industrial sectors such as textiles, clothing, and food (Bejarano 1978b). In the early 1950s expansion in these sectors was still in low-income markets, displacing traditional artisan and household production, but firms in these sectors later also oriented themselves toward higher income markets (ibid.; Misas 1975b).

To analyze the regional pattern of change, I have carried out a shift and share analysis and also an analysis of the regional export base. These studies have been conducted for the periods 1945–1958 and 1958–1967. In the first period industrialization was still largely a Colombian affair. In the second, particularly after 1961 when conditions for foreign investment were made more attractive, much of the industrial growth was due to foreign firms.

## Regional Industrialization Patterns: 1945–1958

Table 5.11 summarizes the results of the analysis carried out for the period 1945–1958. The first two columns give the value added generated by the manufacturing industries in 1945 and 1958, respectively. Expected levels of net output are calculated for 1958 by applying the national growth rate to each region. This expresses a situation in which further regional differentiation would not have occurred during that period. The difference between the actual value at the end of the period and this estimated value constitutes the "net shift" of regional output change vis-à-vis the national average. This figure is presented in the third column. In the fourth column the percentage distribution of the total negative and the total positive net shifts are presented, and the fifth column gives the net shift in terms of the "expected" level of net output, indicating its importance within each region. In the sixth and seventh columns the net shift of each region is broken down into the industrial mix—denoting that part of the net shift attributable to differences between the region and the nation in sectoral structure—and the residual regional share component, respectively. The regional pattern of output growth in this period reveals some very clear changes. Whereas industry in Antioquia, the oldest industrial region, grew at a rate slightly below the national average, Cali (Valle) became firmly established as the third industrial center of the country. Cali's extraordinary growth of output was largely due to the expansion of the Buena Ventura harbor on the Pacific Coast, which made Cali an attractive location as a transshipment point, at the cost of Barranquilla (Atlantico). A second important reason was the development of agroindustry, particularly sugar refining. Valle, together with the capital-city region of Cundinamarca, contained almost the entire positive shift. In other words,

TABLE 5.11
Shift and Share Analysis of Regional Industrial Output and Growth in Colombia, 1945–1958

| | Output (VA) 1945 | Output (VA) 1958 | Net shift | Relative distribution | | Comparative shift | Breakdown Net shift | |
|---|---|---|---|---|---|---|---|---|
| | | | | – | + | | Industrial composition | Regional residual |
| Antioquia | 36,475 | 801,884 | −13,458 | 5.3 | — | −1.7 | −101,265 | 87,808 |
| Atlantico | 18,882 | 292,570 | −129,508 | 51.2 | — | −30.7 | −30,097 | −99,411 |
| V. Bolivar | 4,759 | 93,569 | −12,811 | 5.1 | — | −12.0 | −8,390 | −4,421 |
| Boyaca | 3,173 | 74,124 | 3,197 | — | 1.3 | 4.5 | −2,502 | 5,699 |
| V. Caldas | 8,693 | 168,280 | −26,038 | 10.3 | — | −13.4 | −23,245 | −2,794 |
| Cauca | 1,564 | 22,738 | −12,223 | 4.8 | — | −35.0 | 3,216 | −15,439 |
| Cundin'ca | 36,601 | 875,945 | 57,787 | — | 22.8 | 7.1 | −73,858 | 131,644 |
| Huila | 506 | 11,864 | 553 | — | 0.2 | 4.9 | −1,914 | 2,467 |
| V. Magdalena | 1,326 | 20,051 | −9,590 | 3.8 | — | −32.4 | −2,306 | −7,284 |
| Narino | 0,970 | 18,202 | −3,481 | 1.4 | — | −16.1 | −2,267 | −1,214 |
| Norte San. | 1,623 | 29,674 | −6,606 | 2.6 | — | −18.2 | −4,461 | −2,145 |
| Santander | 7,665 | 172,464 | 1,125 | — | 0.4 | 0.7 | 240,866 | −239,742 |
| Tolima | 3,916 | 48,143 | −39,393 | 15.6 | — | −45.0 | −715 | −38,679 |
| Valle | 18,242 | 598,216 | 190,445 | — | 75.2 | 46.7 | 6,936 | 183,509 |
| Total | 144,395 | 3,227,724 | 0 | 100.0 | 100.0 | 0 | — | |

*Note:* Values in millions of current pesos.
*Source:* Helmsing (1983b).

significant processes of concentration favored the established industrial centers, but within this group a reallocation occurred away from Barranquilla and toward Cali.

This regional restructuring of output growth is also clearly reflected in the breakdown of the net shift in each region. Only for Valle are the mix and share components favorable. In other words, Valle not only had a favorable sectoral structure (proportionally more of the fast-growing sectors) but these sectors grew faster in Valle than elsewhere.

Peripheral regions such as Narino, Norte Santander, Bolivar, Tolima, and Magdalena not only had relatively unfavorable industrial structures, but their performance also was worse than elsewhere. This applied also to regions without any clearly peripheral status, such as Viejo Caldas.

Given the fact that the period 1945–1958 was one in which industry was protected against foreign imports, the relative interregional changes could be interpreted entirely in the context of the domestic market. That is to say, there may be a relation between the high growth in the established industrial regions and the relatively poor industrial performance in the periphery.

As indicated, industrial firms displaced artisan production in the period 1945–1958, but this is extremely difficult to study at a disaggregated level. The only study, by Urrutia and Villalba (1969), shows that rural artisan manufacture declined in almost all regions although with considerable variation. Artisan production in the towns increased, as could be expected.

To enable the pattern of regional specialization to be assessed, the regional manufacturing economic base is estimated for each region (cf. Helmsing 1983b).[4] Two indices have been calculated: an export dependency index, which is the inverse of the base multiplier and which expresses the share of manufacturing export-base production in the total of regional manufacturing output, and the Gibbs–Martin index of trade diversification.

Tables 5.12 and 5.13 present the computed indices and Figure 5.1 summarizes the results for this period. A number of conclusions may be drawn. In 1945 almost all regions had a relatively low dependence on exports to the rest of the world. Regional specialization was varied, though on the whole limited, and the majority of the regions had a fairly diversified export base. However, while the industrial core regions maintained high levels of diversification (with the exception of Antioquia), almost all peripheral regions experienced reductions in export diversification. The analysis seems to support the hypothesis that during this period, when changes in the manufactur-

4. The economic or export-base model postulates the existence of two sectors in a region's economy. The basic or export sector sells its output to the rest of the world. The nonbasic sector caters exclusively to the region's internal demand. Income in this sector depends on the income level of the regional economy as a whole. It follows that the basic sector ultimately determines that income level.

TABLE 5.12
Regional Industrial Export Base Dependency Ratio, by Region, Colombia, Selected Years, 1945–1980

| | *Series A*[a] | | *Series B*[a] | | |
|---|---|---|---|---|---|
| | *1945* | *1958* | *1958* | *1967* | *1980* |
| Antioquia | 25 | 32 | 33 | 32 | 30 |
| Atlantico | 25 | 18 | 20 | 22 | 25 |
| V. Bolivar | 33 | 35 | 35 | 53 | 63 |
| Boyaca | 46 | 57 | 64 | 69 | 71 |
| V. Caldas | 33 | 39 | 39 | 36 | 24 |
| Cauca | 45 | 60 | 60 | 61 | 62 |
| Cordoba | (1) | (1) | 55 | 58 | 59 |
| Cundin'ca | 18 | 18 | 19 | 21 | 22 |
| Huila | 38 | 49 | 51 | 56 | 69 |
| V. Magdalena | 40 | 54 | 55 | 61 | 51 |
| Meta | na | na | 56 | 64 | 73 |
| Narino | 18 | 41 | 41 | 58 | 70 |
| Norte Santander | 32 | 43 | 46 | 54 | 51 |
| Santander | 44 | 59 | 59 | 53 | 63 |
| Tolima | 39 | 48 | 48 | 54 | 40 |
| Valle | 15 | 28 | 29 | 30 | 32 |
| Total | 25 | 29 | 30 | 32 | 34 |

[a]Series A is formulated according to 1945 Census of Manufacturing Production; Series B according to 1958 Census.

*Notes:* (1) included under Bolivar; n.a. = not available

Methodology: For each region the manufacturing export base has been calculated by the following formula:

$$OB(i) = \frac{Lq(i)-1}{Lq(i)} O(i) \qquad \text{for} \quad Lq(i) \geqslant 1$$

if $Lq(i)<1$ then $OB(i) = 0$, where, $OB(i)$ is the export base portion of sector $(i)$ and $Lq(i)$ the location coefficient of sector $(i)$. The export dependency ratio of the region concerned $E(r)$ can now be formulated as follows: $E(r) = \Sigma_i OB(i)/\Sigma_i O(i) \star 100$

*Source:* Helmsing (1983b).

ing export base occurred entirely within the context of interregional trade, the integration process negatively affected the peripheral regions. Increased export dependence, reduced diversification, and relatively poor growth performance all occurred together. The peripheral regions became more integrated into the national market but on a narrower basis.

Changes in the industrialized core regions were more heterogeneous. Only Cundinamaca diversified its industrial export base without coming to depend more on external demand; simultaneously, it gained from the inte-

TABLE 5.13
Regional Industrial Export Base Diversification Index, by Region, Colombia, Selected Years, 1945–1980

| | Series A[a] | | Series B[a] | | |
|---|---|---|---|---|---|
| | *1945* | *1958* | *1958* | *1967* | *1980* |
| Antioquia | .20 | .24 | .26 | .32 | .37 |
| Atlantico | .73 | .62 | .79 | .83 | .78 |
| V. Bolivar | .79 | .59 | .59 | .55 | .24 |
| Boyaca | .52 | .36 | .33 | .51 | .29 |
| V. Caldas | .13 | .40 | .40 | .60 | .80 |
| Cauca | .56 | .48 | .48 | .44 | .27 |
| Cordoba | (1) | (1) | .57 | .31 | .38 |
| Cundin'ca | .66 | .83 | .85 | .80 | .89 |
| Huila | .46 | .41 | .45 | .24 | .21 |
| V. Magdalena | .27 | .02 | .07 | .49 | .16 |
| Meta | na | na | .24 | .45 | .00 |
| Narino | .69 | .66 | .66 | .59 | .01 |
| Norte Santander | .69 | .47 | .52 | .52 | .50 |
| Santander | .79 | .59 | .41 | .38 | .02 |
| Tolima | .39 | .50 | .51 | .52 | .57 |
| Valle | .75 | .67 | .69 | .72 | .72 |
| Total | .86 | .88 | .89 | .90 | .88 |
| Range of index: | 0 < index < 0.93 | | 0 < index < 0.95 | | |

[a]Series A is formulated according to 1945 Census of Manufacturing Production; Series B according to 1958 Census.

*Note:* (1) included in Bolivar.

Methodology: The index, known as the Gibb–Martin index of trade diversification, applied here at the regional level $GM(r)$ is formulated as follows:

$$GM(r) = 1 - \frac{\Sigma OB(i)^2}{[\Sigma OB(i)]^2},$$

where $OB(i)$ is defined as above. The upper boundary varies with the adopted number of sectors ($i$) (cf. Hammond and McCullagh 1974).

*Source:* Helmsing (1983b).

gration process with above-average rates of growth, thereby consolidating its dominant industrial position.

## Regional Industrialization Patterns: 1958–1967

Whereas before 1958 industrialization largely had been undertaken and controlled by Colombian groups, in the period 1958–1967 foreign investment and multinational firms became more important, particularly after 1961. The basically open attitude toward foreign enterprise was related to the fact that

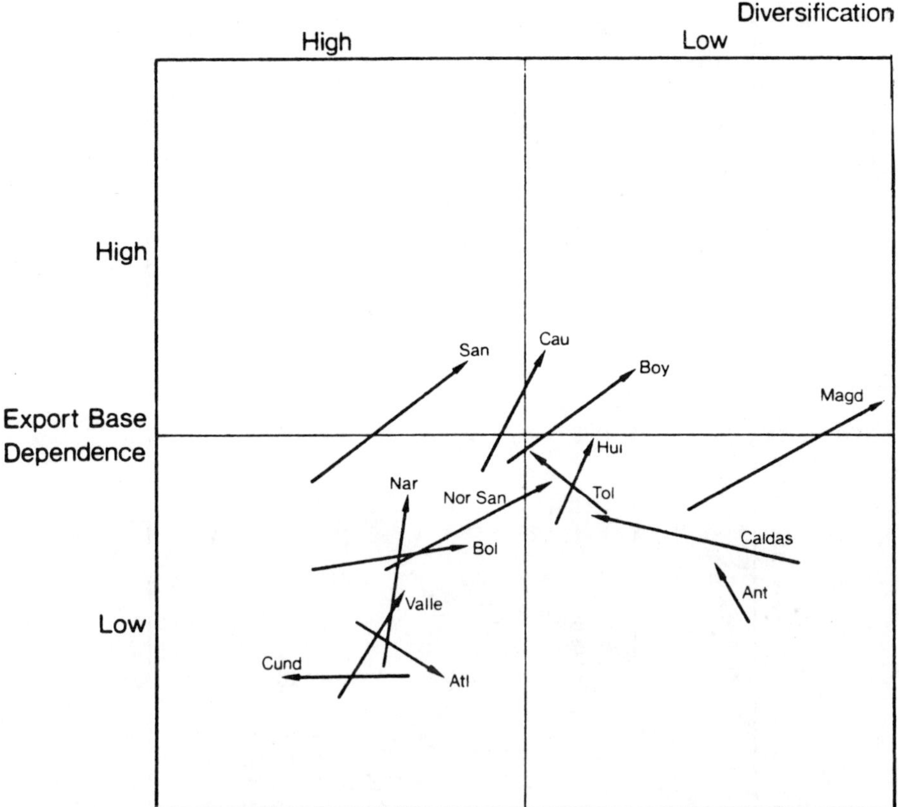


FIGURE 5.1. Changes in the industrial export base of Colombian Regions, 1945–1958.

Colombian industrial expansion at that time was moving more into consumer durables and intermediate and capital goods (Bejarano 1978b). The fastest-growing sectors were furniture, metal products, nonelectrical appliances, rubber, oil, and oil derivatives. Basic consumer goods industries clearly fell behind in this period (Montes and Candelo 1981). The pattern of regional industrial growth is summarized in Table 5.14. Within the industrial core, consisting of the four main established industrial regions, the indicated sectoral pattern is reflected in a minor relative decline in Antioquia where the slow growth of "first stage" industries, notably textiles, showed itself in a large negative industrial-mix component, and in Cundinamarca, where the growth of "second stage" industries did not entirely compensate the fairly heavy decline in beverages, tobacco, and clothing industries. The third

TABLE 5.14
Shift and Share Analysis of Regional Industrial Output Growth in Colombia, 1958–1967

| | Output (VA) 1958 | Output (VA) 1967 | Net shift | Relative distribution | | Comparative shift | Breakdown net shift | |
|---|---|---|---|---|---|---|---|---|
| | | | | – | + | | Industrial composition | Regional residual |
| Antioquia | 801,884 | 3,590,703 | −161,499 | 26.3 | — | −4.3 | −400,898 | 239,399 |
| Atlantico | 292,570 | 1,258,480 | −110,523 | 18.0 | — | −8.1 | 53,602 | −164,125 |
| V. Bolivar | 88,633 | 566,920 | 152,186 | — | 24.8 | 36.7 | −34,871 | 187,056 |
| Boyaca | 74,124 | 383,258 | 36,415 | — | 5.9 | 10.5 | −25,447 | 61,861 |
| V. Caldas | 168,280 | 691,919 | −95,502 | 15.6 | — | −12.1 | −29,041 | −66,462 |
| Cauca | 22,738 | 119,483 | 13,087 | — | 2.1 | 12.3 | −4,331 | −17,418 |
| Cordoba | 4,936 | 24,438 | 1,341 | — | 0.2 | 5.8 | −1,916 | 3,257 |
| Cundin'ca | 875,945 | 3,908,677 | −190,074 | 31.0 | — | −4.6 | 98,410 | −288,484 |
| Huila | 11,864 | 57,441 | 1,927 | — | 0.3 | 3.6 | −3,222 | 5,148 |
| Magdalena | 20,051 | 151,833 | 58,010 | — | 9.5 | 61.8 | −6,739 | 64,749 |
| Meta | 5,072 | 56,199 | 32,466 | — | 5.3 | 136.8 | −1,510 | 33,975 |
| Narino | 18,202 | 94,164 | 8,993 | — | 1.5 | 10.6 | −6,227 | 15,220 |
| Norte San. | 29,674 | 135,879 | −2,973 | 0.5 | — | −2.1 | −9,965 | 6,993 |
| Santander | 172,464 | 839,426 | 32,427 | — | 5.3 | 4.0 | 120,206 | −87,779 |
| Tolima | 48,143 | 172,114 | −53,158 | 8.7 | — | −23.6 | −8,799 | −44,359 |
| Valle | 598,216 | 3,076,071 | 276,879 | — | 45.1 | 9.9 | 260,747 | 16,132 |
| Total | 3,232,796 | 15,127,005 | 0 | 100.0 | 100.0 | — | — | — |

*Note:* Values in millions of current pesos.
*Source:* Helmsing (1983b).

region, Valle, clearly benefited from the expansion in intermediate industries that had started in the preceding period, accounting for 45% of the positive shift in the period 1958–1967. The fourth region, Atlantico, continued to lose out, for reasons already indicated.

Most peripheral regions, notwithstanding their unfavorable industrial structures, experienced above-average growth (e.g., Magdalena and Meta). The considerable expansion in Bolivar should be viewed in the context of the political decision to establish the new petrochemical complex in Cartagena rather than Barrancabermeja (Santander).

On the whole, it seems feasible to conclude that regional differentiation in 1958–1967 was not only less marked than in the previous period but also was differently shaped. Whereas regional differentiation in the period 1945–1958 tended to be more in accordance with the center-periphery model of regional development (except for the reallocation between Cali and Barranquilla), it now took place much more within the industrial core and within the periphery. Of the four core manufacturing regions, three grew more slowly and one more quickly than the national average. In the periphery, Boyaca, Magdalena, Narino, and Santander grew faster, but Caldas, Tolima, and Norte Santander grew more slowly than the national average.

In the pattern of regional specialization, various tendencies seemed to occur simultaneously (see Tables 5.12 and 5.13 and Figure 5.2). Dependence on the manufacturing export base increased in all peripheral regions, most of which also had above-average rates of growth. At the same time, however, in some peripheral regions the export base diversified, whereas in others the opposite occurred. A similar sort of internal variation has already been noted with respect to the industrialized core of the country.

## Agricultural Development

A number of factors must be taken into account for an understanding of developments in agriculture. In some regions the *Violencia* had devastating effects, not only helping to uproot traditional tenure relations but also to change the distribution of land ownership. Many peasant smallholders and tenants left their holdings, most of them unwillingly and often never to return (Oquist 1978). The resulting fall in land prices eventually caused an even more skewed distribution of land ownership. The rural exodus of perhaps more than two million people from the areas of violence was mostly toward the towns but it also led to the settlement of new land in tropical regions such as Caqueta, Putumayo, Meta, and Medio Magdalena (Helmsing 1983a).

A major role was also played by the new technology that became available

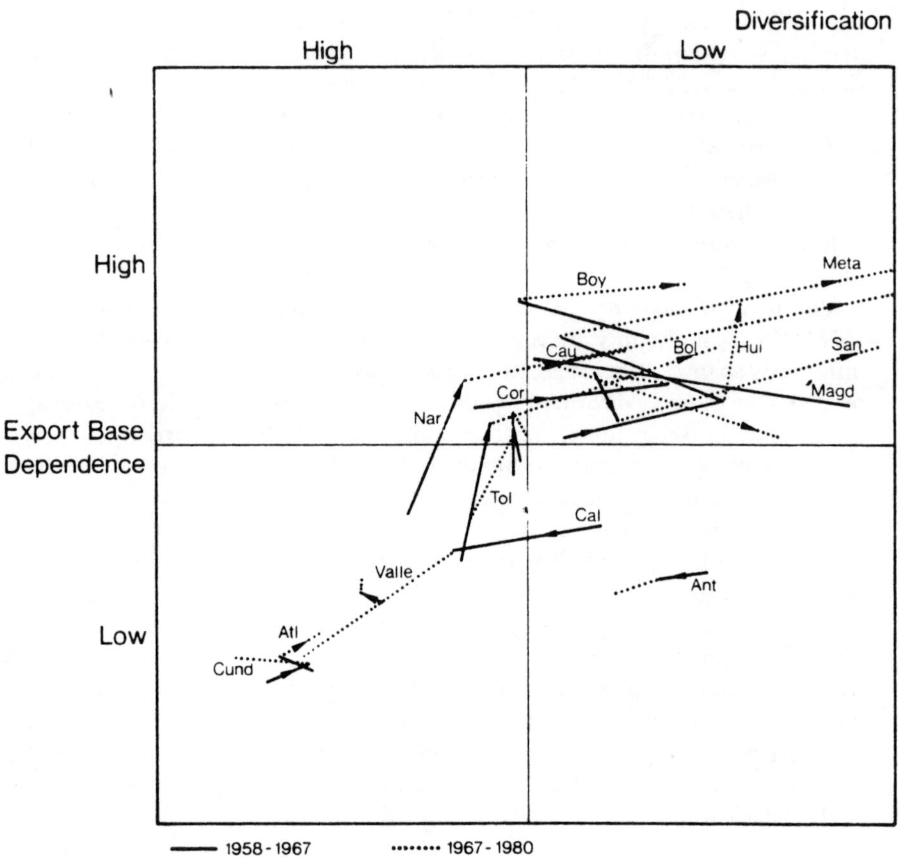


FIGURE 5.2. Changes in the industrial export base of Colombian regions, 1958–1967, 1967–1980.

after World War II and made large-scale manager-managed production feasible. Supply conditions now shifted in favor of the landowners, particularly the *hacendados*.

A third factor was the considerable increase in the demand for agricultural products. During the intercensal period 1951–1964 urban growth was as high as 5.7% per annum. The proportion of the population that went to live in the towns rose from 39% in 1951 to 53% in 1964. Furthermore, the growth of industry stimulated the demand for agricultural output, but the latter did not occur automatically. Only after the domestic market became shielded from foreign competition could the agricultural import-substitution process begin (cotton, soya, sorghum, and African palm oil).

The fourth factor to be singled out concerns the state. The agricultural support system was built up during the 1950s, although its development can be traced back to the preceding decade. It can be summarized under three headings.

1. *Marketing and prices.* Price controls were issued for industrial raw materials such as sugar and cotton. Given the fact that elaborate negotiations were held between government and the agricultural and industrial interest groups, it is perhaps more appropriate to speak of negotiated prices. A government marketing agency created in 1944 intervened in commercialization of food crops (wheat, maize, rice, and beans). Because on the whole the market share of industrial raw materials was reduced (< 10%), it seems that the main objective was to smooth urban market provision and prices (FEDESARROLLO 1975).

2. *Credit.* In 1959 the commercial banks were required to allocate an amount of credit to agriculture equivalent to at least 15% of "call" and "term" deposits. This system of enforced transfer of credit was further developed in 1966 and 1973. In addition to the commercial banks, the agrarian bank (Caja Agraria) was active in providing (some) credit to peasants.

3. *Technology and extension.* Although some of the experimental stations dated from earlier than 1950, it was only later that these activities were undertaken on a large scale by the Instituto de Crédito Territorial (ICA).

The fifth and final factor is the producer associations that became important vehicles for the rapid diffusion of technological innovations as well as for the distribution of industrial inputs, seeds, technical assistance, and credit. In some cases these associations emerged in response to the oligopolistic structure of agricultural product markets caused by industry or trade (e.g., cotton, bananas and to some extent rice). In other cases, in an attempt to secure, control, and/or expand or improve the supply of raw materials, the industry set up such organizations (e.g., barley, coffee and, for a period of time, cacao). In Chapter 6 I will elaborate on the role of these associations. Suffice it to say here that they constitute a key link between the individual producer and the organized market. Table 5.15 gives the main aggregate features of agricultural development.

The so-called commercial crops (those predominantly used as inputs for industry) have been the most dynamic elements in the transformation of Colombian agriculture. Their share in the value of crop production increased between 1951 and 1973 with a factor of almost two-and-a-half, from 10% to 24%, and continued to grow thereafter, albeit at a slower pace. The fact that

TABLE 5.15
Agricultural Production, Employment, and Cultivated Area, by Type of Land Use, Colombia, 1951, 1964, 1973

| | | *Value Output* | | *Employment* | | *Cultivated Area* | | | |
|---|---|---|---|---|---|---|---|---|---|
| | | *Millions of 1970 Columbian Pesos* | *Percent dist.* | *Thousands of Persons* | *Percent dist.* | *Thousands of hectares* | *Percent dist.* | *Output ÷ Employment* | *Output ÷ Area* |
| Agriculture[a] | 1951 | 10,952.5 | 61.4 | 1,236.7 | 71.7 | 2,836 | 11.1 | 8.856 | 3.876 |
| | 1964 | 16,206.1 | 59.7 | 1,600.6 | 74.1 | 3,798 | 13.2 | 10.125 | 4.267 |
| | 1973 | 19,464.8 | 52.3 | 903.3 | 63.2 | 4,667 | 14.2 | 16.851 | 4.171 |
| Commercial crops[b] | 1951 | 1,093.6 | 10.0 | 75.1 | 6.1 | 281 | 10.0 | 14.562 | 3.892 |
| | 1964 | 3,078.5 | 19.0 | 216.5 | 13.5 | 712 | 18.7 | 14.219 | 4.324 |
| | 1973 | 4,663.4 | 24.0 | 136.3 | 15.1 | 896 | 19.2 | 34.214 | 5.205 |
| Mixed crops | 1951 | 2,680.9 | 24.5 | 391.0 | 31.6 | 976 | 34.5 | 6.850 | 2.747 |
| | 1964 | 3,317.1 | 20.5 | 429.0 | 26.8 | 1,167 | 30.7 | 7.732 | 2.342 |
| | 1973 | 3,082.0 | 15.8 | 171.0 | 18.9 | 1,053 | 22.6 | 18.023 | 2.917 |
| Traditional crops | 1951 | 2,432.8 | 22.2 | 360.1 | 29.1 | 669 | 23.7 | 6.756 | 3.636 |
| | 1964 | 3,388.0 | 20.9 | 415.1 | 25.9 | 740 | 19.5 | 8.162 | 4.578 |
| | 1973 | 3,646.8 | 18.7 | 258.7 | 28.6 | 929 | 19.9 | 14.097 | 3.926 |

| | | | | | | | | | |
|---|---|---|---|---|---|---|---|---|---|
| Plantation crops | 1951 | 3,459.7 | 31.6 | 350.7 | 28.4 | 698 | 24.7 | 9.865 | 4.957 |
| | 1964 | 4,544.0 | 28.0 | 466.7 | 29.2 | 908 | 23.9 | 9.736 | 5.004 |
| | 1973 | 4,744.1 | 24.4 | 272.6 | 30.2 | 968 | 20.7 | 17.403 | 4.901 |
| Minor crops | 1951 | 1,285.6 | 11.7 | 59.5 | 4.8 | 202 | 7.1 | 21.607 | 6.364 |
| | 1964 | 1,878.5 | 11.6 | 73.5 | 4.6 | 271 | 7.1 | 25.558 | 6.932 |
| | 1973 | 3,328.5 | 17.1 | 64.7 | 7.2 | 821 | 17.6 | 51.445 | 4.054 |
| Livestock | 1951 | 5,297.0 | 29.7 | 328.8 | 19.1 | 12,123 | 47.5 | 16.110 | 437 |
| | 1964 | 8,795.2 | 32.4 | 385.3 | 17.8 | 15,686 | 54.4 | 22.827 | 561 |
| | 1973 | 13,613.6 | 36.6 | 251.8 | 17.6 | 18,425 | 56.1 | 54.065 | 739 |
| Other uses[c] | 1951 | 1,587.5 | | 160.0 | | 9,767 | | | |
| | 1964 | 2,144.4 | | 174.6 | | 6,917 | | | |
| | 1973 | 4,169.1 | | 275.6 | | 5,414 | | | |
| Fallow land | 1951 | | | | | 798 | | | |
| | 1964 | | | | | 2,454 | | | |
| | 1973 | | | | | 4,364 | | | |
| Total | 1951 | 17,837.2 | 100.0 | 1,725.5 | 100.0 | 25,514 | 100.0 | 10.337 | 699 |
| | 1964 | 27,145.8 | 100.0 | 2,160.5 | 100.0 | 28,855 | 100.0 | 12.565 | 941 |
| | 1973 | 37,246.5 | 100.0 | 1,430.2 | 100.0 | 32,870 | 100.0 | 26.043 | 1.133 |

[a]Excluding silviculture, hunting and fishing.

[b]Commercial crops: rice, cotton, sorghum, soya, barley, sesame and sugar cane; mixed crops: maize, potato, tobacco and wheat; traditional crops: beans, plantain, cassava, panela; plantation crops: banana, cacao, coffee; minor crops: vegetables and fruits.

[c]Includes housing and other rural construction, land improvements, irrigation and construction for agriculture and livestock, marginal and supplementary crops.

*Source:* From DNP (1977:158).

initially neither land nor labor productivities changed very rapidly indicates that a considerable geographical widening of the base of the transformation must have occurred. Only in the 1960s and early 1970s did a strong deepening (productivity growth) take place.

The production of basic foodstuffs such as maize, cassava, plantain, and potato remained within the realm of peasant production. Given the fact that productivity increases were very low, the only way in which increased supply can be explained is by the continued market incorporation of peasant agriculture and, to a lesser extent, to the extension of peasant production by means of land settlement.

As regards the regional dimensions of the emerging structure of agricultural production, I have already indicated that an expansion of the agricultural frontier occurred (2% per year increase of land under cultivation and with livestock). The word *frontier* here has a double meaning. On the one hand, it refers to transformation of the traditional and often extensively used estates into capitalist agricultural production enterprises. On the other hand, it refers to peasant land settlement. The former occurred particularly in the interior and later on the Atlantic Coast. Peasant land settlement took place on a fairly considerable scale in the south and southeast but extended essentially into all tropical areas of the country (Helmsing 1982b).

On the basis of regional land-use data for the 16 principal crops, it has been possible to examine the regional dimension for the later part of the period 1958–1967. The computed indices are summarized in Table 5.18 and 5.19. It can be concluded that agricultural production expanded most strongly in the regions of the Costa Atlantica in the north, mostly in industrial crops such as cotton, sorghum, and rice. In addition, the agricultural frontier extended considerably in several regions, for example, Meta.

With regard to crops for industrial use, some of the existing specialized production areas switched to other and more profitable crops, and new specialized production regions emerged (sorghum, barley), partly replacing existing ones (barley, rice, and cotton). Changes in the interregional distribution of production of mixed and traditional crops were much more limited. Either there were no specialized production regions at all (maize and plantain) or, when they did exist (mostly due to climatic reasons), they tended to account for a growing proportion of total production (potatoes, beans, and tobacco).

In the 1960s, the development of agriculture took a great leap forward. First, production increases produced exportable surpluses (cotton, rice, and sugar). Second, new technological developments in high-yielding varieties and related technological packages raised the capital requirements of production and threatened to marginalize the participation of smallholder farmers.

In the following decade, the number of small holdings, as well as agricultural employment which had increased in the 1950s, dropped again.

Thus, as industrial growth slackened and the employment absorption capacity of industry declined, capitalist agriculture started to expel rural labor and peasant agriculture threatened to become marginalized. Two policy solutions were put forward to deal with the social problem (cf. Bejarano 1978a; Fajardo 1983). One was to keep the peasants in the countryside. Recognizing the social function of land ownership, land reform would be the principal instrument with which to do this. The second was an urban solution via a program of (labor-intensive) urban housing construction. Successive liberal and conservative governments experimented with both alternatives.

Although differences arose with regard to the social issue, there also were remarkable similarities in the ways in which the economic problem was tackled. Rather than stimulation of domestic demand by means of some redistributive measures, the goal was a reorientation toward external demand. A number of reforms aimed at this goal were introduced in 1968.

## Exports and Internationalization of the Economy

In 1968, a number of reforms were introduced with the intention of encouraging exports as a new source of accumulation and growth; to this end, a structural reform of the economy became imperative. The key elements of this reform included the following:

1. A change in the exchange-rate system, the existing system of relatively stable but multiple exchange rates being replaced by the flexible "crawling peg" system. Frequent and small devaluations avoided serious balance-of-payments problems that would necessitate large devaluations. The persistent overevaluation of the currency, which tended to favor imports over exports, was now avoided. Moreover, imports were liberalized.
2. Fiscal incentives for exports (by means of corporate tax-reduction certificates) were increased. At first these were for manufactures only, but in 1970 they were extended to cover nontraditional agricultural exports.
3. New export-promotion institutions were created, such as the export-promotion fund, and free trade zones were established in all major towns.
4. The Andean Pact, with its common external tariff, provided additional market leeway (Bejarano 1978a).

Later governments extended this policy in a neoliberal fashion by considerably lowering tariffs on manufactured imports, partly inspired by other and new events, in particular the coffee price "bonanza" of 1975–1976 and the growing drug trade (Piedrahita 1980). Together with the economic reorientation, institutional reforms were introduced, which considerably expanded the role of national semi-autonomous public agencies. The effects of the new policy on the growth of manufacturing industry are shown in Table 5.16.

During the two subperiods of 1967–1974 and 1974–1980, exports clearly became a much more important source of growth. For the sector as a whole, exports contributed 9% and 10%, respectively, to the average real rates of growth, climbing from the previous 1% (see pp. 135–151). The share of manufactures in total exports also rose to as high as 46 percent in 1974, but fell again to 29% in 1979 (DANE Census of Manufacturing Industry 1981: 132–134).

Domestic demand had not become less important; on the contrary, its significance as a source of growth even increased somewhat. The problem was that trade liberalization had a negative effect, particularly in the second period. Without going into much detail, the rhythm of capital accumulation declined in the second part of the 1970s, not only because of the world recession but also because of the restrictive policies of government intended to curb the inflationary effects of the coffee and drug trade booms (Piedrahita 1980).

The change in economic policy attracted a considerable increase in foreign investment. By 1974, firms with varying degrees of foreign participation contributed no less than 45% of total manufacturing exports (Arango 1976). In this respect there was a clear link between the changing participation of Colombia in the international division of labor and the role played by the foreign firms active in the country. Foreign presence was strongest in the intermediate and capital-goods sectors such as paper, chemicals, rubber, glass, nonferrous metals, and transport machinery. The most important

TABLE 5.16
Composition of Annual Growth Rate of Manufacturing Industry, by Economic Use, Colombia, 1967–1974 and 1974–1980

| | *1967–1974* | | | | *1974–1980* | | | |
|---|---|---|---|---|---|---|---|---|
| | *Total change* | *Domestic change* | *Export change* | *Import substitution* | *Total change* | *Domestic change* | *Export change* | *Import substitution* |
| Light consumer goods | 5.35 | 4.92 | 0.61 | −0.18 | 5.18 | 4.64 | 0.67 | −0.12 |
| Cons. durable goods | 9.52 | 6.42 | 0.65 | 2.46 | 7.95 | 8.98 | 1.02 | −2.05 |
| Intermediate goods | 10.92 | 10.30 | 0.92 | −0.28 | 5.57 | 5.57 | 0.27 | −0.40 |
| Capital goods | 10.00 | 6.79 | 0.35 | 2.96 | 6.30 | 8.67 | 0.64 | −3.04 |
| Total manufacturing | 8.52 | 7.48 | 0.74 | 0.30 | 5.63 | 5.90 | 0.54 | −0.82 |

*Source:* Chica Avella (1983:83–84).

change with respect to the previous period was that past orientation had been primarily toward the domestic market, with foreign firms operating in alliance with Colombian groups. The most common strategy for a foreign company was to "buy in" in a company owned by a Colombian group that often maintained majority control (Parra Sandoval 1977). In the 1970s, foreign ventures in Colombia came increasingly under control of the multinational companies themselves. In 1969 only 45% of all foreign participations were major participations (>50%); by 1974, however, this figure had risen to 72% (Arango 1976). Rather than being a final market, Colombia became a node in transnational networks.

The export-promotion strategy was quite successful in terms of employment. In the period 1967–1975, employment growth averaged more than 6% per annum, but later it dropped strongly. Success in terms of employment was at the cost of real wages, which fell fairly considerably from 1970 until 1977, when the coffee bonanza made its impact. Not only did the (imported) inflation rise dramatically, but for their export strategies to be successful, companies had to keep wages down. This became an essential prerequisite, all the more so because imported intermediate and capital goods made it impossible to avoid cost inflation. This had various important implications for relations between agriculture and industry, as shown subsequently.

The major growth sectors during this period were chemicals, printing and publishing, basic metallurgical and transport industries. In contrast, the traditionally most important consumer-goods industries showed a relative lag. This sectoral reorientation of the economy produced a new tendency toward interregional differentiation.

## Regional Industrialization Patterns

Table 5.17 summarizes regional shifts in industrial output and allows a number of conclusions to be drawn. *Within* the industrial core, a recentralization occurred that favored Bogotá (Cundinamarca). Cundinamarca's very favorable industrial structure was the main reason for its above-average growth performance. The Valle region lagged considerably, even more than Antioquia. Moreover, Barranquilla (Atlantico) apparently benefitted little from the export drive, despite its favorable location. On the contrary, the region continued to trail behind and was responsible for 28% of the negative shift.

The trend toward differentiation within the periphery continued, with Bolivar and Santander together accounting for 65% of the positive shift. In both cases, this was almost entirely due to their inclusion as producers of

TABLE 5.17
Shift and Share Analysis of Regional Industrial Output Growth in Colombia, 1967–1980

| | Output (VA) 1967 | Output (VA) 1980 | Net shift | Relative distribution | | Comparative shift | Breakdown Net shift | |
|---|---|---|---|---|---|---|---|---|
| | | | | − | + | | Industrial composition | Regional residual |
| Antioquia | 3,590,703 | 76,276,976 | −3,683,832 | 15.1 | — | −4.6 | −4,197,454 | 513,625 |
| Atlantico | 1,258,480 | 21,060,216 | −6,964,680 | 28.5 | — | −24.9 | −1,952,347 | −5,012,336 |
| V. Bolivar | 566,920 | 20,930,328 | 8,305,675 | — | 34.0 | 65.8 | −1,518,665 | 9,824,335 |
| Boyaca | 383,258 | 8,630,374 | 95,661 | — | 0.4 | 1.1 | −2,827,111 | −2,731,449 |
| V. Caldas | 691,919 | 16,441,389 | 1,033,152 | — | 4.2 | 6.7 | −1,040,275 | 2,073,428 |
| Cauca | 119,483 | 2,088,794 | −571,954 | 2.3 | — | −21.5 | −258,510 | −313,444 |
| Cordoba | 24,438 | 506,274 | −37,932 | 0.2 | — | 7.0 | −54,886 | 16,954 |
| Cundin'ca | 3,908,677 | 94,267,728 | 7,226,008 | — | 29.6 | 8.3 | 6,604,916 | 621,078 |
| Huila | 57,441 | 1,230,992 | −48,153 | 0.2 | — | −3.8 | 48,424 | −96,577 |
| V. Magd'na | 151,833 | 2,106,994 | −1,274,152 | 5.2 | — | −37.7 | −140,162 | −1,133,989 |
| Meta | 56,199 | 1,222,996 | −28,491 | 0.1 | — | −2.3 | −41,606 | 13,115 |
| Narino | 94,164 | 1,330,215 | −766,709 | 3.1 | — | −36.6 | −40,515 | −726,194 |
| Norte San. | 135,879 | 3,264,395 | 238,527 | — | 1.0 | 7.9 | −70,898 | 309,425 |
| Santander | 839,426 | 26,212,662 | 7,519,614 | — | 38.0 | 40.2 | −1,389,029 | 8,908,638 |
| Tolima | 172,114 | 3,620,486 | −212,294 | 0.9 | — | −5.5 | −195,388 | −16,906 |
| Valle | 3,076,071 | 57,670,088 | −10,830,456 | 44.4 | — | −15.8 | 1,419,255 | −12,249,718 |
| Total | 15,127,005 | 336,860,928 | 0 | 100.0 | 100.0 | — | — | — |

*Note:* Values in millions of current pesos.
*Source:* Helmsing (1983b).

intermediate and resource-based output (chemicals, oil, and oil derivatives). The other peripheral regions of Cauca, Narino, Magdalena, Tolima, Cordoba, and Meta all stayed behind, primarily due to an unfavorable industrial structure.

Data available for 1974 for foreign investment and companies show that 80% of the net output of firms with foreign participation was concentrated in the three industrial core regions, well in excess of the participation of these regions in total net manufacturing output (68% in 1975). It cannot be concluded, however, that foreign firms accentuated or were the primary cause of concentration, because foreign investment became relatively more important to Valle and to Antioquia than to Cundinamarca (Arango 1976). In other words, the increasing presence of foreign firms mitigated rather than fostered the differentiation within the industrial core.

Tables 5.12 and 5.13 give the results of the export-base analysis of the regions for the period 1967–1980. These results are also summarized in Figure 5.2. The pattern of change in this period undoubtedly was affected by the growing significance of international as against interregional trade. On the basis of the present data, however, it is impossible to isolate interregional from international export-base activities. In other words, the impact of each on the pattern of regional change cannot be individually assessed.

Some interesting conclusions about the overall pattern of change can nevertheless be drawn. First, there is a very strong tendency toward specialization (less diversification) in the manufacturing export base of the peripheral regions, as well as increased dependency on that base. Second, no such phenomenon can be observed with regard to the industrial core regions, where export activities have become *more* diversified (except in Atlantico) and the export dependency has risen only slightly. Third, not all regions within either center or periphery have been affected equally by the increased international exposure. Within the core, only Cundinamarca experienced an above-average rate of growth; in the periphery, Santander and Bolivar, and to a lesser extent four other departments, experienced relatively high rates of growth, whereas six others stagnated. In other words, some regions have gained from specialization, others have not. Similarly, some have come to depend more on exports, others not. Finally, some regions that depend more on exports have done well in terms of growth, others not.

## Developments in Agriculture

In the agricultural sector, the new policy orientation aided and strengthened an emerging tendency. In the second half of the 1960s, exportable surpluses already had been produced in such crops as cotton and sugar and, later, rice. The new policy measures offered opportunities for the expansion of capitalist agriculture, which simultaneously experienced important technological improvements.

It is sometimes suggested that the division of labor that developed between capitalist and peasant agriculture was a relatively stable one. In the case of Colombia, small-scale agriculture became marginalized as a result of the growing opportunities created by industrial demand for agricultural products (e.g., cotton), but it cannot be maintained that the production of foodstuffs remained in the realm of peasant agriculture. A number of cases illustrate that if technological conditions are present and the composition of demand turns to industrial demand, large-scale agriculture will enter these product sectors (Helmsing 1983a). In rice production, for example, the displacement of traditional dry rice producers in the urban food markets could clearly be observed (CIDER 1978). Similarly, the industrial processing of cassava for the extraction of starch began on a significant scale in the early 1970s and led quite rapidly to the relative displacement of peasant production. Industrial demand was met by large-scale cultivation (20–50 has) (ibid.:1978). Another case is that of potato growing: Industrial processing has been met almost entirely by large-scale growers who deliver directly to the factories, just as in the case of cassava (DNP 1979:69–125). Although the penetration by large-scale agriculture into basic foodstuff production has been limited, it is by no means unimportant. The preceding examples of what are considered to be typical peasant crops show that relations between the two types of agriculture are not at all static.

Agricultural development in the period 1967–1980 was influenced by three major processes: The first process was the expansion (up to 12% of total exports in 1975) and later the decline of nontraditional agricultural exports, resulting from plunging international market prices and skyrocketing prices of chemical inputs for agriculture in the mid-1970s. Second, the importance of the traditional major export crop, coffee, was greatly affected by the 1975 price export boom following a calamitous frost in Brazil. The share of coffee in total registered exports, which had dropped to 43% in 1974, subsequently rose to 59% in 1980 (Parra Escobar 1982). The third major occurrence was the stagnation of peasant agriculture, in which a number of factors played a role. First, there are some indications that the country has reached or has already passed what Johnston and Kilby (1975) call the "structural transformation point," which happens when the rural or agricultural population declines not only relatively but also in absolute numbers (cf. DNP 1977:27, 29). Similarly, the number of smallholdings (< 5 has) declined from 756,000 in 1960 to 640,000 in 1970. Second, and related to the first point, is the fact that the continued land settlement in outlying tropical regions no longer compensates for the rural exodus in the Andean zones and the older established tropical regions. Third, agricultural policy had for decades neglected peasant *production*. There was no adequate extension or research, nor did much credit or many marketing facilities reach the peasantry in order to raise agricultural productivity (Fajardo 1983). Finally, although capitalist agriculture had made important inroads into the production of traditional and mixed crops, production in these areas was still limited and the recession had brought developments in capitalist agriculture to a halt. Peasant agriculture came to constitute a real economic problem. In 1976 an integrated rural development program was initiated, which is still in existence.

The nonavailability of consistent data greatly confines any examination of the regional dimensions of developments in agricultural activities. My data are limited to the period 1965–1974 and hence do not include the recession. With regard to livestock, a similar problem exists. Taking these limitations into account, however, some tendencies can still be identified. Two tendencies in livestock production appear to have occurred simultaneously. On the one hand, intensification of dairy cattle (e.g., in Cundinamarca) and the displacement of beef cattle took place. In Magdalena and Cesar, where livestock had expanded in the 1950s, it was now partly displaced by the production of industrial crops such as cotton (CIDER 1978). On the other hand, livestock expanded in Cordoba and the Medio Magdalena and in more outlying regions such as Meta, Caqueta, and Casanare.

Considerable regional displacements in agriculture can be detected (see Tables 5.18 and 5.19). Areas of specialized production increased in number, particularly with regard to industrial crops. This tendency toward the spatial concentration of production often was accompanied by important shifts from one major region to another (rice, sorghum, and barley). No such tendencies can be clearly detected for mixed and traditional crops, except for cassava and less strongly for maize. Only in the case of beans is an opposite tendency observed.

If concentration patterns at the regional level are considered (Table 5.19), it will be seen that the urban and industrialized regions became *less* specialized agricultural producers. The agro-regions of the interior and the north show marked tendencies toward specialization in a few crops; moreover, in the interior, switches occurred from one crop to another, whereas in the north, new crops have been added. These two phenomena appear to be related, that is, interregional shifts in concentration (cotton and rice).

In peripheral regions (Cauca, Norte Santander, and Santander), the levels of specialization are considerably lower; more important, these do not increase but remain more or less stable or even decline (Narino and Boyaca). The peasant economies that continue to predominate in these regions maintain a relatively diversified crop pattern.

TABLE 5.18
Share of Specialized Production Regions[a] in Total Crop Area, for Main Crops, Colombia, 1959, 1965, 1974 (percentages)

| | *1959* | *Shifts*[b] | *1965* | *Shifts* | *1974* |
|---|---|---|---|---|---|
| *Industrial crops* | | | | | |
| Sesame | 82 (2) | | 78 (2) | + | 85 (3) |
| Cotton | 77 (4) | ⋆ | 63 (2) | + | 63 (3) |
| Sorghum | 86 (2) | + | 73 (3) | ⋆ − | 51 (2) |
| Barley | 84 (2) | ⋆ + | 91 (3) | ⋆ | 98 (3) |
| Sugar[c] | 20 (1) | | 19 (1) | | 22 (1) |
| Rice[d] | 29 (2) | ⋆ | 36 (2) | ⋆ + | 63 (4) |
| *Mixed crops* | | | | | |
| Maize | 0 (−) | | 0 (−) | + | 10 (1) |
| Potato | 61 (2) | + | 67 (3) | | 67 (3) |
| Wheat | 84 (3) | ⋆ | 93 (3) | ⋆ | 93 (3) |
| Tobacco | 73 (2) | + | 79 (3) | | 83 (3) |
| *Traditional crops* | | | | | |
| Beans | 41 (2) | + | 58 (3) | − | 18 (1) |
| Plantain | 0 (−) | | 0 (−) | | 0 (−) |
| Cassava | 49 (5) | ⋆ − | 27 (3) | ⋆ + | 35 (4) |
| *Tree crops* | | | | | |
| Banana | 46 (2) | − | 37 (1) | + | 70 (2) |
| Coffee | 26 (1) | | 22 (1) | | 21 (1) |
| Cacao | 56 (3) | ⋆ | 49 (3) | | 49 (3) |

[a]Specialized production regions in a particular crop are defined as those regions that have a location coefficient ≥ 2. The calculated index refers to the sum of cultivated area in specialized production regions expressed as a percentage of total cultivated area of that particular crop. Numbers in parentheses refer to the numbers of regions specializing in a particular crop.

[b]Shifts refer to changes in the set of specialized production regions: ⋆ signifies a change in rank order among existing specialized production regions; +, − refer to changes in the number of specialized production regions.

[c]Sugar includes traditional sugar production (*panela*).

[d]Rice includes dry rice (traditional) and irrigated rice.

*Sources:* Calculations are based on 1959 data from Agricultural Census of 1960; calculations for 1965 and 1974 are based on tabulations mimeographed by the Caja Agraria.

## Verticalization of the Regional Economy

From my perspective, four processes provide the key to understanding the regional differentiation process in the postwar period. These processes share a common element, namely, that regional economies fragment into various parts having fewer and fewer interlinkages, but which individually have elaborate extraregional and international links. These processes are (1) agri-

TABLE 5.19
Share of Specialized Production Areas of All Crops in Total Cultivated Area, by Region, Colombia, 1959, 1965, 1974 (percentages)

| | *1959* | *Shifts* | *1965* | *Shifts* | *1974* |
|---|---|---|---|---|---|
| *Core regions* | | | | | |
| Cundinamarca | 31 (3)[a] | ★ | 26 (3) | ★ | 20 (3) |
| Antioquia | 6 (1) | | 6 (1) | + − | 3 (1) |
| Valle | 26 (1) | + | 30 (2) | − | 24 (1) |
| *Interior agro regions* | | | | | |
| Tolima | 23 (2) | − | 7 (1) | ★ + | 33 (2) |
| Huila | 6 (1) | ★ + | 13 (2) | ★ + | 32 (3) |
| *Northern agro regions* | | | | | |
| Atlantico | 52 (3) | − | 54 (2) | + | 82 (4) |
| V. Bolivar | 42 (3) | | 49 (3) | | 47 (3) |
| Cordoba | 42 (2) | − | 39 (1) | + | 90 (4) |
| V. Magdalena | 34 (4) | − | 43 (3) | + − | 41 (3) |
| *Periphery (South-West)* | | | | | |
| Cauca | 0 (−) | + | 2 (1) | | 3 (1) |
| Narino | 20 (3) | + − | 39 (3) | ★ | 31 (3) |
| *Periphery (North-East)* | | | | | |
| Boyaca | 30 (2) | + | 44 (3) | ★ | 35 (3) |
| Santander | 24 (4) | − | 11 (3) | − | 11 (2) |
| Norte Santander | 13 (1) | | 11 (1) | | 13 (1) |
| *Coffee regions* | | | | | |
| V. Caldas | 65 (1) | | 58 (1) | | 65 (1) |

[a]Numbers in parentheses refer to number of crops in which a region is specialized; see also notes for Table 5.18.

cultural specialization and agroindustrial integration; (2) economic concentration in industry, trade, and finance; (3) the extension of foreign enterprise; and (4) centralization within the state sector. Together, these processes are conducive to a verticalization of the regional economy, which does not necessarily imply that the affected regions stagnate. On the contrary, some regions may experience a limited boom in particular fields, whereas others decline. The net result in terms of aggregate economic growth may be positive or negative, depending on the particular economic configuration and on the local/regional responses to these processes. This does not mean that there is no direction in the process. As we shall see, there is a definite tendency toward economic and urban primacy. The evolving regional and urban situation described later in this chapter (see pp. 180–185) will confirm this.

## Agricultural Specialization and Agroindustrial Integration

Earlier, I elaborated on the factors that shaped agricultural development during the years 1950–1980. Of the five factors enumerated, two referred to the "institutional environment" in which agricultural production takes place, that is, the state agricultural support system and the producers associations. Of these two, the former is the least developed, much to the disadvantage of smallholders. Economic transformation at the microlevel—the holding—depends in large measure on access to either of these or both. Access to credit with which to finance annual cultivation expenditures is one thing, access to controlled markets is quite another. I shall elaborate on this in more detail in the case study on cotton and textiles.

The key point seems to be that the level at which markets for agricultural products are organized moves from local to regional to (inter)national markets. Naturally, this does not all take place at the same time for all products. Agricultural products used by industry tend to be the first (in our case, cotton and rice), together with internationally traded products (coffee). For example, prior to World War II, individual textile companies made isolated and local attempts to stimulate cotton production (Montenegro 1982). In the 1950s, when textile companies became nationally organized, they formed a national buyers' organization (cartel). Prices were determined nationally rather than regionally. A similar phenomenon occurred in the case of coffee: the Federación established a uniform price system and abolished the hitherto existing regional price differences (Palacios 1979). A similar process occurred, but much more slowly, in the intermediation of unprocessed agricultural commodities, as large trading companies developed alongside traditional small-scale intermediaries (cf. DNP 1979:124).

Livestock production also showed such a tendency. In the marketing of cattle for meat, three previously regional fairs have assumed a national character (Medellin, Neiva, and Bucaramanga), not only in terms of volume traded but also in price-setting behavior for other and regional market fairs (San Martin, Facatativa, La Dorada, Cartago (Cali), and Pasto) (cf. Montes and Candelo 1980).

On the input side a broadly similar process occurred. In the 1950s, import substitution took place in the production of intermediate agricultural inputs. Producers were relatively small in number, however, and produced for the entire national market. Such was the case, for example, with the production of fertilizer. Although the country is still dependent on the import of a large proportion of basic ingredients and types of fertilizer, national production is undertaken by only three companies. Similarly, no more than 30 firms are engaged in the production of improved seeds and the lion's share is produced by only 7 companies, of which 1 is state owned (Cresemillas), 2 are producer associations (Fedearroz and Fedealgodon), and 2 are industry based (Malterias Unidas and Colsemillas). Finally, with regard to farm implements, four companies produce 80% of the national production and, thanks to import-substitution measures, can nowadays meet almost the entire national demand (DNP 1979:49–63). It seems reasonable to conclude, therefore, that agricultural production in any given area, but varying depending on the prevailing composition of peasant and capitalist agriculture, relies less and less on local inputs but increasingly must obtain these inputs from nationally operating firms and trade channels.

The same can be said, although with less strength, with regard to agricultural output, particularly that purchased by industry. Processes of specialization at farm, enterprise, and regional levels are interrelated, and a transformation of the institutional environment constitutes the organizational linkage between the two processes. Prices are less often set in what might have been competitive local markets and become more administered, fixed by nationally operating industrial and trading companies. The transformation from peasant to farmer, or from estate to agroenterprise, has this double connotation of a changing microeconomic unit in a simultaneously changing institutional environment, which in turn becomes organized at *higher* spatial scales. The individual unit becomes inserted in a complex web of relations that increasingly, but in varying degrees for different products, find their raison d'être outside the region in which the unit is located.

## Economic Concentration and the Formation of Conglomerates

I have shown earlier that the creation of the national industrial base implied the emergence of large firms operating nationally, in product markets that, given the characteristics of the product concerned, could be considered national (e.g., textile products), or have achieved a dominant position in various regional product markets via the creation of subsidiaries or branch plants (e.g., beer or cement).

The economic and physical integration of the nation through the extension of roads and railways, nationally operating banks and trading houses, and so forth, and improved transport technology, eroded the geographical and local political protection that regional firms had often enjoyed. Oligopolistic advantages of scale of production and size previously acquired by companies in the largest regional markets encouraged the formation of national oligopolies. The integration of the other less-developed regions into the national market at a later stage helped to consolidate oligopolistic structures. For example, after establishing itself in the largest regional marekts, Bavaria, the beer brewing and soft drinks company, within three years

FIGURE 5.3. Early regional integration.

FIGURE 5.4. Banco de Bogotá (1920–1960), geographical expansion of branch office network.

extended its network of branch plants to the smaller markets of Girardot, Bucaramanga, Buga, Ibague, Villavicencio, Neiva, Manizales, Armenia, and Ipiales (cf. Bavaria 1966).

The basic integration of regional markets was completed in the 1950s (Misas 1975b). Artisan and small-firm manufacture were displaced; the small firms concerned were sometimes taken over or they turned to product types or lines ignored by the large firms or intended for local regional markets only (Misas 1975b:61–69). On the other hand, once import substitution became virtually complete for existing products in the now-national market, new products frequently were introduced on the basis of foreign technologies but within preestablished oligopolistic market structures. Advantages obtained in one field were thus carried over into another. Finally, the introduction of entirely new products in new fields (e.g., intermediate products) meant that national oligopolistic structures were brought into existence almost directly.

To some extent, the processes of sectoral and regional concentration are two dimensions of the same process, the one reinforcing the other. Expansion of industry in a particular region requires and stimulates the further development of basic infrastructure such as electricity, water, and other public services. Agglomeration and inmigration are additional elements in such a cumulative process.

On the level of economic concentration, the present data are rather sketchy. In his study of the history of trade unionism, Urrutia concludes that the industrial product-market structure was highly monopolistic, a single firm usually controlling the production of one product or a group of products (Urrutia 1969:150). His conclusion is based on the estimated share of "unlimited companies" *(sociedades anonimas)* in total sales for 1959–1961. Misas (1975), in his study based on the manufacturing census of 1968, concludes that industry was characterized by a high degree of concentration; depending on the type of economic sector, this varied from a highly concentrated oligopoly for products that are nationally traded, to "atomized" oligopolies in industrial sectors which, due to the product characteristics, produce for local regional markets. Although Urrutia's empirical data refer to companies and those of Misas mostly to establishments, both correctly emphasize that the degree of economic concentration supersedes the level of product markets. In particular, due to the closed domestic market and the limited ability of government to control prices effectively, especially outside the larger towns, firms are able to administer additional price mark-ups. The rate of accumulation then soon extends beyond the growth of the market and firms rapidly expand their activities beyond their original scope. Several alternative strategies and combinations thereof can be followed. A firm may extend into geographical markets that are not yet incorporated, integrate vertically in forward or backward direction, or diversify into other related or unrelated fields of investment.

The case of Bavaria is illustrative. Even before the company went national it had moved into the production of bottles (Fenicia) and the mining of raw materials for glass manufacture (minas de Zipacon). After establishing its basic national network, Bavaria set up factories for the manufacture of malt and bottle tops. In the 1960s, it integrated further by setting up factories specialized in machine repairs and the making of spare parts and by moving into the commercialization and seed improvement of barley. In the same decade, Bavaria moved into real estate, urban construction, livestock, and other manufacturing-industry sectors (Bavaria 1966).

As we shall see, similar processes of vertical integration occurred in varying degrees for other companies—in textiles (Coltejer, Fabricato, Tejicondor), leather (Colcurtidos), metal making (Industrias Modernas), beverages (Postobon), tobacco (Coltabacos), comestibles (Cia Nal Chocolates), and building materials (Samper, Eternit Colombia). The 1961 tax reform made it more interesting to diversify and to form new companies for new investments rather than to keep all activities under one legal unit, the parent company. Therefore, the 1960s saw the development of conglomerates of companies.

The *Superintendencia de Sociedades* (1978) published a major study on conglomerates in industry and trade, based on analysis of the linkages between the 3,102 limited companies that had been registered in 1975. Conglomerates were identified on the basis of direct and indirect company control. Majority control was achieved in various ways. One company could control or dominate another via a majority share obtained directly or through other companies, via the application of specific norms for the decision-making quorum, or via the use of representational powers (having ensured the voting powers of other shareholders). In addition to companies that were thus controlled, the *Superintendencia* identified those that belonged to the "area of influence" of a conglomerate because of their minor participations.

In this way, 24 conglomerates were identified encompassing 311 enterprises, 300 of which were limited companies. Statutory limitations prevented the *Superintendencia* from doing more than partially incorporating the relations between conglomerates and banks. It is known, for instance, that many conglomerates have created their own credit institutions through which they are interpenetrated by banking and insurance conglomerates. Also, known links with the mass media were not explored in detail in the *Superintendencia de Sociedades's* report.

The 24 conglomerates and their manufacturing activities that produced 20% of manufacturing output in 1975 do not form a homogeneous set. Three subgroups were identified: two "superconglomerates"—a Medellin-based financial group (SurAmericana) encompassing 8 conglomerates and the Santo Domingo investment group incorporating 4 conglomerates. At a second level, 8 conglomerates were organized as an investment group. Finally, another 4 were organized around one or more families (*Superintendencia* 1978:328–329).

To examine the extent to which these conglomerates have extended nationally by incorporating companies or branch offices/plants, I have traced the location of all companies and their respective branches with the aid of Colombia's industrial yearbook for 1982. By this means I have been able to locate not only the companies but also their (registered) branch offices and plants.

This analysis is consistent with my emphasis, which is not on product-market classifications but on the extent to which a conglomerate as an organization either has become transregional or continues to operate exclusively from a single base In the former case, investment decisions and intrafirm trade influence interregional economic and trade structures and encourage the verticalization of the regional economies. My analysis includes only a small proportion of all transregionally operating firms. Given the economic importance of the conglomerates, however, this analysis may serve as a useful and important indicator.

Finally, I was unable to trace 40 of the 311 companies listed by the *Superintendencia*. These may have been eliminated or reconstituted, or perhaps had changed their names in the meantime. In the Appendix to this chapter each conglomerate is briefly described. Their geographical scales of operation are shown in Table 5.20.

The Appendix shows that the formation of conglomerates or economic groups is not limited to industrial firms but extends also in transport and trade. In banking and insurance, similar processes have taken place. Unfortunately, much less detailed and systematic information is available about these (cf. Colmenares 1977, 1983; Camacho Guizado 1975). In this context it is appropriate to refer also to agriculture. The *Federación Nacional de Cafeteros*, in view of the fact that it is controlled by a small group of coffee growers, may qualify here. Apart from its direct activities of commercializing and exporting coffee, the Federation has had since the 1950s economic interests in shipping, banking, insurance, and a number of semipublic agencies (Machado 1982; Palacios 1979).

It should be emphasized that concentration processes are not only intrasectoral. For several reasons such a process may advance more in one type of activity than in another; the sparse information presented shows that the conglomerates move across sectoral lines just as they move across the bound-

TABLE 5.20
Conglomerate Networks (Companies and Branch Plants/Offices)

| | Antioquia | Atlantico | V. Bolivar | Boyaca | V. Caldas | Cauca | Cordoba | Cundin'ca | Choco | Guajira | Huila | V. Magda'na | Meta | Narino | Nor. San. | Santander | Tolima | Valle | Ter. Nac. | Total |
|---|---|---|---|---|---|---|---|---|---|---|---|---|---|---|---|---|---|---|---|---|
| Moris Gutt (Bogotá) | | 3 | | 1 | | | | 12 | | | | | | | | 2 | 1 | 1 | | 20 |
| Echevarria (Bogotá) | 10 | 2 | 2 | 1 | 1 | | | 15 | | | | | | | | 1 | | 3 | | 35 |
| Espinosa (Bogotá) | | 4 | | | 3 | | | 13 | | | | 1 | | | 1 | | 1 | 2 | | 25 |
| Puyana (Bogotá) | 2 | | 2 | 1 | | | | 6 | | | | | | | | 2 | | 1 | | 14 |
| Cementos Esp. (Bogotá) | | | | | | | | 4 | | | | | | | 2 | 1 | | | | 7 |
| Tejidos Unica (Manizales | | | | | 4 | | | | | | | | | | | | | | | 4 |
| ColCurtidos (Bogotá) | 3 | 1 | | | | | | 5 | | | | 1 | | | 1 | 1 | | 1 | | 13 |
| Ind. de Gaseosas (Medellin) | 7 | 1 | 1 | 3 | | | | 4 | | | | 1 | | | 1 | | 1 | 2 | | 22 |
| Cementos Samper (Bogotá) | | | | | | | | 12 | | | | | | | | | | | | 12 |
| Cadenalco (Medellin) | 8 | 2 | 1 | 2 | 3 | 1 | 1 | 3 | | | | 2 | 1 | 1 | 2 | 1 | | 4 | | 32 |
| Eternit Col. (Bogotá) | 3 | 2 | | 1 | | | | 7 | | | | | | | | | | 3 | | 16 |
| Manuelita (Palmira) | 1 | 2 | 1 | | 1 | | | 3 | | | | | | 1 | | 1 | | 14 | | 24 |
| Confecc. Col. (Medellin) | 6 | | | | | | | | | | | | | | | | | | | 6 |
| Tejicondor (Medellin) | 8 | | | | | | | | | | | | | | | | | 1 | | 9 |
| Cia. Nac. Choc. (Medellin) | 4 | 1 | 1 | | 3 | | | 3 | | | | | | | | 2 | | 2 | | 16 |
| Coltabacos (Medellin) | 7 | 4 | | | | | | | | 2 | | 1 | | | | 2 | 3 | 2 | | 21 |
| Fabricato (Medellin) | 6 | | | | | | | | | | | | | | | | 1 | | | 7 |
| Argos (Medellin) | 6 | 7 | 1 | | 1 | | 1 | 1 | | | | | | | | | | 5 | | 22 |
| Postobon (Medellin) | 3 | 2 | 1 | 2 | 2 | | 1 | 4 | | | 1 | 2 | 1 | 1 | 1 | 2 | 1 | 2 | | 26 |
| Coltejer (Medellin) | 23 | | 1 | | | | | | | | | | | | | | | 2 | | 26 |
| Santo Domingo (B'quilla) | 6 | 19 | | | 2 | | | 7 | | | | | | | | 2 | | 2 | | 38 |
| Avianca (Bogotá) | 3 | 3 | 4 | | 2 | | 1 | 7 | | | | 1 | | 1 | 2 | 1 | | 4 | 3 | 32 |
| Colinsa (Barranquilla) | 2 | 10 | | | | | | 7 | | | | | | | | | | | | 19 |
| Bavaria (Bogotá) | 3 | 15 | 3 | 2 | 4 | 1 | 1 | 29 | | | | 2 | | | 1 | 4 | | 4 | | 69 |

aries of the various regional economies, although some still seem to operate almost exclusively from their historical regional base.

Only 3 of the 24 identified conglomerates still operated exclusively from a regional base—in Caldas, Antioquia, and Bogotá. Of the 5 conglomerates that had subsidiaries and branches in 10 or more regions, 3 operated in 15 or more regions of the country. This is an extremely simplified view, but it does indicate the transregional importance of these conglomerates, which can reshape regional economic structures through their decisions concerning investment allocation and intrafirm trade.

## Foreign Investment and Enterprise

The importance of foreign enterprises in the verticalization of the regional economy needs little elaboration, as the topic has been well covered in the literature (cf. Holland 1976; Hayter and Watts 1983). Multinational firms, in search of raw materials and/or cheap labor, mostly have quite restricted local regional linkages. The import content of production tends to be high, and a large proportion is exported to extraregional markets. Production and investment decisions are made outside the region and in the context of international rather than local considerations. Multinational corporations are sometimes characterized as "runaway" industries, when even local fixed investments are kept very low by means of location in an industrial estate or export zone.

In the case of Colombia, foreign investment played a limited role in the process of early industrializtion. With the exception of petroleum, the presence of direct foreign investment and firms was relatively small. The volume of investment climbed in the 1950s, reaching a peak early in the following decade when a reform lowered barriers and introduced incentives to foreign investment. In the early 1970s, the volume of foreign investment again increased after the 1968 reform, which provided important incentives to nontraditional exports (cf. Matter 1977; Arango 1976).

Foreign investment traditionally has been concentrated in chemicals and pharmaceuticals, machinery, paper, and food industries, as well as in commerce (including hotels) and banking. After the 1968 reform there was a marked shift toward chemicals, plastics and rubber, furniture, machinery industries, and financial activities, consistent with the changing market orientation.

Up to the 1960s, foreign investment in Colombia mainly had been oriented to the domestic market, but in that decade it also catered to export markets. Whereas firms with foreign investment contributed more than others to the exports of intermediate and capital goods, their share in the exports of consumer good was less. In terms of the share of exports in value added, however, the total for manufacturing industry and for firms with foreign participation showed little difference, namely 14% versus 15%, respectively, in 1974.

It has been shown that the share of imported material inputs of production was considerably higher, although it varied greatly among various sectors of activity. For manufacturing as a whole, Arango has estimated the share of imported inputs in the total of material inputs at 25% and that for firms with foreign (major and minor) participation at 37% (Arango 1976:150). Measured in terms of value added, however, the average difference is not that great, namely 11% versus 15%.

In terms of economic concentration, foreign firms are in many ways ahead of the national firms. By using large-scale sophisticated technology in sectors that hitherto were only weakly developed if at all, as in the case of a number of intermediate and capital goods, monopoly positions were fairly easily achieved (Matter 1977). Arango has shown that more than one third of the production in 302 establishments took place under "absolute" monopoly conditions, in which 75% to 100% of national production was realized by a single company. Another 22% of national production took place in circumstances whereby one company produced between 50% and 74% of the national output of the products in question. Thus, 57% of production by these firms was intended for markets in which they held 50% or more (Arango 1976:129). Furthermore, in a number of cases, one company produced various products under monopoly conditions.

Foreign enterprise may enter a country such as Colombia in various ways. It may negotiate a joint venture based on capital or other inputs, for example, technological, either with or without a majority share, or it may create a new subsidiary. In the case of Colombia, it seems that joint ventures with existing Colombian companies formerly were quite frequent, but that as the orientation toward exports spread, subsidiary companies with complete or majority ownership were preferred (Arango 1976). Parra Sandoval reports, however, that in Colombia, 57% of the establishments of American transnational corporations and 68% of non-United States transnational corporation establishments were directly created by the foreign parent company, and the remainder were established through the acquisition of existing companies (Parra Sandoval 1977:246). Depending on the definition of foreign enterprise that is used, the two findings need not contradict each other.

All authors agree on the regional distribution of foreign enterprise. Foreign investment and enterprise in manufacturing is mostly located in four cities (Matter 1977; Parra Sandoval 1977; Arango 1976). The activity of foreign firms in these cities is considerably greater than is the share of the cities in total manufacturing activities; on balance, therefore, foreign enterprises and investments contributed to greater geographical concentration of manufacturing activity. Table 5.21 illustrates this conclusion. As stated earlier, the significance of foreign enterprise has grown in Cali and Medellin, whereas in Bogotá it has actually decreased, so that in this respect the centralization tendency of foreign-based industrialization does not agree with the overall trend.

This partially explains why it is difficult to sustain Parra Sandoval's (1977) thesis that the principal cause for the process of urban primacy is the growing importance of foreign enterprise. I agree with Gilbert that manufacturing industry in Colombia is quantitatively too small a sector to explain the changes at the top and bottom of the urban structure (Gilbert 1970:388); moreover, insofar as foreign enterprise is concerned and in relation to the top of the urban size structure, the variables move in opposite directions: Bogotá receives a *smaller* share of foreign manufacturing activity.

As a whole, apart from the geographical concentration, foreign investment and enterprises that became more export oriented with a somewhat higher import content of production, helped to verticalize regional economic structures in Colombia. These firms are less integrated in the local regional economy than are their national counterparts. In this context it is important to refer to international intrafirm trade of the multinational corporations.

TABLE 5.21
Geographical Distribution of Foreign Enterprise Manufacturing and Total Manufacturing in Colombia, 1969 and 1975 (in percentages)

| | *1969* | | | | *1978* | | | | | |
|---|---|---|---|---|---|---|---|---|---|---|
| | *No. firms* | | *Employment* | | *No. firms* | | *Employment* | | *VA* | |
| | *All* | *Foreign* | *All* | *Foreign* | *All* | *Foreign* | *All* | *Foreign* | *All* | *Foreign* |
| Bogotá | 29 | 58 | 27 | 46 | 33 | 37 | 29 | 24 | 27 | 21 |
| Medellin | 16 | 12 | 25 | 17 | 18 | 16 | 22 | 17 | 19 | 22 |
| Cali | 15 | 19 | 17 | 28 | 10 | 15 | 12 | 29 | 14 | 23 |
| B'quilla | 8 | 4 | 9 | 3 | 7 | 8 | 8 | 8 | 8 | 8 |
| Subtotal | 68 | 93 | 78 | 94 | 68 | 76 | 71 | 78 | 68 | 74 |
| Rest of country | 22 | 7 | 22 | 6 | 32 | 24 | 29 | 22 | 32 | 26 |
| Total | 100 | 100 | 100 | 100 | 100 | 100 | 100 | 100 | 100 | 100 |

*Note:* Although both Arango and Matter employ a broad definition of firms with foreign participation, one that does not stipulate a majority share ownership, the former uses a sample whereas the second draws on records of the *Oficina de Cambios*. Given this difference, caution should be exercised in drawing conclusions from a comparison.

*Sources:* 1969 data from Matter (1977:372); 1975 data on firms with foreign participation from Arango (1976:223); Data on total manufacturing from DANE: *Censo Industrial* (1975).

With regard to imports, and measured in relation to total private Colombian imports, this trade was estimated at 29% at the height of the export drive in 1975; later, in 1979, the figure declined to 21% (Misas 1983:51).

## Centralization of the State

The state functioned in considerable disarray in the early 1950s due to the *Violencia*. The first attempt at controlling this was made by Gen. Rojas Pinnilla, who took over the government from Gomez in 1953. His peaceful coup was welcomed in a way by most factions of the elite who could no longer control the violence to which they had contributed. However, when Rojas attempted to create and consolidate his own political movement—(ANAPO), the "third force," modelled after Peron—he was removed in 1957 by a caretaker military junta, paving the way for a return to civilian government, which was to be based on a cooperation pact between Liberals and Conservatives. The two parties agreed to alternate the presidency, to share public posts equally, and to exclude third parties from elections for a period of 16 years. In a plebiscite held at the end of 1957, the constitution was amended to allow for the formation of what became known as "national front" governments. Such was, and still is in large measure, *la democracia Colombiana,* the existence of which increased the ongoing (re)centralization tendencies.

To improve the legitimacy of the state and its stability, efficiency, and performance, the public administration was modernized. A 1958 reform created so-called decentralized agencies; in spite of their name, however, these public institutions are directly accountable to the president. In addition, by emphasizing technical competence and continuity of office in these agencies, the attempt was made to reduce clientelist and thus regionalist influences from Congress (Ruiz 1982). In 1968, a second reform of the public administration perfected and extended this system, reproducing it at the local and regional levels. The central planning agency founded in 1951, which became the National Planning Department (DNP), and the *Consejo Nacional de Politíca Económica y Social* (CONPES) coordinated state intervention at the national level.

Decentralized agencies soon proliferated in all main sectors of the economy: agriculture, industry, natural resources, physical infrastructure, housing, banking, and so forth. In 1980, fiscal statistics listed 164 national agencies; the major ones are listed in Table 5.22. These decentralized agencies were in fact the main vehicles of centralization of the Colombian state, not only away from Congress but also away from the departmental and local levels of government.

TABLE 5.22
Major Decentralized Agencies, Colombia

| *Acronym/title* | *Sector* | *Function* |
|---|---|---|
| PROEXPO | Internat. trade | Export promotion |
| IDEMA | Agriculture | Marketing |
| Caja Agraria | Agriculture | Credit |
| Banco Ganadero | Agriculture | Credit |
| Corp. Aut. del Cauca | Agriculture | Irrigation |
| INCORA | Agriculture | Agrarian reform, irrigation |
| HIMAT | Agriculture | Irrigation |
| INDERENA | Agriculture | Renewal of natural resources |
| INGEOMINAS | Mining and energy | Geological research |
| CARBOCOL | Mining and energy | Coal |
| ECOPETROL | Mining and energy | Oil |
| CORELCA | Mining and energy | Electricity supply |
| ICEL | Mining and energy | Electricity supply |
| IFI | Economic development | Industrial investment |
| ICEE | Economic development | Energy |
| ICSS | Public health | Health and insurance |
| Caja Nal. de Prevision | Public health | Health and insurance |
| TELECOM | Transport and communication | Telephone, telegraph |
| INRAVISION | Transport and communication | Television, radio |
| COLPUERTOS | Transport and communication | Ports |
| FFCC | Transport and communication | Railroads |
| Fondo Nac. Vial | Transport and communication | Roads |
| ICBF | Social welfare | Social work |
| ICT | Social welfare | Housing |
| INSFOPAL | Social welfare | Infrastructure |
| SENA | Education | Training |
| Banco de la Republica | Banking | Central bank |
| Banco Central Hip. | Banking | Mortgages |

*Sources: Contraloria General de la Republica* (1983); *Estadistica Fiscal del Estado 1977–1981*; and Kline (1983:70).

Two processes happened simultaneously. First, government institutions became more technocratic, barring clientelism and patronage to a certain point, but this was almost entirely at the central or national level, at which government expenditures rose considerably. Second, *nationally* organized economic pressure groups became important mechanisms, influencing and even participating in the making of government policies. This could occur directly, when pressure groups participated in the boards of decentralized agencies or coordinating committees, or more indirectly and informally. The principal pressure groups include ANDI (industry), FEDEMETAL (industry), ACOPI (small and medium industry), SAC (agriculture), FEDECAFE (coffee), FEDEGAN (livestock), FEDEARROZ (agriculture, ASOCANA (sugar), FEDEALGODON (cotton), FENALCO (commerce), CONFECAMARAS (commerce), CAMACOL (construction), ANIF (finance), ASOBANCARIA (banking), FASECOLDA (insurance), and also the labor unions (CTC, UTC, CSTC).

The Colombian state was modernized in a particular and selective way, mostly at the center, which as a result became top heavy. Table 5.23 summarizes the distribution of income and expenditures—total, current, and investment—by level of government.

National ministries and above all the decentralized agencies account for the greater part of expenditures, particularly investment expenditures. Local and regional (departmental) governments became less and less involved in the allocation of government expenditures, particularly investment expenditure. Most decisions about infrastructural investment in the regions are made and implemented by national agencies. The relevant local and regional governments and the local and regionally operating firms, farms, and groups are allowed little influence.

By the end of the 1970s, the state sector had grown so lopsided and was so inadequate at the local level that calls from towns and regions for decentralization became louder. The emerging fiscal crisis as well as political factors may have induced central government to develop initiatives intended to strengthen departmental and municipal finance and performance (cf. Wiesner and Bird et al. 1981).

Centralization had other regional consequences. First, with regard to the allocation of government expenditures, it is important to note that the head offices of most national decentralized agencies are located in Bogotá, as is the coordinating bureaucracy. Bogotá is therefore the indicated location for access to and influence over the allocation process of decision making, for which face-to-face contacts and informal circuits are essential.

The regional effects of government expenditure, not only on investment but also on consumption, are closely related. A number of estimates show that national government investments, on the whole, have a positive effect; that is, they are distributed in favor of the relatively less-developed regions (cf. Blanco and Blanco 1981:113–115; Garcia Merlano 1976:65; Leon and Richter 1979:208).

With regard to government consumption, which tends to have *higher local* multiplier effects, there is less clarity, which is mostly a result of inadequate data and study. A very approximate indication may be obtained by examining the evolution of public employment. According to the National Ac-

TABLE 5.23
Distribution of Income and Expenditures by Government Level, Colombia, Selected Years, 1950–1980 (percentages)

| | *1950–1952* | *1959–1961* | *1964–1971* | *1975* | *1980* | |
|---|---|---|---|---|---|---|
| | | | *Income* | | | |
| National | 59.0 | 58.4 | 44.5 | 41.3 | | |
| Dentralized agencies | 3.2 | 8.6 | 33.4 | 39.4 | | |
| Subtotal | 62.2 | 67.0 | 77.9 | 80.7 | | |
| Departmental | 14.8 | 9.5 | 9.2 | | | |
| Municipal | 17.3 | 18.2 | 12.6 | 10.1 | | |
| Total | 100.0 | 100.0 | 100.0 | 100.0 | | |
| | | *Total Expenditure* | | | *(1)* | *(2)* |
| National | 59.5 | 58.9 | 43.8 | 41.2 | 28 | 81 |
| Decentralized agencies | 3.4 | 8.9 | 34.8 | 39.7 | 65 | – |
| Subtotal | 62.9 | 67.8 | 78.6 | 80.9 | 93 | 81 |
| Departmental | 20.2 | 15.4 | 9.5 | 8.9 | 5 | 13 |
| Municipal | 16.9 | 16.8 | 11.9 | 10.2 | 2 | 6 |
| Total | 100.0 | 100.0 | 100.0 | 100.0 | 100 | 100 |
| | | *Current Expenditure* | | | *(1)* | *(2)* |
| National | 57.0 | 56.6 | 46.7 | 34.3 | 28 | 79 |
| Decentralized agencies | – | 13.4 | 28.5 | 33.1 | 64 | – |
| Subtotal | 57.0 | 70.0 | 75.2 | 67.4 | 92 | 79 |
| Departmental | 27.1 | 15.5 | 13.4 | 17.9 | 6 | 14 |
| Municipal | 15.9 | 14.5 | 11.4 | 14.7 | 2 | 6 |
| Total | 100.0 | 100.0 | 100.0 | 100.0 | 100 | 100 |
| | | *Investment Expenditure* | | | *(1)* | *(2)* |
| National | 61.8 | 61.8 | 42.3 | 47.7 | 24 | 78 |
| Decentralized agencies | 8.8 | 2.7 | 37.7 | 42.4 | 63 | – |
| Subtotal | 70.6 | 64.5 | 80.0 | 90.1 | 87 | 78 |
| Departmental | 13.4 | 16.2 | 6.7 | 3.2 | 12 | 19 |
| Municipal | 16.0 | 19.3 | 13.3 | 6.8 | 1 | 3 |
| Total | 100.0 | 100.0 | 100.0 | 100.0 | 100 | 100 |

*Note:* The 1980 distribution has been calculated in two ways to allow for comparison with data on earlier years. The estimate under (1) follows the same methodology as DNP(1977), grouping all decentralized agencies. The estimate under (2) redistributes the decentralized agencies to the level at which they are inserted in the system. In the 1970s, the decentralized agencies expanded particularly at departmental and municipal level, so that the assumption valid for most of the 1950s and 1960s, that these were all national-level agencies, could no longer be sustained.

*Sources:* 1950–1952 to 1975 from DNP (1977):261–278; 1980 from *Contraloria General de la Republica* (1983).

counts, compensation to employees constitutes approximately 80% of final government consumption (United Nations 1981). Again, one is faced with considerable data deficiencies. Only for 1960 and 1970 has it been possible to make complete regional estimates for all levels of government. Table 5.24 shows that total public-sector employment became more concentrated. In 1960 the capital city region enjoyed 27% of all public employment. By 1970 this had risen to 34%, and there is little reason to assume that any reversal of this trend occurred during the rest of that decade. Table 5.24 also indicates the role of central government in causing this skewed regional distribution. Almost 50% of central government employment is estimated to have been in the capital city. Therefore, it seems reasonable to conclude that the development of the state itself consituted part of the regional problem, not only insofar as centralization in decision making was concerned but also with regard to the concentrating effects of government consumption.

## Responses by Local and Regional Enterprises and Households

I have discussed several processes that have reshaped the structure of local regional economies, calling the resulting change a process of verticalization of local and regional economies. In the countryside, nonagricultural activities are still being displaced, while a specialization process takes place in agriculture that lifts the rural economy out of its local setting and places it in (inter)nationally operating agroindustrial and trade structures. The process of specialization is always selective, however, distributing unevenly opportunities for agricultural development. Large-scale capitalist production inevitably has advantages over small farm and household production. The process is also selective in that it encourages specialization into production areas, thus reducing regional diversification.

With regard to the urban economy, we have seen that in various industrial and service activities economic concentration has led to the establishment of multicity and multiregional conglomerates. Although the bulk of their activities is in a few towns in the most developed regions of the nation, these conglomerate structures extend into almost all larger towns throughout the nation. Given their oligopolistic nature, their actions shape decision making by local and regionally operating firms.

The entry and expansion of foreign enterprise has contributed to this process of verticalization, particularly since the end of the 1960s, when they began to use Colombia as a base for international exports. With a slightly higher import and export content of production, and probably a much higher

TABLE 5.24
Public-Sector Employment, by Level and by Region, Selected Years, Colombia, 1950–1980

| | *Public Employment by Level of Government* | | | | | | | |
|---|---|---|---|---|---|---|---|---|
| | *1950* | | *1960* | | *1970* | | *1980* | |
| | *No.* | *(%)* | *No.* | *(%)* | *No.* | *(%)* | *No.* | *(%)* |
| Central | 47,037 | 40 | 54,329 | 36 | 178,338 | 53 | 258,572 | — |
| Departmental | 47,420 | 40 | 61,483 | 40 | 106,891 | 32 | n.a. | — |
| Municipal | 23,993 | 20 | 35,974 | 24 | 52,638 | 15 | n.a. | — |
| National | 118,450 | 100 | 151,786 | 100 | 337,867 | 100 | n.a. | — |

| | *Estimated Total and Central Government Employment, by Region* | | | | | | | |
|---|---|---|---|---|---|---|---|---|
| | *Total Public-Sector Employment* | | | | *Central Government Employment* | | | |
| | *1960* | | *1970* | | *1960* | | *1970* | |
| | *No.* | *(%)* | *No.* | *(%)* | *No.* | *(%)* | *No.* | *(%)* |
| Antioquia | 20,010 | 13 | 46,370 | 14 | 5,173 | 9.5 | 20,408 | 12.1 |
| Atlantico | 6,723 | 4 | 15,662 | 5 | 2,926 | 5.4 | 9,618 | 5.7 |
| V. Bolivar | 7,088 | 5 | 13,358 | 4 | 1,447 | 2.7 | 4,886 | 2.9 |
| Boyaca | 5,047 | 3 | 8,740 | 2 | 166 | 0.3 | 622 | 0.4 |
| V. Caldas | 9,508 | 6 | 12,162 | 3 | 149 | 0.3 | 330 | 0.2 |
| Cauca | 3,284 | 2 | 4,825 | 1 | 211 | 0.4 | 468 | 0.3 |
| Cordoba | 3,031 | 2 | 6,007 | 2 | 286 | 0.5 | 1,130 | 0.7 |
| Cundin'ca | 41,740 | 27 | 113,691 | 34 | 26,981 | 49.8 | 85,164 | 50.6 |
| Choco | 2,507 | 2 | 1,925 | 0.6 | 27 | 0.0 | 93 | 0.0 |
| Huila | 2,006 | 1 | 7,391 | 2 | 364 | 0.7 | 6,005 | 3.6 |
| V. Magdalena | 4,952 | 3 | 7,555 | 2 | 1,609 | 3.0 | 1,995 | 1.2 |
| Meta | 2,756 | 2 | 9,290 | 3 | 733 | 1.3 | 6,876 | 4.0 |
| Narino | 4,821 | 3 | 6,765 | 2 | 557 | 1.0 | 1,262 | 0.7 |
| Norte San. | 4,772 | 3 | 8,590 | 2 | 1,133 | 2.1 | 3,045 | 1.8 |
| Santander | 8,012 | 5 | 13,083 | 4 | 1,874 | 3.4 | 4,810 | 2.9 |
| Tolima | 8,755 | 6 | 29,395 | 9 | 4,219 | 7.8 | 7,541 | 4.5 |
| Valle | 17,693 | 12 | 29,007 | 9 | 6,475 | 12.0 | 14,085 | 8.4 |
| Total | 152,705 | 100 | 333,816 | 100 | 54,329 | 100.0 | 168,338 | 100.0 |

*Note:* Data for municipal and departmental public employment for 1960 and 1970 are published by DANE in the *Annuarios Fiscales y Financieras* for the corresponding years. The *Contraloria General de la Republica* discontinued this series from 1972 onward. Employment provided by central government is given only as an aggregate. The regional distribution of central government employment has been estimated in proportion to the *nomina nacional* distributed by department, as given by INANDES (1977:221–222).

proportion of intrafirm trade, these internationally operating firms illustrate the reshaping that took place in the local regional economy.

The economic and physical integration caused state responsibilities to increase because infrastructure was needed with which to sustain these processes, but at the same time this necessitated centralization of the state. As a consequence, the restructuring of the state contributed to the verticalization of local regional economies.

The question that now must be addressed concerns the responses of local and regional firms, farms, and households to this verticalization. Responses were various, some readily observable, others not. Three of the most obvious included (1) migration of the population and, by implication, of small firms and artisans; (2) regionalist movements; and (3) civil strikes. Less readily observable reactions involved local diversification of activities among members of a household or by a regionally operating firm. I shall now discuss the three easily observable responses.

The decision to migrate is usually a reaction to reduced chances of securing a livelihood in one's area of residence, whether rural or urban, as much as to expectations of better opportunities elsewhere. In explanations of migration, a distinction often is made between "push" and "pull" factors. To search for a single push or pull factor would be futile in this context. By definition, migration has an origin and a destination, hence there are always two sides to the issue.

In the intercensal period 1938–1951, the regions that experienced the greatest net migration were Valle, Atlantico, Cundinamarca, Narino, Caldas, Magdalena, and the land settlement areas of the Territorios Nacionales. In contrast, Antioquia, Cauca, Bolivar, Norte Santander, Tolima, Choco, Huila, and Santander all had a negative migration balance (R. Berry 1965).

Table 5.25 summarizes the net migration indices for the last two intercensal periods. Regions that are net receivers of population have reduced in number from seven to six to four; among these, three departments have shown continual positive migration growth rates since 1938, namely Cundinamarca, Valle, and Atlantico. Antioquia, Magdalena, and Choco first experienced positive and later negative net migration records, whereas Norte Santander showed the reverse. A persistent loss of migrants occurrred in Bolivar, Boyaca, Caldas, Cauca, Huila, Narino, Santander, and Tolima (Gilbert 1970; Linn 1979).

According to Shaw (1976), there is a definite relation in Colombia between the importance of *minifundio* and population pressure on the land, and rural outmigration. To this it may be added that the specialization process has left fewer alternate means of livelihood in the countryside, which explains why most migration is rural-to-urban. The main exception concerns migration to regions of land settlement. The analysis is less clear with regard to in-

TABLE 5.25
Indices of Net Migration within Colombia, by Department, 1951, 1964, 1973

| | | Annual Net Migration as Percentage of Initial-Year Population | | Index of Net Migration 1973 | |
|---|---|---|---|---|---|
| | | *1951–1964* | *1964–1973* | *Department* | *Departmental capital* |
| Antioquia | (Medellin) | 0.21 | −0.08 | 2.9 | 43.6 |
| Atlantico | (Barranquilla) | 0.64 | 1.61 | 41.8 | 42.4 |
| Bolivar | (Cartagena) | −0.51 | −0.43 | −18.6 | 28.8 |
| Boyaca | (Tunja) | −0.71 | −1.55 | −67.2 | −13.4 |
| Caldas | (Manizales) | −0.92 | −1.52 | −35.2 | 0.9 |
| Cauca | (Popayan) | −0.14 | −2.45 | −32.4 | 3.7 |
| Cesar | (Valledupar) | (a) | (a) | 32.5 | 39.5 |
| Cordoba | (Monteria) | (b) | −1.21 | −26.2 | −3.3 |
| Cundin'ca | | | | −49.8 | |
| | | 1.42 | 2.16 | 29.2 | 64.8 |
| Bogotá | | | | 64.8 | |
| Choco | (Quibdo) | 0.72 | −2.22 | −22.4 | −10.5 |
| Huila | (Neiva) | — | −0.85 | −20.4 | 6.7 |
| Guajira | (Rio Hacha) | (c) | (c) | 35.4 | 56.9 |
| Magdalena | (Sta. Marta) | 0.8 | −1.19 | −29.9 | 16.0 |
| Meta | (Villav'cio) | (c) | (c) | 16.0 | 11.3 |
| Narino | (Pasto) | −0.58 | −0.96 | −60.1 | 22.6 |
| Nor. San. | (Cucuta) | −0.12 | 0.58 | −2.1 | 46.4 |
| Santander | (B'manga) | −0.53 | −0.52 | −28.6 | 14.2 |
| Quindio | (Armenia) | (d) | (d) | −14.2 | −8.7 |
| Risaralda | (Pereira) | (d) | (d) | −15.7 | −2.4 |
| Sucre | (Sincelejo) | (b) | (b) | −47.5 | 7.0 |
| Tolima | (Ibague) | −1.62 | −1.15 | −39.3 | 2.9 |
| Valle | (Cali) | 0.35 | 0.77 | 25.4 | 42.8 |

*Notes:* 1. Annual net migration estimation based on age cohort specific survival ratio. For estimation see Linn (1979).
2. Index net migration based on change of residence during lifetime of 1973 census population. Index is derived as the ratio of net migration over the sum of gross in- and outmigration for each department (capital), expressed as a percentage.
3. (a) included in Magdalena; (b) included in Bolivar; (c) no census taken; (d) included in Caldas.

*Source:* Linn (1979:30).

migration, except that there is a positive relation between size of the receiving city and volume of migrants.

No clear linkage can be established between industrialization and migration, because the increased employment in industry constitutes too small a fraction of the migration volume (Gilbert 1970). For this reason, Gilbert has sought to explain migrational movements by the centralization of government and the physical integration of the country. In a way, it could be argued simply that the larger the city, the more numerous are *small* and local opportunities for survival.

Another way to approach this issue is to examine changes in the distribution of population active in artisan and small-scale activities. Table 5.26 presents some estimations of regional distribution and changes therein in the period 1953–1974. In the early part of this period, when the integration process was still in high gear, only one region experienced an absolute decline of artisan and small-scale activity. In all other regions, total rural artisan and small-scale activity declined in varying proportions, but increased more in the towns (Urrutia and Villalba 1969). Although the majority of the more peripheral regions experienced only small increases, expansion was not limited to core regions such as Cundinamarca, Valle, and Atlantico, but also occurred in regions where considerable agricultural growth was taking place (Tolima, Caldas, Viejo Magdalena). During the 1960s and early 1970s, artisan and small-scale activities (though small in volume) increased mostly in the agricultural frontier regions of the south and in the Santanderes. In the core regions, differentiation was remarkable in the sense that at first only two and then only one region continued to show above-average growth of such activities. The tendency toward economic and physical primacy of Bogotá was reflected in the changing distribution of small-firm and household artisan production.

A second response to verticalization of the local regional economy was voiced in movements for more regional autonomy (cf. Ruiz 1982). Two distinct phenomena can be distinguished. One was the creation of new territorial units of government, such as a new department hived off from an existing department (e.g., Cesar), or, as in land settlement areas, the upgrading of the level of government (e.g., Caqueta). At a lower level, the second phenomenon concerned the creation of new municipalities. The creation of territorial units of government enabled newly emerged local and regional elites to consolidate their economic and political power. Moreover, the creation of a new government always implies an important infusion of economic activity, because government consumption in particular will increase through the expansion of government bureaucracy.

The third response in Colombia was civil protest *(paro civico)*. During the period 1971–1981, the mass media recorded 128 civil strikes (Santana 1983). These strikes, usually consisting of a local or regional paralysis of activities for one day plus demonstrations, mostly concerned demands for the improvement of public services such as water supply, sanitation, and the like, and local regional development issues such as transport and the need for (state) economic activities. According to Santana, most civil protest movements

TABLE 5.26
Estimated Population Economically Active in Artisan and Small Industry, Absolute Numbers, Percentage Distribution and Average Growth Rates, by Region, Colombia, 1953–1974

| | *1953* | *1960* | *1967* | *1974* | *1953* | *1960* | *1967* | *1974* | *1953–1960* | *1960–1967* | *1967–1974* |
|---|---|---|---|---|---|---|---|---|---|---|---|
| Antioquia | 26,772 | 32,624 | 31,498 | 30.412 | 9.2 | 9.2 | 8.1 | 6.6 | 2.9 | −0.5 | −0.5 |
| Atlantico | 14,626 | 22,439 | 18,601 | 15,419 | 5.0 | 6.4 | 4.8 | 3.3 | 6.3 | −2.6 | −2.6 |
| Bolivar | 19,899 | 24,300 | 20,056 | 27,576 | 6.8 | 6.9 | 5.2 | 6.0 | 2.9 | −2.7 | 4.7 |
| Boyaca | 14,554 | 16,533 | 15,164 | 13,909 | 5.0 | 4.7 | 3.9 | 3.0 | 1.8 | −1.2 | −1.2 |
| V. Caldas | 22,084 | 28,438 | 29,596 | 32,021 | 7.6 | 8.1 | 7.6 | 6 9 | 3.7 | 0.6 | 1.1 |
| Cauca | 7,497 | 7,897 | 8,363 | 8,858 | 2.6 | 2.2 | 2.2 | 1.9 | 0.7 | 0.8 | 0.8 |
| Cordoba | (a) | 7,005 | 11,561 | 19.084 | (a) | 2.0 | 3.0 | 4.1 | (a) | 7.4 | 7.4 |
| Cundin'ca | 47,915 | 11,638 | 8,281 | 5,893 | 16.5 | 3.3 | 2.1 | 1.3 | −18.3 | −4.7 | −4.7 |
| Bogotá | (b) | 49,576 | 63,417 | 81,130 | (b) | 14.0 | 16.3 | 17.6 | (b) | 3.6 | 3.6 |
| Choco | 1,361 | 2,011 | 1,584 | 1,248 | 0.5 | 0.6 | 0.4 | 0.3 | 5.7 | −3.4 | −3.3 |
| Huila | 7,448 | 7,679 | 8,900 | 10,128 | 2.6 | 2.2 | 2.3 | 2.2 | 0.4 | 2.1 | 1.9 |
| V. Magd. | 11,169 | 14,323 | 15,407 | 16,714 | 3.8 | 4.1 | 4.0 | 3.6 | 3.6 | 1.0 | 1.2 |
| Meta | 0 | 1,864 | 3,261 | 5,709 | 0.0 | 0.5 | 0.8 | 1.2 | 0.0 | 8.3 | 8.3 |
| Narino | 41,431 | 32,994 | 35,893 | 39,047 | 14.3 | 9.3 | 9.2 | 8.5 | −3.2 | 1.2 | 1.2 |
| Nor. San. | 7,995 | 10,162 | 13,326 | 17,478 | 2.8 | 2.9 | 3.4 | 3.8 | 3.5 | 3.9 | 4.0 |
| Santander | 17,596 | 19,095 | 27,455 | 39,478 | 6.1 | 5.4 | 7.1 | 8.5 | 1.2 | 5.3 | 5.3 |
| Tolima | 12,462 | 15,319 | 15,813 | 16,326 | 4.3 | 4.3 | 4.1 | 3.5 | 3.0 | 0.5 | 0.5 |
| Valle | 34,295 | 46,490 | 53,344 | 61,217 | 11.8 | 13.2 | 13.7 | 13.2 | 4.4 | 2.0 | 2.0 |
| Terr. Nac. | 3,530 | 2,595 | 7,278 | 20,411 | 1.2 | 0.7 | 1.9 | 4.4 | −4.3 | 15.9 | 15.9 |
| Total | 290,634 | 352,982 | 388,798 | 462,058 | 100.0 | 100.0 | 100.0 | 100.0 | 2.8 | 1.4 | 2.5 |

*Notes:* (a) included in Bolivar; (b) included in Cundinamarca.

*Sources:* 1953 from Urrutia and Villalba (1969); 1960–1974 from Inandes (1977), *Anexo metodologico*, Table 71. The Inandes estimates incorporate the earlier Urrutia and Villalba estimates.

were organized by civic committees comprising various groups and organizations, such as community development organizations *(Accion Comunal),* trade unions, merchants and traders, local sections of economic pressure groups, and the church, as well as local politicians and even mayors (Santana (1983:150). These protests addressed not just the malfunctioning and inadequate supply of public services, but also the lack of local self-determination and participation in the functioning of government.

For our purpose, the urban and regional distribution of these civil strikes is interesting (see Table 5.27). In the period 1971–1981, strikes were most important in the poor peasant and land-settlement regions of the south, in the eastern frontier regions, in the Costa Atlantica and, more surprisingly, the Caldas coffee region.

A comparison of the civil strikes by urban size classes clearly shows that their relative significance was greater in the smaller towns. Although this reflects the fact that such towns may have a greater need for infrastructural

TABLE 5.27
Urban and Regional Distribution of Civil Strikes, Colombia, 1970–1980

| | *No. of Strikes* (1) | *Percentage Distribution* (2) | *Percentage of total population involved* (3) | *Ratio (2)/(3)* (4) |
|---|---|---|---|---|
| | | *Regional Distribution* | | |
| Southern regions (Nar./Cau./Put./Vau./Caq.) | 25 | 19.5 | 7.2 | 2.7 |
| Meta/Llanos | 5 | 3.9 | 2.1 | 1.8 |
| Boyaca | 10 | 7.8 | 4.7 | 1.6 |
| Costa Atlantica | 31 | 24.2 | 16.5 | 1.5 |
| Viejo Caldas | 9 | 7.0 | 6.4 | 1.1 |
| Other | 2 | 1.5 | 1.6 | 0.9 |
| Santander/Nor. San. | 9 | 7.0 | 7.9 | 0.9 |
| Tolima/Huila | 7 | 5.4 | 5.9 | 0.9 |
| Antioquia | 14 | 10.9 | 12.9 | 0.8 |
| Valle | 8 | 6.2 | 9.6 | 0.6 |
| Cundinamarca | 5 | 3.9 | 17.3 | 0.2 |
| | | *Urban Size Distribution* | | |
| <10,000 | 51 | 39.8 | 7.2 | 5.5 |
| 10–20,000 | 21 | 16.4 | 6.8 | 2.4 |
| 20–50,000 | 33 | 25.7 | 19.5 | 1.3 |
| 50–100,000 | 10 | 7.8 | 14.0 | 0.5 |
| >100,000 | 13 | 10.0 | 52.5 | 0.2 |

*Source:* Santana (1983:122–130).

improvements and more economic impulses, it may also be that civic protest movements are more easily organized in smaller than in larger towns.

## Evolving Urban and Regional Situations

Over the 30-year period 1950–1980, Colombian economic and regional structures underwent considerable change. In terms of per capita income, four groups of regions can be distinguished (see Table 5.28). At one end of the scale are a number of very rich regions: Bogotá, Valle, Atlantico, Meta, and Cesar. At the other end are very poor regions such as Choco, Cauca, Narino, and Huila, which increasingly lag behind. In between these extremes are a number of intermediate regions: first, the frontier regions that are in the process of being incorporated, and second, a large group of regions that show fluctuating behavior, catching up in one period, falling back in another, and vice versa. These features have led several authors (e.g., Thoumi 1983) to conclude that the Colombian regional structure is characterized by stability. In my opinion, however, stability is more apparent than real. Not only has considerable migration reduced the interregional gaps, but important qualitative changes have the common effect of cutting across regions; I have synthesized these changes under the term *verticalization of the regional economy*. Finally, as shown earlier, often there are opposing tendencies. For example, a weakening of the industrial structure may be accompanied by high rates of regional industrial growth. This may in part explain the large intermediate group of fluctuating regions. Similarly, fast-growing capitalist agriculture and a stagnating peasant economy may be found side-by-side. In this way, aggregate indicators sometimes hide more than they actually reveal.

In this context, it is also of interest to show the changes in regional participation in international trade (see Tables 5.29 and 5.30). During the 1950s, exports were completely dominated by coffee, which originated mostly in the two regions of Caldas and Antioquia, but in the 1960s a process of diversification began that extended regional participation in international exports to such regions as Atlantica, Bolivar, and Valle.

The most remarkable changes, however, occurred on the import side. Cundinamarca, the capital-city region, showed a persistent tendency to dominate international imports, increasing its share from 31% in 1950 to 49% in 1967 to more than 60% in the 1970s (Table 5.30). In all other regions, with the exception of Boyaca and Santander, direct participation declined. I do not have detailed information on the sectoral composition at the regional level, but it appears that this change, as regards imports, cannot adequately be explained only by the general process of urbanization and regional agricul-

TABLE 5.28
Regional Product per Capita in Relation to National Average of Colombia, by Department, Colombia, 1960–1975

| | *Difference relative to national average* | | | *Annual growth rate by period (percentages)* | | | | | |
|---|---|---|---|---|---|---|---|---|---|
| | | | | *1960–1967* | | | *1967–1975* | | |
| | *1960* | *1967* | *1975* | *GDP* | *Population* | *GDPC* | *GDP* | *Population* | *GDPC* |
| Choco | 70.3 | −72.1 | −76.3 | 3.3 | 2.5 | 0.8 | 3.5 | 2.3 | 1.1 |
| Cauca | 41.9 | −44.2 | −45.3 | 2.9 | 1.8 | 1.1 | 3.8 | 0.9 | 2.9 |
| Narino | 40.8 | −49.3 | −51.0 | 1.6 | 2.2 | −0.6 | 5.2 | 2.4 | 2.7 |
| Huila | −22.8 | −24.3 | −25.8 | 3.9 | 2.5 | 1.4 | 5.2 | 2.3 | 2.9 |
| Group 1 | 40.1 | −44.4 | −46.2 | 2.8 | 2.2 | 0.6 | 4.7 | 1.9 | 2.7 |
| Sucre | −30.4 | −31.5 | −20.8 | 4.2 | 2.8 | 1.4 | 4.1 | 3.1 | 1.0 |
| Guajira | −25.3 | −27.1 | −10.3 | 5.0 | 3.8 | 1.3 | 10.7 | 4.9 | 6.5 |
| Boyaca | −21.5 | −35.0 | −32.5 | 0.9 | 1.9 | −1.0 | 5.1 | 1.4 | 3.6 |
| Magd'na | −18.8 | −10.7 | −17.9 | 6.3 | 3.3 | 3.0 | 3.6 | 1.5 | 2.1 |
| Cordoba | −14.0 | −31.2 | −22.5 | 2.4 | 4.0 | −1.6 | 7.7 | 3.0 | 4.7 |
| Tolima | −13.0 | −13.0 | −8.7 | 3.3 | 1.6 | 1.7 | 5.8 | 2.1 | 5.7 |
| Quindio | −12.4 | −19.0 | −32.0 | 2.6 | 2.1 | 0.5 | 2.8 | 1.9 | 0.9 |
| Cund'ca | −9.7 | −9.7 | −4.5 | 3.1 | 1.4 | 1.7 | 5.1 | 2.1 | 3.0 |
| Risaralda | −9.3 | −11.6 | −4.6 | 3.5 | 2.2 | 1.3 | 5.5 | 1.4 | 4.1 |
| Nor. San. | −8.3 | −16.0 | −38.4 | 3.4 | 3.0 | 0.4 | 2.9 | 3.6 | −0.7 |
| Caldas | −5.5 | −10.5 | −20.5 | 2.6 | 1.7 | 0.9 | 2.5 | 0.8 | 1.7 |
| Santander | −5.1 | 4.9 | −0.5 | 5.2 | 2.1 | 3.1 | 4.4 | 1.9 | 2.5 |
| Antioquia | −2.5 | −0.5 | −2.3 | 5.1 | 3.2 | 1.9 | 5.5 | 2.6 | 2.9 |
| Bolivar | 6.3 | −6.1 | 4.4 | 3.2 | 3.3 | −0.1 | 7.4 | 2.9 | 4.5 |
| Group 2 | −9.3 | −10.8 | −11.8 | 4.0 | 2.5 | 1.4 | 5.2 | 2.2 | 3.0 |
| Nat. Terr. | −47.7 | 0.4 | 18.6 | 16.0 | 5.2 | 10.8 | 9.9 | 4.7 | 5.2 |
| Atlantico | 23.6 | 16.4 | 24.0 | 5.0 | 4.2 | 0.8 | 7.7 | 3.7 | 4.0 |
| Meta | 24.1 | 35.4 | 21.4 | 9.3 | 6.3 | 3.0 | 6.8 | 5.1 | 1.7 |
| Cesar | 26.1 | 25.2 | 8.0 | 7.9 | 6.4 | 1.5 | 7.4 | 6.1 | 1.3 |
| Valle | 26.5 | 23.9 | 13.8 | 4.8 | 3.4 | 1.4 | 5.4 | 3.3 | 2.1 |
| Bogotá | 81.2 | 69.4 | 60.2 | 7.0 | 6.2 | 0.8 | 8.2 | 5.8 | 2.4 |
| Group 4 | 45.1 | 40.8 | 34.8 | 6.1 | 4.8 | 1.3 | 7.2 | 4.6 | 2.6 |
| Total for Colombia | (5,088) | (5,719) | (7,352) | 4.8 | 3.1 | 1.7 | 6.1 | 2.9 | 3.2 |

*Note:* Numbers in parentheses refer to Gross Domestic Product per capita in 1970 pesos.
*Source:* DNP (1977:64).

TABLE 5.29
Value of International Exports, by Region, Colombia, 1950–1980 (in thousands of Colombian pesos; constant 1970 prices)

| | *1950* | *1955* | *1960* | *1965* | *1970* | *1975* | *1980* |
|---|---|---|---|---|---|---|---|
| Antioquia | 1,584,158 | 1,956,327 | 1,855,164 | 2,441,220 | 3,620,975 | 4,013,024 | 5,917,748 |
| Atlantico | 50,901 | 41,203 | 145,413 | 392,924 | 474,306 | 649,627 | 973,113 |
| Bolivar | 65,089 | 71,026 | 247,207 | 902,649 | 508,048 | 1,691,232 | 1,091,847 |
| Boyaca | 40 | 17,980 | 59,639 | 291,723 | 47,407 | 43,786 | 367,565 |
| Caldas | 2,788,851 | 3,823,948 | 4,421,967 | 3,469,948 | 5,004,032 | 5,266,215 | 8,375,452 |
| Cauca | 64,248 | 14,993 | 83,757 | 93,048 | 95,992 | 123,668 | 363,591 |
| Cordoba | 0 | 7,752 | 43,577 | 45,551 | 26,947 | 71,482 | 33,779 |
| Cund'ca | 887,614 | 1,003,614 | 454,511 | 692,194 | 725,607 | 2,381,956 | 2,242,734 |
| Choco | 31,495 | 33,993 | 9,311 | 42,621 | 43,607 | 17,570 | 4,113 |
| Guajira | 1,307 | 105 | 266 | 2,584 | 4,797 | 27,962 | 11,837 |
| Huila | 27,139 | 2,980 | 9,151 | 0 | 162 | 191 | 135 |
| Magdalena | 263,337 | 326,804 | 334,292 | 512,617 | 469,962 | 954,212 | 673,543 |
| Meta | 0 | 0 | 0 | 25,800 | 11,127 | 3,787 | 14,906 |
| Narino | 35,218 | 55,673 | 143,630 | 134,242 | 79,616 | 126,015 | 67,478 |
| Norte San. | 579,129 | 623,176 | 1,006,466 | 821,660 | 250,243 | 127,680 | 91,684 |
| Santander | 517,703 | 259,412 | 474,252 | 473,767 | 175,049 | 111,442 | 90,468 |
| Tolima | 328,812 | 300,438 | 270,292 | 35,638 | 7,324 | 104,404 | 144,285 |
| Valle | 413,584 | 1,001,294 | 177,734 | 545,702 | 1,093,667 | 2,198,875 | 1,983,970 |
| Total | 7,638,624 | 9,540,719 | 9,736,629 | 10,923,888 | 12,638,868 | 17,913,128 | 22,502,246 |

*Source: Anuario de Comercio Exterior* (DANE, Bogotá, various years).

tural and industrialization processes. The growing concentration of import trade firms in Bogotá, resulting in large measure from the growing importance of central government regulations, may be the principal reason for the observed change.[5]

The changes in Colombia's urban structure merit independent research, if only to dispel some of the conventionally held beliefs about that structure. In particular, opinion about the stability of the urban size distribution and the importance of so-called intermediate cities can afford a change. The growth of the 30 largest cities and metropolitan areas is summarized in Table 5.31. At least two conclusions can be drawn from these data.

First, urban population growth was most intense during the first intercensal period. Second, the gap between growth of towns of various sizes widened over the entire period and particularly towards the end. Bogotá

5. A similar phenomenon and implied problem of definition can be said to apply also to exports. However, on the basis of my general knowledge and other sources of statistical information, I have reason to assume this not to be the case.

TABLE 5.30
Value of International Imports, by Region, Colombia, 1950–1980 (in thousands of Colombian pesos; constant 1970 prices)

| | *1950* | *1955* | *1960* | *1965* | *1970* | *1975* | *1980* |
|---|---|---|---|---|---|---|---|
| Antioquia | 1,587,267 | 1,659,621 | 1,403,225 | 1,092,584 | 1,928,415 | 2,041,141 | 4,207,730 |
| Atlantico | 1,494,802 | 1,715,167 | 1,112,283 | 704,542 | 1,273,006 | 937,254 | 1,774,649 |
| Bolivar | 395,151 | 404,818 | 328,803 | 245,273 | 141,384 | 218,022 | 713,093 |
| Boyaca | 40,860 | 85,583 | 67,464 | 48,530 | 90,394 | 62,999 | 34,898 |
| Caldas | 434,814 | 505,523 | 302,719 | 280,139 | 315,898 | 367,263 | 638,585 |
| Cauca | 10,930 | 15,750 | 5,819 | 1,426 | 19,322 | 7,900 | 20,758 |
| Cordoba | 0 | 21,621 | 7,458 | 2,024 | 18,413 | 2,577 | 23,371 |
| Cundin'ca | 2,551,349 | 5,544,122 | 4,279,198 | 4,503,938 | 9,243,784 | 9,651,307 | 19,095,350 |
| Choco | 7,744 | 6,705 | 3,733 | 922 | 5,337 | 2,722 | 55 |
| Guajira | 140 | 659 | 244 | 1,550 | 3,533 | 9,489 | 1,440 |
| Huila | 12,523 | 24,682 | 13,789 | 5,554 | 4,755 | 5,596 | 13,661 |
| Magdalena | 68,593 | 90,015 | 131,072 | 223,791 | 33,533 | 54,252 | 227,937 |
| Meta | 1,058 | 4,091 | 814 | 2,163 | 12,833 | 3,276 | 23,319 |
| Narino | 54,012 | 61,015 | 32,161 | 11,727 | 103,548 | 31,696 | 50,493 |
| Norte San. | 130,558 | 92,189 | 22,150 | 14,671 | 22,329 | 33,394 | 61,034 |
| Santander | 151,953 | 264,341 | 232,219 | 338,275 | 183,171 | 167,486 | 821,215 |
| Tolima | 83,000 | 122,106 | 59,689 | 24,038 | 27,172 | 83,176 | 144,468 |
| Valle | 1,239,698 | 2,043,205 | 1,335,594 | 1,383,281 | 1,841,147 | 2,285,299 | 3,314,414 |
| Total | 8,264,453 | 12,661,213 | 9,338,437 | 8,884,427 | 15,236,326 | 15,964,850 | 31,166,474 |

*Source: Anuario de Comercio Exterior* (DANE, Bogotá, various years).

experienced the highest growth rate throughout the entire period and the 7 intermediate cities actually had the lowest rate in the second period. Linn (1979) correctly concludes that one cannot speak of a process of "polarization reversal" in the case of Colombia. On the contrary, progress toward the primacy of Bogotá is clearly recognizable, even if somewhat different size-class definitions are used (cf. Florez and Gonzalez 1983).

The dimension of the urban structure presented in Table 5.31 represents only one part of the changes—those at the upper end of the size structure. An examination of all municipalities shows that in the period 1938–1951, 28 towns at least doubled their populations, particularly the largest towns. Urban growth was highest in the departments of Cundinamarca, Santander, Boyaca, Tolima, Antioquia, Caldas, and Valle. In the next intercensal period (1951–1964), which was of the same duration, no less than 130 towns at least doubled their population. These were of all sizes: 100 were located in Boyaca, Cundinamarca, Valle, Caldas, and Antioquia, and the remainder were dispersed throughout the south and on the Costa Atlantica. The extraordinary growth of towns in this period must be seen in the context of another factor,

TABLE 5.31
Relative Rates of Growth of Population of the 30 Largest Cities and Metropolitan Areas in Colombia, by Size Class, 1951–1973

| Size class[a] | Number of cities | Total Population by Size class (in thousands) | | | Intercensal Average Comp. Growth rate (%)[b] | | | |
|---|---|---|---|---|---|---|---|---|
| | | *1951* | *1964* | *1973* | *1951–1964* | *Ratio* | *1964–1973* | *Ratio* |
| 30–89 | 13 | 302 | 635 | 873 | 6.1 | 1.9 | 3.3 | 1.3 |
| 90–149 | 6 | 232 | 496 | 672 | 6.0 | 1.9 | 3.4 | 1.3 |
| 150–499 | 7 | 598 | 1,242 | 1,599 | 5.8 | 1.9 | 2.8 | 1.1 |
| 500–1499 | 3 | 940 | 2,112 | 3,092 | 6.4 | 2.1 | 4.3 | 1.6 |
| ≥1500 | 1 | 665 | 1,673 | 2,719 | 7.0 | 2.2 | 5.3 | 2.0 |
| total urban population[c] | | 4,469 | 9,093 | 12,847 | 5.4 | 1.7 | 3.7 | 1.4 |
| total population | | 11,548 | 17,484 | 22,264 | 3.1 | 1.0 | 2.6 | 1.0 |

[a]Size (in thousands); grouping of cities according to 1973 distribution.
[b]Ratio growth rate of size category divided by growth rate total.
[c]Urban population refers to that of the *cabeceras municipales*.
*Source:* Linn (1979:24).

namely, that 200 municipalities in Tolima, Valle, and Caldas lost population in absolute terms as a result of the *Violencia* and the rural exodus. Finally, in the last and shorter intercensal period (1964–1973), 24 towns at least doubled their populations. These were in three main areas: the regions of agricultural expansion on the Costa; the land-settlement regions; and Cundinamarca, where considerable intensification and diversification of agricultural activities took place (Urbano Campo 1977). Some authors argue that a strong correlation exists between urbanization, rural exodus, the *Violencia,* and the central coffee region (ibid.:50).

If anything, industrialization, together with other factors such as centralization of the state and enterprise, may help to explain these changes, particularly at the upper end of the urban-size stucture. On the other hand, rural and agricultural factors are essential for an understanding of urban growth and decline at the lower end. The composite index of social and economic indicators calculated by Richter et al. (1979) is given in Table 5.32. This index gives a broad view of aggregate regional changes over the period 1951–1973.

Table 5.32 presents only general and average indicators, but they reveal considerable differentiation in social conditions experienced by the population of various regions of the country, which no doubt will influence future population migrations.

TABLE 5.32
Index of Socioeconomic Development, by Department, Colombia, 1951, 1964, 1973

| 1951 | | | 1964 | | | 1973 | | |
|---|---|---|---|---|---|---|---|---|
| *Rank* | *Department* | *Index* | *Rank* | *Department* | *Index* | *Rank* | *Department* | *Index* |
| 1 | Atlantico | 1.79 | 1 | Atlantico | 1.61 | 1 | Cundin'ca | 1.51 |
| 2 | Cundin'ca | 1.39 | 2 | Cundin'ca | 1.60 | 2 | Atlantico | 1.38 |
| 3 | Valle | 1.23 | 3 | Valle | 1.13 | 3 | Valle | 1.29 |
| 4 | Antioquia | 0.98 | 4 | Antioquia | 0.90 | 4 | Caldas | 0.86 |
| 5 | Caldas | 0.93 | 5 | Santander | 0.23 | 5 | Antioquia | 0.78 |
| 6 | Norte San. | −0.20 | 6 | Norte San. | 0.20 | 6 | Santander | 0.18 |
| 7 | Tolima | −0.24 | 7 | Huila | 0.14 | 7 | Norte San. | −0.05 |
| 8 | Santander | −0.28 | 8 | Caldas | 0.08 | 8 | Tolima | −0.09 |
| 9 | Narino | −0.43 | 9 | Tolima | −0.17 | 9 | Huila | −0.13 |
| 10 | Magdalena | −0.57 | 10 | Magdalena | −0.51 | 10 | Magdalena | −0.53 |
| 11 | Huila | −0.62 | 11 | Bolivar | −0.79 | 11 | Boyaca | −0.69 |
| 12 | Bolivar | −0.67 | 12 | Boyaca | −0.83 | 12 | Cauca | −0.77 |
| 13 | Cauca | −0.85 | 13 | Cauca | −0.85 | 13 | Narino | −0.85 |
| 14 | Boyaca | −0.90 | 14 | Narino | −0.85 | 14 | Bolivar | −0.99 |
| 15 | Choco | −1.53 | 15 | Choco | −1.88 | 15 | Choco | −1.89 |

*Notes:* Caldas includes Quindio and Risaralda; Cundinamarca includes Bogotá DE; Bolivar includes Cordoba and Sucre; Magdalena includes Cesar; National Territories and Meta were excluded due to lack of data.
*Source:* Richter et al. (1979:20).

## Some Conclusions

In this chapter I have endeavored to highlight, in an interpretive manner, the main interactions between economic and regional change in Colombia during the twentieth century. The aim of the analysis has been to illustrate and further develop some of the principal arguments developed in Chapter 4. The framework elaborated in that chapter is a skeletal one; in this chapter I have fleshed it out with detail taken from reality. The analysis, which is divided into various periods and subperiods, generally follows recognized phases of economic development. Each of these periods could be considered of sufficient length to enable long-term processes of regional change to be discerned.

I provide base-line characterization of late-nineteenth century Colombia, in order to put into context the changes that occurred at the beginning of the present century. After independence early in the nineteenth century, there was little to unite the various regions of what is presently known as Colombia. The economy was in a poor state, as was external trade. There was not much need for a strong central state, nor could such a state be economically sustained. The country was an economic and political archipelago: the shift in the mid-nineteenth century toward a federal political administrative structure confirmed this constitutionally, but such a characterization does not mean that all "islands" were homogeneously poor and uniformly organized. On the contrary, there were significant political and economic differences. In some regions, traditional haciendas and *hacendado-generals* dominated the economic and political scene. But other, less-populated regions, where haciendas were not strongly developed, had structures that were less rigid and authoritarian. In regions such as Santander and Antioquia, processes of land settlement were important insofar as these encouraged more open economic and political structures.

Towns grew slowly and mostly on the basis of conspicuous consumption by the landed rich. In addition, some towns were established and expanded in relation to land settlement processes. These points illustrate the argument put forward in Chapter 3 that the development and growth of towns cannot be considered as independent of, or separate from, processes of rural change.

The archipelago-like character of Colombia was altered by several factors. First, the import of (European) manufactures undermined artisan household textile production in the eastern region, notably in Santander. Second and more important, coffee production and exports developed at different rates in various regions. Not only was the balance of power between groups from the east and the west altered, but a force was set in motion to strengthen the central state and to develop some basic (national) economic and physical infrastructure on behalf of this new export activity. However, a prolonged civil war and virtually dictatorial administrations were needed to defeat traditional regional powers and to start the construction of central state institutions. Former federal states were reduced to regions, and some were subdivided to reduce the bases of power. I view the development of a national export staple grown in several regions (coffee) as the main cause of the development of the central state.

The expansion of coffee production should not be seen only as a sectoral phenomenon. Coffee, together with the early industrialization to which it greatly contributed, required and resulted in multiple processes of economic and political change that extended far beyond sectoral confines and, furthermore, had considerable spatial implications. Coffee required a basic infrastructure that was lacking in most areas. Roads, railways, import and export trade activities, banking, transport, and processing facilities are all essential and expansion could not take place without them. Coffee required and brought about considerable local regional transformations. A similar point can be made with respect to early industrialization.

Coffee developments stimulated early industrialization in several direct and indirect ways. Industrialization internalized the growth effects of coffee and increased its dynamic impact on the economy as a whole, both in and near the coffee regions. The Great Depression and the two world wars, as temporary interruptions of competitive imports, gave additional impetus to this domestic process. In addition to the coffee trade, industrial enterprises and groups became a pressure force for further national integration.

Although coffee production did not displace other agricultural activities on any large scale, and had an impact on the rural labor market only in some regions (notably in the east) indirectly, via public works and industrialization, it generated a demand for both rural labor and agricultural products. No processes of regional specialization could be observed, however; the development of the agroindustrial complex was yet to come. The fact that the processes of economic change were mostly restricted to a few regions only meant that at the end of the period 1900–1950 a number of regions had few if any international trade links. These included not only distant frontier regions but also old, established, predominantly subsistence regions.

The development of the country as an agricultural mono-exporting but industrializing economy led to the emergence of a regional division of labor, albeit incomplete, and had profound effects on the internal political structure of the country, which hitherto had been dominated by various regionally based groups. The implications of this are spelled out in this chapter (see pp. 134–135). With the development of coffee production and trade, and industry, new groups came to the fore which, although their interests were not identical, coincided in their need for the physical and economic integration of the country; to this end, a strengthening of the central state was necessary.

The establishment of new central government institutions was accompanied by administrative reforms that curtailed some local and regional government competences. I have shown that the share of central government in total government revenues and expenditures (particularly investment) rose considerably in the 1920s and 1930s: the centralization process had begun.

Government centralization did not stand on its own. Although evidence is only fragmentary, there are signs of unmistakable trends toward economic concentration in banking, industry, trade, and transport, resulting in the emergence of the first transregionally operating enterprises. The formation of these enterprises and their nationally organized lobbies called for a strengthening of state institutions at the top, but very little reform and restructuring took place at the regional level. Moreover, the particular political conditions of the era made central government intervene actively in issues that were partly regional, or which arose in only a few regions. As a consequence, the system of government at this level was severely undermined. The *Violencia* can be seen in part as a reaction to the collapse of government in various regions.

I conclude the analysis of the pre–World War II period with a broad characterization of the various regional situations. On the basis of the fragmentary evidence available, I conclude that these situations were quite heterogeneous. The central regions, in which most coffee and industrial developments took place, came to spearhead the emerging capitalist regional division of labor.

I divide the post–World War II years into two periods: 1945–1967 and 1968–1980, in accordance with changes in economic policy orientation. The improved, though far from adequate, statistical data base that came available in this period has been used for a description of sectoral and regional patterns in industry and agriculture.

With regard to manufacturing industry, I argue that the so-called import-substitution policy (1950–1967) was more effective in protecting existing industrial enterprises than in promoting import-substituting industrialization. I propose that domestic demand has been the single most important source of demand, and the expansion of existing consumer goods industries the predominant feature.

In the period 1945–1958, the regional pattern more or less conformed the center–periphery model. Integrative processes negatively affected output growth in peripheral regions; increased export-base dependence, reduced export-base diversification, and poor growth performance all went together. Peripheral regions were integrated but on a narrower basis. Within the core of central regions some differentiation occurred, mostly to the advantage of Valle. During the 1960s, the changes in the regional pattern were not only less marked but also less along the lines of the center–periphery model, despite foreign investment and enterprise.

I identify five factors in my description of developments in agriculture in the period 1950–1967: the effects of the *Violencia* on the agrarian structure; new technology that favored large-scale mono-cultivation; the growth of urban and industrial demand for agricultural products; government policy; and the role played by producer associations.

Both land and labor productivity growth were very low and therefore the pattern of growth was based on a geographical widening of production areas, particularly in the so-called commercial crops. This also applied, though less dramatically, to the mixed and the traditional crops, which points to the continued incorporation of peasant agriculture as well as to the expansion of peasant agriculture via land settlement.

The beginning of agroindustrial integration, noticeable in commercial crops, led to regional specialization cum displacement of other, presumably less profitable, land uses (cattle raising). Such patterns were not observed for mixed and traditional crops, thus lending support to my propositions regarding the differential nature of integration processes.

After 1967, exports became a more significant source of growth for manufacturing industry, but import liberalization in the second half of the

1970s did away with much of these effects. The economy became more open and eventually internationalized. The growing role of foreign enterprise accentuated this change even further. Notwithstanding this change toward greater opening up, the center–periphery pattern was less applicable to regional change during the 1960s, and ceased to be relevant in the following decade, when differentiation within core and periphery became predominant. Although industrial export-base dependence increased and specialization became narrower in peripheral regions, some regions gained in terms of growth while other did not. Within the core a recentralization toward Bogotá could be observed.

Export booms, first in nontraditional agriculture and later in coffee, and continued agroindustrial integration were the major features of the 1960s. However, peasant agriculture became increasingly marginalized as a result of these processes. Peasant production stagnated, and the absolute number of smallholdings, which had continued to increase through the 1950s, now declined significantly. The limited data available for only part of the period considered here show that processes of specialization and displacement continued. Commercial crop production shifted from one region to another, and cattle raising was further displaced toward recently settled regions. No such tendencies could be detected for traditional or mixed crops. It is also interesting that overall agricultural diversification in urban–industrial regions remained high or even increased, as in the peripheral regions where peasant agriculture continued to predominate. These patterns support my revised Von Thuenen-type interregional land-use model postulated earlier.

After describing these macro-sectoral and regional patterns, which do not appear to conform to accepted regional theory, I examine four processes in accordance with the theory elaborated in Chapter 4 (see pp. 84–101): agroindustrial integration; economic concentration and the formation of economic conglomerates; extension of foreign enterprise; and centralization within the state. Together, these four processes are conducive to a verticalization of the regional economy.

Agroindustrial integration resulted in markets organized on a national and also, since the late 1960s, on an international basis. Prices came to be determined nationally rather than locally or regionally. On the input side, more inputs must be obtained from (inter)nationally operating firms and trade channels. Processes of farm and regional-level specialization became interrelated. The transformation from peasant to farmer and from estate to agroenterprise has this double connotation of microeconomic change within a simultaneously changing institutional environment that becomes organized on a larger spatial scale.

Up to a certain point, sectoral and regional patterns accompany economic concentration processes, and reinforce one another. However, within a protected internal market, particularly one of a relatively small size, enterprises soon surpass sectoral and regional confines. Several strategies may be followed, but because micro-level data are extremely limited and fragmented, I have not been able to fully investigate temporal and spatial dimensions of these strategies. At the sectoral level, several studies confirm the process of concentration and the emergence of variously structured oligopolistic market forms. At the firm level, the 24 largest industrial conglomerates have been examined and their multiplant/office networks established. The results show that conglomerates have moved across sectoral lines as much as they have crossed regional boundaries, although some still operate largely from their historical regional base. The investments and (intrafirm) trade decisions of conglomerates have allowed them to shape interregional economic and trade structures and, in this way, to contribute to verticalization of the regional economies.

Demonstration of the role of foreign enterprises in the verticalization of the regional economy perhaps requires less argumentation, in that it has been well documented both theoretically and for Colombia. I show that more material inputs are imported from abroad by foreign enterprises: both their import and export content is somewhat higher than that of other companies. As a result, they are even less integrated in their respective local regional economies. Even more than for their national counterparts, extraregional considerations determine their local decision making.

With regard to centralization within the state, it is important to emphasize that the National Front government, created in response to the *Violencia,* did not resolve one of its main causes—the collapse of local/regional government in the *Violencia* regions. To the contrary, further centralization resulted. Administrative reforms in 1958 and 1968 and the creation of decentralized agencies are mentioned in this context. Two processes occurred simultaneously. Government became more technically competent and technocratic, barring clientelism up to a point, but did so almost exclusively at the central level where national organized pressure groups could become effective. At the same time, the bulk of revenues and expenditures were concentrated at the central level. The Colombian state was modernized but in a selective way, that is, only at the center.

Regional consequences were not limited to the effect of centralization in government decision making, however. The same process also resulted in regional concentration. Estimates of the regional distribution of government employment as the single largest component of government consumption show that it was increasingly concentrated in the capital city. Therefore, the centralization of government is very much part of the regional problem.

After showing the processes that induce verticalization of the regional economy, I examine the responses of small firms and housholds (see pp.

173–180). Three responses are found to be relevant. The first of these is migration by small firms, artisans, and households. Although there are always two sides to migration, it can be shown with regard to the net-migration pattern that the number of net-receiving regions has dropped from 7 in 1938 to 4 in 1973. Fewer regions became foci of migration, and only Cundinamarca, Valle, and Atlantico currently continue to be such foci. Estimates of the population normally active in artisan and small industry reveal that these local and regionally operating firms and businesses have come to focus more and more on Bogotá. Large relative increases of these small firms and households are also found in the land-settlement and agro-regions of the country. A second interesting reaction is the demand for more local and regional autonomy through the creation of new towns and departments. The creation of a new territorial unit of government enables new local and regional elites to consolidate their economic and political power. Moreover, an infusion of economic activity, sometimes sizable, is caused by the expansion of the local government bureaucracy. Third, civil strikes, together with calls for more local autonomy in decision making, can be viewed as a reaction against the local/regional malfunctioning of the central state.

The overall review of regional and urban development (see pp. 180–185) shows a growing proliferation of regional socioeconomic situations as well as more pronounced urban primacy.

## APPENDIX: CONGLOMERATES IN COLOMBIA

Unless otherwise specified, the following information has been obtained from Superintendencia de Sociedades (1978).

### *1. Conglomerate Moris Gutt*

This is a family-type conglomerate based in Bogotá; in 1975 it consisted of 16 companies, 15 of which were controlled by the conglomerate. Production is concentrated in the manufacture of fats and oils, food concentrates, and chemical detergents and soaps. Some degree of vertical integration is evidenced by the incorporation of plantations of African palm trees and the processing of subproducts. However, the group has also diversified considerably into metal working and real estate. Although the conglomerate operates mainly from its Bogotá base, where it has 8 companies, it also has subsidiaries and branch plants in four other regions.

### *2. Conglomerate Echevarria*

This is also a family-controlled conglomerate that is almost exclusively dedicated to the manufacture and distribution of a wide range of ceramic products. It is the country's largest producer of porcelain and chinaware, with an estimated 47% market share. In 1975, the conglomerate comprised 31 companies, 22 of which were under some form of control by the parent company. Although the group is concentrated in and around Bogotá, it operates with branches and companies in all major industrial centers, with a clear bias toward Medellin.

### *3. Conglomerate Espinosa*

In 1975, this family-type conglomerate comprised 26 companies, 23 of which were under its control. It is dedicated to the processing of vegetable oils and animal fats, processing and packing of meat, processing of milk, and also to the distribution of these products. Although agroindustry constitutes the core in which it is vertically integrated, the conglomerate has diversified into a number of other lines, particularly the import and assembly of vehicles and parts and agricultural machinery, metal making and related products and machinery, and real estate. Although the conglomerate has concentrated most of its activities in Bogotá, where most of its companies are located, it operates firms and branches in seven other regions of the country.

### *4. Conglomerate Puyana*

This family-type conglomerate is basically a trading group. In 1975, the conglomerate comprised 11 companies, 9 of which were controlled by it. The main trading activities are in metal, printed products, and food products. Like almost all other conglomerates, it has diversified into real estate and urban development. The group operates largely from its Bogotá base but has branches and companies in four other major towns.

### *5. Conglomerate Cementos Especiales*

This conglomerate is relatively new. The parent company was founded in 1957 in Bogotá (Silva 1976). The conglomerate has grown mainly in the production of building materials, particularly cement. It is characterized by vertical integration around this base, with expansion into steel and metal working. In addition, the conglomerate has diversified into tourism and reforestation. In 1975 it incorporated 9 companies, of which it controls 7. It operates mainly from its Bogotá base and has extended into the northeast market for building materials, with one company in Santander and two in Norte Santander.

### *6. Conglomerate Tejidos Unica*

This conglomerate has long historical roots. The parent company was founded as Tejidos del Occidente in 1929 in Manizales. It is based on the manufacture of textile fibers and fabrics and has developed some vertical integration around this base via the making of machines and machine parts. The conglomerate, which operates regionally, has diversified in a number of other branches: machines for ice making, mining and quarrying, building materials, and construction. The strong regional base of this conglomerate, which controls 9 companies, is evidenced by the key role played by the Corporación Financiera de Caldas since the mid-1960s. The conglomerate operates entirely from its base in Caldas.

### *7. Conglomerate Colcurtidos*

This is a relatively small conglomerate whose parent company was founded in Bogotá in 1913. Its main line is the processing of hides and the manufacture of leather products for the domestic market and, since the 1960s, also for export. The parent company had already acquired a leading position in the mechanized processing of leather in the mid-1940s when, after absorbing an Antioqueño competitor, it had a 63% market share (Gallo 1976). In the 1970s its dominant position grew stronger: Gallo estimates that 2 companies within the conglomerate produced 80% of value added for the 18 companies active in this branch. He also indicates that in addition to these 18 companies, 839 artisan establishments were estimated to contribute only 25% of the national production (Gallo 1976:39–40). In 1975 the conglomerate controlled 5 companies in the two main industrial centers of Bogotá and Medellin. One of these companies specializes in the buying of hides and has branches in the principal livestock centers.

### *8. Conglomerate Industrial de Gaseosas*

This Medellin-based conglomerate is dedicated mainly to the production and distribution of soft drinks, for which it holds licensing links with Coca Cola, among others. The conglomerate comprises 15 companies, 12 of which are under its control. The other 3 companies, in which it holds only a minor share, provide raw material inputs. The conglomerate operates nationwide, with branches in many major towns.

### *9. Conglomerate Cementos Samper*

The parent company of this conglomerate was founded as early as 1905. It is dedicated mainly to the production, distribution, and sales of building materials. The group has also vertically integrated downward by engaging in the mining and quarrying of key raw material inputs. In 1975 the conglomerate consisted of 15 companies, of which it controlled 12. It operates mainly in the Bogotá regional building materials market, which is also reflected in the location of its constituent companies.

### *10. Conglomerate Cadenalco*

The parent company of this relatively new conglomerate was founded in 1959. The base consists of a large chain of department stores, with establishments all through the country. Around this retail-trade core, some backward vertical integration has been developed by the incorporation of wholesale activities and also the manufacturing of products such as clothing. Also, the group has moved into real estate for the purpose of renting out shops. This conglomerate operates nationwide, with branches in all major towns. Most subsidiary companies, however, are concentrated in the main industrial and commercial centers, notably Medellin.

### *11. Conglomerate Eternit*

The parent of this group was founded in 1942 in Bogotá by Eternit International (a North American firm), with a 40% participation by Colombians, who soon obtained a majority share. In 1944, in response to high transport costs, the parent company founded subsidiary companies in Cali and Barranquilla. Until 1968, the company had a monopoly on asbestos cement products. In the mid-1970s, a competing firm established in 1967 in Manizales (Colombit SA) entered the market and managed to obtain a 20% market share (Samper 1976).

In 1975 the conglomerate comprised 13 companies, 7 of which were under majority control. Although its main line is building materials, around which it is vertically integrated (from asbestos mining to final products), the group has diversified into closely related lines such as metal structures. The conglomerate operates from all four major industrial centers of the country.

***12. Conglomerate Manuelita***

Although the company that presently constitutes the parent of this conglomerate was founded in 1947, the Hacienda Manuelita is of much earlier origin (1864). The conglomerate has developed on the production of sugar, alcohol, and molasses. At its core are 5 large integrated sugar plantations/mills. The conglomerate has moved into the manufacture of needed chemical inputs and packing materials, as well as transport and the export trade of sugar, and has diversified into food products, particularly comestibles and conserves. In 1975 it comprised 15 companies, 8 of which it controlled. In view of its agro-base, most companies are located in the Valle, its area of origin. Through diversification, the conglomerate has begun to operate companies and branches in 7 other regions.

***13. Conglomerate Confecciones Colombia***

The parent company of this relatively small conglomerate comprising 5 companies was established in 1940. The group's main activity is clothing (Everfitt). It has integrated vertically from agricultural production of some raw materials, to a retail distribution chain. Its major center of operations is Medellin.

***14. Conglomerate Tejicondor***

This is a vertically integrated group of companies dedicated to the production of textile fibers and fabrics. It has developed a wide range of textile products, both natural and synthetic. The vertical integration has been strengthened by the incorporation of machine and tool making and the commercialization of production, both at home and abroad. The conglomerate is composed of 9 companies, 5 of which it controls, and operates almost exclusively from its Antioqueño base.

***15. Conglomerate Compañia Nacional de Chocolates***

The basis for this conglomerate was laid in 1920, with the founding of the parent company in Medellin. By 1941, two subsidiary factories had been established in Bogotá and Manizales, and during the same period the company developed its own national distribution network. At the end of the 1950s, the company moved into the production of its principal raw material, cacao. A few years later it diversified into coffee roasting for the domestic market. In the early 1970s, further diversification took place into food products (vegetable oils and fats) (Forero 1976). In 1975, the conglomerate comprised 6 companies all of which were under majority control. This conglomerate operates companies and branch plants in the core regions as well as in other regions.

***16. Conglomerate Coltabacos***

The parent company of this conglomerate was founded in 1919 in Medellin. The conglomerate is almost exclusively dedicated to the production and commercialization of cigars and cigarettes. It is vertically integrated around the commercialization of "light tobacco" (in which it has a monopoly position) and the making of cigarettes and required inputs such as paper, glue, and so forth. The conglomerate has diversified around this integrated core into tourism, real estate, mining, and the metallurgical industry. In 1975 the conglomerate comprised 16 companies, 9 of which it controlled. It operates companies and branches in all four major industrial centers and in the tobacco areas.

***17. Conglomerate Fabricato***

The origin of this textile conglomerate can be traced back to the first decades of Colombia's industrial development. Its parent company was founded in 1923 in Medellin after a merger of companies (Brew 1977). The group is dedicated to the processing of raw cotton fibers and to the manufacture of natural, artificial, and mixed fibers and fabrics. As part of a vertical integration process, the group extended into machine making and the production of machine parts. In 1975, it was composed of 9 companies, 5 of which it controlled. Historically, the group is of Antioqueño origin and has always remained Antioqueño. Almost all its constituent companies are located in and around Medellin.

***18. Conglomerate Argos***

The base of this sizable conglomerate was laid in 1934 when its parent company, Cementos Argos, was founded in Medellin (Silva 1976). The conglomerate's basic core developed in building materials, cement making, cement products, and brick making. It has achieved a dominant position not only in its own region, but also, via subsidiaries, in the Costa and Valle regions. In addition, it has diversified into tourism and real estate development. In 1975 the conglomerate contained 19 companies, 11 of which it controlled. The economic strategy of Argos is reflected in the location of its constituent companies, in that almost all of these are found in the three regions previously mentioned.

***19. Conglomerate Postobon***

This is a relatively homogeneous and vertically integrated group of 20 companies dedicated to the production and distribution of soft drinks, and to the production of ingredients, bottles, taps, transport, publicity, etc. The parent company is one of the oldest companies in the country, having been founded in 1904 under the name Posada Tobon. The element of geographical market control is reflected clearly in the locational pattern of this conglomerate, which operates branch plants and subsidiary companies in 19 of the 23 departments that existed in 1975.

***20. Conglomerate Coltejer***

This conglomerate also has a long history. Its parent company was founded in 1907 in Medellin and fairly soon achieved an oligopolistic leadership position in the manufacture of textile fibers and fabrics, on the basis of which an elaborate integrated group of companies was developed. With these companies, the conglomerate has moved in both a backward (machine and machine part making) and forward direction (marketing of textile and clothing products). At a later stage, it diversified into a number of other branches of activity such as paper pulp, agroindustry, iron and aluminum, parts for car making, and so forth. However, textiles has remained its main base. The 7 companies in this conglomerate engaged in textile and clothing contributed 16% of total national production in these two sectors. Of the total production of all textile conglomerates listed previously, the Coltejer conglomerate alone participated with 49% in 1975. Notwithstanding its strong national position, the conglomerate continues to operate from its Antioqueño base. Twenty three of the 26 companies that could be traced are found in and around Medellin.

***21. Conglomerate Santo Domingo***

Unlike most of the conglomerates enumerated herein, this conglomerate, which has an important historical development in the Costa Atlantica, is a diverse group of companies without any clear pattern of vertical integration or diversification. Early fortunes were made in food products produced under licence (Colmenares 1977). In 1975 the group produced food products, beverages, transport and metal products. In that year the conglomerate was composed of 37 companies, 19 of which were "shared" with other conglomerates, notably Colinsa and Bavaria.

Although its historical regional orientation toward the Costa Atlantica is still clearly visible in the sense that more than half the companies are located in Barranquilla, the conglomerate presently owns companies in all major industrial centers, with a notable concentration in Bogotá and Medellin.

***22. Conglomerate Avianca***

The Avianca conglomerate's main activity is air transport. It was founded in 1919 as Scadta by German immigrants in Barranquilla. During World War II, Avianca was nationalized and its seat moved to Bogotá. The company was granted a monopoly for postage by airmail. In the 1970s, the conglomerate managed to control 75% of air travel and more than 80% of air cargo through its various airline companies (Colmenares 1983:179). In 1975 it comprised 15 companies, 9 of which were under majority control. Apart from its main transport activity, the conglomerate has diversified into the tourist industry, real estate, and development. The conglomerate operates on a nationwide scale by means of branch offices or subsidiary companies in most of the more populated regions.

***23. Conglomerate Colinsa***

The parent company of this conglomerate was founded in 1933. It has a very similar structure to that of the Santo Domingo conglomerate. It has become an investment group holding a variety of subsidiary companies, and has its historical base in the Costa Atlantica. These similarities are not very surprising if one recalls that there are strong financial and personal interlinkages between the two conglomerates. In 1975 Colinsa was active in agroindustry; livestock; paper products; printing; beverages; chemical, metal, and nonmetallic mineral industries; transport, finance, and real estate. It included 20 companies in 1975, 10 of which were under majority control.

The historical development within the Costa Atlantica is still clearly visible in the sense that 10 companies owned by the conglomerate are located in Barranquilla. The remaining 10 companies are located in the other two principal industrial centers, Bogotá and Medellin.

### *24. Conglomerate Bavaria*

The Bavaria conglomerate has a long and complex development history (Bavaria 1966 and personal interviews). In 1889 its parent company was established in Bogotá, by a German immigrant, after a first trial in San Gil, Santander, under the name Koop's Deutsche Brauerei Bavaria. In an earlier section (see pp. 131–132), I described the historical pattern in which this company established its oligopolistic leadership by means of a national network of breweries, and how vertical integration played a key role in this process. In the 1960s the company engaged in a massive process of diversification into agroindustry, metal working, real estate, petrochemicals, plastics, etc., which established the basis for the present conglomerate. In 1975 Bavaria comprised 63 companies, 35 of which were under its control. The historical regional base of this conglomerate is still visible in that almost 50% of the affiliated companies are located in Bogotá. From this elaborate base the conglomerate has extended into a number of major towns. The close interlinkages between Bavaria and the Santo Domingo and Colinsa conglomerates, together with the Avianca group, form one superconglomerate. This is reflected in the relatively large number of companies in Barranquilla.

# CHAPTER SIX

# COTTON AND TEXTILES: A CASE STUDY OF RURAL AND REGIONAL CHANGE

## Introduction

In this chapter I discuss the development of cotton production in more detail, as a case study of rural and regional change. Since the early 1950s, cotton production has developed from a situation in which it constituted only a mere fraction of domestic demand to one in which it met this demand completely, becoming in the mid-1970s the single most important nontraditional export crop—excluding the equally nontraditional but nonlegal crops such as marijuana and coca.

The production of cotton underwent considerable change both at the microlevel and in the institutional setting in which it took place. Not surprisingly, a considerable spatial reallocation of cotton production also occurred, which in turn had important dynamic implications at the level of particular regions. This combination of factors operating simultaneously and interacting with each other makes it an interesting case to study from the perspective put forward in Chapter 4.

This chapter is organized as follows. After a brief overview of main trends in cotton production, I discuss the changing market and institutional setting in which production has developed. I argue that the simultaneous occurrence of three factors conditioned the rapid expansion of that production: namely, the consolidation behind protective barriers of the textile industry; the role of government in providing the general economic and specific physical infrastructural conditions as well as in mediating between industrial and agricultural interests; and, the organization of cotton producers at the national level. Only by organizing nationally rather than locally could the cotton growers counterbalance the monopsonic power of the textile companies.

Success, in terms of the rapid spread and growth of cotton production and development of exports, culminated in internationalization of cotton production. This, in turn, called for a rearrangement of the institutional setting in which the role of government was considerably altered and reduced. When textile companies also became export oriented, the prime justification for the national organization of cotton growers disappeared, because prices were determined internationally. A proliferation of associations resulted, to some extent in response to technological changes in production.

I then analyze the changes in the structure of production (1950–1980), with respect to both the producers and the producing regions. With regard to the latter, a shift occurred toward the Costa Atlantica, in which almost two-thirds of total production came to be concentrated. This shift was due to three factors: the displacement of cotton by other (more profitable) crops in the interior, the availability of low-cost labor and land, and the reorientation of production toward international exports.

Changes in the structure of production are analyzed mainly for the Costa Atlantica. Until the end of the 1960s cotton was produced in all size classes, although more in the medium-sized class than others. Small-scale production declined in importance in the 1970s, not only in relative, but also in absolute terms. A second phenomenon was the growing significance in the Costa Atlantica of land rental and of "urban" cotton growers, which are seen to be interrelated. The increasing technicalization of production meant that know-how and the timely access to specialist services and inputs became key requirements. The small rural producer lost out on both counts and was replaced by urban capitalists and agricultural specialists.

I then discuss some of the principal impacts of cotton production in the Costa Atlantica, contrasting the developments in the departments of Cesar and Cordoba. In the former, a number of new developments were triggered, ranging from formation of the new department to the expansion of government, commerce, personal services, and industry. The comparison with Cordoba gives rise to the conclusion that, given the rather regressive distribution of direct benefits from cotton production, the positive impact in Cesar was due to the generation of indirect effects and to the externalization of some of the negative effects to other departments.

## Overall Trends and Organizing Forces

Until the 1950s, cotton growing in Colombia was fairly limited in scale, although its origins can be traced back to the precolonial era. Traditionally, cotton was a peasant crop, a perennial interplanted with major food crops. It was found in three regions (Leurquin 1966): Santander/Boyaca, where its cultivation dates back to precolonial times; the north of Antioquia, where it is of much more recent origin, partly grown in response to the locally expanding textile industry; and the Costa Atlantica, where it was mostly grown by peasants who had received land in tenure from big cattle owners with the obligation to turn the land into pasture at the end of the contract period (3 to 4 years). The perennial cotton gave a short fiber which, due to primitive cultivation practices, was not very suitable for large-scale manufacturing textile production. Attempts had been made as early as the 1930s to develop annual and monocultivation varieties, but except during World War II, neither textile companies nor government were sufficiently interested to stimulate domestic production.

Some of the main indicators are summarized in Table 6.1. Four main periods can be identified. In the first, 1923–1950, the growing demand for cotton was met by a growing volume of imports. The second period (1951–1960) was one in which cotton production grew much faster than did domestic demand. The third (1960–1967) was an intermediate period in which cotton import substitution developed into surplus production for export. The situation changed again at the end of the 1960s (fourth period), when the textile companies also sought to expand through exports. Not only domestic supply but also domestic demand now became influenced by international market conditions.

Supply conditions as well as market conditions changed over time, in terms of both technology and organization of production. Improved varieties and cultivation practices helped to bring about considerable increases in yields. The adoption of these innovations made possible and stimulated changes in the organization of production. In the following sections I show how these changes came about and what their consequences were in terms of the production structure.

The remainder of this section is devoted to the three main organizing forces: the textile industry—the principal user of cotton fiber; the cotton growers associations; and the government as mediator between group interests and as provider of infrastructural facilities.

### Textile Companies and Demand

Textile manufacturing as distinct from artisan craft production began its development at the beginning of this century, after a long period of repeated failures (Ospina Vasquez 1974). Historically, its development concentrated in Antioquia. In the period 1902–1920, some 12 manufacturing firms were founded in and around Medellin (Brew 1977:395–403), but textile firms were also established in other parts of the country, for example, in Samaca (Boyaca), Cartagena, Barranquilla, Bogotá, and Cali (Montenegro 1982).

TABLE 6.1
Main Cotton Indicators for Colombia, 1923–1983 (metric tons)

| *Year* | *Production* | *Imports* | *Exports* | *Apparent consumption* | *Apparent consumption per capita* | *Fiber exports in fabrics* | *Total demand* |
|---|---|---|---|---|---|---|---|
| 1923 | 2,137 | 62 | | 2,199 | | | |
| 1924 | 2,263 | 405 | | 2,668 | | | |
| 1925 | 2,976 | 628 | | 3,604 | | | |
| 1926 | 2,850 | 1,049 | | 3,899 | | | |
| 1927 | 2,790 | 1,551 | | 4,341 | | | |
| 1928 | 2,664 | 6 | | 2,670 | | | |
| 1929 | 2,108 | 468 | | 2,576 | | | |
| 1930 | 2,463 | 196 | | 2,659 | | | |
| 1931 | 2,700 | 934 | | 3,634 | | | |
| 1932 | 3,001 | 1,351 | | 4,352 | | | |
| 1933 | 2,510 | 2,225 | | 4,735 | | | |
| 1934 | 3,142 | 2,494 | | 5,636 | | | |
| 1935 | 2,862 | 33,666 | | 36,528 | | | |
| 1936 | 4,450 | 2,568 | | 7,018 | | | |
| 1937 | 5,841 | 3,368 | | 9,209 | | | |
| 1938 | 6,281 | 4,268 | | 10,549 | | | |
| 1939 | 7,047 | 6,721 | | 13,768 | | | |
| 1940 | 2,860 | 8,168 | | 11,046 | | | |
| 1941 | 3,850 | 17,575 | | 21,405 | | | |
| 1942 | 4,922 | 19,002 | | 23,924 | | | |
| 1943 | 4,420 | 17,093 | | 21,513 | | | |
| 1944 | 5,731 | 17,742 | | 23,473 | | | |
| 1945 | 4,738 | 14,977 | | 19,715 | | | |
| 1946 | 4,832 | 20,702 | | 25,534 | | | |
| 1947 | 6,392 | 15,634 | | 22,026 | | | |
| 1948 | 6,080 | 16,675 | | 22,755 | | | |
| 1949 | 6,637 | 16,457 | | 23,094 | | | |
| 1950 | 8,473 | 21,485 | | 29,958 | | | |
| 1951 | 6,474 | 13,849 | | 20,323 | | | |
| 1952 | 10,567 | 18,235 | | 28,802 | | | |
| 1953 | 17,031 | 15,108 | | 32,139 | | | |
| 1954 | 27,884 | 5,719 | | 33,603 | | | |
| 1955 | 24,672 | 2,404 | | 27,076 | 2.05 | | |
| 1956 | 22,529 | 12,407 | | 34,936 | 2.56 | | |
| 1957 | 20,573 | 14,738 | | 35,311 | 2.51 | | |
| 1958 | 25,873 | 10,864 | | 36,737 | 2.53 | | |
| 1959 | 56,408 | 6,181 | 1,003 | 61,586 | 4.12 | | |
| 1960 | 68,732 | 717 | 29,113 | 40,336 | 2.61 | | |
| 1961 | 71,509 | 337 | 24,608 | 47,238 | 2.96 | | |
| 1962 | 80,050 | 564 | 26,010 | 54,604 | 3.32 | | |
| 1963 | 64,507 | 1,726 | 2,850 | 63,383 | 3.74 | | |
| 1964 | 63,381 | 3,040 | 13,697 | 52,724 | 3.01 | | |

TABLE 6.1 *(Continued)*

| *Year* | *Production* | *Imports* | *Exports* | *Apparent consumption* | *Apparent consumption per capita* | *Fiber exports in fabrics* | *Total demand* |
|---|---|---|---|---|---|---|---|
| 1965 | 58,328 | 8,914 | 10,462 | 54,675 | 3.04 | 2,105 | 56,780 |
| 1966 | 75,360 | 6,528 | 12,552 | 62,568 | 3.38 | 6,708 | 69,336 |
| 1967 | 96,582 | 530 | 35,782 | 55,043 | 2.90 | 6,287 | 61,330 |
| 1968 | 120,137 | 904 | 58,222 | 54,388 | 2.79 | 8,431 | 62,819 |
| 1969 | 125,238 | 902 | 62,353 | 54,620 | 2.72 | 9,167 | 63,787 |
| 1970 | 127,784 | 1,463 | 57,656 | 61,014 | 2.96 | 10,577 | 71,591 |
| 1971 | 112,328 | 904 | 42,095 | 56,108 | 2.65 | 15,029 | 71,137 |
| 1972 | 144,436 | 1,003 | 67,834 | 55,394 | 2.54 | 22,211 | 77,605 |
| 1973 | 114,847 | 6,551 | 37,692 | 60,379 | 2.68 | 23,327 | 83,706 |
| 1974 | 145,782 | 897 | 49,654 | 74,143 | 3.23 | 22,882 | 97,025 |
| 1975 | 138,910 | 786 | 80,015 | 38,081 | 1.62 | 21,600 | 59,681 |
| 1976 | 142,085 | 945 | 61,435 | 61,395 | 2.53 | 20,200 | 81,595 |
| 1977 | 160,287 | 693 | 74,527 | 65,153 | 2.62 | 21,300 | 86,153 |
| 1978 | 110,417 | 392 | 34,510 | 53,799 | 2.10 | 22,500 | 76,299 |
| 1979 | 97,155 | 7,526 | 28,543 | 57,538 | 2.19 | 18,600 | 76,138 |
| 1980 | 121,205 | 4,255 | 49,601 | 54,859 | 2.03 | 21,000 | 75,859 |
| 1981 | 124,084 | 638 | 63,041 | 43,681 | 1.57 | 18,000 | 61,681 |
| 1982 | 52,076 | NA | 4,166 | 33,910 | 1.18[a] | 14,000 | 47,910 |
| 1983 | 51,797 | NA | 3,590 | 34,307 | 1.16[a] | 13,900 | 48,207 |

*Note:* [a]estimated. There are small differences in the data presented by INTRA and by Montenegro for the period 1934–1947. I have followed the INTRA version.
*Sources:* INTRA (1972); Federacion Nacional de Algodoneros *Informe* (various years); Montenegro (1982:162).

World War I like the earlier War of a Thousand Days (1899–1902), stimulated domestic supply; the earlier occasion had in fact already effectively destroyed Santander's important artisan textile production.

The development of textile production was characterized by two features: the formation of a national oligopolistic structure, and the geographical concentration in and around Medellin. The growth of Medellin as a center of textile production was due to a number of factors. First, an entrepreneurial elite in the region had accumulated capital, first in gold mining and later in the coffee trade. Second, as part of the gold mining past, an embryonic capital market existed that enabled the industrialists to expand their capital through the emission of shares (Brew 1977:396). Third, the Antioqueño colonization and the growth of coffee exports had stimulated the emergence of an important regional market for textiles (Urrutia 1979). Fourth, the agro-processing of coffee in the towns had generated experiences of factory work and of industrial wage-labor relations on the part of the new industrialists and also in terms of the formation of an urban working class (Montenegro 1982:119). Fifth, in the non-coffee northern part of the department in particular, a relative overpopulation developed in the rural areas that was in search of income opportunities. Textile companies therefore were able to obtain the predominantly unskilled and female labor force that they needed. Finally, the attractiveness of the Medellin area for textile activities was enhanced by the availability of hydraulic power as a source of energy, which other regions lacked. The following quotation gives an idea of this early geographical concentration: "In 1923 there were some 1,600 looms and 30,000 spindles in the country, of which some 650 looms and 16,500 spindles were located in the Medellin area" (Ospina Vasques 1974:497; translation mine). This geographical concentration is an important ingredient of the process of oligopoly formation. It should be emphasized, however, that Antioqueño firms were not always the largest: in 1924 the Fabrica de Hilares y Tejidos de Obregon, located in Barranquilla, was the largest company in the country (ibid.: 475).

It is surprising to see how quickly the process of oligopoly formation developed, particularly in view of the difficulty of communications (Poveda Ramos 1970). Even before World War II, two companies—Coltejer and Fabricato—had taken leading positions in the regional market of Antioquia through the acquistion of rival firms; during the war they consolidated their position nationally, by taking over firms in other regions. In 1942, Coltejer, acquired the Compañia de Tejidos de Rosellon, which in 1919 absorbed the Compañia Unidad de Tejidos and the Fabrica de Tejidos de Antonio Hernandez (all Antioqueño companies). Coltejer acquired Sedeco in Barranquilla in 1944, and in 1959 it acquired Fatanesa in the same town (Colmenares 1977). The second leading firm, Fabricato, took over the Compañia de Tejidos de Medellin in 1939, which, in turn, had acquired the Compañia Antioqueño de Tejidos in 1940. In 1941 Fabricato absorbed the Compañia de Tejidos Santa Fe (Cundinamarca), and in 1946 the Fabrica Colombiana de Hilados de Lana (Filana) and Paños Vicuna Ltda (ibid).

What caused this process of concentration? It seems that the main reason was the temporary reduction of competitive imports during the world wars and the similar effect of the reduced capacity to import during the Great Depression, both of which amplified the market and profit opportunities for Colombian firms. However, because it was difficult to expand total production capacity, due to the equally great difficulty of importing machinery from England or the United States, a firm gained greater benefit from the profitable market situation by taking over rival firms, thus increasing its own market share. Such an action also strengthened the firm's capacity to compete for scarce foreign exchange to enable it to continue to import vital inputs (including cotton from Peru), machine parts, and equipment (Montenegro 1982:149).

The existence of a large regional home base certainly favored the emergence of leading firms from Antioquia. In 1945, the two firms employed 9,000 of the 15,000 workers in the Antioquia textile industry. The import substitution policies of the 1950s helped to further consolidate this oligopolistic market structure. The regional distribution of the textile industry continued to be biased toward Antioquia. In 1945, 55% of value added in this sector was generated there; in 1958 this rose to 67% and in 1968 to 69%.

The post–World War II development of the textile industry can be characterized by three elements: the introduction into the country of synthetic-fiber production; the appearance of foreign companies; and the development of textile exports by the late 1960s. The introduction of chemical textile production was largely related to the entry of foreign enterprises (Misas 1973). In 1942 artificial fiber production had been started by Indurayon, in which Tejicondor had a minor share. In 1950 Celanese was founded, with 75% foreign and 25% Colombian capital, but it was not until the 1960s that synthetic fibers started to become important. In 1964, Enka de Colombia, Polimeros, and Nylon de Colombia were founded. Colombian textile firms held important capital participations in the latter two (DANE 1972:191). The share of these artifical fibers in total artificial and natural fiber demand increased from 6.5% in 1966 to 30% in 1974 and 38% in 1978 (Soler & Prieto 1982). In other words, the competition of these fibers with cotton became real only in the second half of the period considered here. In the same period, however, manufactured exports of textiles increased, so that total demand for cotton fibers continued to grow.

The oligopolization of textile firms had obvious implications for the structure of the cotton market: "Cotton yarn is produced in 15 plants of which 13 belong to companies employing more than 100 persons. The majority of these plants are integrated (spinning and weaving). A very high degree of concentration can be observed. In 1968, 77 percent of the production of cotton yarns was realized by two firms" (DANE 1972:181). These two firms were Coltejer and Fabricato. In 1980 these still held a dominant position, although their share had declined to 65% probably as a result of a relatively greater use of artifical fibers. Nevertheless, a concentrated monopsonistic market structure continued to prevail: 4 firms buy 83% of the cotton, the remainder is bought by 20 other firms (Soler and Prieto 1982:149).

The development of the textile industry did not automatically generate the development of cotton production. After the early establishment and growth of the industry, imports of cotton fibers rapidly increased in importance. Statistics presented by Montenegro (1982) show that imports rose more rapidly in the mid-1920s, declined at the beginning of the Great Depression, and rose again thereafter. Others have calculated a similar trend but with a higher starting share of imports. For instance, the data presented by Ospina Vasquez for the years 1925–1930 indicate that the volume of imported raw cotton and fibers was on average 43% of domestic cotton production (Ospina Vasques 1974:493). This proportion subsequently increased, as can be concluded from the following observation made in 1946: "The extent of this crop in the country and the volume of cotton production are not proportional to the importance which the manufacture of cotton yarns has acquired, since national cotton producers supply only one fifth of the 20,000,000 kilos consumed by manufacturing industry" (Contraloria 1946:192). The relative importance of cotton imports over time is shown in Figure 6.1. Figure 6.1 shows that the share of cotton imports rose to a maximum of 78% in the mid-1940s. Only *after* 1953 did their importance start to decline relatively quickly. In other words, the growth of the industry, which took place largely *before* the 1950s, did not immediately stimulate cotton production, for several reasons. First, there were technological reasons to import cotton: local perennial cotton was not of a uniform and high quality and long fiber was not locally produced. Second, given the conditions under which perennial cotton was produced, it surely must have been rather supply inelastic. Third, during most of the 1930s international prices were relatively low (Montenegro 1982). This may also explain why textile companies resisted attempts by

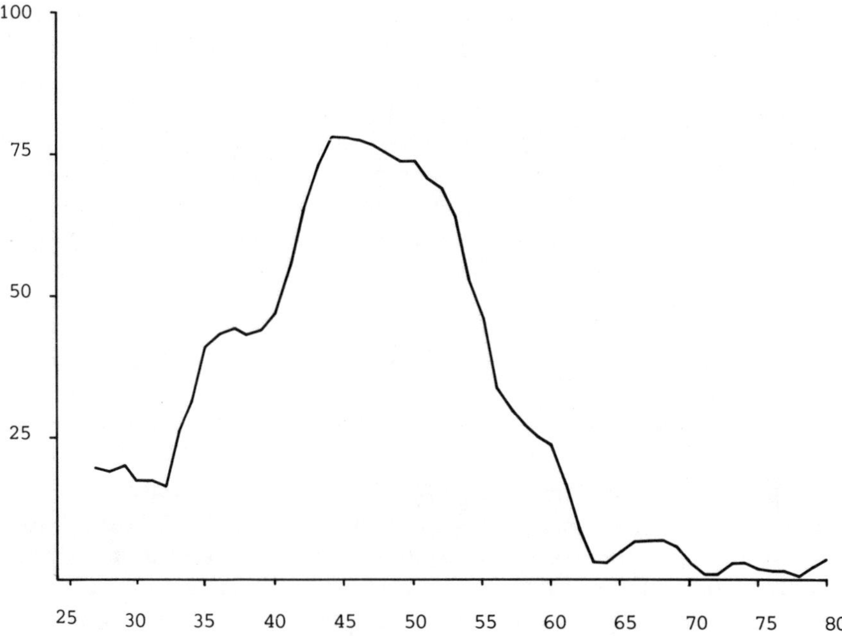


FIGURE 6.1. Cotton imports share in total domestic demand, 1932–1980, Colombia (moving average $n = 5$). *Note*: Based on Table 6.1.

government and local (annual) cotton growers to stimulate domestic production, much to the frustration of the growers (pp. 212–216).

The situation changed during the 1950s, when textiles firms shifted from a heavy bias toward imports to almost complete reliance on domestically produced cotton. In 1947, the three major textile companies—Coltejer, Fabricato and Tejicondor—founded the Instituto de Fomento Algodonero (IFA) in Medellin and in 1950 they set up DIAGONAL to buy, transport, store, and distribute cotton. The IFA was converted into a public agency for the classification of domestic cotton qualities and also to operate cotton gins in the country. Three factors can explain this change. The first is related to government policy. In 1950, as part of its import substitution cum protection policy, the Colombian government established high tariffs on imported cotton fabrics and in 1952 it prohibited imports of cotton fabrics altogether. In other words, the national market was more or less at the disposal of the domestic textile industry. Once the market was protected, the companies could accept the eventual higher costs and/or lower quality of domestically produced cotton. Given the concentrated market structure, higher costs could subsequently be passed on to the Colombian consumer. A second factor was the rise of international prices due to the "Korea boom," which no doubt stimulated the textile industry to look for domestic substitutes. Third, the devaluation of 1957, by raising the local price of imported fibers, undoubtedly also helped to change the attitude of the textile companies.

## Government and Infrastructural Provisions

With regard to the role of the state vis-à-vis the development of agriculture in general and cotton production in particular, three phases can be identified.

The first, which continued until 1950, was characterized by very limited and experimental direct government interference. The second, which lasted into the mid-1960s, was marked by the establishment and further development of a support system for modern agriculture. The overall orientation was toward import substitution in both industry and agriculture, in an attempt to cope with the recurrent balance-of-payments problems. This closed-shop orientation inevitably created conflicts of interest between industrialists and agriculturalists as intersectoral integration proceeded, and government thus became a mediator. During the third and last period (1965–1980), both agriculture and industry have developed an international market orientation. The internationalization of cotton and textile production also brought external determination of the conflicts of interest; this had a profound effect on the role of government in that its intermediation activities were no longer needed.

In the first decades of the twentieth century, Colombian economic development was completely dominated by the rapid expansion of coffee exports. If there was any agricultural policy at all, it consisted of improving the physical infrastructure for coffee exports and some ad hoc measures with which to deal with rural conflicts caused by its production. The growing problems of food supply and rising urban food prices resulting from rapidly increasing urban demand induced government to take active steps toward stimulating agricultural development. Some experimentation and research was sponsored (the first experimental station was set up at Espinal in 1930), and the Agrarian Bank was founded in 1931. In 1944, agricultural policy acquired a new dimension with the creation of the marketing agency INA *(Instituto Nacional de Abastecimiento)*. Although INA was mainly concerned with the supply of urban food, it is significant in marking the beginning of a new trend to create specialized public agencies. The agricultural support system was expanded in 1950 with the previously mentioned IFA and in 1956 the Department for Agricultural Research (DIA), which in 1962 was converted into the Colombian Institute for Agriculture (ICA). ICA expanded IFA's research on and extension of new varieties, and more specialized field stations were set up. In 1968, INA was replaced by the Institute for Agricultural Marketing (IDEMA), which also took over operation of the network of cotton gins that IFA had been developing since 1948. IFA also disappeared in the reorganization, partly reflecting the strength that producer associations had meantime acquired in the distribution of know-how, inputs, and machinery.

Finally, the Agrarian Bank played only a limited role in relation to cotton credits. Of considerable significance, however, was Law 26 of 1959, which is considered "the first formal attempt to incorporate private capital in the financing of the agricultural sector, by means of obliging the commercial banks established in the country, to direct 15% of the deposits at sight and on term to agriculture, livestock and fishery" (FEDESARROLLO 1975:34). In 1966, the Agricultural Financial Fund (FFA) was created. This organization complemented the financial arrangements stipulated in Law 26 and had the specific purpose of improving credit facilities for annual crops. In 1973, this system of "enforced" commercial credit was unified in the Agriculture and Livestock Fund (ALF), financed through the emission of bonds that commercial banks are required to underwrite on the terms stipulated in Law 26. Although the Central Bank administers the ALF, the commercial banks deal with fund applications in the same way as normal credit applications, requiring collateral, and so forth. The main effect of these government measures was to ensure an adequate supply of credit at subsidized rates of interest.

Although the government does not intervene at all in food crops, except by means of intervention (minimum) prices, which do not differ greatly from market prices, a different situation has developed in the cotton (and sugar) industries. Prior to 1962, cotton prices were negotiated directly by cotton growers' associations and by DIAGONAL. Government intervention in price fixing occurred occasionally on an ad hoc basis, and at the insistence of the cotton growers association. In 1962 this intervention became institutionalized, thus marking the success of the cotton growers in catering almost entirely to internal demand (see Figure 6.1). In that year, the Superintendencia de Regulación Económica was set up to determine not only the price of cotton but also that of cottonseed. The determination by decree of the new prices was preceded each year by extensive consultations with both cotton growers' associations and the textile companies.

Cotton surpluses had been produced since the early 1960s. A national Cotton Fund was created (financed by a mark-up over cost of cotton ginning) and IFA was authorized to dump any surpluses on external markets and to finance the losses out of the new fund. By 1965, however, it had become evident that surpluses not only had become a permanent feature but also that they were growing rapidly. New government measures, in particular the 1967 devaluation and the export-subsidy scheme, stimulated exports (Jaramillo 1977). As a result of the devaluation, the international price level rose above the internal price level, thus making cotton exports competitive. The share of cotton exports in total production rose rapidly from 18% in 1965 to 45% in 1970, reaching a peak of 58% in 1975. These changes had considerable implications for the internal price system. The favorable international market conditions caused the cotton growers associations to press for elimination by government decree of the system of price setting, which was entirely geared to the domestic market. The government yielded, and in 1970 the price-control system was abolished and replaced by direct negotiations under government supervision between the cotton growers associations and DIAGONAL (*libertad vigilada*). Because the textile companies had also developed export markets, they began to support the exporting cotton growers in their bid to have international cotton prices (Liverpool index) determine the domestic price level. In 1974, domestic prices were denationalized, or, rather, internationalized, and negotiations between industry and the cotton growers were restricted to specification of the quality grade scheme for domestic cotton.

Until 1973 the international market for cotton was relatively stable, in no small degree a result of the stabilization policy of the United States government. This policy was suspended in 1973 and accumulated stocks were sold, putting pressure on the international price. The oil crisis and the emerging economic recession intensified the deep plunge in cotton prices that began in 1975 (UNCTAD 1981). Rising costs of production, compounded by very low yields in 1977 when a record of cultivated area was registered, all contributed to a major loss for the Colombian cotton growers. This severe crisis, with its accumulated debts, caused the cotton growers' associations to push for the reintroduction of negotiated prices. In 1978, exerting considerable political pressure, the associations managed to achieve an agreement with the textile companies, signed in 1979, setting a minimum or bottom price linked to the Liverpool index. This agreement was reached without government intervention, although pressure was brought to bear on government to ease the effects of the debt crisis by providing special credit facilities.

Early in the 1970s the cotton growers associations reached the apex of their power, based on the internal market in which they countered the virtual monopsony of the textile companies by a virtual monopoly of producers. Their growing strength meant that less government intervention was wanted. In fact, the growth of the associations was based partly on the displacement of government activities. The move into the international market structurally undermined the position of the cotton growers, whose associations became price takers in a market in which they were marginal producers (the Colombian share in world production has never exceeded 1.5%). Direct government intervention disappeared altogether when the associations took over the cotton ginning installations.

This brief overview of the role of government allows several conclusions to be drawn. First, it is quite evident that the Colombian state did not impose any specific orientation or restriction on the development of cotton production. On the contrary, from the early 1950s in particular, government actively encouraged commercial agriculture by sponsoring development of the agricultural support system (IFA, ICA, IDEMA, Credit Funds). Direct government intervention in relations between textile companies and producer associations, through price controls and the cotton-ginning operation, was geared toward mediation of conflicts within a protected market. With the internationalization of production, first among the cotton growers and then the textile companies, this role of government no longer had any rationale. The state withdrew from direct intervention and reduced its role to general measures of support and promotion.

On the whole, government policies *followed* rather than preceded developments. With the possible important exception of management of the exchange rate, the state served rather than shaped developments in agriculture.

## Producer Associations and the Micro-Organization of Production

The foregoing analyses show that the cotton growers' associations were a powerful force vis-à-vis the government and the textile industry, and it might be concluded that they were a key factor in the fast growth of cotton production. Although this is partially true, it cannot in itself explain why these associations were so successful in the first place.

In the first section of this chapter, I show that the textile industry underwent a rapid process of oligopoly formation leading to an oligopsonistic organization of the domestic cotton market. The creation of DIAGONAL further strengthened the position of the textile companies into a virtual monopsony. Because they were long able to import cotton without government restriction, it is clear that cotton producers were at a disadvantage right from the start. Only through organization could they try to break the market power of the textile companies and to negotiate better price and marketing conditions. This situation was made clear in the report of the first Congreso Algodonero, held in 1957:

> From the moment that the cultivation of annual cotton was initiated in the country, the farmers in the area of Armero [Tolima] realized that they would encounter many obstacles and difficulties in selling their product to strong and organized buyers who were protected by the State and who, in a free market, would impose prices and conditions that would put the producer in an inferior position, short of economic resources and in need of government assistance. (quoted by Ruiz 1973:85–86)

Attempts toward *local* organization had been made in Tolima since the 1930s, for example, the Tolima cooperative in 1936 and the marketing company SOPRALGODON in 1949. The creation of a permanent *national* organization was not given serious consideration until 1951; in the same year the initiative was taken in Tolima to set up the National Federation of Cotton Growers—in short, the Federation. SOPRALGODON's funds and installations were transferred to the new Federation, which became a legal entity in 1953.

The Federation remained the only association of cotton producers until the mid-1960s, but later in that decade and in the 1970s associations proliferated. Before discussing the causes of that proliferation, it will be useful to examine first the role played by the Federation and later by the other associations.

From its inception the Federation not only undertook output marketing activities, but started to purchase and distribute inputs with credit facilities and later also machinery, and to provide technical assistance and extension through its regional committees. Furthermore, existing producers placed no barrier to the entry of new producers, for the simple reason that the size of the domestic market left room for expansion. Moreover, every new producer helped to strengthen the bargaining power of the Federation vis-à-vis textile companies and government.

To appreciate the role of the associations, it is perhaps useful to consider the economic and organizational implications of annual cotton production. First, monocultivation rather than interplanting carries higher risks. Second, a key problem in cultivation is the control of insects, requiring specific knowledge of the (timely) treatment of pests and diseases with pesticides, and so forth. Finally, cotton growing has a strong seasonal labor-demand component, particularly at harvest time. In brief, it is a capital-using and management-intensive production, the latter not least because of the growing number of specialized agencies in the cotton support system. The producer associations not only provided credit, inputs, know-how, and marketing facilities, but above all eased the managerial bottleneck, thus enabling microeconomic development into managerial production at the farm level. The association constituted an intermediate link between individual producers and the specialized external environment. Unlike other industries, the association *preceded* rather than followed the growth of the sector, which perhaps explains the spectacular increase in cotton production during the 1950s and 1960s. Table 6.2 illustrates the role of the associations.

The activities undertaken by the associations naturally developed over time, increasing as both their membership and the area under cultivation grew. At first the associations were active in service and material inputs and in domestic fiber marketing; later, new activities were added. In the 1960s they took over export intermediation from IFA. Aerial crop spraying became another concern (ASOCESAR). In the early 1970s the Federation of Cotton Growers started its own research and seed development programs on its new experimental station. Moreover, it has recently moved into agroindustrial activities, particularly the processing of cotton seeds. The Federation acquired the Graseral Company, and ASOCESAR established Aceites del Cesar. Plans were made to develop backward linkages, for example, the

TABLE 6.2
Institutional Environment of Cotton Production

| | *Public agencies* | | | | | *Producer* | *Private companies* | | | |
|---|---|---|---|---|---|---|---|---|---|---|
| *Institution* | *ICA* | *INCORA* | *IDEMA* | *CAJA* | *PROEXPO* | *associations* | *Banks* | *Aviation* | *Inputs* | *Marketing* |
| Function | | | | | | | | | | |
| Techn. dev. | × | | | | | × | | | × | |
| Seeds | × | | | | | × | | | | |
| Extension | × | × | | | | × | | | × | |
| Credit | | × | | × | | × | × | | | |
| Mat. inputs | | (×) | | | | × | | | × | |
| Spraying | | | | | | × | | × | | |
| Ginning | | | × | | | (×) | | | | |
| Marketing | | | | | | × | | | | × |
| Exports | | | | | × | × | | | | × |
| Register | × | | × | | | × | | | | |

manufacture of pesticides. The cotton crisis brought an abrupt end to these plans, however. Finally, some of the smaller associations, notably in the department of Cesar, have developed closed and multiproduct service organizations; these have been founded by small groups of (large) farmers in order to pool their investments in a way that could not profitably be done at the individual farm level. Economies of scale are realized in fixed investments such as drying sheds, storage silos, cotton-ginning installations, and heavy machinery—an illustration of the advanced stage of Colombia's agrobusiness development.

I have yet to discuss the proliferation of producer associations. Why did this occur when it seems to contradict our earlier statements on the role of the associations? Table 6.3 summarizes the situation for the Costa Atlantica region, where 10 associations existed at the end of the 1970s. The Federation was the first national association founded by producers in the interior (Tolima), which was then the only area producing annual cotton. In 1964, the Corporación Algodonera del Litoral (CORAL) was formed. Although its separation from the Federation was justified on the grounds of regionalism (cotton growers from the Costa Atlantica wanted to free themselves from the domination by those of the Interior who controlled the Federation), this apparently resulted from a conflict of interest. As we shall see later, by 1963 the Costa had become the largest producer and was interested in developing cotton exports. Given their geographical location, the producers in the

TABLE 6.3
Distribution of Number of Cotton Growers, Cultivated Area, and Average Size of Cultivation, by Association, Costa Atlantica, 1977–1978

| | *Growers* | | *Cult. Area* | | *Average size* |
|---|---|---|---|---|---|
| | *No.* | *(%)* | *has* | *(%)* | *(ha)* |
| Federation | 6,021 | 71.6 | 169,748 | 60.0 | 28 |
| Coral | 1,456 | 17.3 | 51,816 | 18.3 | 35 |
| Asocesar | 279 | 3.3 | 26,400 | 9.3 | 95 |
| Asosinu | 243 | 2.9 | 6,425 | 2.3 | 26 |
| Coalcesar | 207 | 2.5 | 8,500 | 3.0 | 41 |
| Cooperar | 82 | 1.0 | 7,500 | 2.6 | 91 |
| Coocesar | 81 | 1.0 | 5,850 | 2.1 | 72 |
| Coadeco | 23 | 0.3 | 1,600 | 0.6 | 70 |
| Agrupar | 10 | 0.1 | 2,700 | 0.9 | 270 |
| Agrumag | 4 | 0.05 | 2,600 | 0.9 | 650 |
| Total (approx.) | 8,406 | 100.0 | 283,000 | 100.0 | 34 |

*Source:* Oficina Coordinadora de Algodon, Medellin (1978).

interior were expected to continue to concentrate on the domestic market and hence were less interested in a deregulation of prices.

The formation of ASOCESAR by growers who separated from CORAL in 1968 is often presented as a problem of representation, that is, the functioning of the association on the principle of "one man one vote," in a situation where production is highly concentrated. The conflict this implied between large and small producers previously had played a minor role, first, because there had been room in the past for marginal producers whose entry was welcomed because it enabled a collective counterbalance to the monopsony of the textile industry. Second, because associations incorporated more functions, indivisibilities and potentials for economies of scale created problems of distribution of costs in relation to private benefits.

The crisis in the second half of the 1970s, which affected cotton production in the Costa rather badly, stimulated the creation of a *Costeno* front, if only to lobby for government support (rescheduling of private debt). In 1980, the Confederación Colombiana de Algodon (CONALGODON) was formed by 11 associations in the Costa as an umbrella organization. There are now two national associations, the Federation and CONALGODON, each representing roughtly 50% of the cultivated area.

## Changes in the Structure of Cotton Production

In this section, I analyze the changes in the structure of cotton production, first at the national level, concentrating on the interregional division of labor. The principal change in this respect was a reorientation toward the Costa Atlantica, which became the largest production area. First, the causes of this change are examined. I then examine the changes in the productive structure in the Costa Atlantica. Although small producers continued to participate fairly significantly in the expansionary process, they became marginalized in the 1970s and in part were replaced by urban producers. I examine these issues and relate them to each other.

### Interregional Division of Labor

Analysis of the evolution of production at the level of the main production regions shows a striking coincidence between changes in the interregional distribution and the general orientation of production. Until the end of the 1950s, the share of cotton production in the Costa Atlantica declined relative to that of the Interior region, due to the simultaneous displacement of perennial cotton in the Costa and the fast expansion of annual cotton in the Interior (see Table 6.4). In the Costa, net cultivated area actually declined, but the volume of production showed a net growth as a result of the higher yields of annual cotton. The expansion in the Interior (Tolima and Valle) was quite logical in view of the fact that access to the main centers of domestic consumption (Medellin and Bogotá) was relatively easy. Expansion in the

TABLE 6.1
Cultivated Area, Production of Fiber and Yields, by Main Region, Colombia, 1951–1980

| | *Costa Atlantica* | | | *Interior* | | | *Colombia* | | |
|---|---|---|---|---|---|---|---|---|---|
| *Year* | *Cult. area (ha)* | *Fiber (ton)* | *Yield (per ha) (kg)* | *Cult. area (ha)* | *Fiber (ton)* | *Yield (per ha) (kg)* | *Cult. area (ha)* | *Fiber (ton)* | *Yield (per ha) (kg)* |
| 1951 | 26,500 | 3,693 | 139 | 11,400 | 2,465 | 216 | 6,474 | 39,700 | 163 |
| 1952 | 30,600 | 4,590 | 150 | 22,483 | 5,589 | 249 | 10,567 | 55,163 | 192 |
| 1953 | 35,500 | 5,352 | 151 | 29,200 | 11,328 | 388 | 17,031 | 67,080 | 254 |
| 1954 | 34,259 | 8,635 | 253 | 46,478 | 18,923 | 407 | 27,884 | 82,280 | 339 |
| 1955 | 38,226 | 6,554 | 171 | 44,581 | 17,160 | 385 | 24,005 | 84,050 | 286 |
| 1956 | 20,948 | 3,541 | 169 | 44,660 | 18,226 | 408 | 22,529 | 68,578 | 329 |
| 1957 | 19,370 | 5,649 | 292 | 42,914 | 14,781 | 344 | 20,573 | 63,000 | 327 |
| 1958 | 22,873 | 8,033 | 351 | 53,773 | 17,634 | 328 | 25,873 | 77,000 | 336 |
| 1959 | 39,665 | 14,661 | 370 | 90,305 | 41,522 | 460 | 56,408 | 131,371 | 429 |
| 1960 | 59,580 | 24,817 | 417 | 91,424 | 43,583 | 477 | 68,732 | 152,150 | 452 |
| 1961 | 56,150 | 22,662 | 404 | 94,609 | 48,204 | 510 | 71,347 | 152,341 | 468 |
| 1962 | 66,812 | 28,552 | 427 | 108,693 | 51,148 | 471 | 80,050 | 177,085 | 452 |
| 1963 | 76,334 | 31,328 | 410 | 63,863 | 32,400 | 508 | 64,394 | 142,056 | 453 |
| 1964 | 91,883 | 36,358 | 396 | 49,085 | 23,378 | 476 | 63,381 | 150,044 | 522 |
| 1965 | 90,491 | 39,296 | 434 | 34,030 | 15,940 | 468 | 58,328 | 134,249 | 434 |
| 1966 | 116,743 | 46,728 | 400 | 39,186 | 25,726 | 657 | 75,360 | 164,876 | 457 |
| 1967 | 121,332 | 59,924 | 494 | 47,167 | 34,559 | 733 | 96,582 | 174,538 | 553 |
| 1968 | 119,694 | 64,302 | 537 | 74,128 | 53,652 | 724 | 120,137 | 198,879 | 604 |
| 1969 | 150,814 | 82,560 | 547 | 77,325 | 39,877 | 516 | 125,238 | 236,060 | 531 |
| 1970 | 196,367 | 84,737 | 432 | 61,905 | 40,102 | 648 | 127,784 | 266,665 | 479 |
| 1971 | 158,454 | 74,875 | 473 | 55,299 | 35,204 | 637 | 112,350 | 218,970 | 513 |
| 1972 | 156,989 | 89,833 | 572 | 79,415 | 51,756 | 652 | 144,435 | 242,268 | 596 |
| 1973 | 189,991 | 79,453 | 418 | 54,189 | 30,544 | 564 | 114,861 | 252,648 | 455 |
| 1974 | 182,643 | 99,371 | 544 | 64,254 | 41,239 | 642 | 145,798 | 268,501 | 543 |
| 1975 | 239,341 | 111,767 | 467 | 30,692 | 19,336 | 630 | 138,737 | 291,816 | 475 |
| 1976 | 206,279 | 96,031 | 466 | 62,679 | 40,890 | 652 | 142,089 | 283,358 | 501 |
| 1977 | 233,058 | 96,866 | 415 | 115,004 | 52,658 | 458 | 160,287 | 377,246 | 425 |
| 1978 | 253,768 | 77,977 | 307 | 44,827 | 24,029 | 536 | 110,417 | 327,842 | 337 |
| 1979 | 110,559 | 49,499 | 448 | 57,641 | 40,401 | 701 | 97,155 | 188,400 | 516 |
| 1980 | 143,728 | 78,581 | 547 | 60,671 | 36,545 | 603 | 121,205 | 220,629 | 549 |

*Sources:* IDEMA, Tabulados, Oficina de Planeacion, various years; Federacion Nacional de Algodoneros, Annual Report, various years.

Costa started in 1959 and continued without interruption for an entire decade. The Costa was not initially the largest exporter, but it had assumed this position by the end of the 1960s (see Table 6.5). Some additional factors must be taken into account, however, in the explanation of the shift. Table 6.4 shows that physical yields in the Costa were consistently lower than in the Interior. At the same time, however, land in the Costa was relatively more abundant than in the Interior. As Vergara observes: "The transfer of crops from areas in the interior and Valle to the Litoral [Costa], has been a phenomenon which can be explained by the availability of land in the Litoral, cheap and with low opportunity costs, and cheap labor. These factors give the Litoral a comparative advantage with respect to the Interior and Valle cotton production" (Vergara 1970:80; translation mine). Much in the same line, Leurquin (1966) earlier found that land rents around Valledupar were only 25% of those in the Interior. More detailed estimates of yields and costs per hectare, available from 1966 for the two main regions (see Table 6.6), show that the higher per-hectare costs in the Interior continued to be more than compensated by higher yields leading to lower costs per ton of raw cotton, although these differences tended to narrow somewhat over time.

Although we can agree with the substance of Vergara's conclusion, except for the fact that it is preferable to speak of an absolute advantage, an additional factor must be taken into account, which is that more profitable crop production alternatives had presented themselves in the Interior and effectively displaced cotton. First of all, Valle has sugar cane production which, following the United States embargo on Cuban sugar, has become a Colombian export product. Second, the "green revolution" has caused rice to become a more profitable crop for the irrigated areas of Tolima. In other words, apart from pull factors there also were powerful push factors that moved cotton production to the Costa.

TABLE 6.5
Geographical Distribution of Cotton Exports and Share of Cotton Exports in Total Production, by Main Region, 1966, 1970, 1976, 1980 (percentages)

| | *1966* | | *1970* | | *1976* | | *1980* | |
|---|---|---|---|---|---|---|---|---|
| | *Vol.* | *Value* | *Vol.* | *Value* | *Vol.* | *Value* | *Vol.* | *Value* |
| Costa/Meta | 28 | 25 | 82 | 77 | 74 | 69 | 64 | 58 |
| Interior | 72 | 75 | 18 | 23 | 26 | 31 | 34 | 42 |
| Share of exports (%) | 17 | 14 | 43 | 55 | 43 | 43 | 41 | 41 |

*Source:* Federation (various reports).

TABLE 6.6
Estimated Average Cost per Ton of Cotton Fiber, Costa Atlantica and Interior 1967–1980 (current Colombian pesos)

| | *Costa Atlantica* | | *Interior* | | *Ratio* |
|---|---|---|---|---|---|
| *Year* | *Value* | *Index* | *Value* | *Index* | *Costa/Interior* |
| 1967 | 9,829 | 100 | 6,854 | 100 | 1.43 |
| 1968 | 9,269 | 94 | 7,901 | 115 | 1.17 |
| 1969 | 11,238 | 114 | 12,593 | 183 | 0.89 |
| 1970 | 15,301 | 156 | 10,396 | 151 | 1.47 |
| 1971 | 15,857 | 156 | 11,870 | 173 | 1.34 |
| 1972 | 13,708 | 139 | 12,785 | 186 | 1.07 |
| 1973 | 21,227 | 216 | 19,752 | 287 | 1.07 |
| 1974 | 23,809 | 242 | 27,415 | 399 | 0.87 |
| 1975 | 36,047 | 367 | 35,039 | 510 | 1.03 |
| 1976 | 44,879 | 456 | 36,814 | 536 | 1.22 |
| 1977 | 67,466 | 686 | 77,164 | 1,125 | 0.87 |
| 1978 | 131,664 | 1,339 | 63,897 | 930 | 2.06 |
| 1979 | 83,527 | 849 | 58,190 | 847 | 1.43 |
| 1980 | 88,986 | 905 | 98,654 | 1,437 | 0.90 |

*Note:* Calculated on basis of average cost per hectare and average yield given for each region.
*Source:* Federación Nacional de Algodoneros (various years).

After 1958, cotton production in the Costa Atlantica region experienced continuous growth. In 1976, just prior to the national cotton crisis, the cultivated area was ten times larger than it had been in 1958, and the volume of production had increased twelve times, fluctuating at around 70% of national production. Within the region, annual cotton production was first initiated in Cordoba in the area of the Alto Sinu (Cerete) and on the Atlantic coast, and subsequently spread to Magdalena, Cesar, and the Guajira. The government first built cotton-ginning stations in Cerete, Rio Hacha, and Barranquilla. During the period 1958–1975, the number of cotton-ginning agencies and districts (each with its own installed ginning capacity) rose from 7 to 20.

Although cotton has become the region's most intensive and important crop, it is not its main agricultural activity. The data presented in Table 6.7 indicate its relative importance.

## Changes in the Composition of Producers

Until the end of the 1960s, *all* size classes of cotton growing increased, though some faster than others; in the 1970s, however, a considerable scale

TABLE 6.7
Cotton and Agricultural Activity in the Costa Atlantica, Some Indicators, 1959–1960 and 1970–1971

| | *1959–1960* | *1970–1971* |
|---|---|---|
| Cotton farm holdings | 3,301 | 2,313 |
| Total farm holdings | 179,111 | 166,246 |
| Percentage | 1.8 | 1.4 |
| Cultivated area cotton (has) | 38,815 | 151,159 |
| Total agricultural land (has) | 6,972,437 | 7,914,190 |
| Percentage | 0.6 | 1.9 |
| Cotton cultivated area[a] | 102,210 | 151,159 |
| Cultivated area main crops[b] | 665,965 | 658,870 |
| Percentage | 15 | 23 |
| Cotton cultivated area | 38,815 | 151,159 |
| Cultivated area annual crops | 318,922 | 447,893 |
| Percentage | 12 | 34 |

[a]1965
[b]Sesame, cotton, rice, banana, cocoa, coffee, sugar, barley, beans, maize, sorghum, potato, tobacco, wheat, and cassava.
*Sources:* Censo Agropecuario 1960 and 1970–1971 (DANE, Bogotá); Tabulations, Caja Agraria (Bogotá; mimeo).

TABLE 6.8
Evolution of Cotton Production by Farm Area of Cultivation, Colombia, 1961–1974 (has)

| *Range (has)* | *1961* | *(%)* | *1966* | *(%)* | *1969* | *(%)* | *1974* | *(%)* | *1961–1969* | *1969–1974* |
|---|---|---|---|---|---|---|---|---|---|---|
| 1–<5 | 9,060 | 6 | 9,893 | 6 | 11,800 | 5 | 9,039 | 3 | 30% | −23% |
| 5–<20 | 21,141 | 14 | 19,785 | 12 | 33,040 | 14 | 30,571 | 12 | 56% | − 7% |
| 20–<50 | 31,711 | 20 | 31,326 | 19 | 49,560 | 21 | 51,702 | 20 | 56% | 4% |
| 50–<100 | 24,161 | 16 | 36,273 | 22 | 56,240 | 24 | 58,026 | 22 | 133% | 3% |
| 100–<200 | 33,221 | 22 | 32,975 | 20 | 49,560 | 21 | 56,937 | 23 | 49% | 15% |
| ⩾200 | 31,710 | 21 | 34,624 | 21 | 35,400 | 15 | 52,225 | 20 | 11% | 47% |
| Total | 151,004 | 100 | 164,876 | 100 | 236,000 | 100 | 258,500 | 100 | 56% | 9% |

*Source:* Soler & Prieto (1982:93); Tabulations, IDEMA (1974; mimeo)

increase occurred. Table 6.8 summarizes these overall trends. This table clearly shows that medium-sized cultivation grew most rapidly in the 1960s and that small-scale production also expanded considerably. In the 1970s there was a clear bias toward the rapid growth of large-scale production; small-scale production declined in absolute terms, whereas middle-sized production expanded at only half the national rate. Considering the period as a whole, we find a declining share of small-scale production, a growing share of medium-sized production, and a stable share of large-scale production. In comparing the two main production regions for size structure (Table 6.9), it is important to recall that not only a relative but also an absolute reallocation of production took place in the 1960s, away from the Interior toward specialization in Costa Atlantica. The data presented in Table 6.9 show that in the Interior large-scale production in particular switched to other crops, whereas in the Costa the greatest relative increase was registered in intermediate production. Small-scale production in the Interior has been

TABLE 6.9
Cotton Cultivated Area, by Size of Cultivation, All Producers, 1961, 1969, and 1974; Federation Members, 1974 and 1983, Costa Atlantica, Interior, and Colombia

| | *All producers* | | | | | | *Federation only* | | | |
|---|---|---|---|---|---|---|---|---|---|---|
| *Size (ha)* | *1961* | *(%)* | *1969* | *(%)* | *1974* | *(%)* | *1974* | *(%)* | *1983* | *(%)* |
| 0.1–<5 | 9,060 | 6 | 11,800 | 5 | 9,039 | 4 | 4,909 | 3 | 3,128 | 7 |
| 5–<20 | 21,141 | 14 | 33,040 | 14 | 30,571 | 12 | 18,833 | 12 | 10,620 | 24 |
| 20–<50 | 31,711 | 20 | 49,560 | 21 | 51,702 | 20 | 32,948 | 20 | 8,648 | 20 |
| 50–<100 | 24,161 | 16 | 56,240 | 24 | 58,026 | 22 | 35,635 | 22 | 7,914 | 18 |
| 100–<200 | 33,221 | 22 | 49,560 | 21 | 56,937 | 23 | 37,218 | 23 | 7,636 | 17 |
| ⩾200 | 31,710 | 21 | 35,400 | 15 | 52,225 | 20 | 31,338 | 19 | 6,103 | 14 |
| Total | 151,004 | 100 | 236,000 | 100 | 258,226 | 100 | 160,881 | 100 | 44,049 | 100 |
| **Interior** | | | | | | | | | | |
| 0.1–<5 | 7,384 | 8 | | | 6,242 | 10 | 2,955 | 6 | 2,360 | 15 |
| 5–<20 | 16,101 | 17 | | | 12,021 | 19 | 7,668 | 15 | 3,556 | 23 |
| 20–<50 | 23,193 | 25 | | | 16,615 | 26 | 12,408 | 24 | 3,609 | 23 |
| 50–<100 | 15,704 | 17 | | | 14,024 | 22 | 11,604 | 23 | 2,823 | 18 |
| 100–<200 | 0 | 0 | | | 9,585 | 15 | 9,511 | 19 | 2,264 | 14 |
| ⩾200 | 29,524 | 32 | | | 5,771 | 9 | 6,316[x] | 13 | 1,059 | 7 |
| Total | 91,906 | 100 | — | — | 64,258 | 100 | 50,102 | 100 | 15,671 | 100 |
| **Costa Atlantica** | | | | | | | | | | |
| 0.1–<5 | 1,833 | 3 | | | 1,786 | 1 | 917 | 1 | 222 | 1 |
| 5–<20 | 4,345 | 8 | | | 15,259 | 8 | 7,996 | 8 | 2,683 | 12 |
| 20–<50 | 6,197 | 12 | | | 30,230 | 16 | 15,947 | 16 | 4,188 | 19 |
| 50–<100 | 8,212 | 16 | | | 41,830 | 23 | 22,011 | 22 | 4,971 | 22 |
| 100–<200 | 0 | 0 | | | 47,083 | 26 | 27,537 | 28 | 5,372 | 24 |
| ⩾200 | 31,107 | 60 | | | 46,454 | 26 | 25,022 | 25 | 5,044 | 22 |
| Total | 51,694 | 100 | — | — | 182,643 | 100 | 99,452 | 100 | 22,480 | 100 |

*Note:* [x] = error in original publication
*Sources:* 1961–1974, Colombia: Soler and Prieto (1982:93); 1961, Interior and Costa: Currie (1963); 1974, Interior and Costa: IDEMA: Tabulados (Oficina de Planeación, Bogotá); 1974 and 1983, Federación Nacional de Algodoneros: Tabulados (Division de Estudios Económico, Bogotá).

less sensitive to the specialization process: contrary to overall trends, its share increased.

Cotton suffered its worst crisis during the second half of the 1970s and it would be interesting to see its effects on the production structure. Unfortunately, as a result of the transfer of the cotton-ginning network to the associations, IDEMA no longer keeps an annual register of cotton producers. Only the Federation systematically collects and makes available such records. Although in 1974 the growers associated with the Federation were still a fairly representative sample of the national production structure, this was no longer the case in later years because of the growing proliferation of associations, first in the Costa and later also in the Interior. The average cultivation size of non-Federation growers in the Costa increased from 48 has in 1975 to 71 has in 1982, whereas that of Federation growers remained around 35 has. In the Interior, the average cultivation size of Federation members dropped to the level of non-Federation growers (approximately 17 has). For the Federation as a whole, the share in total cultivated area declined, not surprisingly, from 62% in 1974 to 42% in 1982 (Federación 1983). It is impossible to draw any firm conclusions from an analysis of this period of international boom and bust, based only on Federation data. (Note that Soler and Prieto (1982) overlooked this, and by applying the Federation size distribution to the national total, they came to the conclusion that small producers increased not only their relative but also their absolute participation in the total cultivated area.) These data show that in the period 1974–1983, large-scale production was heavily affected, and small-scale production much less so, relatively speaking (see Table 6.9). Taking regional figures on average cultivation size into account, it can tentatively be concluded that relatively more large-scale cotton growers survived in the Costa than in the Interior. This is understandable because there are more profitable production alternatives in the Interior than in the Costa. Interior producers can switch to rice or sugar, particularly if they have irrigated fields. In the Costa the principal alternative is a less land-intensive livestock production, but this requires considerable capital investment that is not easily financed in times of heavy debt.

A second important aspect of the changing structure of cotton production is that of tenancy. The principal data on tenancy are summarized in Table 6.10. During the 1960s, a very considerable increase occurred in the importance of renting land for cotton production. Again, it is interesting to observe the differences in the two regions. In the Interior, where cotton was substituted for other crops during the 1960s, land rentals declined much more than did production under ownership. In the Costa, the rapid increase in production was largely realized through increased land rental. Moreover, the average size of a rented holding in the Costa was 1.5 times larger than in the Interior. On the basis of the limited data available for the 1970s, it seems that the cotton crisis affected tenant and owner producers more or less equally.

TABLE 6.10
Tenancy of Cotton Producers, Costa Atlantica, Interior, and Colombia, 1961, 1974, 1983

| | *1961* | | *1974* | | *Change* | |
|---|---|---|---|---|---|---|
| | *O* | *LR* | *O* | *LR* | *O* | *LR* |
| | | | **All cotton producers** | | | |
| Colombia | 3473 | 3712 | 4195 | 4436 | 34% | 26% |
| Interior | 2471 | 3226 | 2242 | 2120 | −9% | −34% |
| Costa | 1002 | 486 | 1478 | 2015 | 47% | 315% |
| | | | **Federation members** | | | |
| Colombia | 2339 | 2420 | 1122 | 1144 | −52% | −53% |
| Interior | 1136 | 1112 | 753 | 713 | −34% | −36% |
| Costa | 740 | 1019 | 188 | 305 | −74% | −70% |

O = owners; LR = land-renting tenants

*Source:* IDEMA: Tabulados (various years; mimeographed); Federación: Annual Reports (various years); Currie (1963).

There is also a qualitative change that should be taken into account. During field visits in the Costa, several informants in various positions and occupations emphasized the growing importance of "urban" cotton growers who usually rent a small- or medium-sized holding. According to our informants, these urban cotton growers also hold an urban occupation in (professional) public or private services or trade. Although this phenomenon is reported to be general, it is found particularly in the eastern part of the Costa, which was opened up with cotton production and hence did not have a fully developed agrarian structure.

How can we explain the observed changes in the cotton structure? A number of factors come to mind. First, there has been increasing technicalization of cotton cultivation, particularly in relation to disease control and quality improvement. The consequences of this go beyond the narrower but related issue of mechanization. In regard to mechanization, the necessity for mechanical ploughing at the beginning and end of the growing season in order that the roots may be ploughed under constituted an effective barrier to entry for many small farmers. Very little use is made of animal traction in cultivation practices in the Costa, whereas the commercial renting of tractors and equipment is very limited and is often a complementary business conducted by large-farm managers. The more-recently instituted mechanical harvesting practices constitute the principal economy of (very) large-scale production, which was only introduced in the 1970s. Its principal significance is the small amount of labor it entails (one mechanical harvester displaces 50 to 60 cotton pickers).

However, for small growers, the problems of technification usually are not related to mechanization, but to the growing problems of disease control. Although there is very little scale bias in the means for disease control (if we disregard for a moment aerial spraying, for which 20 hectares has come to constitute a minimum size), the know-how necessary to diagnose disease does have a scale bias. In this context it is important to stress once more that in the 1960s the Costa was relatively disease free (Leurquin 1966), but as soon as cotton production developed on a large scale, the problem of controlling proliferation of insects became more and more important. In the late 1960s, the negative effects of the failure to control pests and disease induced government to impose stringent controls on ploughing the *socas,* conditional on access to government-instituted credit funds. In the mid-1960s less than five applications of pesticides were made each year in the Costa, but they had tripled a decade later, despite continuous improvements that reached the point of becoming lethal to the workers. The share of pesticides in total costs per hectare increased from 23% in 1967–1968 to a disastrous 39% in 1977–1978, after which it declined somewhat (Federación, various years).

Time is an important element in insect control. On some occasions less than 24 hours passes between the diagnosis and a cost-and-yield effective control. Although disease control in cotton generally has been problematic, it is not the same for small and for large producers. The latter, being a large buyer, usually has less problems in gaining timely access to pesticides. Moreover, through their associations, large producers have been better able to protect themselves against speculative behavior by major importers and domestic trade firms. In fact, their problem has often been one of unrestricted and excessive applications, reducing the effectiveness of the foliants through insect immunity. The small producer faced an altogether different, double-edged, problem which affected his crop yields. As a small producer he was often left "in the queue," poorly attended, and in need of pesticides; but he also faced a problem of diagnosis know-how as new diseases continuously developed. The use of specialized agronomist services, available mostly on a commercial basis, has the same time-coordination element. The large producers were able to employ their own agronomists directly or via their associations, but the small producers lost out in this respect. This problem worsened in the 1970s, when problems of insect control caused the government to make access to credit funds to be conditional on the existence of a certificate of extension, which supposedly ensured that each cotton grower had the services of a qualified agronomist at his disposal. Various researchers have shown that yields on large farms are considerably higher than on smaller ones, although a linear curve has not always been found (e.g., Currie 1963; Atkinson 1970). Although it is true that differences in land productivity often are caused by differences in the quality of the land cultivated, it also appears that the issue of access to credit funds further widens the gap between large and small farmers.

The problem was made worse by the growing shortage of credit. Not only was access increasingly tied to nonfinancial conditions, such as the certificate of extension and control over the *socas,* but the quantitative availability of credit did not keep pace with the growing volume of production and rising prices (inflation). During the period 1966–1967, the costs per hectare rose by an average of 18.5% per annum. The average proportion of costs financed with credit dropped from 34% in 1968–1969 to a mere 19% in the middle of the cotton crisis (1977–1978). Although almost all producers received some financing in the 1960s through the agricultural credit funds (FEDESARROLLO 1975), in the following decade the coverage of the fund dropped from approximately 85% in 1976 to an all-time low of 61% in 1978, to recover again to 75% (Federación 1981:84). With less collateral to offer, the small producers could rarely expand beyond these proportionally declining limits.

The reported appearance of new cotton-producing tenants appears to be related in some way to the issues of disease control and credit. The ability to manage insect and disease control became, as we have seen, an increasingly vital production resource. Many of the new urban entrants possess this technological advantage directly, or have assured their access to it through an association. In this context it is perhaps interesting that calculations based on the IDEMA tabulations of 1974 show that small- and medium-sized land hiring tenants (<50 has) have higher physical yields than do their landowning counterparts. Because the urban cotton growers were found to be primarily in the medium-sized category, this may be seen as an interesting indication, but in the absence of additional data it has not been possible to pursue this issue further.

The fact that many of these urban agriculturalists continue their town occupations as professional, lawyer, civil servant, and the like, is also relevant in facilitating their access to capital and credit. Without the highly organized and specialized external environment in which the associations have played a key role, however, this type of selectively easy entry to agricultural production would not have been possible.

## Cotton Production in the Costa Atlantica

Although the number of cotton growers exceeded 17,000 in the country and 7,600 in the Costa only at the peak in 1977, the changes that were triggered and their direct and indirect effects on the Costeño economy have been considerable. In this section I discuss some of these impacts, concentrating on three issues. The first is the effect of cotton production on the sociopolitical structure. The development of cotton production enabled an accumulation of wealth in relatively few hands, and it is interesting to consider the political implications of the emergence of this cotton elite. The second issue discussed is the urban effects of the development of cotton production. Earlier, I stressed the importance of agricultural development for understanding urban change, and this issue also merits discussion in this case study. The third issue I briefly consider is the effect of cotton production on the rural labor market.

In my earlier discussion of rural and regional change, I argued that the effects of processes of change often depend on the historical evolution of the situation in which they occur. For this reason, I have chosen to adopt a comparative perspective—that is, I focus on developments in Cesar, the main production area of the Costa Atlantica, but will contrast these with developments in the department of Cordoba, where annual cotton was first introduced but which had a markedly different initial socioeconomic setting.

The agrarian structure in Cordoba very much resembed the classical *latifundium–minifundium* structure. Large cattle estates and some export plantations were surrounded by a growing *minifundio* population (Fals Borda 1976). There was and is heavy rural population pressure, causing outmigration, mostly to other places in the Costa or, lately, to Venezuela. In 1959–1960, Cordoba held 20% of the total area cultivated in the region in cotton. Growth of production was relatively slow, and by 1975–1976 this figure had declined to just under 10%. The average farm area under cotton cultivation is fairly small, reflecting the agrarian structure of the region.

The eastern part of the original department of Magdalena, which now forms the department of Cesar, is of much more recent settlement. Although settlement in some areas dates back to precolonial and early colonial periods, most of the land remained virtually unutilized. Extensive livestock estates predominated in a sparsely inhabited and relatively isolated area. *Minifundio* was comparatively unimportant. The area was opened up in the 1950s and cotton production was rapidly undertaken. By 1959–1960, Cesar held more than half the total cultivated area of the Costa, a proportion that it maintained thoughout the period under study. The average size of cultivation is three to four times that in Cordoba.

## Cotton Growers and Local/Regional Elite Formation

Even before the development of cotton growing, Cordoba had a local/regional landed elite who dominated livestock production and trade, first to Cartagena in the north and later to Medellin in the south (CIDER 1978). To this elite, cotton represented a means for diversifying its economic and political power. Land-rental prices rose after cotton had been introduced in the Sinu Valley; at the same time, however, the continued land fragmentation caused by generalized population pressure made it difficult for small growers to benefit from this opportunity. Cotton provided considerable rural employment, but only for three or four months each year, in view of its very high seasonal component. In a way, cotton production enabled many rural households to hold on to their mini-holdings, but it did not ease rural conflict; to the contrary, it may even have worsened them. In this context it is perhaps not surprising that land invasions were very numerous in Cordoba (cf. Fals Borda 1976).

The situation in Cesar showed a great contrast, the development of cotton production there being directly responsible for the emergence of a regional elite. For this elite, already potentially rooted in the ownership of land, cotton constituted the economic base on which it could develop its own interests and break away from the old Santa Marta elite, thereby making its influence felt on a national scale. The key to the success of this elite was the creation of Cesar as a department in 1967. This enabled rapid expansion of public employment, because a new departmental government and various central government field offices had to be established in the new departmental capital of Valledupar. The region's growing national influence was evidenced by the fact that during the 1970s a number of cotton growers from Valledupar were elected to ministerial and other high positions in national government, particularly under the Michelsen Administration (Soler and Prieto 1982). The new elite also succeeded in getting the plan for the new northeastern highway changed so that it would pass through Valledupar (CIDER 1978). The fact that the elite has rapidly diversified its sources of wealth is shown by the fact that important *algodoneros* (cotton growers) have major direct commercial interests and influence others through their local growers' associations (Perdomo 1978). Asocesar has a major financial interest in a new commercial airline, fully owns an air-spraying company, and has founded a factory for the processing of cotton seeds. Indeed, the vast expansion of cotton in Cesar has permitted a greater internalization of benefits there than in Cordoba. In general, cotton production itself produces an extremely skewed distribution of income, but the additional effects triggered by cotton, in terms of public and private employment and income opportunities, have made the overall income-distribution effects in Cesar far more positive and accumulative than in the western area. The growing power of the elite in Cesar has therefore been supported by an expanding economic base.

## Cotton, Migration, and Urbanization

Although the level of urbanization in the Costa was comparatively high before the development of annual cotton, mainly because of its historical transshipment function, this was mainly concentrated along the coastline (Cartagena, Barranquilla, Santa Marta etc.). In the interior, the degree of urbanization was comparatively low and was based on the Magdalena river as the principal means of transport (Uribe Echevarria 1979). The difference between the two main cotton-growing departments is fairly clear: Cesar had so far experienced only incipient urbanization and intensive settlement of the area had hardly began; Cordoba, on the other hand, had an extensive but little-developed urban network, much in line with the historical rural development of larger concentrations of *minifundio* and landless populations.

As shown in Table 6.11, population growth in the Costa during the intercensal period 1959–1964 was somewhat higher than the national average (4.6% against 3.5%). Within the Costa, however, there were significant differences.

The cotton-growing departments of Cordoba and Cesar experienced a demographic growth considerably in excess of the regional average (6.4% and 6.6% respectively). This was reflected particularly in a fairly high urban rate of growth. Cesar stands out very clearly (12%), having more than doubled its share of urban population between 1938 and 1964. The underlying migratory processes in the two departments wee different. Cesar, together with Atlantica (Barranquilla), was a net receiver of population, whereas Cordoba had a negative migration balance. On this basis, one may expect that the urban population growth was mainly of domestic origin. Migration was primarily rural–urban. In Cesar, however, the inmigratory flow not only stimulated urban growth but generated increases in the rural population. Data from the 1964 census, when cotton production was in full development, show that 36% had an urban and 64% a rural destination. In the same year, 65% of the economically active population migrated into the department. This situation continued at a reduced level in the 1964–1973 inter-

TABLE 6.11
Annual Growth Rates of Total and Urban Population, Costa Atlantica Departments and Colombia, 1938–1973 (percentages)

| | *Total Population* | | | *Urban Population* | | | *Share Urban Population* | | | |
|---|---|---|---|---|---|---|---|---|---|---|
| | *1938–1951* | *1951–1964* | *1964–1973* | *1938–1951* | *1951–1964* | *1964–1973* | *1938* | *1951* | *1964* | *1973* |
| Cesar | 2.9 | 6.6 | 3.0 | 5.0 | 12.1 | 6.6 | 19 | 25 | 65 | 65 |
| Cordoba | 0.5 | 6.4 | 1.1 | 0.6 | 8.4 | 3.5 | 25 | 25 | 40 | 40 |
| Costa Total | 2.1 | 4.6 | 2.0 | 2.2 | 5.4 | 3.1 | 50 | 53 | 61 | 68 |
| Colombia Total | 2.0 | 3.5 | 2.1 | 4.3 | 5.7 | 4.4 | 29 | 39 | 53 | 62 |

*Sources:* Population censuses corresponding years, in CIDER (1977); DNP (1977).

censal period, although at the end of this period the migration flow gradually shifted toward the towns. In 1973, 74% of the population of the new departmental capital, Valledupar, was in-migrant, this city having taken up almost one third of all migrants to Cesar in this period. Together with Bogotá and Meta, Valledupar was the principal focus of internal migration in the country (ASCOFAME 1978).

The importance of cotton development as an explanatory factor in the process of urban growth can also be seen in quantitative terms, although the dynamics of the situation in Cesar go beyond a simple linear regression. Nevertheless, the data presented in Table 6.12 show a significant correlation between cotton production and migration. It is reasonable to conclude that cotton production has been important, directly and indirectly (through spin-off effects), in stimulating population growth in both town and countryside. The massive expansion of cotton cultivation in Cesar could not have taken place without a considerable in-migration. This contrasted with the situation in Cordoba, where cotton growing could not even stem the out-migration process, which revealed itself particularly with regard to the rural labor market.

TABLE 6.12
Volume of Migration and Cotton Production
Cesar, 1968–1977

| *Year* | *Immigrants* | *Cotton Production (tons)* |
|---|---|---|
| 1969[a] | 718 | 115,483 |
| 1970 | 2,725 | 154,745 |
| 1971 | 1,145 | 167,161 |
| 1972 | 1,865 | 150,914 |
| 1973 | 1,859 | 170,611 |
| 1974 | 2,576 | 178,246 |
| 1975 | 3,440 | 192,329 |
| 1976 | 4,152 | 176,702 |
| 1977 | 2,291 | 168,198 |

[a]Immigrants recorded in 12–month period January to January.

*Sources:* Migrants: Survey, ASCOFAME (1978); Cotton: Federación (various years).

OLS regression: $Y = -3298.15 + 0.0346X$ $R^2 = 0.51$
*SE* (798.129) (2070.7) (0.01268)
(−1.5927) (2.7299)

## Cotton and the Rural Labor Market

The impact of cotton on the rural labor market has various aspects. First, it clearly helped to increase considerably the demand for rural labor. Data presented in Table 6.13 show that in the period 1951–1964, estimated agricultural employment growth was greatest in the two cotton-production areas of Cesar and Cordoba (7.2% and 6.6%, respectively). In the period 1964–1973, estimated decrease in these two departments was less than the regional average. The effects naturally depend also on the particular conditions of labor availability: in this respect, considerable differences exist between the two departments. The best indicator available is the data collected on rural daily wages (Table 6.14). The impact exerted by cotton also depended largely on labor-market conditions that existed before its introduction. High rural population pressure in Cordoba and the growing number of landless families (CIDER 1977) created a great need for farm labor and enabled wages to be kept low. In spite of out-migration rural wages continued to lag for a long time, creating a growing gap in relation to the regional average, although there was some improvment in the 1970s.

To see the effect of cotton on the seasonality of the rural labor market, I have attempted to estimate the demand for rural labor. Data available are extremely limited, requiring that assessments be made on the basis of crop-specific labor requirements, estimates of cultivated area per crop, and the local agricultural calender indicating growing seasons. The data cover only the 16 major crops. Therefore, my results should be seen as indicative only. Finally, it was not possible to make a reasonable estimate of livestock production, but because no major seasonal component is involved in this activity this exclusion does not affect my interpretation.

TABLE 6.13
Estimated Agricultural Employment, Annual Growth Rate and Share in Total Employment, Costa Atlantica, Interior, and Colombia, 1951, 1964, 1973

| | *Agricultural Employment* | | | *Annual Growth* | | | *Share in Total* | | |
|---|---|---|---|---|---|---|---|---|---|
| | *1951* | *1964* | *1973* | *1951–1964 (%)* | *1964–1973 (%)* | *1951–1973 (%)* | *1951 (%)* | *1964 (%)* | *1973 (%)* |
| Cesar | 16,300 | 40,524 | 29,934 | 7.2 | −2.3 | 2.8 | 57.6 | 57.1 | 27.7 |
| Cordoba | 45,911 | 105,971 | 87,743 | 6.6 | −2.1 | 2.9 | 60.1 | 68.1 | 49.6 |
| Costa | 270,742 | 422,499 | 303,204 | 3.5 | −3.6 | .05 | 50.8 | 51.0 | 29.7 |
| Total Colombia | 1,963,700 | 2,354,400 | 1,876,500 | 1.4 | −3.6 | 0.5 | 53.5 | 48.2 | 31.3 |

*Source:* INANDES (1977).

TABLE 6.14
Evolution of Daily Rural Nominal Wages, Costa Atlantica Departments and Colombia, 1950–1978 (wage in hot climate without food)

| | *1950* | *1960* | *1970* | *1976* | *1978* |
|---|---|---|---|---|---|
| Cesar[a] | 2.90 | 5.85 | 24.70 | 79.0 | 137.0 |
| Cordoba | 2.50 | 4.80 | 11.70 | 48.0 | 85.0 |
| Total Costa Atlantica[b] | 2.60 | 5.31 | 19.25 | 64.3 | 108.0 |
| Total Colombia | 2.69 | 5.83 | 18.21 | 66.5 | 122.0 |

[a]1950 and 1960 figures refer to Magdalena as a whole;
[b]Unweighted average of all departments.
*Source:* DANE (1979).

In Cordoba, demand for labor on cotton farms increased from 22% in 1966 to 30% in 1974. Despite this moderate growth, the seasonality of the labor market actually declined a little. The share of the peak month in the total decreased from 14.3% to 13.6%. Figure 6.2 presents the overall picture, from which it can be seen that the greatest peak is not due to cotton but to rice harvesting. The situation in Cesar was markedly different. Table 6.14 shows that wages there rose faster than did the regional average. Apparently, in-migration did not keep pace with the growing demand for rural labor. In a way, this is not surprising, given the large seasonal fluctuation of demand. The significance of cotton labor demand in Cesar rose from 53.5% in 1966 to 65% in 1974, and as Figure 6.3 shows, the greatest peak in the demand for labor was almost completely caused by the cotton harvest. In effect, the expansion of cotton caused a large flow of seasonal migrant labor.

A survey conducted by ASCOFAME (1978) has shown that some 60%–70% of cotton pickers were seasonal migrant labor, the greater majority (90%) coming from other departments of the Costa, in particular from Atlantica and to a lesser extent from Bolivar, Magdalena, and Cordoba! The survey also shows that a large part of the population normally resides in urban centers (particularly in Atlantico), notwithstanding the fact that farm work constituted the principal occupation throughout the year. Although this seasonal labor force must suffer considerable periods without gainful work, the people do not form part of a transmigrant rural proletariat that moves between the coffee, cotton, and rice harvests in the various regions, as has been suggested (cf. Velez 1975). To the contrary, most of the migrant cotton pickers interviewed came directly from, and would return to, their place of residence (AFSCOFAME 1978).

In brief, cotton contributed considerably to employment in the region, both directly and indirectly. However the directly generated employment

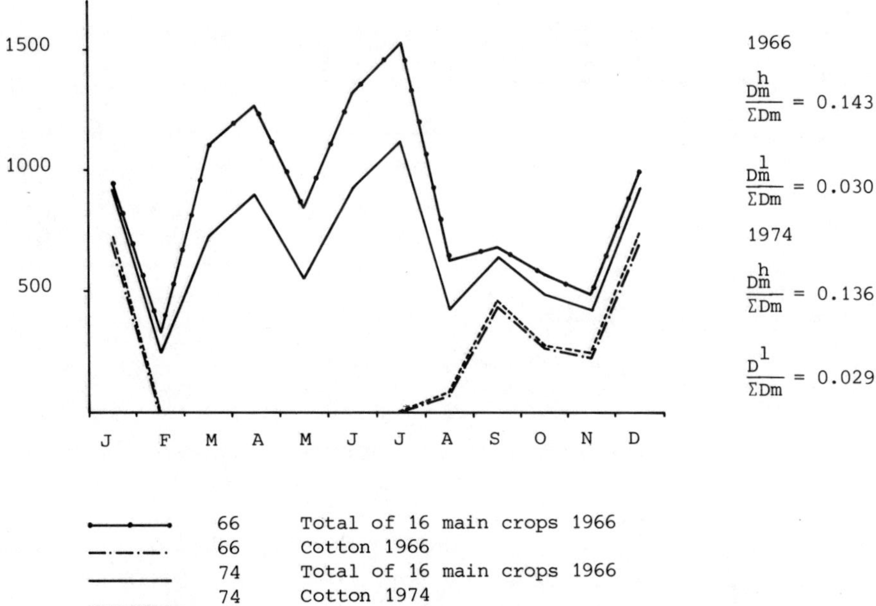


FIGURE 6.2. Estimated demand for labor, cotton and total of 16 main crops, Cordoba, 1966 and 1974. Seasonality is measured by two indices, One expresses the highest monthly demand ($D_m^h$), the other the lowest monthly demand ($D_m^l$), as share of the total estimated demand ($\Sigma D^m$).

has a high seasonal component: almost 60% of labor demand was concentrated in the short harvesting season. In the case of Cordoba, the relative oversupply of labor from the many *minifundio* and the landless population prevented cotton production from bringing any substantial improvement to the living conditions of the labor force, as may be judged from local rural wage behavior. In Cesar, on the other hand, the large expansion and heavy specialization in cotton production created a large but highly seasonal demand for labor, calling forth a migrant labor force. With the exception of a small minority, however, this temporary labor force was unable to settle permanently in the area, because of the lack of alternative employment in the remainder of the year. In this respect, this least remunerative part of cotton employment has been externalized and at best has served to reduce rural underemployment in other areas. The direct generation of permanent employment in Cesar most likely has been fairly small, in comparison with the indirect and induced employment in personal services, trade, manufacturing, and government (CIDER 1977, 1978).

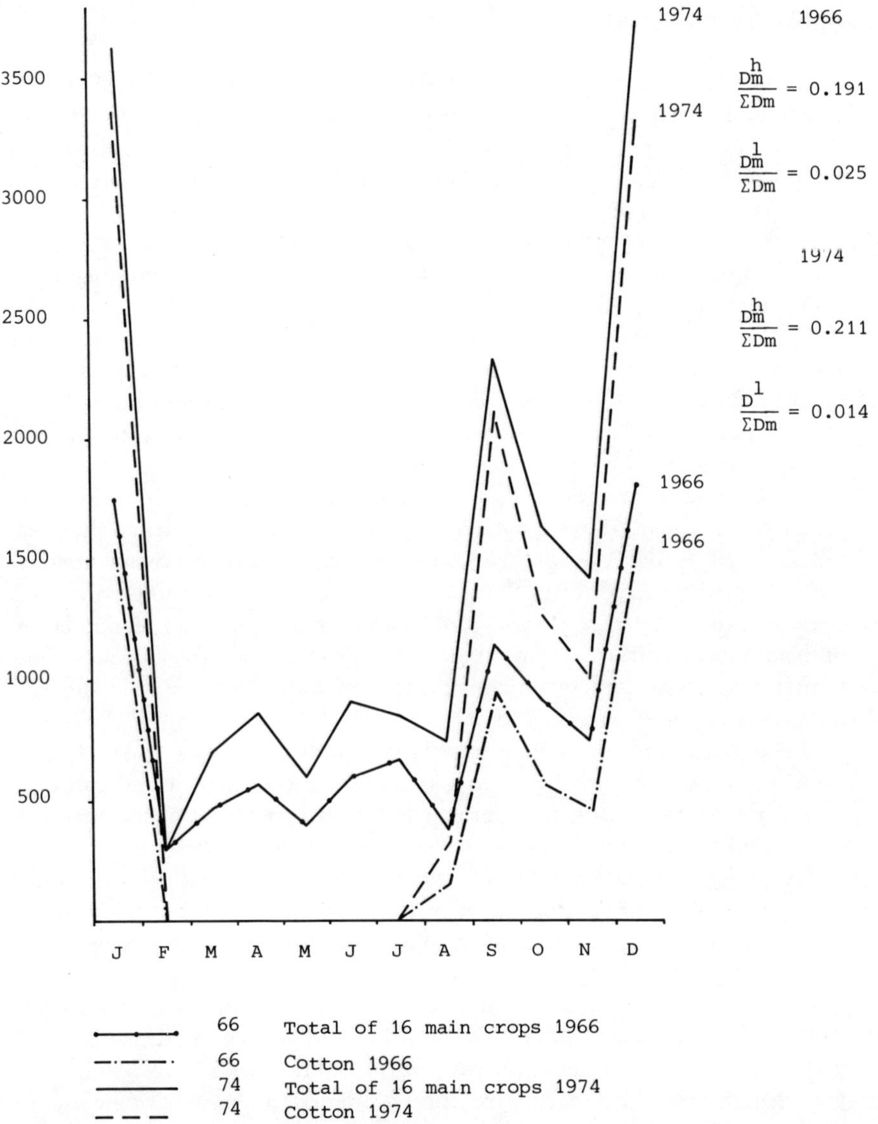


FIGURE 6.3. Estimated demand for labor, cotton and total of 16 main crops, Cesar, 1966 and 1974.

## Some Conclusions

Over time, cotton production has moved from one kind and scale of organization to another. Perennial cotton produced by peasant households was largely a local/regional affair. Once the organizational conditions had been set, production became organized at the national level. Cotton ceased to be a perennial crop and peasant household production was displaced. In its place came annual cotton, which had long been grown by various kinds of growers, big and small. In fact, it was in the interests of all to strengthen their collective market position.

My analysis of the roles of the textile industry, government, and producer associations has shown an interesting dynamic in which the national organization of textile companies called forth an organization of the cotton growers. Government played an important supplementary and mediating role in this process, creating some of the critical infrastructural and market conditions for the domestic expansion of cotton production. The growth of domestic production, which led to exportable surpluses, brought a reorientation in the relations between cotton growers, textile companies, and government, as well as among the growers themselves. As cotton associations started to operate in the (favorable) international market, they pushed for deregulation of the domestic market in response to the new international conditions. This change was completed when the textile companies also began to develop their own export markets.

Relations among cotton growers changed in three respects. First, changes occurred in the relations between growers from the Interior and from the Costa. Given their different regional situations (in terms of international access) and favorable international prices, the Costeños were most interested in developing international exports, whereas the Interior producers remained more oriented toward the domestic market and hence were less interested in deregulating the market. Second, relations between small and large producers changed. Their former common interest disappeared as a result of their differences in market orientation. Moreover, the increasing disadvantages of small-scale production, more than the advantages of large-scale production, helped to erode the earlier cooperation between the two groups. Third, the high degree of institutional organization facilitated the entry of a new type of "urban" cotton farmer–manager. More cotton associations were created, but these developed more in the direction of agrobusiness enterprises, losing their original open and developmental character.

The changes in the interregional division of labor cannot be understood in isolation from the development of the institutional organization of cotton production, without which the rapid regional reallocation of production would not have been possible. At the same time, I have just concluded that the emerging regional specialization contributed to a recasting of that institutional framework.

At the Costa Atlantica level, I analyzed the impact of the introduction of cotton production, contrasting developments in Cesar with those in Cordoba, each of which had a different initial situation. In Cesar, which became the largest production area, cotton triggered a number of new developments, including the creation of a new department and expansion of both the government sector and commerce, personal services, and industry, leading to cumulative growth. In Cordoba, however, cotton production did not significantly contribute to changing the social and economic structure. Comparison of the two regions leads to the conclusion that, given the rather regressive distribution of direct benefits of cotton production, the causes of the positive impact in Cesar should be sought in the indirect local effects that were triggered by its expansion, and in the externalization of some negative effects through the labor market, via the use of seasonal wage labor.

# CHAPTER SEVEN
# ANTIOQUEÑO REGIONAL DEVELOPMENT RECONSIDERED

## Introduction

Not without reason, the economic development of Antioquia has attracted considerable attention in the literature of general and regional development. It is cited as one of the few cases in Latin America of autonomous industrialization in the region, and as such poses a challenge to both nationally minded modernizationists and internationally oriented dependency theorists. Regional theorists have studied the Antioqueño phenomenon not only as a case of successful regional economic development but also in an attempt to explain several specific aspects of the Colombian decentralized regional structure, such as regionalism in Colombian politics, the decentralized urban system, and so forth. Antioquia's development poses a challenge to us in much the same way, but I do not aim at achieving another analysis of Antioquia as a success story (or failure for that matter). Although developments in Antioquia were in many ways remarkable, indeed exceptional, I mainly wish to examine the case from my own perspective, as a test case of my hypotheses concerning regionalism. I argue that despite many exceptional circumstances, my general propositions about the expanding microeconomy, the role and organization of the state, and the verticalization of the regional economy, also apply to developments in Antioquia.

In the second section of this chapter, I give a brief historical description of the main features of Antioquia's economic development. I start by examining the peculiar colonial foundation of the economy, which was characterized by a general weakness of colonial institutions, by the importance of small independent gold mining, and in relation to this, the emergence of small traders, the Antioqueño merchants.

Independence and the abolition of colonial trade monopolies early in the nineteenth century turned the gold-possessing merchants of Antioquia into the principal bankers and traders of the republic, enabling them to obtain considerable privileges and powers that will be analyzed later in this chapter. Under the protection provided by regional autonomy under the Federal Republic (1863–1886), the elite diversified its economic interests in land and

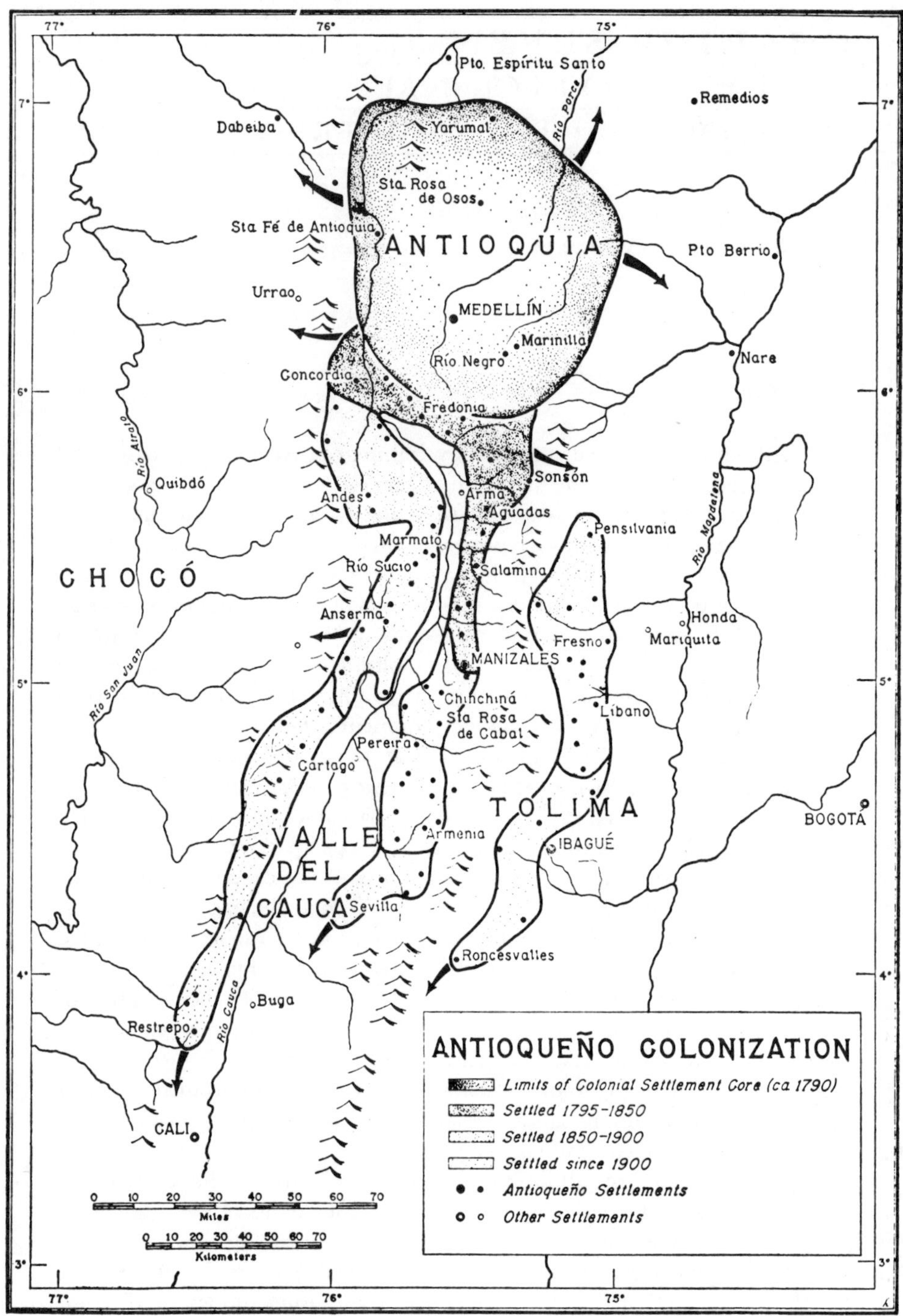


FIGURE 7.1. Land settlement frontiers in Antioquia. (*Source*: Parsons 1950:8.)

livestock, and was aided in this endeavor by the ongoing land-settlement processes (see Figure 7.1). These processes helped both to consolidate the interests of the regional elite and to create a large and independent peasant economy. In such a socioeconomic regional setting, coffee production was able to expand very rapidly after 1870.

If the Antioqueño elite had accumulated numerous mineral, agricultural, and trade interests, why did they move into industrial activities? This question is dealt with in a later section of this chapter (see pp. 247–252) where I submit that their loss of control over gold mining, the emergence of rival groups of traders in other regions, and the related separation of Viejo Caldas, together with other conjunctural factors, made the Antioqueños look for alternative investment opportunities. Accumulated experiences and a number of favorable local conditions made the industrialization process a viable one.

In the third section of this chapter, I discuss the process of national economic integration and regional restructuring. I argue that although the elite formerly had diversified its economic interests mostly within the region, using a strategy of deploying accumulated resources in one field to develop new ones, resources are not used to develop similar activities in other regions. The Antioqueño-led conglomerates operate on a national basis and have come to control national markets. Although these conglomerates are very important to the regional economy, the region itself is no longer so important for the conglomerates, except for selective purposes. A second factor concerns the centralization of government, which is disadvantageous to developments in the region. Finally, the agricultural frontier has ceased to be an important source of small-scale opportunities.

In the last section of the chapter, I review the literature on Antioqueño economic development and draw some conclusions. Several kinds of theories have been put forward with regard to the particular pattern of Antioquia's development. One group of theories centers on the sociocultural values of the Antioqueño people. A second group tries to explain Antioqueño success by the effects of a particular economic activity. A third group stresses the combination of historical events, without attempting to isolate an ultimate cause. I argue along the lines of the last group. Although I recognize historical factors and processes, I also discuss the internally generated limits to regional autonomy. The regional decline is rooted in the success of the regional elite.

## Rise of the Antioqueño Regional Economy

### Colonial Foundations

It is interesting to observe that the colonial occupation by Spain made the area that now forms the region of Antioquia into a border area. The reasons for this were as follows. The area was disputed by two rival columns of Spaniards who advanced upon the region: the representatives of Pizarro, who came from Peru as far as the Valle del Cauca where they founded Cali in 1536, and the adherents of Heredia, who resided in Cartagena and under whose jurisdiction the area of Antioquia originally fell. The cause of the rivalry basically concerned the search for indigenous gold treasures. A number of towns had been established by Jorge Robledo, the representative of Pizarro, and the Royal Court of the Indias decided to bring Antioquia under control of the Province of Popayan, which belonged to the Audiencia of Quito, that is, it was an area under Pizarro's authority. Later, in 1569, Antioquia was separated from Popayan and became an independent *Gobernación,* independent of Popayan and of the Audiencia of Bogotá, which had been established in 1550 (Parsons 1950:39–43). The region became a sort of no-man's territory rather than a focus of colonial control. Its low priority in the eyes of the colonial administration was a result of other reasons also, namely, the difficulty of the terrain, which made the area almost inaccessible, and the low density of indigenous population.

The fact that the area was settled at all rather than left uninhabited was due to the presence of gold. Apart from the excavation of indigenous tombs (by the *huaqueros*), gold was mined in two ways: riverbed mining *(Minería de aluvión)* and the exploitation of auriferal deposits *(minería de veta)*. The latter required considerable investment in capital (slaves) and the state of its technology was very rudimentary. Most gold mining was of the riverbed type, undertaken in two ways: by means of slave labor or by individual independent miners. Given the additional difficulty of foot provisioning, exploitation of deposits with slave labor (*escuadrillas) de esclavos* represented only a small proportion, limited to the richest deposits (West 1972).

A rough idea of the importance of Antioquia in gold production during the colonial period is shown by data collected by Restrepo (1888), and given here in Table 7.1

Important mineral deposits were found in the north in the area of Buritaca, Remedios, Zaragoza, and later in the south, for example, Mariquita. As the exploration of deposits moved southward, Santa Fe de Antioquia lost much of its importance. Medellin and Rionegro came to flourish as administrative and commercial centers provisioning the mining population. Population settlement and growth in the colonial period basically was restricted to the (highland) area defined by these three towns.

A fundamental problem of gold mining was the need to engage in agricultural subsistence activities in order to ensure a basic supply of food. Given the difficulty of transport and the dispersed character of mining operations, it would have been too costly to import all food. The colonial administration attached considerable importance to gold mining, and land was given in

TABLE 7.1
Value of Gold Production, Antioquia and Colombia (Sixteenth–Nineteenth centuries) (in millions of gold pesos)

| | *Antioquia* | *Colombia* | *Share Antioquia* |
|---|---|---|---|
| Second half sixteenth century | 10 | 53 | 18.9% |
| Seventeenth century | 50 | 173 | 28.9% |
| Eighteenth century | 64 | 205 | 31.2% |
| Nineteenth century (to 1886) | 126 | 208 | 60.6% |

*Source:* Based on Restrepo (1888:43, 157).

concession only. In other words, there was considerable restraint in the granting of land for the establishment of traditional haciendas. However, these were not lacking in (highland) Antioquia, as Lopez Toro (1976) has indicated. The small individual miner (the *mazamorrero*), was also protected to some extent: he was free to grow food within a fixed perimeter surrounding his mining operation.

Although these two measures implied that the land frontier remained open, they did not correct the basic poverty of agricultural production in the region. The highlands contained poor agricultural soils, and mining had priority in the lower-altitude and less-healthy lands. Many basic necessities of life, such as meat and salt, had to be imported from elsewhere, as did more luxurious food products such as sugar, cacao, spices, oils, wine, and tobacco. Furthermore, metal was needed for the mining operations and textiles had to be brought in. Given the dispersed character of demand (a thin demand surface), small travelling merchants became key figures in the Antioqueño economy, not only providing these necessities but becoming principal intermediaries in the legal and illegal marketing of gold. Smuggling of gold and of foreign imports always constituted an important but unknown proportion of international trade, in spite of all preventive measures and actions taken by the colonial administrators. However, the Antioqueño traders, who had emerged from the ranks of local people rather than from the colonial self-made aristocracy, were constrained by colonial trade monopolies, so that their real rise would come only after independence (Lopez Toro 1976).

The fundamental problems of the region, characterized by a chronically deficient and expensive food supply for the mining population, a general shortage of land available for agriculture, and at the same time, growing population pressure in the highland areas of early settlement, were recognized by the colonial officials. The most important of these officials was Mon y Velarde, Oidor del Virrey, who came to the region in 1785 (cf. Poveda Ramos 1979). One of the reforms implemented by Velarde was the establishment of so-called agricultural colonies. Approved in 1789, this reform aimed at stimulating land settlement in order to ease population pressure in the highlands but, above all, to increase food supplies to the mining population, which then would be able to expand (Lopez Toro 1976). An agricultural colony typically was a collective form of land settlement, combining the foundation of a new town and the allocation of urban plots to families who also had rural holdings. A number of new settlements were established in this way in towns in the northern part of Antioquia, such as San Carlos and Yarumal, and in the former mining camps of Carolina and Don Matias. These were camps of *mazamorreros* who were thus able to organize themselves as a land-holding rural community (Parsons 1950:62–70).

Under the land-reform laws of Mon y Velarde, which did not respect earlier rights of large traditional landowners, the organized form of collective land settlement soon produced conflicts between settlers and traditional holders of the land (either in property or in concession). Such conflicts became more frequent in the nineteenth century when the southern land-settlement movement began, partly under these laws.

In the late-eighteenth century, and despite the agrarian reforms, mining entered a deep crisis. The easiest deposits of alluvial gold were exhausted, techniques by which to develop auriferal deposits were lacking, the small independent miners became impoverished due to this poor state of affairs and also the squeeze imposed by merchants; also, slave mining stagnated due to its high costs and the shortage of slaves (Poveda Ramos 1979).

**Independence, Federal State, and International Trade**

Independence brought a number of important economic implications for Antioquia. Many marginal miners had left the region and joined Bolivar's liberation armies, as did many of the remaining slaves. In addition, more labor went into subsistence agriculture and into artisan occupations, which previously had been discouraged. Not only were trade monopolies abolished but also the state monopsony on gold exports. The Antioqueño merchants, who controlled a large share of the national production of gold, saw their position rapidly improve. They started to trade directly in Jamaica with English and other European traders, obtaining considerably higher trade margins. Furthermore, they started to provide the new national government with loans in exchange for considerable privileges, such as land and mining concessions and trade advantages. This group of merchants now started to invest in mining based on the new technology brought in by Europeans. As a result, gold production, which had entered a crisis even before Independence, now started to grow again and Antioquia increased its share to about 60% of the national total—an increase that in part was due to the stagnation of gold production in other areas, notably Cauca. The biggest boom took place between 1830 and 1850.

The role played by the Antioqueño elite in national politics was rather discrete, comparable to that of the bankers. The fact that they were not in need of national government resources but, on the contrary, provided loans to the national government, gave the Antioqueños an alternative way of exercising power.

The change to a federal structure in the middle of the nineteenth century was necessary to conserve a minimum of national unity. This change must have suited the Antioqueños very well. Being financially independent and controlling a large portion of international trade, they could mind their own affairs directly *without* too much interference by national government. Under the Berrio administration, centralization of the State of Antioquia, at the cost of local government (the *Cabildos*), further strengthened the power of this merchant class.

As communications improved in the second half of the nineteenth century, Antioqueño traders established direct trade contacts in Europe, thus creating an important barrier to the entry of new members into their class. Small retail merchants who had made considerable profits in the past were able to expand into international trade by investing in Jamaican contacts. When Jamaica was displaced by direct trade with Europe, such a step became more difficult, and the historical ease with which new members could enter and were accepted into the upper ranks of society effectively declined (Brew 1977). The elite became a closed social group.

A regional elite had thus emerged from among the small traders who had accumulated considerable wealth and economic power, and who, as a result of the change to a federal structure, came to control the legal and political administrative apparatus in the area. They were able to ensure the creation of those public goods and services that would promote their own interests, without having to struggle and compromise with elite factions from other regions. However, the result of this political–administrative "closure" was not a rigid social structure, because land settlement had become a new channel for social mobility.

Several factors must be taken into account when considering Antioqueño land settlement processes in the nineteenth century. First, the relatively high demographic growth in Antioquia and the growing population pressure in the older established areas, together with various export staple booms, for example, in cacao, stimulated the settlement of new land. To this domestic component must be added the influx of migrants from Colombian states, escaping the ravages of civil conflict and wars. This factor became more important in the last decades of the nineteenth century, when migrants from Tolima, Cundinamarca, and the two Santanderes arrived in Quindio (Parsons

1950:85). In 1835, the population of Antioquia was no more than 158,000 in an estimated total population in Colombia of 1.68 million. In other words, it constituted 9% of that total. In 1870, just before the large-scale expansion of coffee production, Antioquia had 366,000 inhabitants and its share in total population had risen to 12.5% (Urrutia and Arrubla 1970:30). By 1938, Antioquia's population had grown to 2.2 million, and constituted 26% of the total population of 8.4 million (Parsons 1950:110).

A third and very critical factor concerned the importance the Antioqueño elite attached to land settlement. After the mining boom, which lasted until about 1850, the Antioqueño traders became interested in new export products that would allow them to maintain their position in international trade. This helps to explain their interest in commercial crops such as cacao, tobacco, indigo, and, later, coffee. Land settlement was needed to develop this agriculture. Furthermore, and given pasturage improvements in the second half of the century, the elite also were interested in expanding their herds on the extensive lands they had come to own since Independence. Livestock formerly had been very poorly developed in Antioquia, whereas demand continued to increase. To develop the livestock haciendas, labor was needed to convert the land into pasturage. The merchant elite had an additional reason to be interested in land settlement—great tracts of public land could be obtained in concession from the state government in exchange for road construction. That these roads were especially important to the traders to stimulate trade exchange needs no elaboration.

Three types of land settlement took place during the nineteenth century. The first was the collective type under the land-reform laws created by Mon y Velarde. The more adventurous settlers formed themselves into groups and went south, after obtaining government permission, often still motivated by the search for gold. Towns such as Abejoral (1808), Santa Rosa de Cabal (1844), Neira (1843), and Manizales (1848) were all founded in this manner in the first half of the nineteenth century. A number of others followed, such as Pereira (1863), Armenia (1889), Circasia (1889), and Montenegro (1892). Many of these new settlements were situated in very large land concessions that had been granted in the (colonial) past (e.g., the Villegas and Aranzaru concession), giving rise to prolonged conflicts between groups of settlers and landholders. Villegas gives a detailed description of some of these conflicts, for example, one that concerned the founding of Manizales (Villegas 1978). The Antioqueño merchants who were interested in extending the land frontier were not particularly keen on backing the traditional landowners, and often supported the settlers in their claims against national and, later, federal governments.

A second type of land settlement was organized directly by the Antioqueño commercial elite, for the purpose of establishing livestock estates on their landed properties and in exchange for labor in the road construction projects. In the latter case, road construction workers received small holdings along the newly created road. According to Lopez Toro (1976), the significance of the creation of livestock haciendas as a result of the extension of the land frontier has long been underestimated. To support his claim he shows that in the period between Independence and 1880 the stock of animals expanded more than 20 times. Poveda Ramos provides additional and more detailed evidence, showing that there were some 43.5 thousand head of livestock in 1826. By 1876, this figure had risen to 360,000 and by 1882 to 456,000, after which the stock declined somewhat to 412,000 in 1888 (Poveda Ramos 1979:104). Although the expansion of livestock haciendas does not seem as spectacular as Lopez Toro suggests, these figures nevertheless confirm the growing importance of their development for the land-settlement process.

The construction of roads and, later, railroads, and the private organization of land settlement are clear examples of the work of nineteenth-century land development companies (cf. Christie 1978). For the state, this particular combination was a convenient way to develop infrastructure without having to draw heavily on limited fiscal resources.

The third type of land settlement, that of the individual family, had always existed in connection with, and following, collective colonization efforts. The original group of early settlers who founded a town played a central role, through the *Cabildos,* in allocating land to newly arriving families. This gave the early settlers a considerable social advantage over the new arrivals and helped them to become the local elite in control of trade and local government. A very clear example of such social mobility is the local elite of Manizales, who emerged in this way and grew very powerful through trade in cacao and later coffee (cf. Brew 1977:180ff).

These settler households existed mainly on a subsistence economy, combined with some high value-to-weight cash products (e.g., pigs fattened with maize). The economic viability of these peasant holdings increased greatly from 1870 onward with the growth of coffee production. Within the State of Antioquia, coffee spread to the peasant holdings that had only recently been established and spurred new waves of land settlement southwards. In Chapter 5, I documented the general and spatial pattern of coffee trade expansion and can therefore restrict myself here to the impact of coffee production on the regional social structure.

Individual Antioqueño merchants had shown interest in coffee since 1850 and several early establishments of coffee plantations have been recorded in the northern part of the state (Brew 1977). These were not successful ventures and were mostly given up after some time, but they constituted important entrepreneurial experiences to be made use of in later stages. Furthermore, they may have induced the merchant elite to stimulate coffee production among peasant families in the southern part where agronomic conditions were superior and to concentrate on coffee processing and trade. In this context the efforts of the Uribe Fernandez, Ospina Rodriguez, and Vasquez Jaramillo families in promoting coffee-cultivation technology obtained in Guatemala must be mentioned. By introducing the first threshing machines, these families started to centralize the coffee trade. In addition, by exporting *café verde* instead of *café pergamino* they were able to improve considerably their commercial margins on the exported product. Finally, the commercial elite encouraged the use of hand-driven *despulpadores* (threshers), which enabled the small coffee grower to do the first stage of processing on the farm. This not only improved the quality of the product but also the possibility of storing the coffee for a longer period. These factors, together with the fact that on small family holdings harvesting was done more carefully and in several rounds (selecting ripe fruits only)—whereas on large plantations harvesting was in one or two rounds only—were important also in explaining the higher quality of Colombian coffee over, for example, Brazilian (Brew 1977:270–284). The difference was expressed in smaller variations in quantity and prices in the international market. The favorable demand for Medellin-quality coffee stimulated the growth of Antioqueño coffee production and trade.

As shown in Chapter 5, the expansion of the railroads played a critical role in this process. The first railway connection in Antioquia was between the Rio Magdalena and Medellin, for which the contract was signed by the State of Antioquia and the Cuban engineer Cisneros in 1874. The position of the Medellin merchants was strengthened by these improvements in transport and communications.

However, the great southward expansion of coffee production moved the center of gravity toward Manizales and later to Pereira, and to towns in Tolima such as Ibague. It made it possible for the new local elites to penetrate the coffee trade and to acquire more political power. This is clearly shown by the rise of the Manizales elite (cf. Brew 1977; Ocampo 1972). In their attempt to escape domination by the Medellin traders, the Manizales elite tried to create their own means of access to the sea via the Magdalena river (the famous air cable to Mariquita) or in other ways. This cable and the new railway link with Cali were developed at the start of the twentieth century. The success of the Manizales group in creating their own power base was only achieved when the new department of Caldas was instituted in 1905.

In the last three decades of the nineteenth century Colombia suffered a series of civil conflicts. The federal government, with varying intensity, had adhered to liberal doctrines of free international trade. The ravages caused by war and conflict added to the general state of depression of the national economy, at a time when coffee exports brought new opportunities. Consequently, considerable support was given to a movement, led by Nunez, to reconstitute the Colombian state and economy. His program of "national regeneration" foresaw the reestablishment of a unitary system of government and the creation of a minimum package of central state institutions (see Chapter 5, pp. 107–111). A new constitution was prepared and approved in 1886. The former State of Antioquia became the Department of Antioquia, and functions and prerogatives of the former state government were transferred to the new departmental government. The establishment of a central state government with limited responsibility for the creation and/or improvement of basic interregional (national) transport infrastructure and other trade services found considerable support among the Antioqueño merchant elite. Some of the conditions for accumulation became *national* in scope. It is one thing to export gold that is also the medium of exchange for the acquisition of imports, but quite another to export a large volume of coffee.

As shown in Chapter 5, however, Nunez's proposals met with considerable opposition in various regions with regard to both the general and the specific projects he proposed, such as the Banco Nacional. The War of a Thousand Days (1899–1902), which was the culmination of these tensions, brought the defeat of traditional regional power. The almost-dictatorial administration of General Rafael Reyes which followed, had significant implications for the future development of Antioquia.

## Antioqueño Early Industrialization

Although the central part of Antioquia had experienced considerable population pressure combined with poor soils, artisan activity in the nineteenth century in Antioquia had never reached a high level, compared with that in Santander, for example (cf. Jones 1977). The greater transportation difficulties in Antioquia were most likely the cause, together with alternative (self-) employment in land settlement and mining. The general increase in economic activity nevertheless stimulated artisan development. In 1869, according to the census for that year, there were some 18,000 artisans and 62 *fabricantes* in Antioquia (owners and workers). Most of these were active in pottery, gold work, wood work, clothing, metal forging, and the like—all of which were oriented toward local demand.

In the last quarter of the nineteenth century, factory-type production of textiles, soaps, beer, and metal work was attempted in Medellin and Manizales and also in other towns. The urban growth of Medellin had also made it possible to develop the first building-materials industries (brick making). Finally, the expansion of more capital-intensive mining and coffee production, particularly coffee processing, stimulated the emergence of metal foundries—to make parts and components for imported machines, but also to make coffee threshing and depulping machines. Brew gives a detailed description of a number of firms established in the 1880s and 1890s (Brew 1977:285–392). The 1883 census enumerated 485 *fabricantes* and some 22,000 artisans in Antioquia. According to Poveda Ramos (1979), at the end of the nineteenth century Antioquia already was competing with Santander for the position of second-most industrialized region in Colombia after Bogotá. But as the level of industrial activity in Santander declined and that in Bogotá stagnated, Antioquia showed vigorous expansion (Poveda Ramos 1979:149). What made Antioquia become the foremost industrial region of the country in the period that followed? To understand the Antioqueño development path a number of factors must be considered.

Since the Regeneration, and particularly under Reyes, governments became more nationalistic and more intent on industrialization through protectionist measures. The growth of coffee production stimulated demand in various ways, not only at the level of peasant farms but also through the additional income triggered-off by coffee production, processing, and trade. Furthermore, the coffee infrastructure helped to unify regional markets through drastic reductions in transport costs.

In addition, a number of other factors were specific to Antioquia. First, the War of a Thousand Days, which was not fought in Antioquia, most seriously affected the east of the country. It caused the virtual destruction of industrial activities in the Santanders and provoked capital flight toward Antioquia. Second, thanks to substantial gold deposits, the Antioqueños could protect themselves against government measures to control rampant inflation during and after the war, particularly the massive internal devaluation of the peso. Together with these measures, the war caused industrial activity to decline considerably in Santander, Cundinamarca, Boyaca, and Tolima. Third, mining and coffee had provided important industrial experience, not only in running industrially organized enterprises but also in creating a skilled urban industrial workforce. In this context is is also important to mention the Escuela de Minas (School of Mines), which stimulated technological capacity in the region. Fourth, the region had sources of hydraulic energy available with which people had become familiar through its use in mining.

The most important factor, however, seems to have been the changing outlook of the Antioqueño elite regarding opportunities for accumulation. They had lost ground in several fields, namely, gold mining, coffee-export trade, and import trade, and consequently had to look for new investment opportunities. With regard to gold mining, new technological changes in riverbed (the dragline) and shaft mining, which were instrumental in enlarging the share of North American companies in gold production (Pato Consolidated Mining and Frontino Gold Mines), enabled these companies to displace the larger Antioqueño and early British ventures and, to a lesser extent, the small and independent miners (cf. Melo 1974; Lopez Castano and Arango Restrepo 1977). Important trade in coffee exports and import business was lost to Manizales (coffee) and to Cali (coffee and imports) as a result both of changes in the national transport system and of the administrative reorganization under Reyes that led to the separation of Viejo Caldas from Antioquia (and from some other parts taken from Tolima and Valle)

As other regions were opened-up by coffee and trade, their local elites started to compete with the Antioqueño merchants. As banking and the recently introduced paper money reduced the role of gold in exchange, the merchants lost much of their original monopolistic advantage. During the first two decades of the twentieth century many Antioqueño merchants returned home with their capital, looking for alternative investment opportunities, which clearly were necessary. In effect, favorable national and regional conditions that had presented themselves in industry had given the Antioquia region considerable permanent *and* temporary advantages. In this context, the Antioqueño merchants' long-established contacts in England were no doubt useful in the acquisition and absorption of manufacturing technology.

In Chapters 5 and 6, I discussed early—twentieth century industrialization in general and industrialization of textiles in particular, so I can be quite brief here. Although the region's early period of industrialization was characterized by considerable diversity, the industrial base in Antioquia soon became

TABLE 7.2
Manufacturing Employment in Antioquia, 1924

| | *Men* | *Women* | *Total* | *Distribution (%)* |
|---|---|---|---|---|
| Textile factories | 379 | 981 | 1,360 | 24.7 |
| Beer & soft drinks factories | 124 | 111 | 235 | 4.3 |
| Printing and lithography | 101 | 151 | 252 | 4.5 |
| Chocolate factories | 47 | 12 | 59 | 1.0 |
| Coffee threshing factories | 112 | 1,918 | 2,030 | 36.9 |
| Cigarette factories | 146 | 370 | 516 | 9.4 |
| Tile making factories | 151 | 6 | 157 | 2.8 |
| Sweets and biscuits factories | 35 | 47 | 82 | 1.5 |
| Candle and match factories | 16 | 72 | 248 | 1.6 |
| Leather factories | 141 | 107 | 88 | 4.5 |
| Others | 269 | 209 | 478 | 8.6 |
| Total | 1,521 | 3,984 | 5,505 | 100.0 |

*Source:* Poveda Ramos (1979:172).

dominated by coffee threshing and by textiles, as indicated in Table 7.2. In 1924, one-third of the total and almost one-half of the female labor force was employed in coffee processing (female labor being used particularly in the selection of the beans). This predominance later disappeared, as the textile industry became more capital intensive and coffee threshing and processing became almost entirely mechanized. By 1945, the female labor force had declined to 49% of the total, and later decreased even more.

Table 7.2 shows that in the mid-1920s more than half the industrial workforce was occupied in the two principal sectors. The importance of coffee processing as the largest sector once again stresses the significance of the agroindustrial connection in the early industrialization process (cf. Arango 1977).

It is interesting to recall that the strong push for physical and economic integration under the aegis of the *national* government was initiated under the administration of Pedro Nel Ospina (1922–1926), an Antioqueño industrialist of conservative persuasion. Ospina's program of massive public works in transport infrastructure and his organization of the banking system very much resembled an application to the country as a whole of the Antioqueño concept of the role of government. This "Antioqueñization of Colombia" also represented the *beginning* of the "Colombianization of the Antioqueños" (cf. Fajardo 1966).

The Great Depression played a role in the process insofar as it triggered a number of mergers and acquisitions of enterprises in order to overcome the effects of the crisis and to capitalize on the advantages in terms of a more protected domestic market. Even in the 1930s, a number of firms started to operate on a national basis and it was not long before the industrial bourgeoisie organized itself nationally through the powerful Asociación Nacional de Industrias (ANDI). Moreover, ANDI was founded in Medellin and the Antioqueños played a predominant role in it.

The coffee complex had set up the Federation of Coffee Growers much earlier, and thus the two most important activities of the region became organized at the national level. In my view, this meant that the Antioqueño elite was leaving the territorial and economic confines of Antioquia; as a result, its significance for the region would change.

In the early 1920s, however, considerable differences in development style still existed between Antioquia and the other regions. A comparison between Antioquia and Cundinamarca is interesting: two issues stood out in the 1920s and 1930s, namely, the virtual absence of peasant organization and an important urban–industrial labor movement in Antioquia, and the presence of peasant leagues in Cundinamarca. In fact, almost all conflicts over land at that time occurred in Cundinamarca and Tolima, with the exception of isolated cases in the Costa Atlantica (cf. Tovar 1975; Gaitan 1976). These differences may be explained by differences in the agrarian structure of the two regions—particularly in the organization of coffee production, which was the main cause of conflict in Cundinamarca. As we have seen, coffee in Cundinamarca (and in Tolima) was grown on haciendas, and in Antioquia it was grown by independent peasants. In Cundinamarca, the insecurity of tenure prevented tenant farmers from growing coffee trees, something large coffee growers insisted on in order to have an adequate supply of labor during harvest. This situation simply did not exist in Antioquia.

Industrial labor organization in the country as a whole in the 1940s is shown in Table 7.3. This table shows that the largest and most-developed industrial region had the lowest degree of unionization in manufacturing industry, far below the national average. Although the differences may be partly attributed to variations in sectoral composition, in the sense that more female labor (which is generally underpaid and underorganized) was employed in Antioquia (50% in 1945), the very low degree of organization is still striking. It appears that the industrialists had better control over the labor market. Parsons describes the particular labor-relations climate in Antioquia as paternalistic (Parsons 1950:184). Moreover, the intertwining of agrarian and industrial interests in Antioquia meant that the political cleavages between liberals and conservatives were not as marked there as in Cundinamarca. As a result, the *Revolución en Marcha,* from which the labor movement received support, was less strongly felt in Antioquia and hence labor unions had less chance to develop. However, in the absence of greater insight into the local regional political situation in the 1940s, this last conclusion can only be tentative.

TABLE 7.3
Employment and Union Membership in Manufacturing in Colombia, by Region, 1942 and 1945

| | *Employment 1945* | *Union members 1942* | *Degree of organization (%)* |
|---|---|---|---|
| Antioquia | 34,648 | 445 | 1.3 |
| Atlantico | 14,405 | 2,866 | 19.9 |
| Cund'ca | 27,694 | 3,886 | 14.0 |
| Valle | 17,979 | 1,233 | 6.8 |
| Magdalena | 1,239 | 590 | 47.6 |
| Other departments | 37,328 | 2,527 | 6.7 |
| Total[a] | 135,400 | 11,767 | 8.7 |

[a]Total includes Territorios Nacionales.
*Sources:* Employment taken from DANE: Census of Manufacturing Industry; Union membership from Urrutia (1969:208–209, Table 20).

TABLE 7.4
Manufacturing Industry in Medellin, Antioquia, and Colombia, 1945

| | *Medellin* | *(%)* | *Antioquia* | *(%)* | *Colombia* | *(%)* |
|---|---|---|---|---|---|---|
| Number of establishments | 789 | (10) | 1,288 | (16) | 7,853 | (100) |
| Employment | 23,422 | (17) | 34,648 | (25) | 135,400 | (100) |

*Sources:* DANE: Census of Manufacturing Industry 1945; Poveda Ramos (1979:192)

The national process of industrial expansion continued at a considerable pace. It was interrupted only by the Great Depression, and was stimulated by additional protectionist measures. The process was no longer restricted to Antioquia: the regional as well as the sectoral basis broadened, so that Antioquia's share in total manufacturing industry in effect declined. Some researchers have estimated that that share represented about half the total manufacturing industry in the mid-1920s. However, by 1945, it had dropped to slightly over one-quarter (see Table 7.4).

## National Economic Integration and Regional Restructuring (1950–1980)

We have seen in Chapter 6 that the process of post–World War II economic development extended rapidly over many regions. While early industrialization, changes in coffee growing, and other agricultural changes were limited mostly to Cundinamarca, Antioquia, Viejo Caldas, Valle, and to some extent, Tolima and Atlantico, they were extended during the 1950s–1960s to more regions, most notably to the Costa Atlantica, but also to old subsistence regions in the southwest and northeast and to some newly settled regions such as Meta. The various "frontiers of development" (cf. Henessy 1978) were now found in regions other than Antioquia, which had fallen back several steps in the league of economic and social development indicators. What was the reason for this decline?

In this section, I focus on differences in the patterns of industrial development among the three most-developed regions (Antioquia, Valle, and Cundinamarca), in an attempt to understand the factors that shaped the particular situation in Antioquia. I rely on the analysis presented in Chapter 5, complemented by a number of other regional studies, and argue that at least five factors have played a role: (1) the wearing down of the regional economic base—the loss of part of the coffee trade and also gold-mining, which already had happened but continued to have lasting effects into this period; (2) the growing national orientation of the Antioqueño elite; (3) the protection of the regional economy against entry of unwanted extraregional firms (which is related to the second factor); (4) the centralization of government, which had a negative effect on Antioqua, in terms of both the economic impact of government expenditure and decision-making processes; (5) the closing of the Antioqueño land frontier.

It will be recalled that the settlement of new land previously stimulated by the coffee expansion petered out in the 1950s. Data on the settlement of public lands show that between 1931 and 1941 some 212,000 has of public land were converted into private property in Antioquia/Choco, constituting 33% of the national total. During the next nine years, only some 83,000 has changed title, representing only 8% of the total (DANE 1976). In addition, and particularly during the 1960s and 1970s, considerable concentration started to take place in coffee production. Town-based groups started to acquire coffee holdings. Peasants were displaced by capitalist enterprises as production became increasingly technical and capital using *(caturra)*. The "small man's frontier" that had contributed so much to the economic expansion and social mobility in the region disappeared. Although land settlement acquired renewed significance in the northwest (Uraba) in the 1970s, it had become a "big man's frontier" of developing banana plantations.

In general terms, industrial development during the 1950s and 1960s was particularly marked in Valle and Cundinamarca rather than in Antioquia. Regions with the largest markets benefited from the policy of protecting the national market, but some benefited more than others, for regionally specific reasons. Valle, for example, initially had two additional favorable factors: the improved international access of Cali because of the Buena Ventura harbor, and the expansion of sugar plantations. Many foreign enterprises that came to Colombia during the import-substitution era of the 1950s and 1960s set up industries that nevertheless were import-intensive. They preferred Cali for the reasons just mentioned. The expansion of sugar production brought sugar refining and extension into certain sugar-intensive food-processing industries. As a result, Valle's industrial structure consisted of two clearly identifiable parts: the food processing industries that were in the hands of the local regional *landed* elite (the sugar barons), on the one hand, and a diverse group of foreign-owned consumer and intermediate product industries, on the other (Walton 1977). Since the late 1960s, industrialization in Valle has stagnated, mainly because the centralization of government decision making causes new foreign enterprises to prefer to locate in Bogotá. In fact, some firms based in Cali have relocated for this reason or have set up a national office in Bogotá (cf. Vellinga and Kruit 1983).

Initially, the pattern of Cundinamarca's industrial expansion was similar to that of Valle, insofar as new intermediate sectors were added to the regional industrial base as a result of foreign investment. No similar strong growth occurred in the agroindustry, however; industry became more diversified and, in contrast to developments in Valle, foreign enterprise did not attain any considerable importance.

Finally, industrial growth in Antioquia was not as high as in the other two regions and was differently formed. The greatest expansion took place in the 1950s in sectors in which the region had *already developed a strong base,* namely, tobacco, beverages, clothing and textiles; other sectors, including some that already had been established, lagged behind. This two-fold process caused the regional industrial base to become highly specialized. In the 1960s, there was a general marked slowdown in growth of demand for these traditional consumer-goods industries; it is not surprising that this seriously affected industrial expansion in Antioquia. This pattern remained unchanged throughout the 1970s, despite the short export-led upswing, particularly in textiles and clothing.

The differences in the industrial sector become even clearer after examining the level of diversification of the regional industrial export base (see Figures 5.1 and 5.2). Although the industrial composition of Valle and Cundinamarca is highly diversified, that of Antioquia is heavily specialized. A look at the sectoral composition of the export base sharpens the picture even more (see Table 7.5). In 1945, the textile industry was estimated to represent 89% of the industrial base, and this was virtually the same in 1958 (87%). Over time, the figure declined somewhat but textiles did not lose its dominant position. Since the late 1950s, in fact, there has been little change in the export-base structure. In contrast, the export base in Cundinamarca changed completely, as old export sectors (consumer goods) were replaced by new (intermediate and capital goods). Valle is in an intermediate situation: food processing (agro-based industries) constitutes its single largest component; secondary export bases are varied but consist mostly of intermediate goods. The post-war industrial development pattern in Antioquia seems to have been characterized by expansion and consolidation in the early industrial sectors without any dynamic process of diversification and change.

My analysis of the industrial conglomerates confirms this tendency (see Chap. 5, pp. 161–166). Of the 10 large industrial conglomerates that developed in Antioquia in the 1960s and 1970s, 9 were built up around enterprises in textiles, beverages, clothing, food, and cement. Although all conglomerates operate nationally, those of Antioqueño origin tend to have the highest proportion of enterprises within Antioquia. The other large conglomerates, including Bavaria, Colinsa, Avianca, Echevarria, etc., do not have such strong locational preferences.

Finally, it is striking that the presence of foreign enterprise and investment

TABLE 7.5
Sectoral Composition of Industrial Export Base of Antioquia, Cundinamarca, and Valle, Selected Years. 1945–1980
(three largest export sectors and their respective shares in total)

| Region | *1945* | | *1958(A)* | | *1958(B)* | | *1967* | | *1980* | |
|---|---|---|---|---|---|---|---|---|---|---|
| Antioquia | Textiles | (89%) | Textiles | (87%) | Textiles | (85%) | Textiles | (82%) | Textiles | (79%) |
| | Other manufacturing | (8%) | Tobacco | (6%) | Tobacco | (6%) | Clothing | (6%) | Tobacco | (10%) |
| | Mineral products | (3%) | Clothing | (4%) | Clothing | (6%) | Other manufacturing | (4%) | Clothing | (5%) |
| Cundinamarca | Beverages | (41%) | Beverages | (25%) | Beverages | (23%) | Oil derivatives | (21%) | Rubber | (17%) |
| | Mineral products | (37%) | Mineral products | (23%) | Mineral products | (22%) | Transport equipment | (14%) | Electrical machinery | (16%) |
| | Printing and publishing | (19%) | Paper and paper products | (13%) | Paper and paper products | (12%) | Mineral products | (14%) | Transport equipment | (11%) |
| Valle | Food | (42%) | Food | (44%) | Food | (43%) | Food | (45%) | Food | (45%) |
| | Rubber | (20%) | Oil derivatives | (33%) | Oil derivatives | (32%) | Furniture | (18%) | Paper and paper products | (21%) |
| | Metal products | (13%) | Chemicals | (12%) | Chemicals | (12%) | Oil derivatives | (16%) | Chemicals | (16%) |

*Source:* Based on Helmsing 1983b.

in Antioquia differs somewhat in comparison with other regions. In 1970, Antioquia had only 14.5% of total foreign investment in Colombia. By contrast, Cundinamarca had 37% and Valle 24% (Arango 1976). Moreover, foreign investment in Antioquia was concentrated primarily in a single sector, namely (synthetic) textiles. Considering the regional distribution of *all* enterprises with any foreign participation, it appears that in 1973 they produced 29% of total value added in Antioquia, only 26% in Cundinamarca, and 25% in Valle. Therefore, it seems reasonable to assume that national capital presence in these enterprises in Antioquia is stronger than in other regions (Parra Sandoval 1977:254).

Antioquia's relatively low share of total foreign investment may be explained in various ways: either foreign enterprise preferred not to locate in Antioquia or it was actively discouraged from doing so, except in cases (textiles) where this suited local industrial interests. The former does not seem applicable to Antioquia (other than to Valle), at least until the late 1960s when Bogotá became a favored location, as a result of the continued centralization of government. After all, the region did have and still has a sizable market, good-quality transport and other physical and economic infrastructure, and a large and disciplined labor force. The reason for Antioquia's low share is often sought in the regionalist attitudes of the homogeneous and strongly intertwined Antioqueño industrial elite (cf. Walton 1977; Vellinga and Kruit 1983).

Although many historical and cultural reasons for this alleged regionalistic behavior can be cited, there may clearly be other, economic, motivations. Why would the industrial elite continue to be so regionalist when these conglomerates had obtained strong oligopolistic and in some instances monopolistic positions in the *national* market and when many material inputs were procured from other regions? One plausible answer may be found in the labor market. In other words, in early industrial activities such as textiles and clothing, in which labor costs constitute a relatively large proportion of production costs, control over the labor market may be instrumental in keeping wages down, certainly in a situation where nationally organized collective wage bargaining is unknown, as in Colombia. Such advantages of a stable and relatively low-wage labor force could also be obtained through fencing off the local labor market against unwanted foreign firms, which is made possible by the reputed close links between the industrial elite and the local and regional government.

This same phenomenon could not apply to Valle, where agro-based industry is located throughout the sugar plantation area, and where a different labor-market segment is tapped than is tapped by the foreign enterprises located in Cali. In the case of Bogotá, the large increase in the supply of labor resulting from high immigration would make such a labor-market strategy less necessary. Moreover, in accordance with the sectoral composition of the economy, the labor market would be more diversified in the case of Valle and Cundinamarca.

Table 7.6 compares the share of labor costs in gross production in the various activity sectors for selected years of the postwar period, showing that textiles and clothing were by no means the activities with the greatest share of labor costs. In the 1950s, their labor costs constituted only 15% of total gross value of the respective sectoral outputs. In the 1960s and 1970s, however, this share rose to 21% and 19%, respectively, so that at the end of this period these two sectors had the fifth and sixth highest shares of labor costs. Moreover, in Antioquia these sectors consistently show somewhat higher shares. If we examine the average wage per worker, the labor-market control argument would indicate a relatively low wage level in Antioquia, in comparison with other regions. In Table 7.7 the average regional wage in manufacturing has been calculated for selected years. Because Antioquia ranks in all years among regions with the highest average wage, it seems difficult to support the original hypothesis.

TABLE 7.6
Wages as Percentage Share of Value Gross Output by Sector, Colombia, 1958, 1967, 1980

| | *1958* (%) | *1967* (%) | *1980* (%) |
|---|---|---|---|
| Food | 4.7 | 6.2 | 7.7 |
| Beverages | 10.9 | 13.8 | 11.5 |
| Tobacco | 7.1 | 9.3 | 10.5 |
| Textiles | 15.4 | 21.1 | 18.6 |
| Clothing | 15.4 | 16.3 | 21.3 |
| Wood | 17.6 | 20.6 | 16.3 |
| Furniture | 28.8 | 29.3 | 28.2 |
| Paper | 12.4 | 13.1 | 12.1 |
| Printing | 24.6 | 24.6 | 21.4 |
| Leather | 14.0 | 13.8 | 19.4 |
| Rubber | 16.6 | 21.7 | 15.3 |
| Chemicals | 11.8 | 13.9 | 12.4 |
| Oil and oil derivatives | 6.9 | 6.2 | 4.6 |
| Non-metallurgical minerals | 24.5 | 25.2 | 21.6 |
| Metallurgical | 10.6 | 7.2 | 22.5 |
| Metal products | 17.8 | 21.5 | 17.4 |
| Nonelectrical machinery | 26.9 | 29.0 | 17.7 |
| Electrical machinery | 14.4 | 17.9 | 14.9 |
| Transport equipment | 36.9 | 25.1 | 12.9 |
| Other manufacturing | 21.3 | 19.8 | 18.2 |

*Sources:* 1958 and 1967: CID 1970; 1980: DANE 1980.

TABLE 7.7
Average Nominal Wage per Employee, by Sector and by Region, Colombia, 1958 and 1980 (in thousands of current Colombian pesos)

| | *1958* | *1967* | *1980* |
|---|---|---|---|
| | | **By Sector** | |
| Food | 3,428 | | 176,959 |
| Beverages | 16,951 | | 297,036 |
| Tobacco | 4,849 | | 275,402 |
| Textiles | 5,043 | | 205,793 |
| Clothing | 2,536 | | 111,055 |
| Leather | 2,981 | | 94,726 |
| Wood | 3,357 | | 152,542 |
| Furnitures | 5,192 | | 442,111 |
| Paper | 4,684 | | 312,784 |
| Printing/publ. | 3,928 | | 59,475 |
| Chemicals | 6,333 | | 125,723 |
| Oil & der. | 5,382 | | 713,434 |
| Rubber | 26,447 | | 109,976 |
| Non-metallurgical minerals | 3,845 | | 216,068 |
| Metallurgical | 7,108 | | 316,679 |
| Metal products | 4,010 | | 150,004 |
| Machinery | 4,329 | | 157,826 |
| Elec. Apl. | 4,428 | | 194,869 |
| Transp. eq. | 4,964 | | 218,051 |
| Other Man. | 3,697 | | 157,282 |
| | | **By Region** | |
| Antioquia | 4,805 | 25,208 | 202,102 |
| Atlantico | 4,535 | 17,495 | 192,796 |
| Bolivar | 7,489 | 21,951 | 301,532 |
| Boyaca | 6,319 | 17,825 | 369,448 |
| V. Caldas | 3,259 | 12,768 | 107,387 |
| Cauca | 2,861 | 13,182 | 145,760 |
| Cordoba | 2,896 | 8,515 | 157,218 |
| Cund'ca | 4,741 | 18,756 | 193,317 |
| Huila | 3,706 | 14,142 | 161,522 |
| Magdalena | 3,629 | 20,157 | 201,125 |
| Narino | 2,343 | 9,584 | 162,516 |
| Norte San. | 3,556 | 11,548 | 168,556 |
| Santander | 4,463 | 16,405 | 226,057 |
| Tolima | 4,342 | 13,553 | 138,744 |
| Valle | 4,856 | 20,625 | 212,841 |

*Source:* 1958 and 1967: CID 1970; 1980: DANE 1980.

It will be recalled that unionization was very low in Antioquia. One may argue as an alternative hypothesis that Antioqueño enterprises had succeeded in preventing unionization by paying higher wages. To prevent wages from rising further would certainly create problems for the sectors that were increasingly labor-costs sensitive, such as clothing and textiles. In this way the labor-market strategy may still be relevant. Thus, although the labor-market argument may sound convincing, it is not borne out very strongly by the indicators used.

Another partially overlapping argument to explain the relatively stagnating position of Antioquia is that during the postwar period the Antioqueño elite increasingly operated on a national scale. Instead of continued diversification of economic interests *within* the region, as had previously happened, existing industrial interests were extended nationally. From a historically developed, strong economic and culturally supported base, the industrial elite was able to extend its economic interests into other regions, penetrating markets, acquiring other firms, and so forth, while simultaneously preventing unwanted penetration by extraregional (including international) interests. As shown earlier, numerous present-day conglomerates originated in Antioquia. However, the region has ceased to be the exclusive recipient of investment, employment, and other advantages. Although conglomerates are still very important to the economy of the region, the region has become less important for the Antioqueño-led conglomerates.

It seems reasonable to conclude that several factors explain the relative decline of Antioquia. Some are extraregional factors, such as national policies. Others are connected with the resource base of the region. A third category of factors concerns the relationship between the Antioqueño elite and the regional economy. In essence, the Antioqueño elite stopped being regional and its local and regional political importance may well have contributed to its decline.

## Antioqueño Elite and the Limits of Regional Autonomy: Some Comparisons and Conclusions

Several kinds of theories have been put forward to explain Antioquia's relatively advanced level of development. One group of authors focuses on the particular sociocultural values of (sections of) the Antioqueño people. Others seek the explanation of Antioquia's success in the role of a particular economic activity or sector. A third group of authors stress the importance of the historical combination of events.

Hagen (1962), who belongs to the first group, argues in the context of his general social–psychological theory of change that the Antioqueños were a cultural minority with little if any national prestige; in perceiving this lack of social status after independence in the nineteenth century, they looked for a new identity via economic enterprise. In contrast, the elites of Popayan and Bogotá, who constituted the sociocultural core, aspired to occupations with high social prestige, such as the law, and had no interest in the pursuit of economic gain. Hagen's view has been severely criticized by Safford (1977b) and by others (e.g., Lopez Toro 1976; Brew 1977; Jaramillo Uribe 1982). According to Safford, there is no historical evidence that the Antioqueños were looked down upon or that they perceived themselves as lacking status. Safford reproduces a number of statements made in the mid-nineteenth century in support of his contention. The fact that a great proportion of the gold was produced in Antioquia and controlled by Antioqueño merchants gave them the opportunity to control finance and a large portion of international trade. In this way they developed their entrepreneurial capacities and acquired their particular ethic and personality. Furthermore, their apparent lack of participation in national politics after Independence had little to do with inferior status—they had been the bankers for the early Bogotá governments. In fact, because Antioquia was dominated by a group of thriving capitalists who were accumulating capital at a considerable pace in various activities, there was little need for them to participate in national politics, especially as the State of Antioquia did not depend as much as did other states on the meager national federal budget of that time (Safford 1977b:84).

Fajardo (1966) recognized in the Antioqueños the capitalist virtues that Weber saw in European protestants. In his view, Weber erred in associating such virtues with a religious sect (puritanism): "The development process implies a series of changes in the social organization of a people in fundamental structures such as the family, education, work, group relations, etc., and these changes over generations produced the personality type which coincides with those characteristics presented as 'puritanism' " (1966:21). According to Fajardo, the distinct Antioqueño personality was formed in a situation in which the colonial semifeudal type of social organization implanted by the Spaniards was very weak. There were no *encomiendas* of any importance in the area because there were so few indigenous population. There were neither *encomenderos* nor serfs. The local society was molded instead by pioneering, pioneer towns, and independent small-scale mining. As a result, there was more social mobility in a more egalitarian context. Although Fajardo recognizes that the Antioqueño success story is more complex, including, for example, the agrarian reforms of Mon y Velarde, the Independence war, coffee and land colonization, etc., he singles out as the key factor the weakness of colonial social institutions that caused lack of productivity and passivity in other regions.

The second group of theorists includes Safford, who argues that a key factor was the accumulation of gold by a few Antioqueño traders through trade with the small independent miners. After Independence, gold gave the Antioqueños a decisive advantage over others in controlling international trade. Moreover, they came to act as financiers of the national government in Bogotá and in this way were able to obtain considerable privileges, for example, in land concessions. These concessions were instrumental in enabling this merchant elite to control much of the land-settlement processes, which in turn were important in ensuring future benefit from the subsequent coffee expansion, and so on.

Parsons argues that the Antioqueño success was largely due to the nature of the land-settlement processes, which he was the first to study systematically (Parsons 1950). In his view, gold mining was important insofar as it explains the predominance of mining in land matters. It also explains why the frontier remained open to small settlers. The fast demographic growth and the relatively poor highlands (the area of original settlement) stimulated a considerable migration to, and settlement of, the lower altitudes and the tropical areas, where it eased the supply of agricultural products for the miners. In a way, the merchant elite recognized the convergence of interests and even stimulated land settlement. The emerging independent land-owning peasantry came to constitute the democratic element in Antioqueño agriculture. At the end of the nineteenth century, the development and expansion of coffee cultivation on their holdings boosted internal investment and consumer demand for manufactured products. One reason the merchant elite took this new opportunity for industrialization is because at the turn of the century they had lost much of their control over the western import and coffee trade. This increasingly came into the hands of Cali traders, partly as a result of the changing transport situation (Panama railroad, later canal; the Buena-Ventura port and railroad to Cali, and the Caldas/Antioquia rail connection to Cali).

Urrutia (1972) argues along similar lines, though in slightly different terms. Land settlement gave the agrarian structure a democratic character, and the small farmer/peasant coffee production produced a favorable distribution of income resulting in a comparatively heavy demand for manufactures. McGreevey (1975) draws a similar conclusion about the role of demand created by income from coffee production.

The argument that demand is the principal explanatory factor has been criticized by several authors, including Arango (1977) and Palacios (1982). Arango reasons that one should not attribute so much importance to demand by the small coffee growers because much of the economic surplus was appropriated by traders who controlled the threshing of coffee *(la trilla)*. Instead, he argues that coffee stimulated accumulation by the traders who, through the industrial organization of threshing, acquired the capacity to run fairly large enterprises in the towns. The *trilla* was also the training ground for the urban industrial work force. In the eastern coffee regions where large coffee plantations predominated, coffee was threshed on the estates and did not give rise to any group with industrial managerial experience or to an urban industrial proletariat. Coffee threshing thus constituted a central element of Antioquia's subsequent industrialization.

Palacios supports the first part of Arango's arguments. He estimates the monetary income of small coffee growers in several regions, showing that in fact the income of the Antioqueño and Caldas coffee-growing peasant was much less than that of small coffee growers in Cundinamarca and Tolima (Palacios 1982:91). Palacios, in my view correctly, dissociates himself from the alternative "one equation" explanation offered by Arango. Although Arango certainly brings in a new and relevant dimension (cf. Ocampo 1979), it cannot be considered a complete answer.

This brings us to the third group of authors, who were careful not to participate in the "metaphysics of the ultimate causality" (Jaramillo Uribe 1982). Reference has already been made to Palacios; others include Brew (1977) and Lopez Toro (1976). Lopez Toro's work is admirable for his attempt to combine historiography and (macro)economic theoretical argumentation to achieve an understanding of the broader context of the conditions of social change in Antioquia. Like others before him, Lopez Toro attributes considerable importance to the particular colonial structure of Antioquia, that is, the existence of a social class that did not own much capital or land, but nonetheless combined small-scale mining with subsistence agriculture. This economic activity constituted a real alternative, a safety valve, to the colonial *agregado* or *peon* on the haciendas or in the larger mining companies *(mineria de escuadrilla)*. Out of this social group developed a mercantile class who recovered gold from the dispersed miners in return for basic foodstuffs, clothing, and so forth. According to Lopez Toro, the fundamental disequilibrium between the growing mining sector and a stagnant agriculture enabled a shift in the balance of economic and political power from the traditional colonial elite to this new commercial class, which was able to consolidate itself after independence. Moreover, in the nineteenth century a convergence developed between the interests of settlers, who migrated due to population pressure on the highlands, and those of this dominant class, insofar as the settlement of new land enabled the latter to expand its commercial agriculture and livestock investments and its trade activities.

By the end of the century, land settlement, which had previously taken various forms, became increasingly individual and small scale; with the arrival of coffee, this gave the agrarian structure in the region its particular character of medium-sized and partly-commercialized holdings. The Antioqueño elite, however, began to lose control over mining, which increasingly became a larger-scale shaft mining operation and fell into foreign hands. Moreover, part of its import–export trade was lost to Cali. These factors, together with the political changes of the period, seem to have induced the Antioqueño elite to diversify into manufacturing, taking advantage of the favorable market and production conditions in the region. In the end, Lopez Toro avoids any attempt to single out one particular factor, and his approach is supported by Palacios. The latter stresses the fact that what boosted the demand for manufactures was not so much the growth of demand in a particular group or class, but the entire uplifting of the economy as a result of increases in agricultural production, trade, transport, services, and urbanization and of industry itself (Palacios 1979, 1982). Palacios agrees with the general conclusion reached by Brew (1977) in the latter's very detailed regional history of Antioquia. Brew points to the weakness of colonial structures as a factor that enabled the Antioqueños to make use of international relations rather than be victimized by them, to the importance of small independent mining in creating a small group of merchants, and to the relatively abundant labor force, and then concludes:

> To these favorable circumstances one should add political stability and security; . . . take into account the fortuitous fact that coffee, so successfully planted on the same slopes of the mountains where land settlement had already been accomplished, would be favorable to the development of the market; also, the fast money obtained through speculation during and after the War of a Thousand Days; add further the protectionist effect of the fluctuations of the exchange rate and of the establishment of new tariffs in that time, and one may perhaps have the explanation of why and when the industrialization of Antioquia was initiated. (Brew 1977: 143–144)

One may agree with Brew's conclusion that "the Antioqueños economic success in reality was no more than a historical accident" (ibid.:146). Although in many respects the Antioquia experience was unique and was equalled only in a few other instances (e.g., Monterrey), its uniqueness appears to be particularly a result of the very high level of development that was achieved autonomously (industrialization). This regional success was due to the combined historical occurrence of a number of factors.

If we continue to examine the more recent developments in Antioquia, particularly in the post–World War II period of national integration and restructuring, the following conclusions may be drawn. First, it is important to emphasize the fact that the Antioqueño small man's frontier of opportunities had disappeared. Land settlement declined, and peasants came to suffer strong competition from capitalist enterprises in coffee production. A second and related factor concerns the narrowing of the economic base of the regional economy. Although the economic structure diversified in other (developed) regions, in Antioquia it remained rather static. Third, the centralization of government clearly played a negative role in Antioquia—not only in terms of centralization of decision making, but also in the direct economic effects of government expenditure, which favored the Bogotá economy in particular. Last but most important, emphasis must be placed on the changing role of the Antioqueño elite, which became more nationally oriented and less identified with the regional economy. Whereas in the past the elite had diversifed its economic interests within the region, by means of the strategy of using the accumulated resources of one field of activity to develop new fields in Antioquia, accumulated resources were now more used to finance similar industrial activities in other regions. In fact, the strong links that historically had evolved between homogeneous elite and the regional government may very well have contributed to the relative decline of the regional economy. In other words, the economic success of the elite contained the roots of regional decline.

# PART FOUR
# CONCLUSIONS

# CHAPTER EIGHT
# CONCLUSIONS AND FINAL CONSIDERATIONS

In this study I have attempted to develop and apply a micro-based perspective to rural, urban, and regional dimensions of development. I justify the case for such a perspective on the basis of a critique of the relevance of macro-sectoral and spatial dichotomies and on the recognition of microeconomic heterogeneity and pluriformity.

These dichotomies emphasize the fact that rural and urban processes of change occur simultaneously and in interaction with one another. The empirically observable fact that activities are increasingly urban based cannot be taken as evidence that urbanization is an independent and autonomous process.

In addition to industry-led processes, agriculture-led processes are equally relevant in any explanation of the growth of towns. Similarly, agroindustrial integration cannot take place without expansion of town-based activities. However, these processes do not necessarily coincide spatially. Agroindustrial integration involves a rearrangement of relations at higher national or international levels. In this respect, it is useful to recall some findings of my case studies. The expansion of coffee production exports is an obvious case with which to illustrate these arguments. It required and stimulated multiple transformations that clearly transcended the sector and the regions in which it was situated, and had considerable implications for national economic, political, and physical integration. On a less grand scale, this is also found in the case of cotton, whose development in the Costa triggered a number of further developments in industry, government, and various kinds of service activities, for example, commerce and personal services. It was the combination of the multiple sectoral effects that created such a remarkable impact.

Paraphrasing Von Thuenen (1966), it might be concluded that by using spatial, sectoral dichotomies one tends to separate what in reality is interdependent. For Von Thuenen and for myself, the question is to determine what kind of abstractions are most relevant. I argue in this study that too much emphasis has been placed on bipolar macro-sectoral and spatial divisions. This does not imply, however, an argument in favor of a restoration of unity, for example, between town and countryside or between core and periphery. Rather, higher-level integration and verticalization have resulted. All case studies give supportive evidence in this direction. Before elaborating on this, it is perhaps useful to stress from a somewhat different angle that the institutional setting in which economic development takes place is itself subject to change. An a prior assumption of (inter)*national* frameworks of analysis may result in the loss of an important part of the internal dynamics of processes of change.

The central argument of this study is that conductors and mechanisms of change have come to transcend macro-sectoral, spatial, and spatio-sectoral divisions and dichotomies. Instead of approaching the issues from an aggregate level, whether sectoral or regional, I take a microeconomic approach. I argue that various forms of microeconomic organizations exist that differ among themselves as to goals pursued, internal organization, and spatial scale of operations. In an attempt to capture this microeconomic pluriformity, I identify a working typology consisting of four forms: household, owner-operated, owner-managed, and manager-managed micro-organization of production. If the microeconomic composition of an economy changes, then the mechanisms of rural, urban, and regional development are also altered. In turn, changes in the patterns of rural, urban, and regional development will affect the various microeconomic organizations in different ways. Some types (household, owner-operated) are more affected than others (managed firms) by these changes, and some may be able to adjust (households, managed corporation), whereas others are forced to migrate (households, owner-operated firms). New (managerial) forms of microeconomic organizations have superseded town–country, urban–rural, and regional (core–periphery) divisions, and have themselves become organizing forces of rural, urban, and regional change.

In this context, some conclusions reached in Chapter 5 are pertinent. The (internal) center–periphery model was found applicable to the (macro-) regional pattern of manufacturing change in the 1950s, but ceased to be relevant in the 1970s, when differentiation within core and periphery had become a predominant feature.

Given the surprisingly large gap in development studies of the development of microeconomic organizations, I have taken only small steps toward elaborating the theoretical implications of microeconomic change for macro development. The same applies to my case studies. I have been able to uncover a small part of the ongoing processes of rural, urban, and regional change only at the extremes of household and owner-operated farms and managerial corporations, both Colombian and foreign. The analysis given in Chapter 5 shows the importance of nationally operating conglomerates, which may be seen as indicative of the relevance of my propositions in this respect. The analysis also demonstrates that it would be a considerable oversimplification to dismiss or underestimate the dynamic character of large Colombian conglomerates—some of which have recently gone international—and their role in shaping processes of regional change. The changing composition of cotton producers, in terms of size and location (see the second case study in Chapter 6) also illustrates some micro-level developments at the farm level. At the same time, this study shows that the processes involved are far more complex than had originally been formulated. Microeconomic developments are embedded in an institutional environment that becomes increasingly complex. More research is needed before all these complexities can be unravelled.

The state is a central element in the institutional environment. I have argued, theoretically and empirically, that the growing role of the state and the centralization within it are two dimensions of the same process. I show that the initial outgrowth of the central state in Colombia during the first decades of this century was related to the provision of basic economic and physical infrastructure necessary for the development of coffee exports and early industrialization. Fundamental changes in the political structure resulted—new nationally operating groups displaced regional oligarchies in the control over the (central) state.

Developments in the post–World War II period also lend support to my arguments. Administrative reforms in the late 1950s and the 1960s that resulted in further centralization coincided historically with shifts toward nationalization and internationalization of the (micro-)organization of productive activities. It should be added immediately, however, that the particular political conditions of the era, notably the *Violencia*-instigated National Front agreement, contributed to the selective reorganization of the Colombian state.

Based on these two lines of argument concerning the development of microeconomic organizations and of the state, I have elaborated three partially overlapping processes of rural, urban, and regional change. Nonagricultural activities are being displaced in the countryside, while in agriculture a (multisectoral) process of specialization is taking place that lifts agriculture out of its local setting and inserts it into (inter)nationally operating agro-industrial and trade structures of monopolistic character. The process of specialization is selective, however, and opportunities for agricultural development are unevenly distributed. Because it uses more capital, large-scale managerial production has advantages over small-scale farm and household production. The process is also selective in that it encourages specialization into production areas, reducing local/regional diversification.

With regard to the urban economy, I have shown that economic concentration has led to the development of multisectoral, multicity, and multiregional conglomerates. For historical reasons, many activities may be carried out in a few towns in the most developed regions, but most of these conglomerates have extended into numerous other locations. Given their oligopolistic market positions, the activities of these companies shape decisions made by local and regionally operating firms. Foreign-enterprise establishments are one specific form—transnationally integrated microeconomic organizations, whose local decisions are only in part a function of local conditions. In this respect, these firms are the most advanced but not the only exponents of verticalization processes.

The expanding role of the state and centralization within the state also have important regional implications. I have already mentioned decision making with regard to infrastructure. A second consequence concerns the concentration effects of centralization. The outgrowth of central government institutions in relation to those on a lower level tends to result in greater concentration, particularly of government consumption.

These processes, together with the migratory responses by small firms and households in search of (small) opportunities, have specific urban impacts. Towns cease to be relatively autonomous socioeconomic entities, a phenomenon that occurs in conjunction with a tendency toward urban primacy.

Finally, I discuss the implications of verticalization for regionalism, and reach the conclusion that regionalism may result as a political reaction to this process but may be weakened by several factors, internal and external to the region concerned. The following is a summary of the main findings in relation to these processes. It can be concluded that with the second thrust of national integration in the 1950s and 1960s, verticalization processes became more manifest, and internationalization in the 1960s and 1970s gave it further impulse.

In the cotton-textiles study, I attempt to show the multiple dimensions of rural change. I found that dynamics were not only sectoral but also regional. Relations between cotton growers, textile companies, and the government developed in an interesting way. The organization of cotton growers was called forth by the national and monopsonistic organization of the textile companies. This change in the institutional environment, together with the role of government in providing essential infrastructural facilities, was fundamental in enabling the rapid expansion and regional shift in the production of cotton. Success in terms of increased production and the generation of exportable surpluses pushed for a rearrangement of relations between textile companies, government, and cotton growers, and also interrelations among the latter on regional (Costa vs. Interior) and microeconomic lines (small farms vs. agroenterprises).

The cotton-textile study and the general study of macro and regional developments underline the importance during the postwar period, of agriculture-led in contrast with the frequently emphasized industry-led processes of regional change. Furthermore, I show the importance of local dynamic effects that gave rise to new local regional groups who were able to consolidate their position via the creation of new territorial units of government. The study of the agroindustrial complex demonstrates the regional diversity of processes of rural change. This is directly observable in the cotton case study. For the rest, I examine regional patterns of agricultural production via an a priori categorization of crops according to the predominant form of production. Both studies lend support to propositions concerning regional specialization and displacement of land—uses of land as part and parcel of agroindustrial integration. I observed such changes in the regional patterns only in those crops for which an agro-complex developed. I did not find similar patterns for the other nonincorporated products, and in some cases these even contradicted that pattern. Thus, it seems reasonable to conclude on both theoretical and empirical grounds that a regional diversity of rural situations existed.

With regard to the formation of nationally operating conglomerates, I argue that up to a point the sectoral and regional processes of concentration are two dimensions of the same process—one reinforces the other and vice versa. The relatively closed domestic markets and the limited ability of government to control prices, certainly outside the largest towns, enables firms to administer additional price mark-ups. The rate of accumulation would then soon exceed the growth of the market, so that such firms would expand their activities beyond their original products and markets. Several strategies and combinations thereof are possible: A firm may extend into geographical market areas that are not yet incorporated, it may integrate vertically in forward or backward direction, or it may diversify into related and unrelated fields of investment. Research on Colombia has shown that all strategies have been adopted. Moreover, the transregional character of the large majority of these conglomerates has been clearly established. This lends support to the argument that their investment decisions and intrafirm trade affect interregional economic structures and contribute to verticalization of the regional economies in question.

Similar reasoning can be applied to foreign enterprises. The growing export orientation, in particular, caused extraregional considerations to play a role in local production and investment decisions, even more than in their national counterparts. The proportion of material inputs imported from abroad became greater, and on the whole, the import and export contents of production were also somewhat higher. However, it is unwarranted to conclude, as some have done, that only foreign enterprise shapes the urbanization process. Such a conclusion disregards the dynamic character of Colombian conglomerates.

My case studies have shown that centralization and geographical concentration are very much part of the expanding role of the state. At the same time, it is important to emphasize that the National Front governments created in response to the *Violencia* did not resolve one of its causes, namely, the fundamental weakness of local and regional government. In contrast, further centralization occurred, to some extent in response to the further development of (inter)nationally operating firms and organizations.

The reforms of 1958 and 1968 and the creation of decentralized agencies should be mentioned in this context. Two processes occurred simultaneously. First, government became technically more competent and technocratic, barring clientelism up to a certain point; but, second, it did so almost exclusively at the central level where nationally organized pressure groups had become effective. The regional consequences of this process are not limited to decision-making aspects only. I show in Chapter 5 that centralization was reflected in the growing share of central government in total government revenues and expenditures. In looking at the regional distribution of government expenditures, I found a clear tendency toward concentration in the capital-city region. This shows very clearly for public-sector employment, which constitutes the single largest component of government expenditure. In this way the centralization of government is very much part of "the regional problem."

It seems reasonable to conclude that the case studies provide sufficient indications that propositions concerning verticalization should not be dismissed. In reaching this conclusion, I stress also that verticalization is not synonymous with either stagnation or underdevelopment, but that these may be implied by it. All case studies in this book show that verticalization—a product of the development of micro-organizations and of the state—may go hand in hand with growth.

The case studies only partly illustrate the propositions put forward in Chapter 4 about urbanization. Only to some extent have I been able to identify multilevel organizations in (private) enterprise. Nevertheless, the multicity, multiregional character of the largest conglomerates is clearly established. Furthermore, centralization processes in government, as well as the responses by small firms and households, give support to my analysis of urban primacy, for which I show three indicators, namely migration, growth/decline of population active in artisan and small-scale manufacturing, and local civil protest. Migration focuses increasingly on fewer places, notably Bogotá. Small-firm developments have also concentrated in Bogotá and to some extent in the Valle region, although agricultural and land-settlement processes have also stimulated small-firm activities in other regions. Finally, I found civil protest movements, which tend to be most frequent in the smaller towns, to be primarily a reaction to centralization and a call for increased local government autonomy.

Although there is a broad association between centralization in government and enterprise and urban primacy, there is no reason to adopt a "capital city" versus "rest of country" dichotomy. This would, in fact, underrate the importance of government and enterprises as integrative forces.

All case studies in this volume hint at the importance of both the local and regional dynamics of (new) developments, and local and regional reactions to verticalization. Examples of the former are coffee developments in Antioquia and Caldas and cotton developments in Cesar. Illustrations of the latter include calls for decentralization and the local civil movements of the 1970s. In this context, the conclusion I reach in the Antioquia case study with regard to the role of regionalism (see Chapter 4) is interesting: that is, I identified built-in factors that limited regionalism. During the postwar periods, Antioqueño traders, who had developed multiple economic interests and were considered to be an elite who stimulated and facilitated economic developments in the region, increasingly operated on a national scale. Rather than continuing their diversification within the region, prewar industrial interests were extended nationally. From an historically developed, strong, economically and culturally supported base, this elite was able to expand into other regions, penetrating markets, acquiring other firms, and the like. For the same reason, unwanted entry by extra-regional (including international) enterprises could be prevented. However, the region of Antioquia is no longer the exclusive recipient of investment and employment by the conglomerates that were thus formed. Although these conglomerates are still very important to the economy of the region, the region itself has become less important for the Antioqueño-led conglomerates. Many factors must be taken into account in explaining the relative decline of the economy of Antioquia, but the changing role of the elite, which ceased being regional, has no doubt contributed to it.

This study as a whole has signalled a considerable gap in development studies literature, particularly concerning the development of microeconomic organizations and their implications for (regional) development. Furthermore, when conventional macro-policy prescriptions lose much of their relevance, there is all the more reason to retrace one's steps and to return to the microeconomic building blocks. What are the economic and extra-economic conditions that stimulate or prevent the development of various forms of micro-organizations of production? My typology is only a preliminary one, born out of necessity and certainly open to improvement. More research is needed on individual case histories, for example, by means of composite trajectories of microeconomic develoment. Similarly, comparative research on various regional situations in terms of the composition of microeconomic organizations and the changes therein, may yield more insights in the micro–macro dynamics of (regional) development. Finally, as more groundwork is done at the micro level, it becomes more possible to carry out a more detailed exploration of the forces surrounding centralization in government and enterprises and their implications for rural, urban, and regional change.

The research presented herein is devoted mainly to frameworks for understanding, to theories and possible ways in which they might be improved, rather than to policy and the evaluation of policies. Nevertheless, some general points can be made about the latter. One of my main conclusions is that verticalization of regional economies and their differentiation is very much part of the microeconomic dynamics of (capitalist) development. Although equal access of individuals and groups to economic opportunity remains a laudable goal of regional policy, this does not necessarily lead to "mopping up" areas of out-migration, or to expensive incentives to nationally operating firms to enable these to make only selective use of conditions of production in a particular region. A more relevant option may be more development policy at the level of the regions rather than centrally controlled regional policy, thus providing more local regional room for maneuver. However, we must be careful not to lose sight of the fact that government itself is part of the problem; in other words, such an option is not always feasible in view of the ongoing centralization process.

The argument that firms, when successful, would outgrow the region and become national or even transnational, so that the fruits of the efforts of microeconomic development would largely be lost, should be handled with care. A large but unknown proportion of firms will *remain* regional/national, either because of the objectives they pursue, or because competitive struggles force them to remain within these territorial confines.

# REFERENCES


Abalos, J.A. 1982. "Regional growth versus the community: A case study of collective self-reliance and resilience." Master's thesis, The Hague, Institute of Social Studies.

Abler, R., Adams, J.S., and Gould, P. 1971. *Spatial organization: The geographers' view of the world.* Englewood Cliffs: NJ: Prentice Hall.

Abrams, P. 1978. Towns and economic growth: Some theories and problems. In P. Abrams, et al., eds., *Town in societies.* Cambridge: Cambridge University Press.

Arango, J.A. 1976. Inversion extranjera en la industria manufacturera Colombiana. *Boletin Mensual de Estadistica,* Nos 302 and 303.

Arango, M. 1977. *Cafe e industria 1850–1930.* Medellin: Carlos Valencia Editores.

ASCOFAME. 1978. *Desarrollo de la agricultura comercial y poblacion. Estudio de la zona algodonera del Cesar.* Bogotá: ASCOFAME.

ASOCESAR. Various years. *El Emisor Agropequario.*

Atkinson, J. 1970. *Agricultural productivity in Colombia.* Washington, DC: U.S. Department of Agriculture.

Ayala, H., et al. 1978. Gestion tecnologica en la industria de alimentos de Colombia. *Revista de la EAFIT* 31.

Banaji, J. 1976. Summary of selected parts of Kautsky's *The Agrarian Revolution. Economy and society* 5 (1): 2–49.

Banco de Bogotá. 1960. *Banco de Bogotá trayector a de una empresa de servicio 1870–1960.* Bogotá: Banco de Bogotá.

Bavaria. 1966. *Bavaria (1889–1966) Una tradicion de prestigio y calidad.* Bogotá: Bavaria S.A.

Beavon, K.S.O. 1977. *Central place theory: A reinterpretation.* London: Longman.

Bejarano, J.A. 1977a. Contribucion al debate sobre el problema agraria. In F. Leal et al., eds., *El agro en el desarrollo historico Colombiano, pp 33–85. Bogotá: Editorial Punta de Lanza.*

Bejarano, J.A., ed. 1977b. *El siglo XIX en Colombia visto por historiadores Norteamericanos.* Bogotá: Editorial La Carreta.

Bejarano, J.A. 1978a. *Ensayos de interpretacion de la economia colombiana.* Bogotá: Editorial La Carreta.

Bejarano, J.A. 1978b. Industrializacion y politica economica. In M. Arrubla et al., eds., *Colombia Hoy,* pp 221–271. Bogotá: Siglo Veintiuno Editores.

Bejarano, J.A. 1979. *El regimen agrario de la economia exportadora a la economia industrial.* Bogotá: Editorial La Carreta.

Bejarano, J.A. 1980. La economia. In *Manual de la Historia de Colombia,* vol. 3, pp. 17–83 Bogotá: Colcultura.

Bejarano, J.A. 1984. *La economia Colombiana en la decada del 70.* Bogotá: Fondo Editorial CEREC.

Berry, B.J.L., 1961. City size distribution and economic development. *Economic Development and Cultural Change* (9). Reprinted in J. Friedmann and W. Alonso., eds., 1964. *Regional development and planning.* Cambridge, MA: M.I.T. Press.

Berry, B.J.L. 1967. *Geography of market centers and retail distribution*. Englewood Cliffs, NJ: Prentice-Hall.

Berry, B.J.L. 1971. City size and economic development; Conceptual synthesis and policy problems with special reference to South and South-East Asia. In J. Jacobson and V. Prakash, eds., *Urbanization and national development*, pp 111–156. Beverly Hills, CA: Sage.

Berry, R.A. 1965. *Breve estudio de los determinantes del crecimiento de la poblacion en Colombia*. Bogotá: Universidad de los Andes, Centro de Estudios sobre el Desarrollo Economico.

Bienefeld, M. 1975. The informal sector and peripheral capitalism: The case of Tanzania. *Institute of Development Studies Bulletin* 6 (4): 53–73.

Blanco, A.M. and Blanco, E. 1981. La asignacion regional del presupuesto de inversiones. *Enfoques Colombianos*, 10:105–116.

Boisier, S. et al., eds. 1981. *Experiencias de planificacion regional en America Latina. Una teoria en busca de una practica*. Santiago: ECLA/ILPES/SIAP.

Botero, F. and Guzman, B. 1977. El enclave agricola en la zona bananera de Santa Marta. *Cuadernos Colombianos* 3 (11):309–391.

Brew, R. 1977. *El desarrollo economico de Antioquia desde la Independencia hasta 1920*. Bogotá: Banco de la Republica.

Bromley, R. 1979. Introduction to "The urban informal sector: Why is it worth discussing?" In R. Bromley, ed., *The urban informal sector: Critical perspectives on employment and housing policies*, pp. 1033–1039. Oxford: Pergamon Press.

Bromley, R. and Gerry, C., eds. 1979. *Casual work and poverty in Third World cities*. Chichester, England: Wiley.

Bromley, R.J. et al. 1975. The rationale of periodic markets. *Annals of the Association of American Geographers* 65 (4):530–538.

Butterworth, D. and Chance, J.K. 1981. *Latin American urbanization*. Cambridge: Cambridge University Press.

Bye, P. 1975. *Modalidades de industrializacion en el sector agropequario*. Documento 25, CEDE. Bogotá: Universidad de los Andes.

Caja Agraria. Various years. *Tabulations crop estimates by department*. (mimeographed)

Camacho Guizado, A. 1975. *The social organization of capital centralization: A study of the communities of interests of the Colombian ruling class*. Ann Arbor, MI: University Microfilms International.

Carroll, G.R. 1982. National city size distribution: What do we know after 67 years of research? *Progress in Human Geography* 6 (1): 1–44.

Castells, M. 1973. La urbanizacion dependiente en America Latina. In M. Schteingart, ed., *Urbanizacion y Dependencia en America latina*, pp. 70–92. Buenos Aires: SIAP.

Castells, M. 1977. *The urban question: A marxist approach*. London: Edward Arnold. [Original in French 1972.]

Castells, M. 1978. *City, Class and Power*. London: Macmillan.

Chambers, R. 1984. *Rural development: Putting the last first*. London: Longman.

Chandler, A.D. Jr. 1977. *The visible hand; The managerial revolution in American business*. Cambridge: Belknap Press.

Chandler, A.D. and Daems, H., eds. 1980. *Managerial hierarchies; comparative perspectives on the rise of the modern industrial enterprise*. Cambridge: Harvard University Press.

Chayanov, A.V. 1966. *The theory of peasant economy*. Edited by D. Thorner, R.E.F. Smith, and B. Kerblay. Homewood IL: Richard D. Irwin.

Chelintsev, A.N. 1911. *Sel'sko-khoziaistvennye raiony evropeiskoi Rossii kak stadii sel'sko-khoziaistvennoi evoliutsii i kul'turnyi uroven' sel'skogo khoziaistva v nikh*. Moscow.

Chica Avella, R. 1983. El desarrollo industrial colombiano, 1958–1980. *Desarrollo y Sociedad* 12:19–125.

Child, J. and Arango, M. 1984. *Bancarrotas y crisis*. Bogotá: Editorial Presencia y Biblioteca de El Espectador.

Chisholm, M. 1962. *Rural settlement and land use*. London: Hutchinson.

Christaller, W. 1966. *Central places in Southern Germany* Translated by W. Baskin. Englewood Cliffs, NJ: Prentice-Hall.

Christie, K.H. 1978. Antioqueno colonization in western Colombia: A reappraisal. *Hispanic American Historical Review* 58 (2):260–283.

CID. 1970. *Industria Manufacturera Fabril, monografia estadistica*. Bogotá, Universidad Nacional.

CIDER. 1977. Estudio regional integrado de la Costa Atlantica Colombiana. Vol. I. CIDER, Bogotá: Universidad de los Andes.

CIDER. 1978. Estudio regional integrado de la Costa Atlantica Colombiana. Vol. II. CIDER, Bogotá: Universidad de los Andes.

Colmenares, J.S. 1977. *Los verdaderos duenos del pais*. Bogotá: Editorial Suramericana.

Colmenares, J.S. 1983. *Tras la mascara del subdesarrollo: dependencia y monopolios*. Bogotá: Carlos Valencia Editores.

Connell, J., Dasgupta, B., Laishley, R. & Lipton, M. 1976. *Migration from rural areas; the evidence from village studies* (ILO-WEP). Delhi: Oxford University Press.

Contraloria General de la Republica. 1946. *Geografia economica de Colombia*. Vol. 7, *Tolima*. Bogotá: Editorial Santa Fe.

Controlaria General de la Republica. 1983. *Estadistica fiscal del estado, 1977–1981,* Bogotá: Controlaria General de la Republica.

Corbridge, S. 1982. Urban bias, rural bias, and industrialization: An appraisal of the work of Michael Lipton and Terry Byres. In J. Harriss, ed., *Rural Development,* pp. 94–116. London: Hutchinson University Library.

Cox, K.R., and Reynolds, D.R. 1974. Locational approaches to power and conflict. In K.R. Cox, D.R. Reynolds, and S. Rokkan, eds., *Locational approaches to power and conflict,* pp. 19–41. New York: John Wiley.

Crush, J.S. 1980. On theorizing frontier underdevelopment. *Tijdschrift voor Economische en Sociale Geografie* 71:343–350.

Currie, L. 1963. *El algodon en Colombia—Problemas y oportunidades*. Bogotá: Fundacion para el Progreso de Colombia.

Currie, L. 1966. *Accelerating development—The necessity and the means*. New York: McGraw-Hill.

Currie, L. 1976. *Taming the megalopolis—A design for urban growth*. Oxford: Pergamon Press.

DANE. Various years. Anuario del comercio exterior.

DANE. Various years. Census of agriculture.

DANE. Various years. Census of manufacturing industry.

DANE. Various years. Census of population. Muestra de avance.

DANE. Various years. Estadisticas fiscales y empleo publico.

DANE. 1972. La industria textil en Colombia. *Boletin Mensual de Estadistica,* no. 255–256, pp. 171–199.

DANE. 1979. Los jornales agropequarios. *Boletin Mensual de Estadistica,* no. 336, pp. 18–35.

Davila, C. 1976. Dominant classes and elites in economic development: A comparative study of eight urban centers in Colombia. Bogotá: Universidad de los Andes.

Davis. K. 1969. *World urbanization 1950–1970*. Vol. I, *Basic data for cities, countries, and regions*. Berkeley: University of California, Institute of International Studies.

Davis, K. 1972. *World urbanization*. Vol. II, *Analysis of trends, relationships, and regions*. Berkeley: University of California.

Departamento Nacional de Planeacion. 1975. La produccion alimentaria y el proceso de comercializacion en Colombia. 3 vols. Bogotá: Departamento Nacional de Planeacion.

Departamento Nacional de Planeacion. 1977. La economia colombiana 1950–1975. *Revista de Planeacion y Desarrollo* 3 (9): 7–278.

Departamento Nacional de Planeacion. 1979. *Politica agropecuaria y el sistema de alimentos*. Vols. 1 and 2, *Diagnostico*. Bogotá: Departamento Nacional de Planeacion.

Diot, J. 1976. Colombia economica 1923–1929. *Boletin Mensual de Estadistica*, No. 300.

Djurfeldt, G. 1982. Classical discussion of capital and peasantry: A critique. In J. Harriss, ed., *Rural Development*, pp. 139–158. London: Hutchinson University Library.

Dobb, M. 1978. A reply. In Sweezy, P. et al. *The Transition from Feudalism to Capitalism*. London, Verso. pp. 57–67.

Dorward, N.M.M. 1979. Market area analysis and product differentiation: A case study of the West German truck industry. In F.E.I. Hamilton and G.J.R. Linge, eds., *Spatial analysis, industry and the industrial environment*. Vol. I: *Industrial systems*. Chichester: John Wiley.

Douglass, M. 1984. *Regional integration on the capitalist periphery: The Central Plains of Thailand*. Research Report Series 15. The Hague: Institute of Social Studies.

El-Shakhs, S. 1972. Development, primacy and systems of cities. *Journal of Developing Areas* 7:11–36.

Escorcia, J. 1978. *Historia economica y social de Colombia*. Bogotá: Editorial Presencia.

Ettlinger, N. 1981. Dependency and urban growth: A critical review and reformulation of the concepts of primacy and rank size. *Environment and Planning* 13:1389–1400.

Fajardo, L.H. 1966. *La moralidad protestante de los Antioquenos. Estructura social y personalidad*. Cali: Universidad del Valle.

Fajardo, D.M. 1983. *Haciendas, campesinos y politicas agrarias en Colombia, 1920–1980*. Bogotá: Editoral Oveja Negra.

Fals Borda, O. 1957. *El hombre y la tierra en Boyaca*. Bogotá: Punta de Lanza.

Fals Borda, O. 1976. *Capitalismo, hacienda y poblamiento en la Costa Atlantica*. Bogotá: Editoral Oveja Negra.

Federacion Nacional de Algodoneros. Various years. *El algodonero*. Bogotá.

Federación Nacional de Algodoneros. Various years. *Informe del gerente al congreso nacional de algodoneros*. Bogotá: Federacion Nacional de Algodoneros.

FEDESARROLLO. 1975. La politica agraria en Colombia 1950–1975. Banco de Bogotá Informe de Segundo Semestre. Bogotá: Banco de Bogotá.

Figueroa, A. 1984. *Capitalist development and the peasant economy in Peru*. Cambridge: Cambridge University Press.

Florez, L.B. and Gonzalez, C. 1983. *Industria, regiones y urbanizacion en Colombia*. Bogotá: Editorial Oveja Negra.

Forero, P.M. 1976. *Estudio de caso: Nacional de Chocolates*. Bogotá: Facultad de Administracion, Universidad de los Andes. (mimeographed)

Frank, A.G. 1969. *Latin America: Underdevelopment or revolution*. New York: Monthly Review Press.

Friedmann, J. 1968. A strategy of deliberate urbanization. *Journal of American Institute of Planners* 34:364–373.

Friedmann, J. 1972. A general theory of polarized development. In N.M. Hansen, ed., *Growth Centers in Regional Economic Development*, pp. 82–107. New York: Free Press.

Friedmann, J. 1972–73. The spatial organization of power in the development of urban systems. In *Development and Change*, Vol. 4, No. 3, pp. 12–50.

Friedmann, J. 1973. *Urbanization, planning and national development*. Beverly Hills, CA: Sage.

Friedmann, J. and Alonso, W. eds. 1964. *Regional Development and Planning. A reader*. Cambridge, Mass.: MIT.

Friedmann, J. and Douglass, M. 1978. Agropolitan development: Towards a new strategy for regional planning in Asia. In F.C. Lo and K. Salih, eds., *Growth pole strategy and regional development policy*. pp. 163–192. Oxford: Pergamon, For UNRISD.

Friedmann, J. and Weaver, C. 1979. *Territory and function; The evolution of regional planning*. London: Edward Arnold.

Friedmann, J. and Wulff, R. 1976. *The urban transition*. London: Edward Arnold.

Gaitan, G. 1976. *Colombia: La lucha por la tierra en la decada del treinta*. Bogotá: Ediciones Tercer Mundo.

Galan Gomez, M. 1947 *Geografia economica de Colombia*. Vol. 8, *Santander*. Contraloria General de la Republica. Bucaramanga: Imprenta Departamental de Santander.

Gallo, H. 1976. Estudio de caso: Historia de ColCurtidos S.A. Bogotá: Facultad de Administracion, Universidad de los Andes. (mimeographed)

Garcia, A. 1937. *Geografia economica de Colombia*. Vol. 4, *Caldas*. Contraloria General de la Republica. Bogotá: Imprenta Nacional.

Garcia Merlano, R. 1976. Estructura regional de los ingresos presupuestales y de la inversion publica nacionales. *Revista de Planeacion y Desarrollo* 8 (2):57–70.

Geertz, C. 1963. *Agricultural involution, the process of ecological change in Indonesia*. Berkeley: University of California Press.

Germani, G. 1973. Urbanization, social change and the great transformation. In G. Germani, ed., *Modernization, urbanization and the urban crisis*, pp. 3–58. Boston: Little, Brown.

Gilbert, A. 1970. Industrial growth in the spatial development of the Colombian economy between 1951 and 1964. Ph.D. diss., University of London.

Gilbert, A. 1974. *Latin American development. A geographical perspective*. Harmondsworth: Penguin Books.

Gilbert, A. and Goodman, D. 1976. Regional income disparities and economic development: A critique. In A. Gilbert, ed., *Development planning and spatial structure*, pp. 113–142. London: Wiley.

Gilbert, A. and Gugler, J. 1982. *Cities, poverty, and development—urbanization in the Third World*. Oxford: Oxford University Press.

Giraldo, G. and Obregon, R. 1979. Industria Textil. *Revista de Planeacion y Desarrollo* 11 (2):49–132.

Gomez, M.T. 1935. *Geografia economica de Colombia*, Vol. 1: *Antioquia*. Contraloria General de la Republica. Bogotá: Imprenta Nacional.

Goodman, D. and Redclift, D. 1981. *From peasant to proletarian: Capitalist development and agrarian transitions*. Oxford: Blackwell.

Gore, C. 1984. *Regions in question*. London: Methuen.

Gottmann, J., ed. 1980. *Centre and periphery; spatial variation in politics*. Beverly Hills, CA: Sage Publications.

Gourevitch, P. 1979. The re-emergence of 'peripheral nationalisms.' *Comparative Studies in Society and History*, Vol. 21, 3, 303–322.

Gugler, J. 1982. Urban ways of life. In A. Gilbert & J. Gugler. *Cities, Poverty, and Development*. London, Oxford University Press.

Guzman, G, Fals Borda, O, and Umana, E. 1977. *La violencia en Colombia*. 2 vols. Bogotá: Editorial Punta de Lanza (first edition 1962).

Hagan, E.E. 1962. *On the theory of social change: How economic growth begins*. Homewood, IL: Dorsey Press.

Hakanson, L. 1979. Towards a theory of location and corporate growth. In F.E. I. Hamilton and G.J.R. Linge, eds., *Spatial analysis, industry and the industrial environment*. Vol. I, *Industrial systems*. Chichester: Wiley.

Hall, P., ed. 1966. *Van Thuenen's isolated state: An English edition of Der Isolierte Staat*. Oxford: Oxford University Press. [Originally published in 1826.]

Hamilton, F.E.I. and Linge, G.J.R. eds. *Spatial analysis, industry and the industrial environment.* Vol. II, *International industrial sytems.* Chichester: Wiley.

Hammond, R. and McCullagh, P.S. 1974. *Quantitative techniques in geography.* Oxford: Clarendon Press.

Harloe, M., ed. 1977. *Captive cities, studies in the political economy of cities and regions.* London: Wiley.

Harrison, M. 1982. Chayanov's theory of peasant economy. In J. Harriss, ed., *Rural development,* pp. 246–258. London: Hutchinson University Library.

Harriss, J. 1981. "The mode of production controversy: Themes and problems of the debate." Discussion paper. Norwich: University of East Anglia.

Harriss, J., ed., 1982. *Rural development—Theories of peasant economies and agrarian change.* London: Hutchinson University Library.

Harvey, D. 1967. Models of the evolution of spatial patterns in human geography. In R.J. Chorley and P. Hagget, eds., *Models in geography.* London: Methuen.

Harvey, D. 1973. *Social justice and the city.* London: Edward Arnold.

Harvey, D. 1982. *The limits to capital.* Oxford: Basil Blackwell.

Hayter, R. and Watts, H.D. 1983. The geography of enterprise: A re-appraisal. *Progress in Human Geography* 7(2):157–181.

* Helmsing, B. 1978. *Oligopolio y desarrollo regional.* CIDER, Bogotá: Universidad de los Andes. (mimeographed)

Helmsing, B. 1979. *El desarrollo de la produccion de algodon 1950–1978. Analisis de sus condicionantes, cambios e impactos, con especial referencia a la Costa Atlantica.* CIDER, Bogotá: Universidad de los Andes. (mimeographed)

Helmsing, B. 1982a. *Agriculture and industry in a regional perspective.* Working Paper 4. The Hague: Institute of Social Studies.

Helmsing, B. 1982b. Agricultural production in the periphery: Settlement schemes reconsidered. *Development and Change* 13(3):401–419.

Helmsing, B. 1983a. Agricultura, industria y desarrollo de regiones. *Revista Interamericana de Planificacion* 17(66):91–117.

Helmsing, B. 1983b. *Industrialization and regional division of labour: Analysis of patterns of change in Colombia.* Working Paper 19. The Hague: Institute of Social Studies.

Helmsing, B. 1984a. *Economic structure, trade and regions.* Working Paper 23. The Hague: Institute of Social Studies.

Helmsing, B. 1984b. Colonizacion agricola y asentamiento en el desarrollo colombiano. The Hague: Institute of Social Studies. (mimeographed)

Helmsing, B. 1985. Dependency or differentiation? Regions and industrialization in Colombia. *Tijdschrift voor Economische en Sociale Geografie* 76:121–132.

Helmsing, B. and Uribe, F. 1981. La planificacion regional en America Latina: Teoria o practica? in S. Boisier et al., eds., *Experiencias de planificacion regional en American Latina—Una teoria en busca de una practica.* Santiago: ECLA/ILPES/SIAP

Henessy, A. 1978. *The frontier in Latin American history.* London: Edward Arnold.

Hilhorst, J.G.M. 1971. *Regional planning; A systems approach.* Rotterdam: Rotterdam University Press.

Hilhorst, J.G.M. 1980. *On unresolved issues in regional development thinking.* Occasional Paper 81. The Hague: Institute of Social Studies.

Hilhorst, J.G.M. and Lambooy, J.G. 1974. Urbanization and the spatial concentration of decision making. In H.G.T. Van Raay and A.E. Lugo, eds., *Man and environment Ltd.* pp. 147–165. Rotterdam: Rotterdam University Press.

*A.H.J. Helmsing's earlier publications were published under the name Burt Helmsing.

Hinderink, J. and Sterkenburg, J.J. 1978. Spatial inequality in underdeveloped countries and the role of government policy. *Tijdschrift voor Economische en Sociale Geografie* 69:5–16.

Holland, S. 1976. *Capital versus the regions*. London: Macmillan.

Holton, R.J. 1984. Cities and the transitions to capitalism and socialism. *International Journal of Urban and Regional Research* 8(1):13–37.

Hoselitz, B. 1954. Generative and parasitic cities. *Economic Development and Cultural Change* (3):278–295.

Houston, J.M. 1968. The foundation of colonial towns in Hispanic America. In R.P. Beckinsale and J.M. Houston, eds., *Urbanization and its problems* pp. 352–390. Oxford: Basil Blackwell.

Hymer, S. 1971. The multinational corporation and the law of uneven development. In J.N. Bhagwati, ed., *Economics and world order from 1970s to 1990s*, pp. 113–141. New York: Macmillan.

IDEMA. Various years. *Tabulados area cultivada y produccion fisica por secciones del pais*. Bogotá: Oficina de Planeacion.

INANDES. 1977. *El desarrollo economico departamental 1960–1975*. Anexo Metodologico. Bogotá: FONADE.

INTRA. 1972. *Estudio sobre origen y destino de la carga de algodon*. Bogotá: INTRA.

Jansen, A.C.M. 1974. Elementen van een vestigingsplaatsmodel voor industriele 'multi-plant' ondernemingen. *Tijdschrift voor Economische en Sociale Geografie* 65(3):174–193.

Jansen, K. 1982. *State, policy and the economy*. Research Report Series No. 12. The Hague: Institute of Social Studies.

Jaramillo, O. 1977. El algodon, industria de altibajos. *Revista Nueva Frontera* 55.

Jaramillo Uribe, J. 1982. Vision sintetica de la tarea investigativa desarrollada sobre la region antioquena. In M. Melo, ed., *Los estudios regionales en Colombia: El caso de Antioquia*, pp 1–16. Medellin: Fondo Rotatorio e Publicaciones, Fundacion Antioquena para los Estudios Sociales.

Johnson, E.A. 1970. *The organization of space in developing countries*. Cambridge: Harvard University Press.

Johnston, B.F. 1970. Agriculture and structural transformation in developing countries: A survey of research. *Journal of Economic Literature* 8(2):369–405.

Johnston, B.F. and Clark, W.C. 1982. *Redesigning rural development: A strategic perspective*. Baltimore: Johns Hopkins University Press.

Johnston, B.F. and Kilby, P. 1975. *Agriculture and structural transformation: Economic strategies in late developing countries*. Oxford: Oxford University Press.

Johnston, R.J. 1977. Regarding urban origins, urbanization and urban patterns. *Geography* 62(1):1-8.

Johnston, R.J. 1982. *Geography and the state*. London: Macmillan.

Jones, E.L. 1977. Environment, agriculture, and industrialization in Europe. *Agricultural History*, 51:491–502.

Kalmanovitz, S. 1978a. *Desarrollo de la Agricultura en Colombia*. Bogotá: Editorial La Carreta.

Kalmanovitz, S. 1978b. Problemas del campesinado parcelario. *Enfoques Colombianos* 7:25–36.

Kalmanovitz, S. 1979. El regimen agrario durante el siglo XIX en Colombia. In *Manual de la Historia de Colmbia*, Vol. 2. p. 211–325. Bogotá: ColCultura.

Kathrijn, W.H. 1952. The Agriculture of Colombia. Washington: USDA.

Kautsky, K. 1970. *La Question Agraire*. Paris: Maspero (first published in 1899 as *Agrarfrage*).

Kline, H.F. 1983. *Colombia; Portrait of unity and diversity*. Boulder, CO: Westview Press.

Leal, F. 1973. *Analisis historico del desarrollo politico nacional 1930–1970*. Bogotá: Editorial Tercer Mundo.

Leff, N. 1979a. Entrepreneurship and economic development: The problem revisited. *Journal of Economic Literature*, 17:46–64.

Leff, N. 1979b 'Monopoly capitalism' and public policy in developing countries. *Kyklos* 32(4): 718–738.

Leigh, R. and North, D.J. 1978. Acquisition in British industries: Implications for regional development. In F.E.I. Hamilton, ed., *Contemporary industrialization, spatial analysis and regional development*. London: Longman.

Lenin, V.I. 1964. *The development of capitalism in Russia*. Vol. 3 of *Collected Works*. Moscow: Progress Publishers.

Leon, A. 1982. Dimension territorial de las disparidades sociales: El caso de Colombia. Santiago: ILPES. (mimeographed)

Leon, A. and Richter, C. 1979. Inversiones publicas y desarrollo regional: El caso de Colombia. *Desarrollo y Sociedad* 10:199–209.

Leurquin, P. 1966. Cotton growing in Colombia: Achievements and uncertainties. *Food Research Institute Studies* 4(2):143–181.

Linn, J.F. 1979 Urbanization trends, polarization reversal and spatial policy in Colombia. Washington, DC: World Bank. (mimeographed) Published in Spanish in S. Boisier et al., eds. 1981. *Experiencias de planificacion regional en America Latina*. Santiago: CEPAL/ILPES/SIAP.

Lipton, M. 1968. The theory of the optimizing peasant. *Journal of Development Studies*, 4, 3:327–352.

Lipton, M. 1977. *Why poor people stay poor—A study of urban bias in world development*. London: Temple Smith.

Lipton, M. 1982. Why poor people stay poor. In J. Harriss, ed., *Rural development. Theories of peasant economy and agrarian change*, pp. 66–81. London: Hutchinson.

Lipton, M. 1984. Urban bias revisited. *Journal of Development Studies* 20(3):139–167. (Special issue on rural–urban divide).

Loesch, A. 1954. *The Economies of Location*. New Haven: Yale University Press. Trans. W.H. Woglom.

Long, N. and Roberts, B., eds., 1978. *Peasant cooperation and capitalist expansion in the central highlands of Peru*. Austin and London: University of Texas Press for Institute of Latin American Studies.

Lopez Castano, H. and Arango Restrepo, M. 1977. *La pequena y la mediana mineria aurifera en el Bajo Cauca y en el Nechi*. Medellin: CIE, Universidad de Antioquia. (mimeographed)

Lopez Toro, A. 1976. *Migracion y cambio social en antioquia durante el siglo XIX*. (2nd ed.) Bogotá: Universidad de los Andes-CEDE.

Machado, A. 1977. *El cafe: De la aparceria al capitalismo*. Bogotá: Editorial Punta de Lanza.

Machado, A. 1981. Politicas agrarias en Colombia. In D. Fajardo et al., eds., *Campesinado y capitalismo en Colombia*, Bogotá: CINEP.

Machado, A. 1982. La politica cafetera en Colombia. *Desarrollo y Sociedad* 8:179–200.

Marciales, M. 1948. *Geografia historica y economica del Norte de Santander. Contraloria del Norte de Santander*. Bogotá: Editorial de Santa Fe.

Martinez, F.G. 1979. *El poder politico en Colombia*. Bogotá: Editorial Punta de Lanza.

Massey, D. 1979. In what sense a regional problem? *Regional Studies* 13:233–244.

Matter, K. 1977. *Inversiones extranjeras en la economia Colombiana*. Medellin: Ediciones Hombre Nuevo.

McGee, T.G. 1971. *The urbanization process in the Third World*. London: Bell & Sons.

McGreevey, W.P. 1971. A statistical analysis of primacy and lognormality in the size distribution of Latin American cities, 1750–1960. In R.M. Morse, ed., *The urban development of Latin America*. Stanford, CA: Center for Latin American Studies.

McGreevey, W.P. 1975. *Historia economica de Colombia, 1845–1930*. Bogotá: Editorial Tercer Mundo.

McNee, R.B. 1958. Functional geography of the firm. *Economic Geography,* Vol. 34, 321–337.

Medina, J.R. 1936. *Geografia economica de Colombia.* Vol. 3: *Boyaca.* Contraloria General de la Republica. Bogotá: Imprenta Nacional.

Melo, H. 1974. *El mercado internacional del oro y la explotacion del oro en Colombia.* Bogotá: Universidad Nacional de Colombia—CID.

Melo, O.J. 1979. La evolucion economica de Colombia: 1830–1900. In Vol. 2 of *Manual de la historia de Colombia,* pp. 135–209. Bogotá: Colcultura.

Mennes, L.B.M., Tinbergen, J. and Waardenburg, J.G. 1969. *The element of space in development planning.* Amsterdam: Netherlands Economic Institute/North Holland.

Merrington, J. 1978. Town and country in the transition to capitalism. In P. Sweezy et al., eds., *The Transition from Feudalism to Capitalism.* London: Verso Ed. pp. 179–195.

Meyer, D.R. 1980. A dynamic model of the integration of frontier urban places into the United States system of cities. *Economic Geography,* Vol. 56, No. 2 pp. 120–140.

Misas, G. 1975a. *Contribucion al estudio del grado de concentracion en la industria Colombiana.* Bogotá: Editorial Tiempo Presente.

Misas, G. 1975b. Caracteristicas generales de las industrias regionales en Colombia. *Enfoques Colombianos* 4:61–79.

Misas, G. 1983. *Empresa multinacional y pacto andino.* Bogotá: Editorial Oveja Negra and FINES.

Monsalve, D. 1927. *Colombia Cafetera: Informacions general de la Republica y estadistica de la industria del cafe.* Barcelona: Artes Graficas.

Montenegro, S. 1982. La industria textil en Colombia: 1900–1945. *Desarrollo y Sociedad* 8: 117–177.

Montes, G. and Candelo, R. 1980, Sept./Dec. La economia ganadera en Colombia. *Revista de Planeacion y Desarrollo:* 91–142.

Montes, G. and Candelo, R. 1981. El crecimiento industrial y la generacion de empleo en Colombia: entre la substitucion de importaciones y la promocion de exportaciones. *Revista de Planeacion y Desarrollo* 13(1/2):87–132.

Moore, M. 1984. Political economy and the rural–urban divide. *Journal of Development Studies* 20(3):5–28. (Special issue on rural–urban divide, edited by M. Moore and J. Harriss)

Morillo, J. 1942. *Geografie economica de Colombia.* Contraloria General de la Republica. Bogotá: Editorial El Grafico.

Morrison, B.M. 1980. Rural household livelihood strategies in a Sri Lankan village. *Journal of Development Studies* 16(4):443–468.

Morse, M. 1962. Latin American cities: Aspects of function and structure. *Comparative studies in society and history* 4, 473–493. Reprinted in J. Friedmann and W. Alonso, eds., *Regional development and planning; A reader,* pp. 361–382. Cambridge, MA: M.I.T. Press.

Morse, R. 1971. Planning, history and politics: Reflections on John Friedmann's *The Role of Cities in National Development.* In J. Miller and R. Gakenheimer, eds., *Latin American Urban Policies and the Social Sciences.* pp. 189–200 Beverly Hills: Sage.

Moser, C. 1978. Informal sector or petty commodity production: Dualism or dependence in urban development? *World Development* 6(9/10):1041–1064.

Myrdal, G. 1957. *Economic theory and underdeveloped regions.* London: Duckworth.

Newfarmer, R. 1979. Oligopolistic tactics to control markets and the growth of TNCs in Brazil's electrical industries. *Journal of Development Studies* 15(3): 108–141.

Nichols, T.E. 1973. *Tres puertos de Colombia.* Bogotá: Biblioteca Banco Popular.

Nieto Arteta, L.E. 1975a. *El cafe en la sociedad Colombiana.* Bogotá: Ediciones Tiempo Presente.

Nieto Arteta, L.E. 1975b. *Economia y cultura en la historia de Colombia.* Bogotá: Ediciones Tiempo Presente.

Norcliffe, G.B. 1975. A theory of manufacturing places. In L. Collins and D.F. Walker, eds., *Locational dynamics of manufacturing activity.* London: Wiley.

Ocampo, J.A. 1979. Resena del libro 'Cafe e industria en Colombia 1850–1930' *Desarrollo y Sociedad* 2:293–300.

Ocampo, J.F. 1972. *Dominio de clase en la cuidad colombiana*. Medellin: Editorial La Oveja Negra.

O'Connor, J. 1973. *The fiscal crisis of the state*. New York: St. Martin's Press.

Oficina Coordinadora de Algodon. 1978. Informe de desmote para la Costa Atlantica. Medellin. (mimeographed)

Ogliastri, E. 1976. *Estudio de caso: Bavaria S.A.* Facultad de Administracion. Bogotá: Universidad de los Andes. (mimeographed)

Oquist, P. 1978. *Violencia, conflicto y politica en Colombia*. Bogotá: Biblioteca Banco Popular.

Orlove, B.S. 1977. *Alpacas, sheep and men: The wool export economy and regional society in Southern Peru*. New York: Academic Press.

Ortiz, S.R. 1973. *Uncertainties in peasant farming, A Colombian case*. New York: Humanities Press.

Ospina Vasquez, L. 1974. *Industria y proteccion en Colombia 1810–1930*. Medellin: La Oveja Negra. [Originally published in 1955.]

Palacios, M. 1979. *El cafe en Colombia, 1850–1970: Una historia economica, social y politica*. Bogotá: Editorial Presencia.

Palacios, M. 1981. La fragmentación regional de las clases dominantes en Colombia: Una perspectiva histórica. In G.A. Bank, R. Buve and L. van Vroonhaven, et al., eds., *State and region in Latin America: A workshop*, pp. 41–75. CEDLA Incidentele Publicaties 17. Amsterdam: CEDLA.

Palacios, M. 1982. El cafe en la vida de Antioquia. In H. Melo, ed., *Los Estudios regionales en Colombia* pp. 85–99. Bogotá.

Pardo Pardo, A. 1972. *Geografia economica y humana de Colombia*. Bogotá: Ediciones Tercer Mundo.

Paris Lozano, G. 1946. *Geografia economica de Colombia*. Vol. 7: *Tolima*. Contraloria General de la Republica, Bogotá: Editorial Santa Fe.

Parra Escobar E. 1982. La economia colombiana: 1971–1981. *Controversia* 100:1–97.

Parra Sandoval, R. 1977. Empresa multinacional, urbanizacion y cambios en la estructura ocupacional: 1920–1970. In A. E. Havens et al., eds., *Metodologia y desarrollo en las sciencias sociales: efectos del crecimiento dependiente sobre la estructura social Colombiana*, CEDE Universidad de los Andes, Bogotá: Editorial Presencia.

Parsons, J.J. 1950. *La colonizaction Antioquena en el occidente Colombiano*. Medellin: Imprenta Departamental.

Pearse, A. 1968. Metropolis and peasant: The expansion of the urban industrial complex and the changing rural structure. Reprinted in T. Shanin, ed., 1971. *Peasants and peasant societies*. Harmondsworth: Penguin.

Pearse, A. 1975. *The Latin American peasant*. London: Frank Cass.

Perdomo, G. 1978. *El impacto de la actividad algodonera en el crecimiento urbano de Valledupar y de Aguachica*. Documento de trabajo, IDER. Bogotá: Universidad de los Andes.

Perloff, H. and Wingo, L. 1961. Natural resource endowments and regional economic development. In J.J. Spengler, ed., *Natural resources and economic growth*, pp. 191–212. Washington, DC: Resources for the Future, Inc.

Perroux, F. 1964. *L'economie du XXeme siecle*. Paris: Presses Universitaires du France.

Perry, S. 1983. *La crisis agraria en Colombia 1950–1980*. Bogotá: El Ancora Editores.

Piedrahita, F. 1978. Nuestra industria—El sector textil. *Revista de la ANDI* 38:26–36.

Piedrahita, F. 1980. Desarrollo industrial en la decada de los Setenta. *Revista de la ANDI* 50:35–153.

Poveda Ramos, G. 1966. Problemas y perspectivas de la industria textil en America Latina. *Revista de la ANDI* 1:48–83.

Poveda Ramos, G. 1967. Antecedentes y desarrollo de la industria en Colombia. *Revista de la ANDI* 4:3–23.

Poveda Ramos, G. 1970. Historia de la industria en Colombia. *Revista de la ANDI* 1:1–98.

Poveda Ramos, G. 1979. *Dos siglos de historia economica de Antioquia*. Medellin: Biblioteca Pro Antioquia.

Poveda Ramos, G. 1981. Algunos aspectos sobre descentralizacion industrial en Colombia. *Enfoques Colombians* 10:47–65.

PREALC. 1978. *Sector informal—Functionamiento y politicas*. Santiago: ILO-PREALC.

Quijano, A. 1974. The marginal pole of the economy and the marginalised labour force. *Economy and Society* 3(4), pp. 393–428.

Restrepo, V. 1888. *Las minas de oro y plata de Colombia*. Bogotá: Imprenta de Silvestre y Cia.

Ricaurte Montoya, J. 1936. *Geografia economica de Colombia*. Vol. 2, *Atlantico*. Bogotá: Contraloria General de La Republica.

Richardson, H.W. 1969. *Elements of Regional Economics*. Harmondsworth, Penguin.

Richter, C., Leon, A., Sierra, J.R. and Tirado, N. 1979. *Una clasificacion de los departamentos y cuidades de Colombia segun sus niveles de desarrollo socioeconomico*. CEDE, Documento 056. Bogotá: Universidad de los Andes.

Reveiz, E. and Montenegro, S. 1983. Modelos de desarrollo, recomposicion industrial y evolucion de la concentracion industrial de las cuidades en Colombia (1965–1980), *Desarrollo y Sociedad* 11:95–154.

Roberts, B.R. 1974. The interrelationships of city and provinces in Peru and Guatemala. In W.A. Cornelius, and F.M. Trueblood, eds., *Latin American urban research*, vol. 4, pp. 207–236. Beverly Hills, CA: Sage.

Roberts, B.R. 1975. Center and periphery in the development process. In W.A. Cornelius and F.M. Trueblood, eds., *Latin American urban research*, Vol. 5, pp. 77–107. Beverly Hills, CA: Sage.

Roberts, B.R. 1978. *Cities of peasants*. London: Edward Arnold.

Roberts, B.R. 1982. Cities in developing societies. In H. Alavi and T. Shanin, eds., *Introduction to the sociology of developing societies*, pp. 366–387. London: Macmillan.

Rodriguez, O. 1981. *Efectos de la gran depresion en la industria Colombiana* (2nd ed.). Bogotá: Editorial Oveja Negra.

Ruiz, J. 1982. Administrative reform in Colombia: The limits of decentralization. Master's thesis, The Hague, Institute of Social Studies.

Ruiz, S. 1973. *La fuerza de trabajo en la produccion de arroz y algodon*, vol 1. Bogotá: DANE.

Sack, R.D. 1980. *Conceptions of space in social thought*. London: Macmillan.

Safford, F. 1977a. *Aspectos del siglo XIX en Colombia*. Medellin: Ediciones Hombre Nuevo.

Safford, F. 1977b. Significacion de los Antioquenos en el desarrollo economico colombiano. Un examen critico de las tesis de Everett Hagen. In F. Safford, ed., *Aspectos del siglo XIX en Colombia*. Medellin: Editorial Hombre Nuevo.

Samper, A. 1976. *Estudio de caso: Eternit de Colombia S.A.* Bogotá: Facultad de Administracion, Universidad de los Andes. (mimeographed)

Sanchez Santamaría, I. 1925. *Geografía Comercial y Economica y de los Países con los cuales negocia*. Bogotá: Editorial Ariel.

Santana, P. 1983. Desarrollo regional y paros civicos en Colombia. *Controversia* 107/108. Bogotá: CINEP.

Santos, M. 1979. *The shared space—The two circuits of the urban economy in underdeveloped countries*. London: Methuen. [Original in French, 1975.]

Scherer, F.M., Beckenstein, A., Kaufer, E., Murphy, R.D. 1975. *The economics of multi-plant operation. An international comparisons study*. Cambridge: Harvard University Press.

Schwartz, E. 1983. Crisis of the fiscal crisis. A review of James O'Connor's The fiscal crisis and the state. *Antipode* 15(3):45–50.

Schultz, T.W. 1964. *Transforming traditional agriculture*. New Haven, CT: Yale University Press.

Shanin, T. 1982. Polarization and cyclical mobility: The Russian Debate over differentiation of the peasantry. in J. Harriss, ed., *Rural Development*. Theories of peasant economy and agrarian change. pp. 223–245. London: Hutchinson

Shanin, T. 1973/74. The nature of the peasant economy. *Journal of Peasant Studies* 1(1):63–80 and (2)187–206.

Shaw, R.P. 1976. *Land tenure and rural exodus in Chile, Colombia, Costa Rica and Peru*. Gainesville, FL: University Press of Florida.

Shejtman, A.Z. 1975. Elementos para una teoria de la economia campesina: Pequenos propietarios y campesinos de hacienda. *Trimestre Economico* 42 (2):487–509.

Shejtman, A.Z. 1980. Economia Campesina—Logica interna y articulacion. Santiago: ILPES Doc. PA-1.

Short, J.R. 1982. *An introduction to political geography*. London: Routledge & Kegan Paul.

Silva, E. 1976. *Cementos Diamante S.A.* Bogotá: Facultad de Administracion, Universidad de los Andes. (mimeographed)

Sinclair, S.W. 1978. *Urbanization and labour markets in developing countries*. London: Croom Helm.

Singer, P. 1973. Urbanizacion, dependencia y marginalidad en America Latina. In M. Schteingart, ed., *Urbanizacion y dependencia en America latina,* pp. 93–123. Buenos Aires: Editorial SIAP.

Singer, P. 1974. Campo y ciudad en el contexto historico Latino Americano. *Revista EURE* 4(10):9–22.

Sjoberg, G. 1965. Cities in developing and industrial societies: A crosscultural analysis. In P.M. Hauser and L.F. Schnore, eds, *The study of urbanization,* pp. 213–265. New York: Wiley.

Skinner, G. 1964. Marketing and social structure in rural China: Part I. *Journal of Asian Studies* 24:3–43.

Skinner, G. 1965. Marketing and social structure in rural China: Part II. *Journal of Asian Studies* 24:195–228.

Slater, D. 1975. Underdevelopment and spatial inequality approaches to the problem of regional planning in the Third World. *Progress in Planning* 4 (2):97–167.

Smith, A. 1970. *The wealth of nations,* Vol. 1. New York: Everyman's Library.

Smith, C.A., ed. 1976a. *Regional analysis. Vol. I, Economic systems*. New York: Academic Press.

Smith, C.A., ed. 1976b. *Regional analysis*. Vol. II, *Social systems*. New York: Academic Press.

Soler, Y. and Prieto, F. 1982. *Bonanza y crisis del oro blanco 1960–1980*. Bogotá: Editograficas Ltda.

Solomon, S.G. 1977. *The Soviet agrarian debate: A controversy in social science 1923–1929*. Boulder, Colorado: Westview Press.

Sovani, N.V. 1964. The analysis of 'over-urbanization.' *Economic Development and Cultural Change* 12:113–122. Reprinted in J. Friedmann and W. Alonso, eds., *Regional policy. Readings in theory and applications* 1975. pp. 421–433. Cambridge, Mass.: M.I.T. Press.

Stein, B., Rokkan, S., and Urwin, D.W. 1982. *The politics of territorial identity*. London: Sage.

Stoehr, W. and Taylor, F. 1981. *Development from above or below? The dialectics of regional planning in developing countries*. London: Wiley.

Stoehr, W. and Toedtling, F. 1976. Spatial equity—Some antitheses to current regional development strategy. *Papers of the Regional Science Association* 38:33–53.

Stoehr, W. and Toedtling, F. 1978. An evaluation of regional policies—Experiences in market and mixed economies. In N.M. Hansen, ed., *Human settlement systems,* pp. 85–119. Cambridge, Mass.: Ballinger.

Storper, M. 1981. Toward a structural theory of industrial location. In J. Rees, G.J.D. Hewings and H.A. Stafford, eds., *Industrial location and regional systems* pp. 17–40. New York: Bergin.

Superintendencia de Sociedades, 1979. *Conglomerados de sociedades en Colombia*. Coleccion de la Superintendencia de Sociedades, Documento No. 3. Bogotá: Editorial Presencia.

Suzman, P. and Schutz, E. 1983, April. Monopoly and competitive firm relations and regional development in global capitalism. *Economic Geography:* 161–178.

Sweezy, P. et al. 1978. *The transition from feudalism to capitalism*. London: Verso.

Sylos-Labini, P. 1969. *Oligopoly and technical progress*. Translated from the Italian by E. Henderson. Cambridge: Harvard University Press.

Szelenyi, I. 1981. Structural changes of and alternatives to capitalist development in the contemporary urban and regional system. *International Journal of Urban and Regional Research* 5:1–14.

Szelenyi, I. and Pearse, M. 1983. The city in the transition to socialism. *International Journal of Urban and Regional Research* 8:90–107.

Tangri, S.S. 1982. Family structure and industrial entrepreneurship: The evolution of a field study. In H.I. Sofa, ed., *Towards a political economy of urbanization in Third World countries*, pp. 188–208. Delhi: Oxford Uiversity Press.

Taylor, M. and Thrift, N. 1983. Business organization, segmentation and location. *Regional Studies* 17(6):445–465.

Thoumi, F.E. 1983. La estructura del crecimiento economico regional y urbano en Colombia (1960–1975). *Desarrollo y Sociedad* 10:151–181.

Tirado Mejia, A. 1978. El estado y la politica en el siglo XIX. In *Manual de la historia de Colombia*, vol 2, pp. 327–383. Bogotá: Colcultura.

Tirado Mejia, A. 1981. "Algunas caracteristicas regionales de Colombia." Paper presented at National Seminar on Decentralization, Universidad de los Andes-CIDER and FESCOL, Bogotá, September 1982.

Todaro, M.P. 1969. A model of labor migration and urban unemployment in less developed countries. In *The American Economic Review*, 59, 1, pp. 138–148.

Tokman, V.E. and Souza, P.R. 1976. The informal urban sectors in Latin America. *International Labour Review* 114(3).

Tovar, H. 1975. *El movimiento campesino en Colombia durante los siglos XIX y XX*. Bogotá: Ediciones Libre.

UNCTAD. 1981. Fibres and textiles: Dimensions of corporate marketing structures. TD/B/C.1/219, coor. 1. Geneva: United Nations.

United Nations. 1981. *National accounts handbook*. Vol. 2, *Country data*. New York: United Nations.

Urbano Campo, 1977. *La urbanizacion en Colombia*. Bogotá: Ediciones Suramerica.

Uribe Echevarria, J.F. 1979. El proceso de urbanizacion en la Costa Atlantica. CIDER Bogotá: Universidad de los Andes.

Urrutia, M. 1969. *The development of the Colombian labor movement*. New Haven, CT: Yale University Press.

Urrutia, M. 1972. El sector externo y la distribucion del ingreso en Colombia en el siglo XIX. *Revista Banco de la Republica*, 1974–1987.

Urrutia, M. 1979. *Cincuenta años de desarrollo Economico Colombiano*. Bogotá: Editorial La Carreta.

Urrutia, M. and Arrubla, M. 1970. *Compendio de estadisticas historicas de Colombia*. Bogotá: Universidad Nacional.

Urrutia, M. and Villalba, C.E. 1969. El sector artesanal en el desarrollo Colombiano. *Revista de Planeación y Desarrollo* 1:1–43.

Vapnarski, C.A. 1969. On rank-size distributions of cities: An ecological approach. *Economic Development and Cultural Change* 17(4):584–595.

Velez, H.E. 1975. *Dos ensayos acerca del desarrollo capitalista en la agricultura Colombiana*. Medellin: Ed. 8 de Junio.

Vellinga, M. and Kruijt, D. 1983. *Industrialization and regional development in Colombia*. Incidentele Publicaties No 26. Amsterdam: CEDLA.

Vergara, C. 1970. *Estudio de transferencia del cultivo de algodon y de la asignacion de recursos resultante*. CEDE, Bogotá: Universidad de los Andes.

Villegas, J. 1978. La colonizacion de vertiente en el siglo XIX. *Estudios Rurales Latino Americanos* 3(2):102–147.

VonThuenen, J.H. 1966. *The Isolated State*. London, Oxford University Press; trans. C.M. Wartenberg.

Walker, R. and Storper, M. 1981. Capital and industrial location. *Progress in Human Geography* 5(4):473–510.

Walton, J. 1977. *Elites and economic development; Comparative studies on the political economy of Latin American cities*. Austin: University of Texas Press.

Walton, J. 1982. The international economy and peripheral urbanization. In N.I. Fairstein and S.S. Fairstein, eds., *Urban policy under capitalism*. Beverly Hills: Sage.

Watts, H.D. 1975. The market area of a firm. In L. Collins and D.F. Walker, eds., *Locational dynamics of manufacturing activity* pp. 357–383. London: Wiley.

Webb, R. 1975. Ingreso y empleo en el sector tradicional urbano del Peru. In R. Cardona, ed., *America—Distribucion espacial de la poblacion*. Bogotá: C.C.R.P.

West, R.C. 1972. *La mineria de aluvion en Colombia durante el periode colonial*. Bogotá: Imprenta Nacional.

Westaway, J. 1972. The spatial hierarchy of business organization and its implications for the British urban system. *Urban Studies* 8(2):145–155.

Wiesner, E. and Bird, R. et al., 1981. *Las finanzas intergubermentales en Colombia*. Informe de la Mision Wiesner-Bird. Bogotá: Departamento Nacional de Planeacion.

Wildavsky, A. 1973. If planning is everything maybe it's nothing. *Policy Sciences*, 4(2):127–153.

Williamson, J. 1965. Regional inequality and the process of national development: A description of patterns. *Economic Development and Cultural Change* 13. Reprinted in J. Friedmann and W. Alonso, eds., 1975. *Regional policy, readings in theory and applications*. Cambridge: MIT Press.

Wrigley, E.A. 1978. Parasite or stimulus: The town in a preindustrial economy. In P. Abrams, and E.A. Wrigley, eds., *Town in societies*, pp. 295–309. Cambridge: Cambridge University Press.

# INDEX

C

## M



## N